Qualitative Research in Nursing

Advancing the Humanistic Imperative

Qualitative Research in Nursing

Advancing the Humanistic Imperative

HELEN J. STREUBERT, EdD, RN

Associate Professor and Director
Nursing Program
College Misericordia
Dallas, Pennsylvania

DONA RINALDI CARPENTER, EdD, RN

Associate Professor
Department of Nursing
University of Scranton
Scranton, Pennsylvania

J. B. Lippincott Company
Philadelphia

Sponsoring Editor: Margaret Belcher
Coordinating Editorial Assistant: Kimberly Oaks
Indexer:: Maria Coughlin
Production Service: Berliner, Inc.
Cover Designer: Larry Pezzato
Production Manager: Janet Greenwood
Production Editor: Mary Kinsella
Printer/Binder: RR Donnelly & Sons, Crawfordsville

6 5 4 3 2 1

Library of Congress Cataloguing in Publications Data

Streubert, Helen, J.
    Qualitative research in nursing: advancing the humanistic
    imperative / Helen J. Streubert, Dona Rinaldi Carpenter.
            p.   cm.
        Includes bibliographical references and index.
        ISBN 0-397-55091-X
            1. Nursing—Research—Methodology.   2. Sociology—Research—
    Methodology.   I. Carpenter, Dona Rinaldi.   II. Title.
        [DNLM: 1. Nursing Research—methods.   2. Research Design.   WY
    20.5 S915q 19940]
    RT81.5.S78 1994
    610.73'072—dc20
    DNLM/DLC
    for Library of Congress   94-13709

∞   This Paper Meets the Requirements of ANSI/NISO Z39.48–1992 (Permanence of Paper)

I dedicate this work to Dr. Maxine Greene who has stimulated my insight into feminism, power, and relationships. I also dedicate it to my teachers, mentors, students, friends, and colleagues who have challenged me to go beyond the obvious, to explore parts of my consciousness that were not immediately perceptible. And finally, I dedicate this book to my family who has relentlessly provided me with the space to create a reality that is meaningful, compassionate, and questioning.

HJS

*T*o my parents, Elaine and Vito Rinaldi, my mother-in-law, Jeanne Carpenter, and my husband, Brian. Their support and encouragement continually provide me with opportunities to take risks and explore new horizons. I would also like to acknowledge the contributions of Dr. Patricia Munhall who encouraged, challenged, and gave direction to my written work during my doctoral studies. Most especially, this book is dedicated to my daughter, Emily Joy, who helps me remember what really matters in this life, and who has given me the opportunity to fold back the layers of meaning I have given to my own life and to view once again the world through the eyes of a child.

DRC

About the Authors

Helen J. Streubert, Ed.D., R.N., is Associate Professor and Director of the Nursing Program at College Misericordia, Dallas, Pennsylvania. In addition to this position, she also chairs the division of health science. Her primary research investigations have involved qualitative research methodologies, primarily phenomenologic studies, in the area of clinical education. Her phenomenologic work has been funded, presented nationally and internationally, and published; she has also received advanced preparation in this field. Dr. Streubert teaches qualitative research methods to interdisciplinary health science majors. In addition to her work in qualitative research, Dr. Streubert also has co-authored a text on faculty role development with Dr. Theresa Valiga, which received the AJN Book of the Year Award in 1992.

Dona Rinaldi Carpenter, Ed.D., R.N., is Associate Professor of nursing at the University of Scranton, Scranton, Pennsylvania, where she teaches medical-surgical nursing and the required research course for senior nursing majors. Her research interests focus on doctoral education in nursing, professional commitment, and quality of life. She has authored and co-authored several articles and a book chapter, and has presented her work at national and international meetings.

Contributors

Sandra Beth Lewenson, Ed.D., R.N., is the Associate Director of Accreditation at the National League for Nursing. Her research focus is on nursing's historical relationship with the women's suffrage movement at the beginning of the twentieth century. She has published several books and articles on the topic. In celebration of the National League for Nursing's centennial, she collaborated with other historians on a pictorial display weaving nursing's historical past with America's social, political, and economic history. Currently, she has begun to explore the history of accreditation in nursing.

Joan M. Jenks, Ph.D., R.N., is Associate Professor and Director of the Baccalaureate Division in the Department of Nursing, College of Allied Health Sciences, Thomas Jefferson University. She teaches qualitative research methods to undergraduate and graduate students in nursing and occupational therapy. Her research focuses on decision making using naturalistic approaches. She has researched and published valuable insights about nurse clinical decision making, contributing to the understanding of this complex process.

Preface

Qualitative Research in Nursing: Advancing the Humanistic Imperative presents the essentials of qualitative inquiry as applied to nursing. It offers a sound philosophical and methodological framework from which the researcher interested in using the approaches can initiate a study using one of the approaches offered.

This book arises out of a fundamental need to bring to its readers a sense of direction in the implementation of inquiry methods that value new ways of knowing and celebrate the human experience. As doctoral students struggling to authenticate our own ways of knowing, we found little direction in the existing literature. Some might suggest that the reason we found so little prescription for how we wanted to conduct our research was a direct result of our having chosen a research paradigm that inherently resists linear explanations of inquiry. However, without substantial understanding of the underpinnings of hundreds of years of philosophical debates, we felt lost in a sea of words and contexts unfamiliar to us. We read and read and read in an attempt to gain understanding. During our search, we were privileged to be mentored by scholars who believed that we could find a way of discovering meaning from the experiences of those we sought to understand. Dr. Maxine Greene helped us struggle with the philosophical ideologies that provide the foundation for much of our understanding of human science. Dr. Patricia Moccia provided us a safe place to talk about alternate paradigms and challenged us to explore our inner sense of self as we debated philosophy and methodology. Our colleagues at Teachers College repeatedly asked us to contemplate the real meanings of creating understanding in nursing.

Our understanding of nursing evolves from a belief that nursing is a holistic undertaking. We firmly believe that research out of the context of human experience has the potential to create knowledge that is disconnected to the realities of practice. Further, we believe that pursuing the mastery of any new skill requires fundamental understanding of its history, basic parts, context, and outcomes. Therefore, we have developed this text to speak to the acquisition of qualitative research skills. The book introduces the reader to the "historical background" of the approaches discussed. It shares the "parts" of the approaches, and appropriate "contexts" in which to use them, and the intended "outcomes" that one who uses the approaches should expect. Knowing these parts allows for integration and synthesis, ultimately providing greater understanding of the whole and authentication of the findings of human inquiry.

This book is intended to begin the dialogue for individuals interested in using qualitative inquiry approaches. In order to become competent as a qualitative researcher, one needs to read, study, observe, participate in, and discuss the realities of the art and practice of living. However, it is only through engagement of ideas that one can participate in and contribute to advancing the humanistic imperative.

ORGANIZATION

The text is organized to facilitate the reader's comprehension of each approach and to provide examples of how the approaches have been used in nursing education, administration, and practice. In Chapter 1, "Philosophical Dimensions of Qualitative Research," the reader is introduced to the traditions of science, the interpretations of what constitutes science, perceptions of reality, and characteristics common to all qualitative research approaches.

In Chapter 2, "What Is Nursing Knowledge?," the philosophical discussion is continued and expanded to include how qualitative research approaches have meaning in the practice of nursing. The chapter also contains a description of the common methodological features found in the approaches included in the text.

In Chapter 3, "Phenomenological Research Approach," an in-depth description of philosophical and methodological conceptualizations is offered. An overview of specific phenomenological perspectives provides the framework for choosing and implementing the approach. A table listing the procedural steps for implementing a phenomenological study from the perspective of six phenomenologists provides an excellent resource for the would-be phenomenological researcher.

Chapter 4 is an outstanding complement to Chapter 3, detailing for the reader application of the approach from the perspective of education, administration, and practice. Published works are evaluated for the contributions made to the qualitative phenomenological literature. A particular strength in all of the companion chapters is the use of evaluation guidelines specific to the approach being discussed. In addition, an extensive table at the end of most companion chapters provides the reader with a resource for examining published works using the various approaches discussed throughout the book.

Chapter 5, "Ethnographic Research Approach," Chapter 7, "Grounded Theory Research Approach," Chapter 9, "Historical Research Approach," and Chapter 11, "New Generation Research Approaches," follow the format found in Chapter 3. This includes an in-depth discussion of the philosophical and methodological issues specific to the approach. Data generation and treatment, as well as ethical issues specific to the particular approach, are discussed in detail.

Chapters 6, 8, 10, and 12 repeat the format found in Chapter 4, incorporating a detailed examination of published studies that illustrate a particular approach followed by guidelines for critiquing the approaches used. All of these chapters include tables offering a substantial resource list of studies completed in the areas of education, administration, and practice except for Chapter 10 which incorporates an extensive discussion of a variety of studies within the context of the chapter. Finally, each of these chapters includes a reprint of a selected study that illustrates the qualitative method discussed in that chapter.

Chapters 11 and 12 are a significant addition to the qualitative research literature. These two chapters speak specifically to what we have labeled *new generation research approaches*. Included in these chapters is an extensive description of naturalistic inquiry, action research, and life history approaches for conducting qualitative research. A table detailing computer programs available for data analysis is also included in Chapter 11.

Chapter 13, "Challenges Facing Qualitative Researchers," provides a full description of issues related to funding qualitative research projects and dissemination of qualitative research findings. It details for the reader the potential triumphs and the pitfalls in moving qualitative research into a public forum.

KEY FEATURES AND BENEFITS

The following features are included in the philosophical and methodological framework.

- Description of the philosophical underpinnings of each approach. This description provides more than the "how" of the approach; it presents the underlying assumptions of the approaches.
- Detailed description of procedural steps used in each of the approaches. This offers the reader the opportunity to learn step by step how the approach is implemented.
- Emphasis on the ethical considerations of each approach. This emphasis provides an understanding of the ethical considerations that are specific to the approach used by the reader.
- Tables profiling studies conducted using each of the approaches. These tables offer the reader an excellent resource for further exploring the existing body of knowledge specific to the approach being described.

- In-depth discussion of published research studies that have used the approaches under discussion. This examination shares with the reader not only what has been published but also the attention to implementation of the approach used by the researcher. The critique clearly helps the reader understand the strengths and weakness of the studies reported.
- Specific critiquing guidelines available in all companion chapters for each of the approaches. These guidelines help the reader understand the specific questions that should be asked of research studies that have used or will be using the approach.
- Inclusion of chapters on new generation research approaches. As nursing becomes more comfortable with qualitative research approaches, there is a need to make public new endeavors by researchers who borrow and apply methods used by other human scientists. These two chapters specifically offer the approaches less well known to nurses and not as frequently used by nurse researchers in an effort to stimulate understanding and use of them.
- Inclusion of companion chapters. Companion chapters describing application of each of the approaches included in this text provide strong evidence of the impact these qualitative research methods are having on the discipline of nursing and the potential benefits they will continue to have. These chapters also provide neophyte qualitative researchers with clear descriptions of what is expected from researchers who will evaluate their work.
- Inclusion of tables. The use of tables throughout the text allows the reader quick access to important reference information and offers visual representation of some methodological steps.

A cknowledgments

The authors wish to acknowledge the process of feminist thinking that has influenced the writing of this book. When the chapter authors came together to write this text, there was and continues to be a commitment to another voice, another way of creating meaning. It is through the shared commitment of the authors of this text and that of colleagues and friends who unselfishly gave of themselves to comment, to critique and learn, that this book is available to the nursing public. We wish to acknowledge those who have shaped our thinking and our way of being—our colleagues, teachers, students, friends, and family.

Specifically, we wish to acknowledge those who have been most closely involved in the production of this text. The authors are grateful for the editorial direction and assistance of Margaret Belcher; the technical support of Carolyn M. Tomassoni; the research assistance of Donna West-awski, Cathy Bullick, Suzanne Schick, Adele Lurie, and Andrea Allmer; the peer review activities of Kathy Brown, MSN, RN, Marie O'Toole, Ph.D, RN, Ryda D. Rose, Ph.D, Ann H. Lewis, Ph.D, RN, Marian Farrell, Ph.D, RNC, Nettie Birnbach, Ed.D, RN, FAAN, Ellen Baer, Ph.D, RN, FAAN, Julie Fairman, Ph.D, RN, and Timothy K. Casey, Ph.D; and the expert manuscript review by Ann Grant, Ph.D, RN, Janet F. Sullivan, Ph.D, RN, C, and Mary E. Duffy, Ph.D, RN.

Contents

9 Historical Research Approach   **195**
SANDRA B. LEWENSON

10 Historical Research Approach Applied to   **213**
Nursing Education, Practice, and Administration
SANDRA B. LEWENSON

11 New Generation Research Approaches   **242**
JOAN M. JENKS

Qualitative Research in Nursing

Advancing the Humanistic Imperative

Chapter 1

Philosophical Dimensions of Qualitative Research

The tradition of science is believed to be uniquely quantitative. The quantitative approach has been justified in the success that human beings have encountered in measuring, analyzing, replicating, and applying knowledge gained from this method of inquiry. In more recent history, scientists have been challenged to explain phenomena that defy measurement. The inability to measure some phenomena and the dissatisfaction with the results of measurement of other phenomena have led to an intense interest in seeking other modes of studying particularly human phenomena. This inability to measure human phenomena and dissatisfaction with the results led researchers to ask specific questions about the nature of knowledge and the best way to obtain knowledge that was not accessible through quantitative means. Ultimately, the concern for other means of explaining phenomena not available through traditional means resulted in the utilization of a group of methods that have been labeled qualitative research methods.

The tradition of using qualitative methods to study human phenomena is grounded in the social sciences. The tradition arose as a result of a need to know about parts of the human system that were not amenable to study through measurement. As an example, culture is an important part of human phenomena that was not accessible using quantitative measure; thus, the development of anthropology.

From a philosophical viewpoint, the study of human phenomena is deeply rooted in descriptive modes of research. Truth, as an important element of human existence, in its simplest form may yield to quantitative measurement. However, truth has been an elusive concept perplex-

Qualitative Research in Nursing: Advancing the Humanistic Imperative by Helen J. Streubert and Dona R. Carpenter. Copyright © 1995 by J. B. Lippincott Company.

ing human beings for centuries. The difficulty in defining truth is philo-sophically hindered by an inability to achieve agreement universally on what constitutes it. This is because truth is defined by individuals' belief systems. For example, if an individual states that 60 times 12 is 599.76, quantitative measurement would have us believe that this is not correct. However, philosophically, one could argue that the only truth found in the correct answer is a consensual belief in the measurement defined by human scientists. If, for example, an individual believed that a unit of a number equaled .833, then 60 times 12 does equal 599.76. The question of what is real and true then becomes a commitment to a common belief system. Without a commitment to a common belief system, all truth and thus reality become a matter of individual perception of what is real, rather than a commonly accepted structure. The idea of truth and thus reality may in fact rest more on personal perception or, as Lincoln and Guba (1985) offer, construction of reality rather than on positivistically derived scientific fact.

"Positivism asserts that objective accounts of the world can be given" (Denzin & Lincoln, 1994, p. 15). This paradigm has directed and supported a large amount of research in the world. It has provided many biological scientific discoveries that have strengthened individuals' lives. Also impor-tant is the examination of reality that may not be objective, reducible, quantifiable, and replicable. This type of inquiry also strengthens individ-uals' lives. Qualitative research offers the opportunity to focus on finding answers to questions that center on social experience, how it is created, and how it gives meaning to human life (Denzin & Lincoln, 1994). Know-ing how social experiences construct individuals' reality is important.

Based on the assumption that knowing how social experiences con-struct reality is important, an exploration of ways of knowing is appropriate.

WAYS OF KNOWING

Belenky, Clinchy, Goldberger, and Tarule (1986) have given voice to a viewpoint on knowing that has provided a lens to question why objective science has been accepted as the only truth that has been valued as sci-ence. Their exploration of the way women come to know supports a fem-inist ideology. Unfortunately, feminist ideas frequently are viewed as sub-jective and thus less valuable than traditional positivist science. This is changing as scientists are becoming increasingly comfortable with the diversity in society and richness of exploring and utilizing multiple meth-ods of inquiry to discover particular phenomena.

Although the study conducted by Belenky and colleagues (1986) focused on women, there is a great deal to be learned about how both sexes obtain knowledge from their work. The idea of *received knowl-*

edge is an important premise set forth by these authors. The way individuals learn things is usually by being told, receiving knowledge. All too frequently, the act of being told limits the opportunity to engage the self in a dialogue about what is real. When presented with received knowledge, the receiver of the knowledge should ask, "What are my perceptions about this knowledge as it is presented to me?"

From the time individuals are very young they are told by those who know, adults who are viewed as authority figures, the beliefs or knowledge they should retain. Most of what is shared is presented as truth. These truths are usually facts that have, in some way, been passed on or proven to be correct. The proof of correctness often occurs as a direct result of some objective manipulation of factors or variables.

Empirical scientists believe that if objective measurement cannot be assigned to a phenomenon, then the importance and thus the existence of the phenomenon may be in question. Some contemporary philosophers do not ascribe to this value system, particularly in dealing with human beings and their interactions with other human beings. There is very little available objectively derived measurement that is meaningful when one studies human phenomena within a social context. The concepts of objectivity, reduction, and manipulation that are fundamental to empirical science defy the authentic fiber of human beings and their social interactions.

With the belief that science should inform the lives of people who interact and function in society, all parts of reality must be examined. Individuals engaged in research need to examine the subjective reality as well as its objective counterpart. Knowing in the subjective sense should be acknowledged and be valued equally so that scientific knowledge will represent the views of those who experience life. The early phenomenologists believed that the only reality was that which is perceived. Thus, the measurement of perception challenges the empirical scientist. Perception is not objective. Perception is a way of observing and processing that which is present to the self. For example, two individuals may observe the same lecture and leave the classroom with very different interpretations of what the lecturer said. This is very much based on what is perceived to be reality, a reality developed and constructed over a lifetime of receiving, processing, and interpreting information. The internalization of what becomes known as belief systems comes from perception and construction of what is real for the individual.

WAYS OF KNOWING IN NURSING

Carper (1978), in her seminal work on ways of knowing in nursing, states that there are four fundamental patterns that emerge as the way nurses come to know: empirical knowing, aesthetic knowing, personal knowing, and ethical knowing. Empirical knowing represents the traditional, objective, logical, positivist tradition of science. Empirical knowing and thus empirical science are committed to providing explanations for phenomena and then controlling them. An example of empirical knowing is the knowledge derived from the biological sciences that describes and explains human function. Through the description and explanation of human function, biological scientists have been able to predict and control certain aspects of human structure and function. Treatment of diabetes mellitus is an example of empirical research being applied in the health care field. Biological scientists know from their empirical studies that provision of insulin to individuals with diabetes mellitus *controls* the symptoms created by the non-functioning pancreas.

Nursing's alignment with empirical knowing and subsequent pursuit of this mode of inquiry follow the positivist paradigm which believes that objective data, measurement, and generalizability are essential to the generation and dissemination of knowledge.

Aesthetic knowing is the art of nursing. The understanding and interpretation of subjective experience and the creative development of nursing care are based on the appreciation of subjective expression. Aesthetic knowing is abstract and defies formal description and measurement. Carper (1978) states that

> the aesthetic pattern of knowing in nursing involves the perception of abstract particulars as distinguished from the recognition of abstracted universals. It is the knowing of the unique particular rather than an exemplary class (p. 16).

Aesthetic knowing in nursing provides the framework for the exploration of qualitative research methodologies. Qualitative research calls for a recognition of patterns in phenomena rather than the explication of facts that will be controllable and generalizable. An example of aesthetic knowing is the way a nurse would provide care differently for two elderly women preparing for cataract surgery based on his or her knowledge of their particular life patterns.

The third type of knowing is personal knowing. Personal knowing requires that the individual, in this case the nurse, know the self. Knowing oneself is concerned with the abilities of an individual to self-actualize. Movement toward knowledge of the self and self-actualization requires comfort with ambiguity and commitment to patience in understanding. It is a commitment to authentication of relationships, a "presencing" with others. Presencing is the enlightenment and sensitization that human beings bring to genuine human interactions. Personal knowing deals with the fundamental existentialism of human beings. Existentialism is used here to mean the capacity for change and the value placed on becoming.

Personal knowing also supports the qualitative research paradigm. In the conduct of qualitative inquiry, the researcher is obligated by the philosophical underpinnings of the methodologies used to accept the self as part of the research enterprise and to approach the research participants in a genuine and authentic manner. An awareness of one's beliefs and understandings is essential to fully discover the phenomena studied in a qualitative research inquiry. Further, the qualitative researcher believes that there is always subjectivity in pursuit of the truth. The very nature of human interaction is based on subjective knowledge. In the most objective research endeavor, there are subjective realities that impact on what is studied.

Moral knowing reflects our ethical obligations in a situation or our ideas about what should be done in a given situation. Through the moral way of knowing, individuals come to a realization of what is right and just. As with personal knowing and aesthetic knowing, moral knowing is another abstract dimension of how it is that individuals come to know a situation. Moral knowing is based on traditional principles and codes of ethics or conduct. This type of knowing becomes most important when human beings face situations in which decisions of right and wrong are blurred by differences in values or beliefs. Moral knowing requires an openness to differences in philosophical positions. Ethics and logic are required to examine the intricacies of human situations that do not fit standard formulas for conduct.

The importance of sharing ways of knowing is to offer the reader a context in which to judge the appropriateness of nursing knowledge and the way that nurses develop that knowledge. It is only through examination of current belief structures that people are able to achieve their own standards of what will be best in a given situation.

In the case of qualitative research, it is only through examination of the prevailing ideologies that nurses will be able to decide which ideology most reflects their personal patterns of discovery and creation of meaning.

MEANING OF SCIENCE

Science is defined in a number of ways. Kerlinger (1973) describes science as a "way of explaining observed phenomena" (p. 7). Namenwirth (1986) defines it as "a system of gathering, verifying, and systematizing information about reality" (p. 19).

Guba (1990), in sharing a view of empirical science, articulates the meaning of science as it is practiced within the premise of value-neutral, logical, empirical methods that promise "the growth of rational control over ourselves and our worlds" (p. 317). All three of these definitions are very different. All three statements give us a very different perception of truth.

Most of what individuals know about science in the nursing profession is based on the empirical view of science which places significant value on rationality, objectivity, prediction, and control. The question that arises is whether this view of science is consistent with the phenomena of interest to nurses.

The empirical view of science permeates many aspects of human activity. In adopting this view, a value system is adopted that frequently dispenses with ideas that do not reflect an objective approach to the generation of knowledge. For instance, some empiricists would propose that if a phenomenon is not observable, the question that should be asked is, "Is it real?" If a particular phenomenon does not conform to reality as it is currently known, the statement is made that it is likely irrational and therefore not important. If a phenomenon is studied without controls protecting the objectivity of the study, then it is said to lack rigor or is soft science and therefore results in unusable data. If the findings from an inquiry do not lead to generalization that contributes to the prediction and control of phenomena under study, then the statement may be made that the findings are less than science.

This view of science has permeated society and has structured what is valued. Feminist scholars state that the scientific paradigm that focuses on prediction and control has gained wide acceptance because of its roots in male dominance. Women have played only a small role in the creation of knowledge up to this point. Therefore, the definitions and values of science have been largely created by male scientists who have valued prediction and control over description and understanding.

An empirical, objective, rational science has significant value when the phenomena of interest are not human. But the goals of this type of science, prediction, and control offer less value when the subject of the inquiry is unable to be made objective.

As a result of the limitations that result from a positivist view of science, philosophers and social scientists have offered another view of science, one that has placed value on the study of human experience. In this new model, subjectivity is acknowledged and valued as part of any scientific inquiry. Human values contribute to scientific knowledge; therefore, neutrality is impossible. Prediction is thought to be limiting and capable of creating a false sense of reality. In a human science framework, the best the scientist can hope for in creating new knowledge is to provide understanding and interpretation of phenomena within context. Human science and the methods of inquiry that accompany it offer an opportunity to study and create meaning that will enrich and inform human life.

Objective Versus Subjective World

Empirical scientists believe that the study of any phenomena must be devoid of subjectivity (Namenwirth, 1986). Further, they contend that objectivity is essential in guiding the way to truth. The problem with this position is that no human activity can be performed without subjectivity. And since it is a human quest for knowledge, it is logical to presume that human activity will be necessary to seek knowledge.

Phillips (1987) believes that objectivity is impossible based on his reading and interpretation of Hanson and states, "The theory, hypothesis, framework, or background knowledge held by an investigator can strongly influence what he sees" (p. 9). Kerlinger (1979) also states that "the procedures of science are objective and not the scientists. Scientists, like all men and women, are opinionated, dogmatic, and ideological" (p. 264). Therefore, the idea of objectivity loses its meaning. On some level all research endeavors have the subjective influence of the scientist. Procedural objectivity is the most that can be hoped for; however, even this is biased by the fact that the scientist will interpret the findings. Even if the findings of a study are statistical (thought to be objective measure), the interpretation of the statistical data is carried out by the scientist who comes with opinions and bias about what the numbers say (MacKenzie, 1981; Taylor, 1985).

Human scientists value the subjective component of the quest for knowledge. They embrace the idea of subjectivity in the recognition that human beings are incapable of total objectivity because they have been situated in a reality which is constructed by subjective experiences. Meaning, and therefore the search for truth, are possible only through social interaction. The degree to which the scientist is part of the development of scientific knowledge is debated even by the human scientists. Post-empiricists accept the subjective nature of inquiry but still support rigor and objective study through method. The objectivity post-empiricists speak of is one of context. For example, the post-empiricist scientists would acknowledge their subjective realities and then, always being aware of them, seek to keep them apart from the scientific inquiry.

Constructivist human scientists believe that "knowledge is the result of a dialogical process between the self-understanding person and that which is encountered—whether a text, a work of art, or the meaningful expression of another person" (Smith, 1990, p. 177). As can be seen, subjectivity is acknowledged but the degree to which it is embraced is based on philosophical beliefs.

The important point to make relative to objectivity is that human scientists see objectivity in its empirical definition to be impossible. The

degree to which one can be objective, and therefore unbiased, is determined by the philosophical tradition the human scientist ascribes to. The
very fact that subjectivity is included in the discussion of human science
conveys an understanding that participation in the world prohibits human
beings from ever being fully objective.

Single Versus Multiple Reality

Alluded to throughout these opening remarks is the idea of science being
a pathway to truth. The definitions of science and truth are debatable;
however, human beings have demonstrated a pursuit of truth throughout
time. Truth, for the purpose of this discussion, is defined as reality.

If the position is taken that the search for truth is a search for reality, then the question arises, "Do we believe there is a single reality, only
one truth?". Lincoln and Guba (1985) identify four ontological positions
regarding reality: objective, perceived, constructed, and created. An examination of these ontological positions is important.

Objective reality "asserts . . . that there is a tangible reality, and
experience with it can result in knowing it fully" (Lincoln & Guba, 1985,
p. 82). This level of reality supports empirical research as the way to truth.
Perfect understanding will come from repeated inquiries that will sooner
or later converge in truth. This position supports the whole being equal
to the parts (Lincoln & Guba, 1985).

Perceived reality is based on an ideological position which suggests
that "there is a reality, but one cannot know it fully" (Lincoln & Guba,
1985, p. 83). This level of reality only can be known from a certain viewpoint. The focus for this notion of reality is a reality that will never be
completely known and will be available to individuals only through one
of the parts.

Lincoln and Guba (1985) offer that the differences between objective and perceived reality is that the objective realist believes that at some
point they will know the whole. Perceptual realists believe that they will
never come to know the whole. The similarity between both is that both
positions believe that there is a reality to be known.

Constructed reality is based on the notion that reality is constructed
by individuals. What is real is constructed through cognitive processes.
Constructive realists question whether there is a reality and purport that
it can never be known. They further believe that "no amount of inquiry
can produce convergence on it" (Lincoln & Guba, 1985, p. 83). Additionally, constructive realists believe that there are multiple realities and
that one "true" reality will never be discovered.

Constructed reality depends on individuals' agreement about certain events, people, or experiences. For example, each individual has a different perception of church. The idea of church represents something different for each individual. Although a person or group can set forth a definition of church upon which a larger group may agree, the meaning derived from the definition is based on constructed reality.

Individuals who support the notion of *created reality* believe that there is no reality at all.

> Reality is best understood as a standing wave function that is not *realized* (note the term) until some observer "pops the qwiff" (Wolf, 1981), "qwiff" being a quantum wave function. Until it is "popped," the quantum wave function (or *probable* reality) remains simply probabilistic (Lincoln & Guba, 1985, p. 85).

Lincoln and Guba (1985) support constructed reality as the most meaningful reality because it fosters the idea that there are multiple realities. Their position appears to be the most logical because it supports the position that there is more than one way to know something and that knowledge is context bound.

To illustrate the divergence in the positions of single versus multiple realities, the following is offered in Table 1.1 (Lincoln & Guba, 1985).

TABLE 1.1 COMPARISON OF ONTOLOGICAL POSITIONS

Objective/Positivist	Subjective/Constructed
"Reality is single, fragmented"*	"Reality is multiple, constructed, holistic"*
Duality exists between knower and known	"Knower and known are interactive, inseparable"*
Context free generalizations are possible	"Only time and context-bound working hypotheses are possible"*
All entities can be explained by cause and effect	All entities are in a state of mutual simultaneous development making it impossible to discern cause and effect
"Inquiry is value-free"*	"Inquiry is value-bound"*

*Data from Lincoln & Guba, 1985, p. 37.

The belief in a single reality limits the ability to understand human function. Human beings are part of reality as cognitive, psycho-social beings. For this reason, the position is taken that the belief in multiple realities supports the search for truth in human inquiry.

COMMON CHARACTERISTICS OF QUALITATIVE RESEARCH

In the conduct of research there are attributes which are common to the discovery enterprise. This is true of both qualitative and quantitative designs. In this section, exploration of those common characteristics of qualitative research will be discussed.

Qualitative researchers emphasize six significant characteristics in their research: a belief in multiple realities, a commitment to identifying an approach to understanding that will support the phenomenon studied, commitment to the participant's point of view, conduct of inquiry in a way that does not disturb the natural context of the phenomena of interest, acknowledged participation of the researcher in the research, and conveyance of the understanding of phenomena by reporting in a literary style rich with participant's commentary.

The idea that multiple realities exist and create meaning for the individuals studied is a fundamental belief of qualitative researchers. Instead of searching for one reality, one truth, the researcher committed to qualitative research believes that individuals actively participate in social actions and through these interactions come to know and understand phenomena in very different ways.

Unlike their quantitative colleagues, qualitative researchers are committed to discovery through the use of multiple ways of understanding. Those engaged in this type of research address questions about particular phenomena by finding a method or approach to answering the question which is appropriate. The discovery leads the choice of method rather than the method leading the discovery. The research is therefore said to be inductive rather than deductive.

In some cases more than one approach to phenomena may be employed. For instance, in work completed by Jenks (1993) on clinical decision making, she found that focus group interaction identified the need to observe nurses in practice which then led to individual interviews about practices observed. In this example and in other qualitative research studies, the researcher is committed to the discovering of information. Method and data collection strategies may change as needed, rather than being prescribed before the inquiry begins which is the way positivist science is developed.

Commitment to the participants' point of view is the third major characteristic of qualitative research. Use of unstructured interview, observation, and artifacts grounds the researcher in the real life of those studied. The researcher is a co-participant in the discovery and understanding of what the realities are of the phenomena studied. The qualitative researcher will conduct extensive interviews and observations, searching documents and articles of importance to understand the context of what is researched. The purpose of the extensive investigation is to provide a view of reality that is important to those studied rather than what is important to the researcher. For example, in work reported by Price (1993) on what perceptions of quality nursing care are, she asked parents whose children were hospitalized to describe their perceptions of quality care. Price (1993) focused on what parents believed quality nursing care was rather than providing a quantitative scale or survey. The interviews with these parents allowed them to tell their stories of quality nursing care. Using this approach provides important, rich data that significantly inform nursing practice. It defines the practice of quality nursing based on beliefs of parents (consumers) rather than on the beliefs of nurses (providers).

The fourth characteristic of qualitative research is conduct of the inquiry in a way that does not disturb the natural context of the phenomena studied. The obligation of the investigator is to conduct the study in a way that alters the context of the phenomena as little as possible. Using ethnographic research to illustrate this characteristic, the ethnographer would study a particular culture with as little intrusion as possible. Living among those who are studied is one way to minimize the intrusion and maintain the natural context of the setting. It is unrealistic to believe that the introduction of an unknown individual would not change the context of the relationships and activities observed; however, prolonged presence should have the effect of minimizing the intrusion.

Accepting the participation of the researcher in the research is the fifth characteristic of qualitative research. The use of the researcher as instrument requires an acceptance of the researcher as part of the study. Because the researcher is the observer, interviewer, or interpreter of various aspects of the inquiry, objectivity serves no purpose. Qualitative investigators accept that all research is conducted with a subjective bias. They further believe that the participation of the researcher in the inquiry has the potential to add to the richness of data collection and analysis. Objectivity is a principle in quantitative research that documents the rigor of the science. In qualitative research, rigor is most often determined by the participants in the study. Do they recognize what the researcher has created to be their culture or experience? The acknowledgment of the subjective nature of qualitative research and the understanding that researchers effect what is studied is fundamental to the conduct of qualitative inquiry.

TABLE 1.2   COMPARISON OF QUALITATIVE AND QUANTITATIVE RESEARCH METHODS

Quantitative	Qualitative
Objective	Subjectivity value
One reality	Multiple realities
Reduction, control, prediction	Discovery, description, understanding
Measurable	Interpretive
Mechanistic	Organismic
Parts equal the whole	Whole is greater than the parts
Report statistical analyses	Report rich narrative
Researcher separate	Researcher part of research process
Subjects	Participants
Context free	Context dependent

Whether the approach is phenomenologic, ethnographic, case study, naturalistic, life history, action research, grounded theory, or historical, the qualitative researcher will report the findings of the study in a rich literary style. Participants' experiences are the findings of qualitative research; therefore, it is essential that they be reported from the perspective of those who have lived them. Inclusion of quotes, commentaries, and stories adds to the richness of the report and to the understanding of what the social interactions of those who are studied have been. Table 1.2 offers a simple description of the contrasts between qualitative and quantitative research.

All six characteristics guide the qualitative researcher on a journey of discovery and participation. Doing qualitative research is similar to reading a good novel. When conducted in the spirit of the philosophy that supports it, qualitative research is rich and rewarding, leaving the researcher with a desire to understand more about the phenomena of interest.

SUMMARY

The nature of knowledge and the means of accessing it have been of concern to scientists and philosophers from the beginning of time. The nurse researcher interested in adventuring into the discourse must come to know what perceptions of reality will help to access the knowledge imbedded in life and specifically in practice. It is essential to examine the premises and assumptions that structure the examination of the inherent beliefs of those who care and who are cared for. It is only through searching the assumptions that individuals come to understand the truths that have been communicated. Without clear statements of what constitutes reality, research will remain an academic enterprise without clear application to the practice setting. Research must be based on a philosophical commitment to discover knowledge using the means that most appropriately explain the phenomena of interest.

In the subsequent chapters, the reader will have the opportunity to learn more about what constitutes nursing knowledge and the multiple ways of describing what is embedded in nursing practice, education ,and administration. The authors provide information on the conduct of inquiry using a variety of qualitative research approaches. Companion chapters provide the reader with an opportunity to view how specific qualitative approaches should be used and evaluated. Additionally, most companion chapters are accompanied by a table illustrating a number of studies that have employed the approach. The selection of studies for inclusion in each companion chapter was based on either the contribution the study makes to the field or in some cases the studies presented may include all studies which have been published and are available using a specific approach.

REFERENCES

Belenky, M. F., Clinchy, B. M., Goldberger, N. R., & Tarule, J. M. (1986). *Women's ways of knowing*. New York: Basic Books.

Carper, B. (1978). Fundamental patterns of knowing in nursing. *Advances in Nursing Science, 1*(1), 13–2.

Denzin, N. K., & Lincoln, Y. S. (1994). Introduction: Entering the field of qualitative research. In N. K. Denzin & Y. S. Lincoln (Eds.), *Handbook of qualitative research* (pp. 1 17). Thousand Oaks, CA: Sage.

Guba, E. G. (1990). *The paradigm dialogue*. Newbury Park, CA: Sage.

Jenks, J. M. (1993). The pattern of personal knowing in nurse clinical decision making. *Journal of Nursing Education, 32*(9), 399–405.

Kerlinger, F. N. (1973). *Foundations of behavioral research,* 2nd. ed. New York: Holt, Rinehart & Winston.

Kerlinger, F. N. (1979). *Behavioral research: A conceptual approach*. New York: Holt, Rinehart, & Winston.

Lincoln, Y. S., & Guba, E. G. (1985). *Naturalistic inquiry*. Beverly Hills: Sage.

MacKenzie, D. (1981). *Statistics in Great Britain: 1885–1930*. Edinburgh: Edinburgh University Press.

Namenwirth, M. (1986). Science seen through a feminist prism. In R. Bleier (Ed.), *Feminist approaches to science* (pp. 18–41). New York: Pergamon Press.

Phillips, D. C. (1987). *Philosophy, science, and social inquiry*. New York: Pergamon Press.

Price, P. J. (1993). Parents' perceptions of the meaning of quality nursing care. *Advances in Nursing Science, 16*(1), 33–41.

Smith, J. K. (1990). Alternative research paradigms and the problem of criteria. In E. G. Guba (Ed.), *The paradigm dialogue* (pp. 167–187). Newbury Park, CA: Sage.

Taylor, C. (1985). *Human agency and language.* Cambridge: Cambridge University Press.

Wolf, F. A. (1981). *Taking the quantum leap.* San Francisco: Harper and Row.

Chapter **2**

What Is Nursing Knowledge?

In 1959, Dorothy E. Johnson wrote:

> The question of the existence of a body of substantive knowledge which can be called the science of nursing is a troublesome one for nurses and for members of allied professional groups alike. Yet it is a question of considerable significance for nursing's continued development as a recognized professional discipline. Certainly no profession can long exist without making explicit its theoretical bases for practice so that this knowledge can be communicated, tested, and expanded (Johnson, 1959, p. 291).

These words, written over thirty-five years ago, still echo the challenge nurses face today. It is essential that nurses continue to advance nursing knowledge, but what is this knowledge?

Some practicing nurses would argue that it is not their job to develop knowledge but rather to take care of patients. Others would suggest that nurses cannot take care of patients unless they use nursing knowledge. Still others might offer that they can be nurses and take care of patients without *developing* specific nursing knowledge. Still other groups would take the position that the disciplines such as medicine, psychology, sociology, physiology and social work offer knowledge which is adequate to guide nursing practice.

To enlighten discussion of these comments, it is important to remember that early nurse scientists, the first developers of nursing knowledge, were trained by natural scientists. These scientist instructed early nurses in the ways of their respective advanced degrees which included sciences such as biology, chemistry, and anatomy. Others were educated in the ways of science by anthropologists, sociologists, and psychologists. Nursing knowledge development during the early period was driven by what the nurses' mentors had learned in their respective fields during advanced degree preparation. Thus, the nurse mentor's perception of what was important to study was greatly influenced by what she/he had studied in graduate school. These early nurse scientists were directed to conduct their inquiries to match the interests of their mentors in the basic and social sciences. As years went by these nurse scientists became mentors to other nurses interested in research and were able to guide their students in the ways they had been taught.

It is not surprising to find that much of what was considered early nursing knowledge was grounded in the empirical scientific method which values above all prediction and control. This understanding of science and the adoption of the scientific method by early nursing scientists was justified. Nursing leaders were convinced that the way to develop a profession which had its own unique body of knowledge was to accept the prevailing paradigm which was positivist.

As time went on, the vision of nursing science as empirical was nurtured by those early nursing scholars. Early nurse scientists believed that the way to develop nursing knowledge was to pursue it in an objective, empirical manner.

Today, the question of what constitutes nursing knowledge is no easier to answer than it was at the time Johnson (1959) offered her positions on the problems, issues and concerns facing the development of nursing knowledge. Questions continue to be raised about what constitutes nursing knowledge; What are the concepts which are important to the development of nursing science?; Is nursing a science?; Is nursing a profession?; Can nursing be science if the findings of studies are not generalizable, and don't lead to control and prediction? These questions and others continue to influence the development of nursing knowledge.

Nurses have agreed almost universally that the focus of their activities should be on the holistic care of human beings. With this position stated, it then becomes essential to incorporate the knowledge developed by many scientists including biologists, physiologist, psychologist, sociologist, and anthropologists. If nurses support the notion that holistic care is what they provide, then the bio-psycho-social cultural dimensions of human beings must be understood by all. The activities which will make nursing's knowledge unique will be the application and modification of the knowledge from these disciplines to the humanistic nursing experience (Paterson & Zderad, 1976).

The development of nursing knowledge will require that nurses borrow knowledge from other disciplines. This is because of the profession's commitment to the holistic nature of human beings. The modification and further refinement of the knowledge specific to the human condition of health is what will make this knowledge uniquely nursing's.

To return to the beginning and ask the question: "What is nursing knowledge?" is to return to the issues of what constitutes science and thus truth. Wilson (1985) takes the position that,

> Science and research are indeed the keystones in the edifice of professional nursing practice, but they do not stand alone. Nursing's goal of wisdom, vision, social significance, accountability, fulfillment, collegiality, and excellence can be achieved only when we synthesize the engaged with the analytic—the humanities with the sciences (p. 8).

The idea that nursing knowledge will be created from the synthesis of the humanities and the sciences is an essential one. This synthesis will allow nursing to develop knowledge using the best from the sciences and humanities to support the goal of holistic, humanistic health care. Johnson (1991) cautions, however,

> if nursing science is pursued as an applied science, nurses will be unable to directly pursue scientific nursing problems; instead, the science of nursing will rest with and ultimately be driven by the advancements of other disciplines, not by the needs of nursing practice (p. 12).

This statement must be respected but understood in the context of how Johnson (1991) defines science. As stated earlier, a position such as the one offered by Johnson supports science as grounded primarily in the empirical tradition. Based on Johnson's comments, further exploration of how it is possible to create nursing knowledge is in order.

GROUNDING RESEARCH IN THE REALITY OF NURSING

The metaparadigm in nursing includes four major concepts. These are human beings, health, nursing and society/environment. All four concepts when related to one another represent human interaction. Human beings' bio-physical functioning is somewhat predictable. Their psycho-social, cultural functioning is less predictable. Because most of the work of nursing is found in the realms of the bio-physical, psycho-social, or cultural and in light of the fact that these dimensions of human existence are inter-related, the researcher interested in studying human phenomena is challenged to identify a research approach which reflects the lack of predictability in the human organism.

Munhall and Boyd (1993) share their belief system which reflects the dichotomy between contemporary nursing philosophy and the positivist tradition in science. Logical positivism focusses on reduction, objectivity, manipulation, linear causality, categorization, human and environmental passivity, predication, generalizability and control (Munhall & Oiler, 1986). Current nursing philosophy, by contrast, focuses on humanism, individualism, holism, self determination, relativism, participation and interaction (Munhall & Oiler, 1986; Munhall & Boyd, 1993). This dichotomy in knowledge development and philosophy has the potential to create problems for nurses who choose to operationalize their research interests without careful reflection on the phenomena of interest and the appropriateness of the discovery method to be used. The method of inquiry should fit the question of the research without manipulation of reality. Research questions which are focussed on description, prediction and control are questions which are amenable to quantitative study (Brink & Wood, 1988). For instance if nurses want to know how frequently patients need to be turned in bed to prevent decubitus ulcers, they would design an experiment which would include people with varying disorders, nutritional states, age, body types and sizes. The subjects in the study could be randomly assigned turning times. Based on an adequate sample size, the nurse researcher would be able to determine the appropriate time patients with the characteristics described should be turned to avoid the development of decubitus ulcers. This would be an easily designed and executed research study and could contribute significantly to the body of existing nursing knowledge. Knowing empirically the appropriate time to turn patients to avoid decubitus ulcers would facilitate efficient use of nurses' time and provide a standard of quality care.

Mechanical changes in body position and the effect these changes create are based on bio-physical knowledge. Bio-physical knowledge is often predictable. This is true because if the study controls variables such as age, nutritional status, medical diagnosis and body size and type and has a large enough sample, nurses are able to generalize these findings to the larger population. Control and prediction are important to this type of inquiry.

If however, the nurse researcher is interested in studying the effect of frequent turning on the patient's psychological well-being, the ability to predict and control the behavior becomes more difficult and some would argue impossible. The most appropriate outcome of a study of this type might be identification of patterns of behavior. The level of prediction and control described in the above example will never be possible because of the potential number of uncontrollable variables related to an individual's psychological health.

In order to understand the difficulty manifested in studying the effect of frequent turning on psychological well-being, let's look at some of the inherent difficulties in measurement and control in this type of study. It would be most important to operationalize psychological well-being. The researcher would need to find an instrument which demonstrated reliability and validity in measuring an abstract concept such as psychological well-being. In order to do this, the researcher would need to define the concept of psychological well-being within the context of a concept which has been operationalized. A concept such as mental health might be a reasonable approximation. As can be seen, there already is an obvious leap of faith that the concepts of mental health and psychological well-being are related. Further, if there was an instrument available that measured psychological well-being, and it had been proven to be both reliable and valid, then the researcher using the tool would need to accept that the experts who established its validity were in fact constructing a measure of psychological well-being.

If the researcher chose not to make a conclusive argument that mental health and psychological well-being are related, then the researcher would need to develop an instrument which is capable of measuring psychological well-being. This could be done based on the researcher's review of current literature on the topic of psychological well being which then would be validated by a panel of experts on the concept. Following development, the instrument would need to be extensively used to demonstrate it's reliability. The question which arises from this type of instrument development is: "How do authors of research reports and experts' opinions become the basis upon which knowledge is validated?" How did the panel of experts become authorities on the concept? Do they have first hand knowledge of psychological well-being? If so, how do they define it? Would those who believe that they are experiencing psychological well-being support the position that the instrument measures what they feel?

To eliminate much of the ambiguity in the acceptance of an instrument which purports to measure psychological well-being or a related construct, a qualitative approach could be used to study the concept. Individuals who have personal knowledge of the phenomenon would be asked to explain their experience of psychological well-being.

If the researcher used a phenomenological approach to study the concept of psychological well-being, the findings would illustrate the participants' perceptions of psychological well-being. This description then could be used to develop an instrument which reflects the experience of psychological well-being based on the experiences of those who have lived it. The importance of examining both the qualitative and the quantitative way of deriving meaning from nursing problems illustrates the appropriate use and potential misuse of these research methods.

THE LANGUAGE OF QUALITATIVE RESEARCH IN NURSING

Qualitative research in nursing is a relatively newly accepted form of creating nursing knowledge. Pioneers such as Paterson & Zderad (1976), Leininger (1985) and Munhall and Oiler (1986) first brought this type of inquiry to the forefront through their important textbook publications. Although the idea of including subjective data in research reports has been supported and encouraged for a long period of time, it was not until these distinguished individuals brought the debate of method to the community of nursing scholars that qualitative research began to take its place next to quantitative inquiry. This is not to suggest that qualitative methodology is viewed the same as quantitative research, for indeed, it is not. There are many nursing scholars who remain committed to the belief that science is not truth until it demonstrates predictability and control. It does, however, appear that in the foreseeable future, more nurses dedicated to the positivist paradigm will support the notion that all questions of human science cannot be answered through the study of phenomena using quantitative methods much the same as scientists in the basic and applied sciences have learned. For now, the inclusion of multiple ways of deriving meaning from nursing phenomena is encouraging. More journals than ever before are supporting the inclusion of new ways of creating meaning in nursing. Similarly, nurses using human science methods to investigate phenomena are finding increasing success with funding organizations for their work.

The importance of including new research paradigms in nursing is that it demonstrates that the positivist nursing research paradigm is in question for describing particular human phenomena (Haase & Meyers, 1988; Knaack, 1984; Moccia, 1988; Munhall, 1982; Nagle & Mitchell, 1991; Omery, 1983; Swanson & Chenitz, 1982; Tinkle & Beaton, 1983). This questioning provides an opportunity to create new ways of deriving meaning in nursing. The approaches which will be discussed in the following chapters are not new to science, but they are comparatively new to nursing.

Qualitative research is a paradigm reflecting the value of subjectivity, individualism, holism, relativism, and interpretation. It also addresses the importance of context in creating meaning, the dynamic fluid nature of reality, and the interrelatedness of all phenomenon.

COMMON FEATURES IN THE CONDUCT OF QUALITATIVE RESEARCH

In the following chapters, specific approaches to the conduct of qualitative research will be discussed. Each approach will be considered giving the reader a sound basis from which to develop a qualitative study. Philosophy, process, evaluation and references will be offered. By way of introduction to the approaches discussed, this section will explore the commonalities found across qualitative research methods.

Philosophical Position

The investigator interested in qualitative research approaches the inquiry with a particular philosophical and epistemologic position. The purpose of qualitative research is not prediction and control but rather description and understanding. Since a complete discussion of philosophy occurred in Chapter 1, it will not be repeated here.

Use of the Literature Review

In the development of a quantitative research study, an interested researcher would begin with an extensive literature search on the topic of interest. This review documents the necessity for the study and provides for a discussion of the area of interest and related topics. It helps the researcher decide whether the planned study has been conducted and whether significant results were discovered. Further, it helps the researcher refine the research question and build a case for why the topic of interest should be studied and how the topic will be approached.

Qualitative researchers do not generally begin with an extensive literature review. Purists would argue that no literature review should be conducted before the inquiry begins. Some qualitative researchers accept that a cursory review of the literature may help focus the study. The reason for not conducting the literature review initially is to protect investigators from leading the participants in the direction of what has previously been discovered. For instance, if a phenomenologist is interested in studying the experience of second degree students in nursing education, a review of the literature might document that second degree students are self directed and highly motivated and need little support from their teachers. The researcher then approaches the question with a mind set that second degree students do exhibit these behaviors or they approach the study with the purpose of disproving what they have read. In either case, the objective of discovery is affected by what is already known.

In a qualitative study, generally, the literature review is conducted after the research has been completed and data analyzed. The purpose of reviewing the literature in a qualitative study is to place the findings in the context of what is already known. Unlike a quantitative study, the literature search is not used to establish grounds for the study or to suggest a theoretical or conceptual framework. It's purpose is to tell the intended readership how the findings fit into what is already known about the topic. Further, it is not meant to confirm or argue existing findings.

Explicating the Researcher's Beliefs

Prior to starting a qualitative study it is in the best interest of the researcher to reveal his/her thoughts about the topic as well as personal perceptions and biases. The purpose of this activity is to bring to consciousness and explicate what is believed about a topic. By revealing what the researcher believes, she/he should be in a better position to approach the topic honestly. Explication of personal beliefs makes the investigator more aware of the potential impulsive judgements that may occur during data collection and analysis based on the researcher's belief system rather than on the actual data revealed by participants.

For example, let's say that the topic of interest to the researcher is quality of life in individuals diagnosed with multiple sclerosis. The individual who is conducting the study has an interest in the topic based on a long history of working with individuals with end stage disease. The perception of the researcher is that people with multiple sclerosis live very sad, limited existences. If these perceptions are not explicated, the researcher can lead informants in description of their experiences in the direction of his/her own beliefs. For instance, questions which would lead to answers supporting the researcher's beliefs might be asked. In asking questions to validate the investigator's ideas, the participants may not be heard. The act of expressing one's ideas should help to remind the researcher to listen and see what is real for the informants rather than what is real for the researcher. Schutz (1970) recommended that this process of describing personal beliefs about what is assumed by the researcher will help him/her refrain from making judgements about phenomena based on personal experience.

Once the thoughts, feelings and perceptions about phenomena are revealed, it is recommended that they be *bracketed*. Bracketing is the cognitive process of putting aside one's own beliefs, not making judgments about what is observed or heard and remaining open to data as they are revealed. In qualitative studies this activity is usually carried out before the beginning of the study and is repeated throughout data collection and analysis. In ethnographic work, keeping a diary of personal thoughts and feelings is an excellent way to explicate one's ideas. Once revealed, they can be set aside. By conducting this disclosure, researchers are able to keep their eyes open and to remain cognizant of when data collection and analysis reflects personal beliefs rather than informant's beliefs.

Setting for Data Collection

The setting for qualitative research is the *field*. The field is the place where individuals of interest live, where they experience life. This means that the inquiry will be conducted in the homes, neighborhoods, classrooms, or sites selected by those who will inform the study. The purpose of conducting research in the field is to alter as little as possible the natural settings where phenomena occur. For instance, if the investigator is interested in studying the culture of an intensive care unit, she or he would go to the intensive care unit. If the researcher is interested in studying the clinical decision making skills of nurses, he or she would go to nurses who carry out this skill and ask them where they want to be interviewed or observed.

Being in the field requires a reciprocity in terms of decision making. Participants will decide what access to information they will permit the researcher to have. For instance, if interested in studying the experience of receiving a cancer diagnosis, a researcher would need access to those who have had this life situation. An informant may not wish to share his/her thoughts or feelings in one sitting or at all. In this situation the reader should be able to clearly see the duality of investigator and informants in qualitative research. Negotiation may be possible to obtain information which the participants are reluctant to share. However, the conduct of qualitative research with its requirement of close social interaction may create a situation that can either limit or enhance access to information. It also has the potential to create ethical dilemmas which need careful attention (see Chapter 13). Only through being in the field will the researcher be truly aware of the strengths and potential weaknesses in this common feature of qualitative research.

Selection of Participants

Qualitative researchers generally do not call the individuals who inform their inquiry subjects. The use of the terms participants or informants illustrates the position that qualitative researchers subscribe to. That position is that the individuals who takes part in the research are not acted upon but rather are part of the study. They are active participants in the inquiry and help to inform with the purpose of helping those interested to better understand their lives and social interactions.

In quantitative inquiry, subjects are selected at random if the study is an experimental design and their numbers must be sufficient to establish significance. In a qualitative study, individuals are selected to participate in the research based on their first hand experience with a culture, social interaction or phenomenon of interest. For instance if an ethnographer is interested in studying the culture of a freshman nursing class, then the informants for the study must be those who have experience and participate in the culture. There is no need to randomly select individuals because manipulation and control is not the intent of the inquiry. Similarly, there is no need to determine how many individuals in the group need to be observed or interviewed because the goal is not to generalize the findings. Researchers interested in a freshman nursing class culture should interview as many individuals as they can to obtain a clear understanding of the culture. Lincoln and Guba (1985) and Patton (1990) have labeled this type of sampling, *purposeful*. It has also been called *theoretical* (Glaser & Strauss, 1967; Patton, 1980). Theoretical sampling, used primarily in grounded theory, is sampling on the bases of concepts which have proven theoretical relevance to the evolving theory (Strauss and Corbin, 1992). What both of these terms denote is a commitment to observing and interviewing those who have experience with the culture or phenomena of interest. The concern of the researcher is to develop a rich or dense description of the culture or phenomenon rather than using sampling techniques which support generalizability of the findings.

Saturation

A feature which is closely related to the topic of sampling is a concept labeled *saturation*. Saturation is a term that refers to the repetition of discovered information and confirmation of previously collected data (Morse, 1994). This means that rather than sampling a specific number of individuals to gain significance based on some statistical manipulation, the qualitative researcher is looking for repetition and confirmation of previously collected data. For example in a study conducted by Beck (1992), she was interested in studying the experience of postpartum depression. Her sample consisted of individuals who had experienced this phenomenon. Beck continued interviewing this group of women until she achieved repetition of the salient points (themes). She was able to recognize the repetition and determined that the addition of new informants confirmed her findings rather than adding new information.

Morse (1989) warns that saturation may be a myth. If another group of individuals were observed or interviewed at another point in time, new data may be revealed. The best that a qualitative researcher can hope for in terms of saturation is to saturate the specific culture or phenomenon at a particular point in time.

Data Analysis

Analysis of qualitative research is a "hands on" process. The researcher must become deeply *immersed* in the data. Becoming immersed in data is also called *dwelling* with them. This process requires the inquirer to commit fully to understanding what the data say. It requires a significant degree of dedication to reading, intuiting, analyzing, synthesizing and reporting what is discovered.

Data analysis in qualitative research actually begins when data collection begins. As the researcher conducts interviews and/or observations, records are maintained and they are constantly being reviewed to discover additional questions which need to be asked or to offer descriptions of what is found. Usually these questions or descriptions are embedded in the observations and interviews. The qualitative researcher must "listen" carefully to what is seen, heard and experienced in order to discover meaning. The cyclic nature of questioning and verifying is an important aspect of data collection and analysis. In addition to the analysis which occurs throughout the study, a protracted period of immersion occurs at the conclusion of data collection. During this period of dwelling, the investigator will question all prior conclusions in light of what has been discovered in the context of the whole. Generally this period of data analysis consumes a considerable amount of time. The researcher will spend weeks or months with data based on the amount of data available for analysis.

The actual process of data analysis usually takes the form of clustering data which are similar. These may be referred to as *themes*. Themes are structural meaning units of data. They help the researcher cluster information and discover the meanings intended in what is observed and heard.

Once all themes relevant to the study are explicated, the researcher will write them up in a way that is meaningful to the intended audience. Writing up the findings of a qualitative study are discussed in detail in Chapter 13.

Demonstrating Trustworthiness

Rigor in qualitative research is demonstrated through the researcher's attention to and confirmation of information discovery. The goal of rigor in qualitative research is to accurately represent what those who have been studied experience. There are different terms to describe the processes which contribute to the rigor in qualitative research. Guba (1981) offers the following four terms to describe operational techniques which support the rigor of the work. These include credibility, dependability, confirmability and transferability.

Credibility includes activities which increase the probability that credible findings will be produced (Lincoln & Guba, 1985). One of the best ways to establish credibility is through prolonged engagement with the subject matter. Another way to confirm the credibility of the findings is to return to the participants and see whether they recognize the findings to be true to their experiences (Yonge & Stewin, 1988). Lincoln and Guba call this activity "member checks" (p. 314). The purpose of this exercise is to have those who have lived the described experience validate that the reported findings represent them.

Dependability is a criterion which is met through obtaining credibility of the findings. The question to ask is: "How dependable are these results?" Similar to validity in quantitative research where there can be no validity without reliability, the same holds true for dependability. There can be no dependability without credibility (Lincoln & Guba, 1985).

Confirmability is a process criterion. The way one documents the confirmability of the findings is to leave an *audit trail*. An audit trail is a recording of activities over time which can be followed by another individual. It can be compared to a fiscal audit (Guba & Lincoln, 1985). The objective is to, as clearly as possible, illustrate the evidence and thought processes which led to the conclusions. This particular criterion can be problematic, however, if you subscribe to Morse's (1989) ideas regarding the related matter of saturation. It is the position of this author that another researcher may not agree with the conclusions developed by the original researcher.

Transferability refers to the probability that the findings of the study have meaning to others in similar situations. Transferability has also been labeled fittingness. The expectation for determining whether the findings fit or are transferable rests with the potential user of the findings and not with the researcher (Greene, 1990; Lincoln & Guba, 1985; Sandelowski, 1986). As stated by Lincoln and Guba (1985),

> It is . . . not the naturalist's task to provide an *index of transferability;* it is his or her responsibility to provide the *data base* that makes transferability judgement possible on the part of potential appliers (p. 316).

These four criteria for judging the rigor of qualitative research are important. They define for external audiences the attention qualitative researchers render to their work.

SUMMARY

Nurse researchers are at an important juncture in the creation of nursing knowledge. It is apparent, that new ways of knowing about nurses and nursing increasingly are gaining support. Nurses now are able to ask nursing questions and answer them with research methodologies which foster multiple ways of viewing human phenomena. The opportunity to create nursing knowledge using these methods is exciting. In the following chapters, nurse researchers will be provided with description of qualitative research approaches which offer new ways of creating nursing knowledge which ultimately will lead to new ways of viewing nursing and nursing care.

REFERENCES

Beck, C. T. (1992). The lived experience of postpartum depression: A phenomenological study. *Nursing Research, 42*(3), 166–170.

Brink, P. J., & Woods, M. J. (1988). *Basic steps in planning nursing research* (3rd ed.). Boston: Jones & Bartlett.

Glaser, B. G., & Strauss, A. (1967). *The discovery of grounded theory.* Chicago: Aldine.

Greene, J. C. (1990). Three views on nature and role of knowledge in social science. In E. Guba (Ed.), *The paradigm dialogue* (pp. 227–245). Newberry Park, CA: Sage.

Guba, E. G. (1981). Criteria for assessing the trustworthiness of naturalistic inquiries. *Educational Communication and Technology Journal, 29,* 75–92.

Haase, J. E., & Meyers, S. T. (1988). Reconciling paradigm assumptions of qualitative and quantitative research. *Western Journal of Nursing Research, 10,* 128–137.

Johnson, D. E. (1959). The nature of a science of nursing. *Nursing Outlook, 7,* 291–294.

Johnson, J. L. (1991). Nursing science: Basic, applied, or practical? Implications for the art of nursing. *Advances in Nursing Science, 14*(1), 7–16.

Knaack, P. (1984). Phenomenological research. *Western Journal on Nursing Research, 6,* 107–114.

Leininger, M. (1985). *Qualitative research methods in nursing.* Orlando, FL: Grune & Stratton.

Lincoln, Y. S., & Guba, E. G. (1985). *Naturalistic inquiry.* Beverly Hills: Sage.

Moccia, P. (1988). A critique of comprise: Beyond the methods debate. *Advances in Nursing Science, 10,* 1–9.

Morse, J. M. (1989). Strategies for sampling. In J. M. Morse (Ed.), *Qualitative nursing research: A contemporary dialogue* (pp. 117–131). Rockville, MD: Aspen.

Morse, J. M. (1994). Designing funded qualitative research. In N. K. Denzin, & Y. S. Lincoln (Eds.), *Handbook of qualitative research* (pp. 220–235). Thousand Oaks, CA: Sage.

Munhall, P. L. (1982). Nursing philosophy and nursing research: In apposition or opposition. *Nursing Research, 31,* 178–181.

Munhall, P. L., & Boyd, C.O. (1993). *Nursing research: A qualitative perspective.* New York: National League for Nursing Press.

Nagle, L. M., & Mitchell, G. J. (1991). Theoretic diversity: Evolving paradigmatic issues in research and practice. *Advances in Nursing Science, 14*(1), 17–25.

Omery, A. (1983). Phenomenology: A method for nursing research. *Advances in Nursing Science, 5,* 49–63.

Paterson, J. G., & Zderad, L. T. (1976). *Humanistic nursing.* New York: Wiley.

Patton, M. Q. (1990). *Qualitative evaluation and research methods*. Beverly Hills: Sage.

Patton, M. Q. (1980). *Qualitative evaluation methods*. Beverly Hills: Sage.

Sandelowski, M. (1986). The problem of rigor in qualitative research. *Advances in Nursing Science, 8*(3), 27–37.

Schutz, A. (1970). *On phenomenology and social relations* (H. Wagner, Ed.). Chicago: University of Chicago Press.

Strauss. A., & Corbin, J. (1990). *Basics of qualitative research: Grounded theory procedures and techniques*. Newberry Park, CA: Sage.

Swanson, J. M. & Chenitz, W. C. (1982). Why qualitative research in nursing. *Nursing Outlook, 30*, 241–24.

Tinkle, M. B., & Beaton, J. L. (1983). Toward a new view of science: Implications in nursing research. *Advances in Nursing Science, 2*, 1–2.

Wilson, H. S. (1985). *Research in nursing*. Menlo Park, California: Addison-Wesley.

Yonge, O., & Stewin, L. (1988). Reliability and validity: Misnomers for qualitative research. *The Canadian Journal of Nursing, 20*(2). 61–67.

Chapter 3

Phenomenological Research Approach

Phenomenology has been and continues to be an integral field of inquiry that cuts across philosophical, sociological, and psychological disciplines. The rigorous, critical, systematic investigative method of phenomenology has recently gained recognition as a qualitative research approach applicable to the study of phenomena important to the discipline of nursing. Phenomenological inquiry strives to bring to language perceptions of human experience with all types of phenomena. Since professional nursing practice is enmeshed in the life experience of people, the phenomenological research method is well suited to the investigation of phenomena important to nursing.

Phenomenological inquiry continues to be somewhat new to nursing as a research method. This fact, along with the variety of documented methodological interpretations, often leaves first-time investigators feeling uncertain about what constitutes specific elements and interpretations of this research approach. Chapter 3 explores common phenomenological themes and provides examples of method interpretation currently documented. Finally, methodological concerns specific to conducting a phenomenological investigation are presented. This chapter provides introductory concepts for the researcher interested in phenomenological investigation and should ideally move the researcher to seek out additional readings in the area that are necessary to acquire an in-depth understanding of the approach.

Qualitative Research in Nursing: Advancing the Humanistic Imperative by Helen J. Streubert and Dona R. Carpenter. Copyright © 1995 by J. B. Lippincott Company.

WHAT IS PHENOMENOLOGY?

Phenomenology is a science whose purpose is to describe particular phenomena, or the appearance of things, as lived experience. Merleau-Ponty (1962) answered the question "What is phenomenology?" in the preface to his text *Phenomenology of Perception*. His description reflects the flow of phenomenological thinking and makes clear that to this day, the question "What is phenomenology?" has not yet been answered. Merleau-Ponty (1962) offered the following description:

> Phenomenology is the study of essences; and according to it, all problems amount to finding definitions of essences: the essence of perception, or the essence of consciousness, for example. But phenomenology is also a philosophy which puts essences back into existence, and does not expect to arrive at an understanding of man and the world from any starting point other than that of their "facticity". It is a transcendental philosophy which places in abeyance the assertions arising out of the natural attitude, the better to understand them: but it is also a philosophy for which the world is always 'already there' before reflection begins—as an inalienable presence; and all its efforts are concentrated upon re-achieving a direct and primitive contact with the world, and endowing that contact with a philosophical status. It is the search for a philosophy which shall be a `rigorous science', but it also offers an account of space, time and the world as we `live' them. It tries to give a direct description of our experience as it is, without taking account of its psychological origin and the causal explanations which the scientist, the historian or the sociologist may be able to provide (p. vii).

Herbert Spiegelberg (1975) is perhaps best known as the historian of the phenomenological movement. He defined phenomenology as:

> The name for a philosophical movement whose primary objective is the direct investigation and description of phenomena as consciously experienced, without theories about their causal explanation and as free as possible from unexamined preconceptions and presuppositions (p. 3).

Spiegelberg (1975) and Merleau-Ponty (1962) describe phenomenology as both philosophy and method. Phenomenology is further explained by Wagner (1983) as a way of viewing ourselves, others, and everything else that we come in contact with in life.

> Phenomenology is a system of interpretation that helps us perceive and conceive ourselves, our contacts and interchanges with others, and everything else in the realm of our experiences in a variety of ways, including to describe a method as well as a philosophy or way of thinking (p. 8).

Omery (1983) addressed the question "What is the phenomenological method?" Although this question has been interpreted in a variety of ways, the approach is inductive and descriptive in its design. Phenomenological method is "the trick of making things whose meanings seem clear, meaningless, and then, discovering what they mean" (Blumensteil, 1973, p. 189).

Lived experience of the world of everyday life is the central focus of phenomenological inquiry. Schutz (1970) described the world of everyday life as the "total sphere of experiences of an individual which is circumscribed by the objects, persons, and events encountered in the pursuit of the pragmatic objectives of living" (p. 320). In other words, it is the lived experience that presents to the individual as what is true or real in his or her life. Further, it is this lived experience that gives meaning to each individual's perception of a particular phenomenon and is influenced by everything internal and external to the individual. Perception is important in phenomenological philosophy and method. Merleau-Ponty (1956) explained:

> Perception is not a science of the world, nor even an act, a deliberate taking up of a position. It is the basis from which every act issues and it is presupposed by them. The world is not an object the law of whose constitution I possess. It is the natural milieu and the field of all my thoughts and of all my explicit perceptions. Truth does not "dwell" only in the "interior man" for there is no interior man. Man is before himself in the world and it is in the world that he knows himself. When I turn upon myself from the dogmatism of common sense or the dogmatism of science, I find, not the dwelling place of intrinsic truth, but a subject committed to the world (p. 62).

Phenomenology is as much a way of thinking or perceiving as it is a method. The goal of phenomenology is to describe lived experience. To further clarify both the philosophy and method of phenomenology it is helpful to have some sense of how the movement developed historically. An overview of the phenomenological movement follows. For a more extensive discussion of the history of the phenomenological movement the reader is referred to the works of Spiegelberg (1965), Cohen (1987), and Reeder (1987).

HISTORICAL OVERVIEW AND COMMON THEMES OF PHENOMENOLOGICAL INQUIRY

The phenomenological movement began around the first decade of the 20th century. This philosophical movement consisted of three phases: Preparatory, German, and French. Common themes of phenomenology are described within the context of the three phases of this movement.

The Preparatory phase was dominated by Franz Brentano (1838–1917) and Carl Stumpf (1848–1936). Stumpf was Brentano's first prominent student and, through his work, demonstrated the scientific rigor of phenomenology. Clarification of the concept of intentionality was the primary focus during this time (Spiegelberg, 1965). *Intentionality* means that consciousness is always consciousness of something. Merleau-Ponty (1956) explained that "interior perception is impossible without exterior perception, that the world as the connection of phenomena is anticipated in the consciousness of my unity and is the way for me to realize myself in consciousness" (p. 67). Therefore, one does not hear without hearing something or believe without believing something (Cohen, 1987).

Edmund Husserl (1857–1938) and Martin Heidegger (1889–1976) were the prominent leaders during the German or second phase of the phenomenological movement. Husserl (1931, 1965) believed that philosophy should become a rigorous science that would restore contact with deeper human concerns, and that phenomenology should become the foundation for all philosophy and science. According to Spiegelberg (1965), Heidegger followed so closely in the steps of Husserl that his work is probably a direct outcome of Husserl's. The concepts of *essences, intuiting* and *phenomenological reduction* were developed during the German phase (Spiegelberg, 1965).

Essences refer to elements related to the ideal or true meaning of something. Essences are concepts that give common understanding to the phenomenon under investigation. Essences emerge in both isolation and in relationship to one other. According to Natanson (1973), "Essences are unities of meaning intended by different individuals in the same acts or by the same individuals in different acts" (p. 14). Essences, therefore, represent the basic units of common understanding of any phenomena. For example, in a study on the meaning of commitment to nursing (Rinaldi, 1989), the essences (or basic units of common understanding of the phenomenon of commitment) related to commitment to nursing included altruism, devotion, dedication, caring, being there, trust, loyalty, and nurturance.

Intuiting is an eidetic comprehension, or accurate interpretation of what is meant in the description of the phenomenon under investigation. The intuitive process in phenomenological research results in a common understanding about the phenomenon under investigation. Intuiting in the phenomenological sense requires that the researcher imaginatively vary the data until such time that a common understanding about the phenomenon emerges. Imaginative variation requires that the researcher begin to wonder about the phenomenon under investigation in relationship to the various descriptions generated. To further illustrate, in the study on commitment to nursing (Rinaldi, 1989), the essences of commitment gleaned from the data were varied in as many ways as possible and in comparison to the descriptions given by the participants. From this imaginative variation a relationship between the essences of commitment, and who or what the nurse was committed to, emerged. For example, the nurse may be committed to patients, colleagues, the employing institution, the profession, or to self. Who or what the nurse is committed to is then examined in relationship to the essences of commitment. The researcher might vary the essences of commitment with each example of who or what the nurse is committed to. Some essences may apply when the issue is commitment to patients, and others if the issue is commitment to the institution.

Phenomenological reduction is a return to original awareness regarding the phenomenon under investigation. Husserl specified how to describe, with scientific exactness, the life of consciousness in its original encounter with the world through phenomenological reduction. Husserl (1931, 1965) challenged individuals to go "back to the things themselves" to recover this original awareness. Husserl's reference "to the things" means:

> A fresh approach to concretely experienced phenomena, as free as possible from conceptual presuppositions and an attempt to describe them as faithfully as possible (Spiegelberg, 1975, p. 10).

Phenomenological reduction begins with suspension of beliefs, assumptions, and bias about the phenomenon under investigation. Isolation of pure phenomenon, versus what is already known about a particular phenomenon, is the goal of the reductive procedure. The only way to really see the world clearly is to remain as free as possible from preconceived ideas or notions. Complete reduction may never be possible because of the intimate relationship individuals have with the world (Merleau-Ponty, 1956).

As part of the reductive process, phenomenological researchers must first identify any preconceived notions or ideas about the phenomenon under investigation. Once identified, what the researcher knows or believes about the topic under investigation must be *bracketed* or separated out of consciousness. Bracketing requires the researcher to remain neutral with respect to belief or disbelief in the existence of the phenomenon. This begins the reductive process which must continue throughout the investigation. Essentially, the researcher is setting aside previous knowledge or personal beliefs about the phenomenon under investigation to prevent this information from interfering with the recovery of a pure description of the phenomenon. The reductive process and bracketing continue throughout the research process. This step must be constant and ongoing if descriptions are to achieve their purest form.

Lastly, Gabriel Marcel (1889–1973), Jean Paul Sartre (1905–1980), and Maurice Merleau-Ponty (1905–1980) were the predominant leaders of the French or third phase of the phenomenological movement. The primary concepts developed during this phase were *embodiment* and *being-in-the-world*. These concepts refer to the belief that all acts are con-

structed on foundations of perception, or original awareness of some phenomenon. Lived experience is given in the perceived world and this is
what must be described (Merleau-Ponty, 1956). Munhall (1988) explains
these key concepts originally described by Merleau-Ponty as follows:

> Embodiment explains that through consciousness one is aware of being-
> in-the-world and it is through the body that one gains access to this
> world. One feels, thinks, tastes, touches, hears, and is conscious through
> the opportunities the body offers. There is talk sometimes about expand-
> ing the mind or expanding waistlines. The expansion is within the body,
> within the consciousness. It is important to understand that at any point
> in time and for each individual a particular perspective and/or con-
> sciousness exists. It is based on the individual's history, knowledge of
> the world, and perhaps openness to the world. Nursing's focus on the
> individual and the "meaning" events may have for an individual, is this
> recognition that experience is individually interpreted (p. 24).

Phenomenology is a dynamic philosophy that evolved and changed
throughout the movement. Different philosophers may have different
interpretations of phenomenology as both philosophy and method. The
dynamic nature and evolving interpretations provide the phenomenological researcher with a variety of options to chose from when embarking
on an investigation of this nature. These options, along with other issues
related to actually conducting a phenomenological investigation, follow.

SELECTING THE PHENOMENOLOGICAL APPROACH

How does the researcher decide to use phenomenological method for a
topic needing investigation? What phenomena, important to nursing, lend
themselves to this type of qualitative investigation? The answers to these
questions are grounded in nursing's philosophical beliefs about human
beings and the holistic nature of professional nursing.

Nursing encourages detailed attention to the care of persons as
human beings and grounds its practice in a holistic belief system that
cares for mind, body and spirit. Holistic care and avoidance of reduc-
tionism is at the center of professional nursing practice. The holistic
approach to nursing is rooted in the nursing experience and is not
imposed artificially from without. Just as caring for only part of the patient
is inconsistent with nursing practice, so too is the study of human beings
by breaking them down into parts. The following example illustrates the
nature of holistic nursing practice.

When caring for a patient who has had a mastectomy, the nurse
does not only address body image but also the impact this surgery may
have on family, work, and psychological well being. The nurse might ask,
"How are you feeling about your surgery?" or "What kinds of changes in

your life do you anticipate as a result of your mastectomy?" These questions elicit more about the patient as a person, with a life and feelings, as opposed to a question such as "Do you want to look at the scar?" that deals only with the body part removed. Since phenomenological inquiry requires that the integrated whole be explored, it is a suitable method for the investigation of phenomena important to nursing practice, education, and administration.

Spiegelberg (1965) remarked that phenomenological method investigates subjective phenomena in the belief that essential truths about reality are grounded in the lived experience. What is important is the experience as it is presented, not what anyone thinks or says about it. Therefore, investigation of phenomena important to nursing requires that the researcher study lived experience as it is presented in the everyday world of nursing practice, education, and administration.

A holistic perspective and the study of experience as lived serve as foundations for phenomenological inquiry. A positive response to the following questions will help the researcher clarify if phenomenological method is the most appropriate approach for the investigation.

First, the researcher should ask, "Is there a need for further clarity on the chosen phenomenon?" Evidence to conclude that further clarity is needed may be that there is little if anything published on the subject, or perhaps what is published needs to be described in more depth.

Secondly, the researcher should consider the question, "Will the shared lived experience be the best data source for the phenomenon under investigation?" Since the primary method of data collection is the voice of the people experiencing a particular phenomenon, the researcher must determine that this approach will provide the richest and most descriptive data.

Finally, as in all research, the investigator should consider the issues of available resources, the time frame for the completion of the research, the audience the research will be presented to, and the researcher's own personal style and ability to engage in the method in a rigorous manner.

Topics appropriate to phenomenological research method include those that are central to the life experience of human beings. Examples include feeling happiness or fear, being there, being commited, being a chairperson or head nurse, or the meaning of stress for nursing students in the clinical setting. Health-related topics suitable for phenomenological investigation might include the meaning of pain, quality of life with a particular chronic illness, or loss of a body part. Chapter 4 offers the reader a selective sample of published research using phenomenological research methodology in the areas of practice, education, and administration.

METHODOLOGICAL INTERPRETATIONS OF
PHENOMENOLOGICAL INQUIRY

Phenomenology as a research method is a rigorous, critical, systematic investigation of phenomena. Several procedural interpretations of phenomenological method are available as guidelines to this research approach (Colaizzi, 1978; Giorgi, 1985; Munhall & Boyd, 1993; Paterson & Zderad, 1976; Spiegelberg, 1965, 1975; Streubert, 1991; van Kaam, 1959; van Manen, 1984). Since there is more than one legitimate way to proceed with a phenomenological investigation, method choice should be guided by the appropriateness of the method to the phenomenon of interest. Table 3.1 provides an overview of the various procedural interpretations documented. The reader is referred to Chapter 4 for samples of research that apply the approaches described in Table 3.1.

Spiegelberg (1965, 1975) identified a core of steps or elements that are central to phenomenological investigations. The core steps or main elements of phenomenology detailed by Spiegelberg (1975) include: (1) Descriptive Phenomenology; (2) Phenomenology of Essences; (3) Phenomenology of Appearances; (4) Constitutive Phenomenology; (5) Reductive Phenomenology; and (6) Hermeneutic Phenomenology. A discussion of each of the six elements follows. Important to note, however, is that not all steps must be adopted to be considered method. Very often phenomenological researchers will use only descriptive phenomenology, phenomenology of essences, and reductive phenomenology. Further, hermeneutic phenomenology is an interpretation that really is separate in itself. In the words of Spiegelberg (1965), the purpose is to "present this method as a series of steps, of which the later will usually presuppose the earlier ones, yet not be necessarily entailed by them" (p. 655).

Descriptive phenomenology involves "direct exploration, analysis, and description of particular phenomena, as free as possible from unexamined presuppositions, aiming at maximum intuitive presentation" (Spiegelberg, 1975, p. 57). Descriptive phenomenology stimulates our perception of lived experience while emphasizing the richness, breadth, and depth of those experiences (Spiegelberg, 1975, p. 70). Spiegelberg (1965, 1975) identified a three-step process for descriptive phenomenology that includes intuiting, analyzing and describing.

The first step, *intuiting,* requires the researcher to become totally immersed in the phenomenon under investigation, and is the process whereby the researcher is beginning to know about the phenomenon as described by the participants. The researcher avoids all criticism, evaluation, or opinion and pays strict attention to the phenomenon under investigation as it is being described (Spiegelberg, 1965, 1975).

The step of intuiting the phenomenon in a study of quality of life would involve the "researcher as instrument" in the interview process. The researcher becomes the tool for data collection and listens to individual descriptions of quality of life through the interview process. The researcher then studies the data as they are transcribed, and reviews, over and over again, what the individual has described as the meaning of quality of life.

The second step is *phenomenological analyzing.* This step involves identifying the essence of the phenomena under investigation based on data obtained and how they are presented. As phenomena are distinguished with regard to elements or constituents, relationships and connections with adjacent phenomena are explored (Spiegelberg, 1965, 1975).

As the researcher listens to descriptions of quality of life and dwells with the data, common themes or essences will begin to emerge. Dwelling with the data essentially involves complete emersion in the generated data to engage fully in this analytical process. The researcher must dwell with the data for as long as necessary to ensure pure and accurate description.

The third step is *phenomenological describing.* The aim of the describing operation is to communicate, to bring to written and verbal description, distinct, critical elements of the phenomenon. The description is based on a classification or grouping of the phenomenon. The researcher must avoid attempting to describe phenomena prematurely. Premature description is a common methodological error associated with this type of research (Spiegelberg, 1965, 1975). Description is an integral part of intuiting and analyzing. Although addressed separately, they are often occurring simultaneously.

In a study on quality of life, phenomenological describing would involve classifying all critical elements or essences that are common to the lived experience of quality of life and describing these essences in detail. Critical elements or essences are described singularly and then within the context of their relationship to one another. A discussion of this relationship follows.

Phenomenology of essences involves probing through the data and searching for common themes or essences, and establishing patterns of relationships shared by the particular phenomena. *Free imaginative variation* is used to apprehend essential relationships between essences. This involves careful study of concrete examples supplied by the participants experience and systematic variation of these examples in the imagination. In this way it becomes possible to obtain insights into the essential structures and relationships among phenomena. Probing for essences provides a sense for what is essential and what is accidental in the phenomenological description (Spiegelberg, 1975). The researcher follows through with the steps of intuiting, analyzing, and describing in this second phase (Spiegelberg, 1965, 1975). According to Spiegelberg (1975),

TABLE 3.1   METHODOLOGICAL INTERPRETATIONS

Author	Procedural Steps

van Kaam (1959)	1. Obtain a core of common experiences.
	2. List and prepare a rough preliminary grouping of every expression presented by participants.
	3. Reduction and elimination. Test each expression for two requirements:
	  A. Does it contain a moment of the experience that might eventually be a necessary and sufficient constituent of the experience?
	  B. If so, is it possible to abstract this moment and to label it, without violating the formulation presented by the subject? Expressions not meeting these two requirements are eliminated. Concrete, vague, and overlapping expressions are reduced to more exactly descriptive terms. EXAMPLE: "I feel like I could pull my hair out by the roots" could be reduced to "feelings of frustration".
	4. Tentatively identify the descriptive constituents. All common relevant constituents are brought together in a cluster that is labeled with the more abstract formula expressing the common theme.
	5. Finally, identify the descriptive constituents by application. This operation consists of checking the tentatively identified constituents against random cases of the sample to see whether they fulfill the following conditions. Each constituent must:
	  [a] be expressed explicitly in the description.
	  [b] be expressed explicitly or implicitly in some or the large majority of descriptions
	  [c] be compatible with the description in which it is not expressed.
	  [d] If a description is found incompatible with a constituent, the former must be proven not to be an expression of the experience under study, but of some other experience that intrudes upon it.

Giorgi (1985)	1. Read the entire description of the experience to get a sense of the whole. 2. Reread the description. 3. Identify the transition units of the experience. 4. Clarify and elaborate the meaning by relating them to each other and to the whole. 5. Reflect on the constituents in the concrete language of the subject. 6. Transformation of that concrete language into the language or concepts of science. 7. Integration and synthesis of the insight into a descriptive structure of the meaning of the experience.

TABLE 3.1 (CONT'D.)

Author	Procedural Steps
Paterson & Zderad (1976)	1. Comparing and studying instances of the phenomenon wherever description of it may be found (putting descriptions in a logbook). 2. Imaginatively varying the phenomenon. 3. Explain through negation. 4. Explain through analogy and metaphor. 5. Classification of the phenomenon.
Colaizzi (1978)	1. Description of the phenomena of interest by the researcher. 2. Collection of subject's description of the phenomena. 3. Reading all the subjects' descriptions of the phenomenon. 4. Returning the original transcripts and extracting significant statements. 5. Trying to spell out the meaning of each significant statement. 6. Organizing the aggregate formalized meanings into clusters of themes. 7. Writing an exhaustive description. 8. Returning to the subjects for validation of the description. 9. If new data are revealed during the validations incorporating them into an exhaustive description.
van Manen (1984)	1. Turn to the nature of lived experience by orienting to the phenomenon, formulating the phenomenological question, and explicating assumptions and pre-understandings. 2. Existential Investigation which involves exploring the phenomenon: generating data, using personal experience as a starting point, tracing etymological sources, searching idiomatic phrases, obtaining experiential descriptions from subjects, locating experiential descriptions in the literature, and consulting phenomenological literature, art, etc. 3. Phenomenological Reflection involves conducting thematic analysis, uncovering thematic aspects in life-world descriptions, isolating thematic statements composing linguistic transformations, and gleaning thematic descriptions from artistic sources. 4. Phenomenological Writing includes attending to the speaking of language, varying the examples, writing and rewriting.
Streubert (1991)	1. Explicating a personal description of the phenomenon of interest. 2. Bracketing the researcher's presuppositions. 3. Interviewing participants in unfamiliar settings. 4. Carefully reading the transcripts of the interview to obtain a general sense of the experience. 5. Reviewing the transcripts to uncover essences. 6. Apprehending essential relationships. 7. Developing formalized descriptions of phenomena. 8. Returning to participants to validate descriptions. 9. Reviewing the relevant literature. 10. Distributing the findings to the nursing community.

"Phenomenology in its descriptive stage can stimulate our perceptiveness for the richness of our experience in breadth and in depth" (p. 70).

Phenomenology of appearances involves giving attention to the ways in which phenomena appear. In watching the ways in which phenomena appear, one pays particular attention to the different ways in which an object presents itself. Phenomenology of appearances focuses attention on the phenomenon as it unfolds through dwelling with the data. Phenomenology of appearances "can heighten the sense for the inexhaustibility of the perspectives through which our world is given" (Spiegelberg, 1975, p. 70).

Constitutive phenomenology is studying phenomena as they become established or "constituted" in our consciousness. Constitutive phenomenology "means the process in which the phenomena 'take shape' in our consciousness, as we advance from first impressions to a full 'picture' of their structure" (Spiegelberg, p. 66). According to Spiegelberg (1975), constitutive phenomenology "can develop the sense for the dynamic adventure in our relationship with the world" (p. 70).

Reductive phenomenology, although addressed as a separate process, occurs concurrently, throughout a phenomenological investigation. The researcher continually addresses personal bias, assumptions, and presuppositions and *brackets* or sets aside these beliefs in order to obtain the purest description of the phenomenon under investigation. Suspending judgment can make us more aware of the precariousness of all our claims to knowledge, "a ground for epistomological humility" (Spiegelberg, 1975, p. 70). This step is critical for the preservation of objectivity in phenomenological method.

For example, in a study investigating the meaning of quality of life for individuals with Type I insulin-dependent diabetes mellitus, the investigator begins the study with the reductive process. This is done by identifying all presuppositions, bias, or assumptions the researcher holds about what quality of life means or what it is like to have diabetes. This is done by a critical self-examination of personal beliefs and acknowledgment of understandings that have been gained from experience. The researcher takes all she/he knows about the phenomenon, brackets it, or sets it aside, in an effort to keep what is already known separate from the lived experience as described by the participants.

Phenomenological reduction is critical if pure description is to be achieved. The reductive process is also the basis for postponing any review of the literature until the data have been analyzed. What the researcher knows or believes about the phenomenon under investigation must always be kept separate from the participants' descriptions. Therefore, postponing the literature review until data analysis is complete facilitates the phenomenological reduction.

Finally, *hermeneutic phenomenology* is a "special kind of phenomenological interpretation, designed to unveil otherwise concealed meanings in the phenomena" (Spiegelberg, 1975, p. 57). Gadamer (1976) elaborates by noting that hermeneutics bridges the gap between what is familiar in our worlds and that which is unfamiliar. "Its field of application is comprised of all those situations in which we encounter meanings that are not immediately understandable but require interpretive effort" (p. xii).

Allen and Jenson (1990) illustrate the application of hermeneutical inquiry in their exploration of what it means to have eye problems and to be visually impaired. Their example emphasizes the applicability of hermeneutics in the description and explanation of human phenomenon. According to Allen and Jenson (1990):

> The task . . . of modern hermeneutics is to describe and explain human phenomena (such as health and illness). The purpose of hermeneutical description and explanation is to achieve understanding through interpretation of the phenomena under study. It is the written description of the phenomena (text) that is the object of interpretation (p. 242).

The six core elements characteristic of phenomenological method have been interpreted in several ways. Examples of these interpretations are outlined in Table 3.1. Applying any of these interpretations to a particular investigation also will require a careful examination of the role of the researcher, generation and treatment of data, and ethical issues connected with a phenomenological investigation.

Application of the Approach

Role of the Researcher

As lived experience becomes description of a particular phenomenon, the investigator takes on specific responsibilities in transforming information. Reinharz (1983) articulated five steps that occur in phenomenological transformation as the investigator makes public what essentially was private knowledge.

The first transformation occurs as the experiences of people are transformed into language. During this step the researcher, through verbal interaction, creates an opportunity for the lived experience to be shared (Reinharz, 1983). In the example of research on quality of life for individuals with Type I insulin-dependent diabetes mellitus, the researcher would create an opportunity for individuals living with this chronic illness to share their experiences related to the meaning of quality of life.

The second transformation occurs as the researcher transforms what is seen and heard into understanding of the original experience. Since individuals can never experience what another person has experienced, in exactly the same manner, researchers must rely on the data participants share about a particular experience and from that develop their own transformation (Reinharz, 1983). In this instance, the researcher studying quality of life takes what has been said by participants and produces a description that lends understanding to the original experience shared by participants.

Third, the researcher transforms what is understood, about the phenomenon under investigation, into conceptual categories that are the essences of the original experience (Reinharz, 1983). Data analysis of interviews addressing the meaning of quality of life would involve clarification of the essences of the phenomenon. For example, the data may reveal that quality of life for an individual with diabetes mellitus may center around freedom from restrictions in daily activities, independence, and prevention of long-term complications.

Fourth, the researcher transforms those essences into a written document that captures what the researcher has thought about the experience and reflects the participant's descriptions or actions. In all transformations, information can be lost or gained; therefore, it is important to have the participant review the final description to ensure that the material is correctly stated and that nothing has been added or deleted (Reinharz, 1983).

Finally, the researcher transforms the written document into an understanding that can function to clarify all preceding steps (Reinharz, 1983). This written document is often referred to as the exhaustive description, the intent of which is to synthesize and capture the meaning of the experience into written form without distortion or loss of richness of the data. In other words, the exhaustive description of quality of life would reveal the richness of the experience identified from the very beginning of the investigation as perceived by individuals with Type I insulin-dependent diabetes mellitus.

In addition to the five transformational steps outlined by Reinharz (1983), the investigator must possess certain qualities that will permit access to data the participant possesses. The ability to communicate clearly and help participants feel comfortable expressing their experiences are essential qualities in a phenomenological researcher. The researcher is the instrument for data collection and must function effectively in order to facilitate data collection. The researcher must recognize that personal characteristics, such as manner of speaking, gender, age, or other personality traits, may interfere with data retrieval. For this reason researchers must ask whether they are the appropriate people to access a given person's or group's experiences (Reinharz, 1983).

Data Generation

Purposeful sampling is used most commonly in phenomenological inquiry. This method of sampling selects individuals for study participation based on their particular knowledge of a phenomenon for the purpose of sharing that knowledge.

> The logic and power of purposeful sampling lies in selecting information-rich cases for study in depth. Information-rich cases are those from which one can learn a great deal about issues of central importance to the purpose of the research, thus the term purposeful sampling (Patton, 1990, p. 169).

Sample selection provides the participants for the investigation. Participants, once they have agreed to participate, should be contacted before the interview to prepare them for the actual meeting and to answer any preliminary questions they might have. At the time of the first interview, informed consent and permission to tape record, if this data-gathering instrument is used, can be obtained. Piloting interview skills and having a more experienced phenomenological researcher listen to the tape of an interview can assist in the development of interviewing skills. According to Benoliel (1988):

> Effective observer–interviewer needs to bring knowledge, sensitivity, and flexibility into a situation. Interviewing is not an interpersonal exchange controlled by the interviewer but rather a transaction that is reciprocal in nature and involves an exchange of social rewards (p. 211).

The researcher should help participants describe lived experience without leading the discussion. Open-ended, clarifying questions facilitate this process. Examples include: What comes to mind when you hear the word commitment? or What comes to mind when you think about quality of life? Open-ended interviewing allows the researcher to follow the participant's lead, to ask clarifying questions, and to facilitate the expression of the lived experience by the participant. Interviews usually end when participants believe they have exhausted their descriptions. If interviews are not feasible, participants can be asked to write an extensive description of some phenomenon by responding to a pre-established question or questions. The concern with written responses versus tape-recorded interviews is that saturation may not be achieved. During an interview, the researcher can help the participant to explain things in more detail by asking questions. This valuable opportunity is eliminated when participants write their descriptions.

The interview allows entrance into another person's world and is an excellent source of data. Complete concentration and rigorous participation in the interview process improve the accuracy, trustworthiness, and authenticity of the data. Finally, the researcher must remember to remain centered on the data, listen attentively, avoid interrogating the participant, and treat the participant with respect and sincere interest in the shared experience.

Data generation or collection continues until the researcher believes saturation has been achieved. Data saturation is said to be achieved when no new themes or essences emerge from the participants and the data are repeating. Therefore predetermination of the number of participants for a given study is not possible. Data collection must continue until the researcher is assured saturation has been achieved.

As noted in Chapter 2 of this text, Morse (1989) states that saturation is a myth. She believes that given another group of informants on the same subject, at another time, new data may be revealed. Therefore, the investigator will be able to reach saturation only with a particular group of informants and only during specific times. "The long term challenge for the phenomenologist interested in generating theory is to interview several samples from a variety of backgrounds, age ranges and cultural environments to maximize the likelihood of discovering the essences of phenomena across groups" (Streubert, 1991, p. 121).

Ethical Considerations

The personal nature of phenomenological research results in several ethical considerations for the researcher. Informed consent differs in a qualitative study as opposed to a quantitative investigation. There is no way to know exactly what might transpire during an interview. Issues of privacy must be considered. When preparing a final manuscript the researcher must consider how the data can be presented so that they are accurate yet do not reveal the identity of participants.

Munhall (1988) noted that qualitative research is a moral as well as knowledge-generating activity. Consent should be viewed as an ongoing transactional process.

> Perhaps the most critical, ethical obligation that qualitative nurse researchers have is to describe the experiences of others in the most faithful way possible. The ethical obligation is to describe and report in the most authentic manner possible the experience that unfolds even if contrary to your aims (p. 153).

Cowles (1988) addressed several concerns that may emerge during a qualitative investigation. Awkward, embarrassing events, overidentification with subjects, loss of composure, and personal reactions may all present during an interview, particularly if the phenomenon of interest is of a sensitive nature. The data collection can be energy depleting, and the researcher often needs social support to cope with sensitive or upsetting topics.

Data Treatment

Treatment of the data can be handled in a variety of ways. When using open-ended interviewing techniques, tape recording and verbatim transcription will increase the accuracy of data collection. High-quality tape-recording equipment is essential. The researcher also should make some hand-written notes. Adding hand-written notes to verbally transcribed accounts helps to achieve the most comprehensive and accurate description. A second interview may be needed to give the researcher an opportunity to refer to limited or inadequately described information and assist the participant to clarify and expound on descriptions. Often participants will have additional thoughts about the phenomenon under study after the initial interview. The second interview provides the researcher with the opportunity to expand, verify, and add descriptions of the phenomenon under investigation. Following the interviews, the researcher should immediately listen to the tape, checking that the interview made sense and verifying the need for a follow-up interview. If for some reason, the tape recording fails, immediately following the interview, the researcher should make extensive, detailed notes.

When data collection begins, so too does data analysis. From the moment the researcher begins listening to descriptions of a particular phenomenon, analysis is occurring. These processes are inseparable. Therefore, the importance of the reductive process cannot be overemphasized. Separating one's beliefs and assumptions from the raw data occurs throughout the investigation. Journaling is a method that is helpful in continuing the reductive process. Use of a journal by the researcher can facilitate phenomenological reduction. Writing down any ideas, feelings, or responses that emerge during data collection supports reductive phenomenology. Drew (1989) offers the added perspective that journaling that addresses the researcher's own experience can be "considered data and examined within the context of the study for the part it has played in the study's results" (p. 431).

After data collection and verbatim transcription, the researcher should listen to the tapes while reading the transcriptions for accuracy. This helps to familiarize the researcher with the data and begins immersing the researcher in the phenomenon under investigation.

Data Analysis

Data analysis requires the researcher to dwell with or become immersed in the data. This begins with listening to participants' verbal descriptions and is followed by reading and re-reading the verbatim transcriptions or written responses. As the researcher becomes immersed in the data, significant statements are identified and extracted. These statements can then be transcribed onto index cards for ease of ordering later in the process. Apprehending or capturing the essential relationships among the statements and preparing an exhaustive description of the phenomenon is the final phase. Through free imaginative variation, the researcher makes connections between statements obtained in the interview process. It is critical to identify how statements or central themes emerged and are connected to one another if the final description is to be comprehensive and exhaustive.

Microcomputers and word-processing software can make data storage and retrieval more efficient. Examining software packages that are available for qualitative data analysis may be an appropriate option depending on the researcher's personal preferences. Please refer to Table 11.1, Computerized Qualitative Data Management Programs for an overview of available software for data storage, retrieval, and analysis.

Review of the Literature

The review of literature should follow data analysis. This is different from quantitative research methods which require the literature review prior to the investigation. The rationale for postponing the literature review is related to the goal of achieving a pure description of the phenomenon under investigation. The fewer ideas or preconceived notions the researcher has about the phenomenon under investigation, the less likely the research will be influenced by his/her bias. Once data analysis is complete, the researcher reviews the literature in order to place the findings within the context of what is already known about the topic. A cursory review of the literature may be done to verify the need for the investigation.

TRUSTWORTHINESS AND AUTHENTICITY OF DATA

The issue of trustworthiness in qualitative research has been a concern for researchers engaging in these methods and is discussed at length in the literature (Beck, 1993; Krefting, 1991; Yonge & Stewin, 1988). The issues of rigor in qualitative research are important to the practice of good science.

The trustworthiness of the questions put to the subjects depends on the extent to which they tap the subject's experience apart from the subjects' theoretical knowledge of the topic (Colaizzi, 1978). Consistent use of the method and bracketing prior knowledge help to ensure pure description of the data. To ensure trustworthiness of data analysis, the researcher returns to each participant and asks if the exhaustive description reflects his/her experiences. Content added or deleted by participants should be incorporated into a revised description.

Finally, requesting negative descriptions of the phenomenon under investigation is helpful in establishing authenticity and trustworthiness of the data. For example, in the study investigating the meaning of quality of life in individuals with Type I insulin-dependent diabetes mellitus, the researcher may ask: "Can you describe a situation where you would feel that you did not have quality of life?" This gives opportunity to compare and contrast data. For additional discussion of issues surrounding reliability and validity in qualitative research please see Chapter 2.

SUMMARY

Phenomenology is an integral field of inquiry to nursing, as well as philosophy, sociology, and psychology. As a research method, phenomenology is a rigorous science whose purpose is to bring to language human experience. The phenomenological movement has been influenced by the works of Husserl, Brentano, Stumpf, Merleau-Ponty, and others. Concepts central to the method include intentionality, essences, intuiting, reduction, embodiment, and being-in-the-world.

Phenomenology as a method of research offers nursing an opportunity to describe and clarify phenomena important to practice, education, and research. Selecting this approach for the investigation of phenomena should be based on suitability and a need for further clarification of selected phenomenon. Specific considerations must be given to the issues of researcher as instrument, data generation, data treatment and authenticity, and trustworthiness of data. Investigations that utilize this approach contribute to nursing's knowledge base and can provide direction for future investigations.

REFERENCES

Allen, M. N., & Jenson, L. (1990). Hermeneutical inquiry, meaning and scope. *Western Journal of Nursing Research, 12*(2), 241–253.

Beck, C. T. (1993). Qualitative research: The evaluation of its credibility, fittingness, and auditability. *Western Journal of Nursing Research, 15*(2), 263–265.

Benoliel, J. Q. (1988). Commentaries on special issue. *Western Journal of Nursing Research, 10*(2), 210–213.

Blumensteil, A. (1973). A sociology of good times. In Psathas, G. (Ed.), *Phenomenological sociology: Issues and applications*. New York: John Wiley and Sons.

Cohen, M. Z. (1987). A historical overview of the phenomenologic movement. *Image, 19*(1), 31–34.

Colaizzi, P. F. (1978). Psychological research as the phenomenologist views it. In R. Valle & M. King (Eds.), *Existential phenomenological alternative for psychology*. New York: Oxford University Press.

Cowles, K. V. (1988). Issues in qualitative research on sensitive topics. *Western Journal of Nursing Research, 10*(2), 163–179.

Drew, N. (1989). The interviewer's experience as data in phenomenological research. *Western Journal of Nursing Research, 11*(4), 431–439.

Gadamer, H. G. (1976). *Philosophical hermeneutics.* (David E. Linge, Ed. and Trans.). Los Angeles, CA: University of California Press.

Giorgi, A. (1985) *Phenomenology and psychological research.* Pittsburgh: Duquesne University Press.

Husserl, E. (1931). *Ideas: General introduction to pure phenomenology.* (W. R. Boyce Gibson, Trans.) New York: Collier.

Husserl, E. (1965). *Phenomenology and the crisis of philosophy* (Q. Laver, Trans.). New York: Harper and Row.

Krefting, L. (1991). Rigor in qualitative research: The assessment of trustworthiness. *The American Journal of Occupational Therapy, 45*(3), 214–222.

Merleau-Ponty, M. (1956). What is phenomenology? *Cross Currents, 6,* 59–70.

Merleau-Ponty, M. (1962). *Phenomenology of perception* (C. Smith, Trans.). New York: Humanities Press.

Munhall, P. (1989). Philosophical ponderings on qualitative research. *Nursing Science Quarterly, 2*(1), 20–28.

Munhall, P. (1988). Ethical considerations in qualitative research. *Western Journal of Nursing Research, 10*(2), 150–162.

Munhall, P. L., & Boyd, C. O. (1993). *Nursing research, A qualitative perspective.* New York: National League for Nursing Press.

Morse, J. M. (1989) *Qualitative nursing research.* Rockville, MD: Aspen.

Natanson, M. (1973). *Edmund Husserl: Philosopher of infinite tasks.* Evanston, IL: Northwestern University Press.

Omery, A. (1983). Phenomenology: A method for nursing research. *Advances in Nursing Science, 5*(2), 49–63.

Patton, M. Q. (1990). *Qualitative evaluation and research methods.* Beverly Hills, CA: Sage Publications Inc.

Paterson, G. J., & Zderad, L. T. (1976). *Humanistic nursing.* New York: John Wiley and Sons.

Reeder, F. (1987). The phenomenological movement. *IMAGE: Journal of Nursing Scholarship, 19*(3), 150–152.

Reinharz, S. (1983). Phenomenology as a dynamic process. *Phenomenology and Pedagogy, 1*(1), 77–79.

Rinaldi, D. M. (1989). The lived experience of commitment to nursing. *Dissertation abstracts international,* Ann Arbor MI:

Schutz, A. (1970). *On phenomenology and social relations.* Chicago: University of Chicago Press.

Spiegelberg, H. (1965). *The phenomenological movement: A historical introduction,* 2nd ed., Volumes 1–2. The Hague: Nijhoff.

Spiegelberg, H. (1975). *Doing phenomenology.* The Hague: Nijhoff.

Streubert, H. J. (1991). Phenomenologic research as a theoretic initiative in community health nursing. *Public Health Nursing, 8*(2), 119–123.

van Kaam, A. (1959). A phenomenological analysis exemplified by the feeling of being really understood. *Individual Psychology, 15,* 66–72.

van Manen, M. (1984). Practicing phenomenological writing. *Phenomenology and Pedagogy, 2,* 36–69.

Wagner, H. R. (1983). *Phenomenology of consciousness and sociology of the life and world: An introductory study.* Edmonton, Alberta: University of Alberta Press.

Yonge, O., & Stewin, L. (1988). Reliability and validity: Misnomers for qualitative research. *The Canadian Journal of Nursing Research, 20*(2), 61–67.

Chapter 4

Application of Phenomenological Research in Nursing Education, Practice, and Administration

The acceptance of qualitative methods as legitimate approaches to the discovery of knowledge has grown considerably in recent years. Phenomenology as one approach to qualitative investigations has made a significant contribution to published research in the qualitative arena. As nurse researchers continue to use qualitative methods for the investigation of nursing phenomena, the availability and quality of published research using qualitative methods will continue to grow.

Qualitative methods allow exploration of humans by humans in ways that acknowledge the value of all evidence, the inevitability and worth of subjectivity, the value of a holistic view, and the integration of all patterns of knowing (Chinn, 1985).

This chapter provides an overview and critique of three phenomenological investigations published as journal articles, in the areas of nursing education, practice, and administration. The purpose is to provide examples that demonstrate the applicability of phenomenological research for the investigator interested in using this approach and to amplify the areas inherent in a phenomenological investigation on which the reader should focus.

The studies presented in this chapter were reviewed according to the "Critiquing Guidelines for Qualitative Research" (Streubert, 1994) presented in Table 4.1. These guidelines offer readers of qualitative investigations a guide to recognizing essential methodological points and evaluating the success of a published report in contributing to the scientific

Qualitative Research in Nursing: Advancing the Humanistic Imperative by Helen J. Streubert and Dona R. Carpenter. Copyright © 1995 by J. B. Lippincott Company.

base of nursing knowledge. A reprint of the Phipps (1993) study can be found at the end of this chapter to assist the reader in understanding the critiquing process.

This chapter also provides the reader with a variety of examples of published research using phenomenological method. These examples are presented in Table 4.2 which summarizes significant points of selected phenomenological investigations. Examples of studies that use the method interpretations addressed in Chapter 3 are also included in Table 4.2 (Colaizzi, 1978; Giorgi, 1985; Munhall & Boyd, 1993; Spiegelberg, 1965, 1975; Streubert, 1991; van Manen, 1984; van Kaam, 1959). These examples are provided as a guide for the reader interested in applying one of the various method interpretations. Articles were chosen based on their ability to provide varied examples of method application and serve only as a beginning point of reference. Nursing research articles are continually added to the wealth of data available, and the reader is encouraged to seek out these new and important examples. Finally, the examples provide the reader with a sense of how the method can be used in nursing education and practice. Although phenomenology is very appropriate for studying phenomena important to nursing administration, the approach has not been widely applied in this area.

PHENOMENOLOGICAL METHOD APPLIED TO NURSING PRACTICE

Many nursing interventions performed in clinical settings lend themselves to quantitative measurement. Examples include measurement of blood pressure, central venous pressure, or urine specific gravity. However, nurses enmeshed in practice settings are well aware that much of what is done for patients is subjective and based on how nurses come to know their patients and their life experiences. For example, caring, reassurance, and quality of life are phenomena central to nursing practice, but do not necessarily lend themselves to quantitative measurement. Therefore, subjective phenomena unique to the practice of professional nursing need investigative approaches suitable to their unique nature. Qualitative methods are applicable to the study of subjective interactive experience and have been addressed in relationship to practice areas (Beck, 1990; Oiler, 1982; Omery, 1987; Pallikkathayil & Morgan, 1991; Paterson, 1971; Taylor, 1993). Phenomenology, as a qualitative research method, has been used to explore a variety of practice-related experiences such as postpartum depression (Beck,1992b) caring in acute care settings (Miller, Haber, & Byrne, 1992) and healing in battered women (Farrell, 1992).

TABLE 4.1   CRITIQUING GUIDELINES FOR QUALITATIVE RESEARCH

Statement of the Phenomenon of Interest
1. Is the phenomenon of interest clearly identified?
2. Has the researcher identified why the phenomenon requires a qualitative format?
3. Are the philosophical underpinnings of the research described?

Purpose
1. Is the purpose of conducting the research made explicit?
2. Does the researcher describe the projected significance of the work to nursing?

Method
1. Is the method used to collect data compatible with the purpose of the research?
2. Is the method adequate to address the phenomenon of interest?

Sampling
1. Does the researcher describe the selection of participants? Is purposive sampling used?
2. Are the informants who were chosen appropriate to inform the research?

Data Collection
1. Is data collection focused on human experience?
2. Does the researcher describe data collection strategies? [i.e., interview, observation, field notes]
3. Is protection of human subjects addressed?
4. Is saturation of the data described?
5. Are the procedures for collecting data made explicit?

One example of a phenomenological research study as applied to the practice setting is a study entitled "A Phenomenological Study of Couples' Infertility: Gender Influence" by Phipps (1993). This article was reviewed using the guidelines presented in Table 4.1. When reviewing any piece of published research it is important to consider the fact that the readers of research are most often interested in the findings of the study, as opposed to the literature review or method. Therefore, the findings are usually what will be published in the most detail, with only method and literature review highlights included. If the reader is interested in more detail about the published research it is often helpful to write directly to the author. The article by Phipps (1993) highlights method in enough detail that the reader can following the method implementation in her discussion of the findings.

In her phenomenological investigation of couples' infertility and

TABLE 4.1 (CONT'D.)

Data Analysis
1. Does the researcher describe the strategies used to analyze the data?
2. Has the researcher remained true to the data?
3. Does the reader understand the procedures used to analyze the data?
4. Does the researcher address the credibility, auditability, and fittingness of the data?

   Credibility
   a. Do the participants recognize the experience as their own?

   Auditability
   a. Can the reader follow the thinking of the researcher?
   b. Does the researcher document the research process?

   Fittingness
   a. Can the findings be applicable outside of the study situation?
   b. Are the results meaningful to individuals not involved in the research?
5. Is the strategy used for analysis compatible with the purpose of the study?

   Findings
   1. Are the findings presented within a context?
   2. Is the reader able to apprehend the essence of the experience from the report of the findings?
   3. Are the researcher's conceptualizations true to the data?
   4. Does the researcher place the report in the context of what is already known about the phenomenon?

   Conclusions, Implications, and Recommendations
   1. Do the conclusions, implications and recommendations give the reader a context in which to use the findings?
   2. Do the conclusions reflect the findings of the study?
   3. Are recommendations for future study offered?
   4. Is the significance of the study to nursing made explicit?

Source: Streubert, H. (1994). Evaluating the qualitative research report. In G. LoBiondo-Wood & J. Haber, (Eds.). *Nursing research. Methods, critical appraisal, and utilization* (3rd. ed.). (pp. 481–499). St. Louis: Mosby.

gender influence, Phipps (1993) discovered that although similarities existed in male and female experiences with infertility, changes in self-perception remained unique to women. The experience of infertility was found to be frustrating and painful for both men and women. Feelings of isolation, guilt, powerlessness, and sorrow were at times consuming. The infertility experience was, however, influenced by gender role expectations. The investigation provided an example of the rigor of phenomenological research and the important contribution that phenomenological research can make to nursing practice.

(Text continues on p. 60.)

TABLE 4.2 SELECTIVE SAMPLING OF PHENOMENOLOGICAL RESEARCH STUDIES

Author/Date	Domain	Phenomenon	Method
Appleton, C. (1990)	Education	The meaning of human care and the experience of caring from the perspective of doctoral students during their educational experience in a program of nursing	Not specified
Ashworth, P. D., & Hagan, T.H. (1993)	Practice	The meaning of incontinence for non-geriatric urinary incontinence sufferers	Giorgi
Baillie, L. (1993)	Education	Factors influencing student nurses' learning in a community setting	Colaizzi, with reference to the work of Knaack & Oiler
Beck, C. T. (1991)	Education	Students' perceptions of caring nursing student-faculty experience	Colaizzi
Beck, C. T. (1993)	Education	The meaning of a caring experience between a nursing student and a patient	van Manen
Criddle, L. (1992)	Practice	The experience of healing from surgery	Lincoln & Guba
Farrell, M. (1992)	Practice	The lived experience of healing in women who encountered battering within a relationship with a man	Giorgi

TABLE 4.2 (CONT'D.)

Sample	Data Generation	Findings
Purposive sample of two doctoral students	Interviews	The meaning of caring emerged as a way of being in the world and the process of caring emerged from the descriptions of commitment, involvement, and belonging for the purpose of becoming. A sense of being in place and feeling belonging was related to caring (p. 86).
28 young or middle-aged women who suffered from urinary incontinence	Audiotaped interviews with verbatim transcription	Incontinence was found to be a socially unacceptable topic of conversation. Sufferers react with apathy, guilt, and denial.
8 nursing students	Audiotaped interviews with verbatim transcription	Factors affecting student learning included relevance of the learning experience, variety of experiences, role satisfaction, attitudes, and professional credibility. These factors were related to the students, mentor, and actual placements.
47 junior and senior nursing students	Participants responded in written format to open-ended questions	Caring behaviors identified included compassion, competence, confidence, conscience, and commitment.
22 undergraduate students	Students wrote in-depth accounts	Five essential themes of a caring nursing student-patient experience emerged: authentic presence, competence, emotional support, physical and positive consequences.
9 post surgical patients	Tape recorded interviews transcribed verbatim at one and four weeks post hospitalization	Healing included four overlapping themes: Active Participation, Achieving Balance, Evolving Beyond and Healing Process.
7 participants	Individual audiotaped interviews with verbatim transcription, field notes and demographic data sheets	Healing is a multidimensional phenomenon. Four Major themes of healing were identified: flexibility, awakening, relationship and empowerment. Interventions need to be multilevel and offered over time.

(cont'd.)

TABLE 4.2 (CONT'D.)

Author/Date	Domain	Phenomenon	Method
Field, P. (1981)	Education	The lived experience of giving an injection	Not specified
Forrest, D. (1989)	Practice	Investigation of the phenomenon of caring with hospital staff nurses	Colaizzi
Green-Hernandez, C. (1990)	Practice	The concept of caring as a lived experience from human and nursing perspectives	Colaizzi
Hanna, K. M. (1989)	Education	The meaning of health for graduate nursing students	Not specified
King, T. (1993)	Practice	Experiences of midlife daughters who were caring for their aging mothers	Giorgi

TABLE 4.2 (CONT'D.)

Sample	Data Generation	Findings
10 experienced nurses, 10 under-graduate nursing students, and 4 diabetic patients	Essays and interviews	The experience of administering an injection was addressed in terms of language, the giver, hurting the other, preparing for the injection, the act, responses to the act and experiences with children and unconscious patients. The purpose was to stimulate the reader so that a better understanding of the anxiety nursing students feel about giving an injection is developed.
17 hospital staff nurses	Audiotaped verbatim transcriptions	Thirty theme clusters emerged and were categorized into seven categories under the two broad classifications of what is caring, and what affects caring? The categories included involvement, interacting, oneself, the patient, frustrations, coping, comfort, and support
Purposive sample of 20 nurses that stated they had experience in caring	Audiotaped interviews that were transcribed verbatim	Six themes emerged as descriptive of the lived experience of natural caring and included being there, touching, social support, reciprocity, time/extra effort, and empathy. 14 themes emerged related to professional nurse caring and included holism, touching, technical competence, communication, listening, being there, professional experience, empathy, social support, reciprocity, involvement, time, formal and informal learning and helping.
29 graduate nursing students	Subjects were requested to describe in writing their meaning of health	Sixty-eight descriptive expressions of health were obtained. 33 reflected an awareness of a physical state and 35 reflected a mental state. Three elements composed the physical state and included physical appearance, physical ability, and energy level. Elements in the mental state included happiness/contentment, anticipation/excitement, and clarity of thinking. Participants also described environmental, situational, and developmental conditions.
7 daughters ranging in age from 42 to 69	Tape-recorded interviews transcribed verbatim	A continuum of care framework is described which integrates the themes that emerged from the raw data. These themes included: knowing mother and her needs, responding to mothers needs, deferring to mothers needs, recognizing, grieving, and identifying own fantasies.

(cont'd.)

TABLE 4.2 (CONT'D.)

Author/Date	Domain	Phenomenon	Method
Nelms, T. P. (1990)	Education	The lived experience of nursing education	Work of Maxine Green noted. Specifics of method not addressed.
Rinaldi, D. (1989)	Practice	The lived experience of commitment to nursing	Speigelberg (1965, 1975)
Streubert, H. (1989)	Education	Clinical experience	Streubert modification of Colaizzi, van Manen, and Paterson & Zderad
Warren, L. D. (1989)	Practice	The meaning of the experience of "feeling cared for"	van Manen (1984)

TABLE 4.2 (CONT'D.)

Sample	Data Generation	Findings
17 baccalaureate nursing students	Semi-structured interviews	The phenomenon of the lived experience of being a nursing student is that of a life-pervasive intensive commitment to a personal goal. Students feel that there are almost insurmountable amounts of knowledge to be learned and mastered. Students are continuously aware that the knowledge and skills to be mastered must be done according to criteria and within a certain time frame. The enjoyment of personal commitment and never being able to relax were noted.
20 participants, purposeful sampling	Audiotaped and verbatim transcription	The lived experience of commitment to nursing as perceived by nurses in a nursing world can be said to be an emotional response or feeling that stems from the nurse's sense of obligation and promise to assist others in meeting their health care needs. Descriptive elements included altruism, devotion, dedication, caring, being there, trust, loyalty, and nurturance.
10 nursing faculty and 10 nursing students	Audiotaped and verbatim transcription	Faculty: 8 major themes emerged including (1) student focussed learning activity, (2) faculty responsibility for student learning, (3) relationship development, (4) competent practice, (5) teacher, (6) relationship of past experiences, (7) assessing and evaluating, and (8) faculty development. Students: 10 major themes including (1) environment, (2) hands on skills, (3) theory/clinical relationship,(4) growth, (5) time, (6) learning, (7) participants in the experience,(8) negotiation, (9) facilitated/impede, (10) feelings. Exhaustive descriptions were offered for both groups of participants.
10 healthy adults	Serial open-ended interviews	The phenomenon of cared-for-ness emerged from examples cited from the childhoods and the family experience of the participants, and the situation that most often resulted in the experience of feeling cared for was that of a need being met without one having to ask that it be met. The feelings evoked by the experience were described as good feelings, feelings of being accepted, warm, secure, loved.

(cont'd.)

TABLE 4.2 (CONT'D.)

Author/Date	Domain	Phenomenon	Method
Wolf, Z. R. (1991)	Practice	Nurses' experiences giving post-mortem care to patients who have donated organs	Colaizzi
Wondolowski, C., & Davis, K. D. (1991)	Practice	The meaning of health for the oldest old	van Kaam Modification
Wood, F. G. (1991)	Practice	The experience of caregivers who were providing care to an individual who recently had been discharged from a physical rehabilitation program.	Not specified

Phipps (1993) made explicit for the reader the *phenomenon of interest* and the rationale for a qualitative research format. Phenomenological research method suited the investigation. The phenomenon of interest identified by Phipps was the "common lived experience of infertility for both males and females" (p. 45). Phipps noted that infertility research predominantly focused on the woman and her experience and that few studies addressed "the male experience with involuntary childlessness, or examine the similarities and differences in the infertility experience of spouses" (p. 44). The following study question directed Phipps' work: "How do the essential elements of men's and women's infertility experience compare?" (p.45).

The *philosophical underpinnings* of the research by Phipps (1993) were supported by the work of Colaizzi (1978), Omery (1983), Oiler (1982), and Spiegelberg (1975). Reference to these phenomenologists by Phipps (1993) provided theoretical support for the study. Direction for implementation of phenomenological research methodology was provided by the procedural steps of Colaizzi's (1978) method.

The *purpose* of the research was identification of gender influence and couples' infertility experiences. Phipps (1993) provided a lim-

TABLE 4.2 (CONT'D.)

Sample	Data Generation	Findings
Network convenience sample of 8 registered nurses	Semi-structured interviews, tape-recorded and transcribed verbatim	Nurses are saddened by the donor's death. Postmortem care is an opportunity to achieve closure with the patient and the nurse often becomes kin with the patient's family. Postmortem care is viewed as an opportunity to provide comfort, even after death.
108 subjects	Audiotaped and verbatim transcription	Three common elements emerged: abiding vitality, generating fulfillment, and rhapsodic reverie. Health for the oldest old was an "abiding vitality emanating through movements of rhapsodic reverie in generating fulfillment" (pg. 115).
Convenience sample of 10 caregivers	Semi-structured interviews, tape recorded and transcribed verbatim	Family members believed caregiving was their responsibility. The closeness established has positive and negative results. Caregiving entailed full-time responsibility while continuing with other roles and responsibilities.

ited discussion of infertility; however, she did make clear her rationale for method selection. The investigation is an important phenomenological research contribution to the domain of nursing practice. Phipps noted a void in the research literature dealing with both men and women experiencing infertility. Her discussion of this void established for the reader the need for the investigation and emphasized the appropriateness of phenomenology as method choice for this qualitative investigation.

Phipps (1993) used *phenomenological research method* as described by Colaizzi (1978) to guide her inquiry. Phenomenological methodology as identified by Colaizzi is well suited to the investigation and provided the researcher with direction for data analysis. Phipps followed the procedural steps as they were outlined by Colaizzi (1978) throughout the research process.

A *purposive sample* of eight Caucasian, middle-class couples was used. Purposeful (purposive) sampling provides information rich cases for in-depth study (Patton, 1990). Demographic data related to age, income, religious preference, and educational level was provided. As described by Phipps (1993),

The eight husbands ranged in age from 26 to 40 years, with a median age of 34 years. All were *college graduates* holding white collar jobs; *family incomes were $35,000 per year or above.* The eight wives ranges in age from 23 to 41 years, with a median age of 32 years. All had *completed or attended college.* Six of the eight couple indicated *Protestant as their religious preference; two couples had no religious preference. Four of the couples were actively participating in infertility treatment* at the time of interview. Two of the male informants had *oligospermia,* while the other six had *no identified fertility problems.* One couple had a shared infertility problem (p. 45).

The informants chosen were appropriate to inform the research because of their personal knowledge of the experience under study.

Data collection was accomplished by Phipps (1993) through audio-taped interviews that were transcribed verbatim. Open-ended interviews were conducted. Phipps used the software package "Ethnograph" (Seidel, Kjolseth, & Seymour, 1988) to process her data. She did not address data saturation in her article. Saturation of data is believed to occur when data begin to repeat themselves and no new themes are emerging during the interview. Addressing saturation adds to the study's credibility.

Data analysis was accomplished using the procedural steps described by Colaizzi (1978). The study reflected consistent use of the method for data analysis. Phipps (1993) discusses the findings of her study in relationship to the 10 categories that emerged (p.46.). The categories included:

1. Evaluation of the meaning of childlessness
2. Feelings associated with infertility
3. Coping
4. Marital functioning
5. Gender role
6. Relationships
7. Investment
8. Perserverance
9. Perception of the health care system
10. Self-perception, which was unique to the women in the group of participants

Discussion of each of the categories supplemented with examples of raw data allows the reader to follow how Phipps (1993) proceeded with data analysis.

Credibility can be established by returning the exhaustive description to each participant and asking them to verify the accuracy of the material. Phipps (1993) indicated that the "exhaustive descriptions of the

male and female experiences were submitted to informants for validation and were accepted without revisions" (p. 44).

Auditability refers "to the ability of another researcher to follow the
thinking, decisions and methods used by the original researcher" (Yonge
& Stewin, 1988, p. 64). Phipps (1993) provided boxed information that
helped the reader follow her line of thinking during data interpretation.
For the ten categories that emerged, Phipps (1993) provided a listing of
both common and different themes for the male and female participants
as they pertained to each of the categories.

Fittingness of the research refers to how well the findings fit outside of the study situation. Phipps (1993) addressed the fittingness of
her findings in both the discussion and implications sections of her article. She noted the importance of nurses and other members of the health
care team in helping infertile couples during their experience. Phipps
(1993) emphasized the need for nurses to provide thorough and meaningful information to couples. "Helping couples explore treatment
options, knowing the inherent risks and expenditures, will increase their
feeling of being in control of their lives and facilitate dyadic decision
making" (p. 55).

The *findings* of Phipps (1993) are presented in the context of the
group studied. The data are presented using both the informants words
and author's interpretations. In Phipp's report the reader gets a sense of
the needs of the infertile couple as well as differences in experiences associated with gender.

The *conclusions* of Phipps (1993) focused on the role of the nurse
and other members of the health care team in dealing with gender specific differences related to the experience of infertility. Her conclusions
were supported by the data and have implications for nursing care. The
study by Phipps (1993) is an example of the important contribution phenomenological research makes to nursing practice. Investigation of subjective phenomena unique to nursing practice is needed to expand nursing's body of knowledge and can provide the necessary background to
guide quantitative investigations.

PHENOMENOLOGICAL APPROACH APPLIED TO
NURSING EDUCATION

Nursing education also lends itself to objective and subjective research
interests. Test construction, and critical thinking are education-related
examples that lend themselves to quantitative investigation, although not
exclusively. The educational domain of nursing also lends itself to qualitative investigation in areas such as educational experiences, caring and

the curriculum, or the impact of evaluation on student performance in the clinical setting.

Several authors have used qualitative methods to investigate phenomena unique to nursing education. An overview and critique of the study "Caring Among Nursing Students," by Beck (1992a) are provided as one example of phenomenological method applied to the educational domain of nursing.

Beck (1992a) reported on a study important to nursing education that dealt with caring among nursing students. She identified four necessary constituents of a caring experience: (1) authentic presencing, (2) selfless sharing, (3) fortifying support, and (4) enriching effects. Beck (1992a) noted that along with faculty, nursing students can also be role models for caring.

The *phenomenon of interest* in this study was the meaning of caring among nursing students (Beck, 1992a). Beck described the importance of developing the capacity to care in nursing students and the fact that nursing students can be caring role models for each other. She further noted that currently, research dealing with caring among nursing students is absent from the literature. Beck described the philosophical underpinnings of the research in relationship to van Kaam's (1966) phenomenological methodology.

The *purpose* of the research was made explicit and the projected significance of the work to nursing education was described. Beck's purpose was to discover the necessary and sufficient constituents of a caring nursing student experience as experienced with another nursing student. A qualitative format suited the investigation since the author was interested in discovering covert and embedded aspects of caring. She was interested in studying human experience as lived, making the choice of phenomenology appropriate to her investigation. This is an important contribution to the literature dealing with nursing education (Beck, 1992a).

The *method* of data collection was compatible with the purpose of the research and adequate to address the phenomenon of interest. Beck (1992a) used the six steps identified in van Kaam's (1966) phenomenological methodology for data analysis.

The *sample* consisted of 53 undergraduate nursing students ranging in age from 20 to 59. Forty nine participants were female and four were male. Generic and RN to BSN students were included in the sample. Informed consent was addressed. Students responded in writing during an undergraduate research course to the following statement "Please describe a situation in which you experienced caring from another nursing student. Share all the thoughts, perceptions, and feelings you can recall until you have no more to say about the experience" (Beck, 1992a, p. 23).

Beck does not address data saturation. Although having participants write about their descriptions is clearly an option for data collection, there is at least one drawback. When participants write their descriptions, the researcher has no opportunity to utilize open-ended questioning. Having the opportunity to ask additional questions to clarify and encourage expanded discussion is helpful to ensure exhaustive description and data saturation.

Data analysis proceeded according the steps outlined by van Kaam (1966). Several tables presented in the study offered examples of Beck's (1992a) thinking process regarding themes. Examples of raw data further illustrate this process for the reader.

Credibility, auditability, and fittingness were addressed as credibility, transferability, dependability, and confirmability. Peer debriefing and member checks were two methods used to establish credibility. Transferability was accomplished by providing "thick, rich slices of data" (Beck, 1992a, p. 24). Dependability was accomplished by use of an audit trail (Beck, 1992a). Beck (1992a) further enhanced the trustworthiness of her findings by having a masters prepared nurse, experienced in qualitative data analysis follow the audit trail she used to analyze the data (p. 24).

The *conclusions, implications, and recommendations* offered by Beck (1992a) were related to the enriching effects of caring experiences and the importance of facilitating caring behavior in students. Beck's recommendations for further study focused on the development of quantitative instruments to measure caring among nursing students. She concluded:

> To nuture caring, nursing students need to be surrounded in a caring environment. Caring can be integrated throughout schools of nursing by fostering not only faculty but also student role models of caring. Caring is contagious (p. 27).

PHENOMENOLOGICAL RESEARCH APPROACH APPLIED TO NURSING ADMINISTRATION

The literature dealing with studies related to nursing administration that use a qualitative approach is limited. This is a domain of nursing that is in need of further qualitative investigation. An overview of the study, "A Phenomenological Approach to Understanding the Process of Deaning" by Stainton and Styles (1985), is presented as an example of application of qualitative research in the area of nursing administration.

The *phenomenon of interest* is clearly identified in this study and is focused on gaining an understanding of the process of deaning. Stainton and Styles (1985) identified specific rationale for using a qualitative format as well as the philosophical underpinnings of the research.

The *purpose* of the Stainton and Styles (1985) study was to gain insight into the deaning process. Rationale for use of a qualitative approach included:

> First, there is little empirical evidence available that assists the novice in understanding the role of the dean. Second, deaning involves situational variables, management skills, and personal knowledge that is gained through experience. And third, an expert dean will approach a situation with a host of unexamined or taken-for-granted meanings and practices that define what it means to be a dean in that situation (pp. 269–270).

This study makes a significant contribution to the understanding of the work of the dean as it describes an interpretive, phenomenological approach to gaining a context-based understanding of the process of deaning (p. 269).

The *method* used to collect data was compatible with the purpose of the research and adequately addressed the phenomenon of interest. Stainton and Styles (1985) reported using an interpretive approach to discover the practical knowledge of an experienced dean. This study is presented as an interpretation of hermeneutic phenomenology whose aim is understanding through interpretation of the phenomenon under study. Stainton and Styles (1985) provided clear rationale for their method choice which includes:

> The many variables characteristic of academic settings generate idiosyncratic approaches to interpreting diverse goals and process. Governance structures (and administrative styles) therefore vary both within and among institutions. They are the result of the blend between the personal knowledge of the individual dean and the characteristics of the situational context in which the role is executed (p. 269). The successful interface and interplay between the organizational and interpersonal aspects of the dean's position require continuous interpretation of the individual and contextual variables, neither of which are static. Deans are situated in a specific academic organization and a social-economic-political milieu that provide a background of shared, implicit meaning in the context of which deaning takes place. Deaning, therefore, cannot be understood by objectively studying decanal behaviors alone. An expert dean will approach a situation with a host of unexamined or taken-for-granted meanings and practice that define what it means to be a dean in that situation. Judgements are not based on rule or steps but on a gestalt of the whole (pp. 269–270).

From this rationale, the authors concluded that an interpretive approach is required to discover the practical knowledge of an experienced dean (p. 270).

The *sample* for this study included the two authors, identified as an expert and a novice dean. The research was focused on understanding the process of deaning as explored through the mentorship relationship existing between the two authors. Given the interpretive approach used, the participants were appropriate to inform the research.

Participant and nonparticipant observation are described by the researchers as the method of *data collection*. The procedures for data collection are made explicit. Data were collected over a two-year period to gain understanding of the role of the dean. Stainton and Styles (1985) do not address data saturation. Credibility, auditability, or fittingness of the findings are not specifically addressed.

Stainton and Styles (1985) discussed how the findings might be applicable outside of the study situation and *conclude and recommend* that:

> A phenomenological approach by means of the interpretive method used by expert and novice deans who can work in sympathetic tandem has potential for the preparation and orientation of some deans. This approach may differ from the mentor or modeling approach, as it leads not to rules, imitation, or theoretical formulations, but to enculturation through understanding. Expert deans willing to have their practices studied in this manner by selected doctoral students or newly appointed deans could increase recruitment to and effectiveness in the decanal role (p. 274).

The area of administration in nursing lends itself to phenomenological research. This is an area in which there is a need for more qualitative and specifically phenomenological investigations. Topics that may be appropriate to phenomenological investigation include the experience of being the chair, director of nursing, or head nurse and patient care coordinators.

SUMMARY

This chapter provides examples of phenomenological research applied to the areas of nursing practice, education, and administration. Critiquing guidelines suitable for use with phenomenological investigations are provided and utilized in the review of three phenomenological investigations. Examples of phenomenological research using the method interpretations presented in the preceding chapter have been provided for the purpose of giving phenomenological researchers samples they can review to help clarify method implementation. Finally, a selected sample of phenomenological studies is provided for the reader.

Phenomenology as a research approach provides an avenue for investigation that allows description of lived experiences. The voice of professional nurses in practice, education, and administration can be a tremendous source of data that has yet to be fully explored. Identifying subjective phenomena unique to the domains of nursing education, practice, and administration is important to the ever expanding body of nursing knowledge.

REFERENCES

Appleton, C. (1990). The meaning of human care and the experience of caring in a university school of nursing. In M. M. Leininger and J. Watson (Eds.), *The caring imperative in education* (pp. 77–94). New York: National League for Nursing.

Ashworth, P. D., & Hagan, M. T. (1993). The meaning of incontinence: A qualitative study of non-geriatric urinary incontinence sufferers. *Journal of Advanced Nursing, 18*, 1415–1423.

Baillie, L. (1993). Factor's effecting student nurses' learning in community placements: A phenomenological study. *Journal of Advanced Nursing, 18*, 1043–1053.

Beck, C. T. (1990). Qualitative research: Methodologies and use in pediatric nursing. *Issues in Comprehensive Pediatric Nursing, 13*, 193–201.

Beck, C. T. (1991). How students perceive faculty caring: A phenomenological study. *Nurse Educator, 16*(5), 18–22.

Beck, C. T. (1992a). Caring among nursing students. *Nurse Educator, 17*(6), 22–27.

Beck, C. T. (1992b). The lived experience of postpartum depression: A phenomenological study. *Nursing Research, 42*(3), 166–170.

Beck, C. T. (1993). Caring relationships between nursing students and their patients. *Nurse Educator, 18*(5), 28–32.

Boyd, C. O. (1993). Toward a nursing practice research method. *Advances in Nursing Science, 16*(2), 9–25.

Chinn, P. (1985). Debunking myths in nursing theory and research. *Image: Journal of Nursing Scholarship, 17*(2), 171–179.

Colaizzi, P. F. (1978). Psychological research as the phenomenologist views it. In R. Valle & M. King (Eds.), *Existential phenomenological alternative for psychology*. New York: Oxford University Press.

Criddle, L. (1993). Healing from surgery: A phenomenological study. *Image: Journal of Nursing Scholarship, 25*(3), 208–213.

Farrell, M. L. R. (1992). The lived experience of healing in women who encountered battering within a relationship with a man. *University Microfilms International*, Ann Arbor, Michigan, DAIB 52/12,6645.

Field, P. A. (1981). A phenomenological look at giving an injection. *Journal of Advanced Nursing, 6*, 291–296.

Forrest, D. (1989). The experience of caring. *Journal of Advanced Nursing, 14*, 815–829.

Green-Hernandez, C. (1990). A phenomenological investigation of caring as a lived experience in nurses. In M. M. Leininger & J. Watson (Eds.), *The caring imperative in education* (pp. 111–130). New York: National League for Nursing.

Giorgi, A. (1985). *Phenomenology and psychological research.* Pittsburgh: Duquesne University Press.

Hanna, K. M. (1989). The meaning of health for graduate nursing students. *Journal of Nursing Education, 28*(8), 372–376.

King, T. (1993). The experiences of midlife daughters who are caregivers for their mothers. *Health Care of Women International, 14,* 419–426.

Miller, B., Haber, J., & Byrne, M. (1992). The experience of caring in the acute care setting: Patients and nurses perspectives. In D. Gaut (Ed.), *The presence of caring in nursing* (pp. 137–156). New York: National League for Nursing.

Munhall, P., & Boyd, C. O. (1993) *Nursing research: A qualitative perspective.* New York: National League for Nursing Press.

Nelms, T. P. (1990). The lived experience of nursing education: A phenomenological study. In M. M. Leininger & J. Watson (Eds.), *Caring imperative in nursing education* (pp. 285–297). New York: National League for Nursing.

Oiler, C. (1982). The phenomenological approach in nursing research. *Nursing Research, 31*(3), 178–181.

Omery, A. (1983). Phenomenology: A method for nursing research. *Advances in Nursing Science, 5*(2), 49–63.

Omery, A. (1987). Qualitative research designs in the critical care setting: Review and application. *Heart and Lung, 16*(4), 432–436.

Pallikkathayil, L., & Morgan, S. A. (1991). Phenomenology as a method for conducting clinical research. *Applied Nursing Research, 4*(4), 195–200.

Paterson, J. G. (1971). From a philosophy of clinical nursing to a method of nursology. *Nursing Research, 20*(2), 143–146.

Patton, M. Q. (1990). *Qualitative evaluation and research methods,* 2nd ed. Newbury Park, CA: Sage.

Phipps, S. A. A. (1993). A phenomenological study of couples' infertility: Gender influence. *Holistic Nursing Practice, 7*(2), 44–56.

Rinaldi, D. (1989) The lived experience of commitment to nursing. *Dissertation Abstracts International,* Ann Arbor, Michigan.

Seidel, J., Kjolseth, R., & Seymour, E. (1988). *The ethnograph.* Littleton, OR: Qualitative Research Associates.

Spiegelberg, H. (1965). *The phenomenological movement: A historical introduction,* Vols 1 & 2, 2nd ed. The Hague: Nijhoff, 1st ed.

Spiegelberg, H. (1975). *Doing phenomenology.* The Hague: Nijhoff, 1st ed.

Stainton, M., & Styles, M. M. (1985). *Journal of Professional Nursing,* (Vol. 1). 269–274.

Streubert, H. J. (1989). A description of clinical experience as perceived by clinical nurse educators and students. *Dissertation Abstracts, 50,* 906.

Streubert, H. J. (1991). Phenomenologic research as a theoretic initiative in community health nursing. *Public Health Nursing, 8*(2), 119–123.

Streubert, H. J. (1994). Evaluating the qualitative research report.In G. LoBiondo-Wood & J. Haber (Eds.), *Nursing research: Methods, critical appraisal and utilization,* 3rd ed. (pp.481–499). St. Louis: Mosby.

Taylor, B. (1993). Phenomenology: One way to understand nursing practice. *International Journal of Nursing Studies, 30*(2), 171–179.

van Kaam, A. (1959). A phenomenological analysis exemplified by the feeling of being really understood. *Individual Psychology, 15*, 66–72.

van Kaam, A. (1966). *Existential foundations of psychology.* Pittsburgh: Duquesne University Press

van Manen, M. (1984). Practicing phenomenological writing. *Phenomenology and Pedagogy, 2,* 36–69.

Warren, L. D. (1989). *The experience of "feeling cared for": A phenomenological perspective.* Dissertation Abstracts International, DIAB, 50/18–3408.

Wolf, Z. R. (1991). Nurses' experiences giving post mortem care to patients who have donated organs: A phenomenological study. *Scholarly Inquiry for Nursing Practice: An International Journal, 5(2),* 73–87.

Wondolowski, C., & Davis, D. K. (1991). The lived experience of health in the oldest old: A phenomenological study. *Nursing Science Quarterly, 4(3),* 113–118.

Wood, F. G. (1991). The meaning of caregiving. *Rehabilitative Nursing, 16,(4),* 195–198.

Yonge, O., & Stewin, L. (1988). Reliability and validity: Misnomers for qualitative research. *The Canadian Journal of Nursing Research, 20(2),* 61–67.

A Phenomenological Study of Couples' Infertility: Gender Influence

Su An Arnn Phipps, PhD, RN

Pregnancy and childbearing are considered normative life events in most cultures. Infertility, however, affects one in five couples in the United States or more than 10 million women and men.[1-3] In 1988, over $1 billion were spent on medical care related to infertility.[4] The need for services is projected to increase because of the growing numbers of people of childbearing age, postponement of pregnancy, medical advances, and the silent epidemic of sexually transmitted diseases.[5-11]

Although involuntary childlessness is an unanticipated circumstance that carries psychosocial consequences of varying intensity for both individuals and couples, infertility research predominantly focuses on the woman and her experience.[12,13] Few studies address the male experience with involuntary childlessness, or examine the similarities and differences in the infertility experience of spouses.

The purpose of this study was to identify the common, lived experience of infertility for both males and females using phenomenology, a qualitative research method. Phenomenology has as its primary aim to describe the "total structure of lived experience, including the meanings that these experiences have for the individuals who participate in them."[14(p 50)] To accomplish this goal, the researcher must investigate subjects' perceptions as they experience their world. The researcher sets aside or "brackets"[15] his or her own values, views, and knowledge about this

SU AN ARNN PHIPPS, Assistant Professor, College of Nursing Graduate Program-Tulsa, University of Oklahoma Health Sciences Center, Tulsa, Oklahoma.

This research was funded by a small grants award from the University of Oklahoma nursing faculty.

Reprinted from Phipps, S.A.A., A phenomenological study of couples' infertility: Gender influence, *Holistic Nursing,* Vol. 7:2, pp. 44–56, with permission of Aspen Publishers, Inc., © 1993.

experience. Thereby, the researcher identifies rather than verifies pre-existing notions of reality.[16] These experiences are thought to provide essential truths about reality[17] that are difficult to discover through quantitative methodology.

The study question was, How do the essential elements of men's and women's infertility experience compare?

RESEARCH DESIGN

Subjects

A purposive sample of eight white, middle-class couples was used to identify the common infertility experience of males (husbands) and females (wives). The study method was an interview, which was audiotape recorded. Spouses were interviewed in their homes, separately and in private. The eight husbands ranged in age from 26 to 40 years, with a median age of 34 years. All were college graduates, holding white collar jobs; family incomes were $35,000 per year or above. The eight wives ranged in age from 23 to 41 years, with a median age of 32 years. All had completed or attended college. Six of the eight couples indicated Protestant as their religious preference; two couples had no religious preference. Four of the couples were involved in infertility treatment at the time of interview. Two of the male informants had oligospermia, while the other six had no identified fertility problems. One couple had a shared infertility problem. Couples participating in in vitro fertilization or infertility support groups were excluded from this study.

Data Collection

Informants were recruited from a local fertility center or by referral from individuals known by the researcher. After obtaining approval from the institutional review board, couples were contacted by telephone to determine their willingness to participate and to determine a convenient time for interview. Interviews were audiotape recorded. The only interview question asked was, "What is it like for you as a man or woman not to be able to have an infant when you want to?"[18] No other questions were asked except for purposes of amplification or clarification. Audiotapes were transcribed verbatim onto a computer and Ethnograph,[19] a software package, was used to process the data. Transcriptions were analyzed using Colaizzi's method[20] of phenomenological analysis. The procedural steps consisted of the following:

1. Read informants' descriptions to acquire a feeling for their content.
2. Extract significant statements, defined as phrases and sentences that directly pertain to the investigated phenomenon, from each description.

3. "Spell out" the meaning of each significant statement thereby formulating meanings.
4. Organize clusters of themes from the aggregate formulated meanings. (This step allowed the emergence of themes that were common to all of the informants' descriptions.)
5. Compare theme clusters to the original descriptions to validate the
clusters and to examine discrepancies.
6. Develop an exhaustive description of the phenomenon by integrating the results developed in preceding steps. (The exhaustive
description of the phenomenon is an unequivocal a statement of
its essential structure as possible.)
7. Have informants review the exhaustive description for validation
of the original experience.

An average of 126 significant statements were identified from each of
the 16 interviews. Formulated meanings, theme clusters, themes, and categories were reviewed by a consultant with expertise in phenomenology
and Colaizzi's methodology; they were determined to be consistent with
the data. Exhaustive descriptions of the male and female experiences were
submitted to informants for validation and were accepted without revision.

RESULTS

Nine common categories of the male experience with infertility were
induced, while the female experience included 10 common categories.
Nine male and female categories included:

1. evaluation of the meaning of childlessness;
2. feelings associated with infertility;
3. coping;
4. marital functioning;
5. gender role;
6. relationships;
7. investment;
8. perseverance; and
9. perception of the health care system.

Although similar common categories were found between the genders,
themes and theme clusters from which the categories evolved were often
different. The tenth category, which was unique to women in this group
of informants, was self-perception. A comparison of 7 of the 10 categories
and themes follows. Verbatim excerpts are included to illustrate data. F
and M indicate the female and male excerpts. Pseudonyms of spouses
have been used.

EVALUATION OF THE MEANING OF CHILDLESSNESS

Male	*Female*
Envisioned future with children	Envisioned future with children
Evaluation of options	Evaluation of options
Quality of life	Quality of life
Ambivalence	—
—	Perceptions of infertility

Evaluation of the Meaning of Childlessness

Three of the themes listed (see the box entitled "Evaluation of the Meaning of Childlessness") were shared by the men and women. All had expected pregnancy and children as a subsequent step after marriage. They had envisioned their future as individuals and as a couple to include children. Spouses' evaluation of their options included more treatment, adoption, foster parenting, and childlessness. Gender differences were more pronounced with the quality-of-life theme. Although men considered childlessness as a painful experience, it did not preclude a full and enjoyable life.

> M: I think feeling determination to not get into a mode of, if we can't have a child or if we can't get pregnant that, you know, that we can't be happily married, or we can't have a good life.

Wives spoke of enjoying their quality of life, but described something as missing. They focused more on the outcome of their experience, such as what they were learning about life, or how they were becoming more sensitive to others.

> F: And I think one of the positive things that has come out of this though, is I think many times in my life I used to look at my life as a glass half empty. Always knew what I had, and there were things I wanted. And this has really moved me in a position of looking at my life as the glass half full. And there's a real sense, on a daily basis, of enjoying my life so much more. And enjoying it in such simple ways. I enjoyed life, but it's just better. Life is better having gone through this. That seems real strange to me [laughter].

Men were more ambivalent than their wives, discussing the changes a child would make in their lives or goals. Men were concerned about whether a child was worth the couple enduring the ordeal of treatment.

> M: There was some ambivalence back at that point anyway, even though I basically wanted a child, there was some ambivalence about whether

or not.... We were kind of comfortable in our life style by mid twenties, and so when we were told that there was a problem, and it became more and more apparent that there was a problem, I was in a place where I probably could have accepted not having a child at all. I could have adjusted to that.

Women shared their perceptions of infertility, noting that it overtook other aspects of life. It was a continuous, biopsychosocial, spiritual struggle; a loss; a feeling of being passed by; and a feeling of incompleteness or emptiness.

F: [Crying] And there's that sense that if there was this much of a little girl left, there is no more.

Researcher: The little girl being?

F: Oh, maybe that innocence you know, that innocence about life that I knew life was disappointment and struggles. I have had my own and I deal with enough people that I know that it's not a bed of roses, but, I there's just this little piece of me that was still, I think, a little bit innocent about something so natural as having a child. I guess that's that little piece.

F: Testing and treatment became more and more important and really swamped my life. We found ourselves planning our lives around when I would go to the physician, when I would start my period, when I would ovulate. You would just count those days when you would wait for your period to start or not start.

Feelings Associated with Infertility

Both genders felt sorrow, isolation, urgency, guilt, and powerlessness associated with infertility (see the box entitled "Feelings Associated with Infertility"). Men experienced sorrow over the loss of a child, often a son, and the parent role. This sorrow was felt monthly, as was their wives' loss.

M: The first feeling, of course, was one of sadness and sorrow because we'd been thinking about it a long time, and then had been trying to have a child and then found out we could not. So it was and still is just more than anything, sadness. That would probably be the one thing that sums it up real quick.

Women's sorrow was spoken of more often and more openly. Their experience incorporated a variety of contexts. Sorrow was tied to a loss of fertility and the pregnancy experience, to their role as a mother and a woman, or the loss of a "normally functioning body." They also expressed sorrow at their spouses' and parents' loss of the dream of a child.

F: The core issue is sorrow. For myself as a woman and because I may never be able to give birth to a child, never be able to parent. As my husband says I think I've wanted a child since I was 2 years old. And so it's a real ... it's a dream of just well half of my life. And ... also the sense of not being able to give my husband a child is real sorrowful to me.

FEELINGS ASSOCIATED WITH INFERTILITY

Male	Female
Sorrow	Sorrow
Interplay of sorrow and hope	—
Isolation	Isolation
Sources of hope	—
Urgency	Urgency
Guilt	Guilt
Powerlessness	Powerlessness
—	Loss of control
Anger at unfairness	—

Men described feeling isolated from others and being physically isolated from their spouses as a part of treatment. Although they recognized their circumstances were not unique, their feelings were not lessened.

> M: Infertility is something that is not understood by anybody unless they have gone through it, because the pain and the agony are so deep. It's a very isolating and lonely experience. It's not really something that gets … that you can really overcome.

For the females, isolation also came from feeling that no one could really understand their experience, including their husbands. Other infertile women were described by some as their main source of support.

> F: Feeling kind of alone in not being able to convey to the people who are closest to me—my mother, my husband, and different people. They empathize, but it's something that nobody else can feel clearly but me.

Both genders described feelings of powerlessness to change their circumstances. In males these feelings seemed to arouse more anger at the health care system and physicians. They expressed anger at the unfairness of infertility and at the "injustice" of treatment, which only worsened their or their wives' condition.

> M: That's not to say that I don't have feelings, disappointment, feeling powerless, feeling invaded by all the treatment and by all the people that interviewed us and examined us and whatever. So I definitely feel that I lost some control or some power over my life. And I don't like it. A lot of those things make me very angry.

Women's theme of lack of control related to the loss of control over their bodies and emotions, which was distinctly different from the feeling of powerlessness.

> F: I would struggle when people told me "If you would just relax...." I would struggle with thinking, well is it in my power? Is it something I'm doing to myself or my body or my mind? Or is it something that I just can't do anything about? What can I do about it?

> F: I think I felt significant changes with Pergonal. I remember standing in the bathroom of my home with my husband there screaming at him that I was losing control. That I just—I have in my recollection never feeling that out of control. I just felt like I can't take this any more. I could feel myself emotionally going on a roller coaster—feeling out of control on it.

Coping

Gender differences were very obvious in coping styles and strategies. The male thought processes tended to be those of not having expectations, cognitive dissonance, or preparing themselves for childlessness. They also used avoidance frequently, that is, choosing not to think about it. Believing the outcome was in God's power only and using prayer were common coping mechanisms (see the box entitled "Coping").

> M: How I feel when I don't think I can have a child when I want to is, I feel pretty bad about that. And so the way I don't feel bad about it, is to most of the time not want it. And I say we can do it later or it will happen later.

> M: And I was going through my own disappointment in my own way which was different from hers. I think less emotion and more quiet, but nevertheless intense.

Women coped cognitively through verbalization, information seeking, reading, accepting their bodies, focusing on the future, preparing themselves for childlessness, and concentrating on the positives of not

---

COPING

Male	Female
Cognitive processes	Cognitive processes
Avoidance	Avoidance
Faith in God	Faith in God
—	Verbal expression
—	Humor

being pregnant. Avoidance had more to do with not attending social gatherings where they were reminded of their childlessness.

> M: And then my thoughts as we would sit in church, I would keep crying every time I saw a woman take her baby to the nursing mothers' room or something like that. One of my thoughts was embarrassment, or maybe I just shouldn't come to church for 2 or 3 months.

Women described a need to discuss and experience their feelings and to be able to express negative feelings. When husbands were having difficulty handling their own emotions when coping strategies were synchronous, however, both spouses felt angry, frustrated, guilty, and alone.

> M: For my wife talking was her major outlet. And her preferred way of dealing with it was to talk about it again and again and again. And I would get real, real sick of talking about it again and again. So I became less than patient at some of those times. You know, when she needed me the most.

Humor was used often and arose as an outcome of wives' experience. Faith in God was expressed as placing trust in God and using God as a source of comfort and support. Believing that God is in control was important to both genders (see the box entitled "Coping").

> F: My gut feeling all along has been that God is in control of my life and He's never messed it up yet, and that He will work His will in His timing. And I have to say that as a result of this waiting and praying for a child, I've spent many hours with God that I wouldn't have otherwise.

Perceptions of the Health Care System

Of the eight couples who were interviewed, only one couple spoke positively of the health care they were receiving. When speaking of the health care system, men reported relationships and communication with physicians in a negative manner (see the box entitled "Perceptions of the Health

---

PERCEPTIONS OF THE HEALTH CARE SYSTEM

Male	*Female*
Relationship with physician	Relationship with physician
Perceptions of health care professionals	Perceptions of health care professionals
Perceptions of treatment	Perceptions of treatment
—	Diagnosis and etiology

Care System"). The physicians encountered by these informants were perceived as nonsupportive and devaluing of the males' personhood and needs. Men felt stripped of their limited control and power by paternalistic approaches or patronization. Communication with physicians was seen as not meaningful and contributing to frustration, anxiety, and anger. Men were frequently not actively involved in the planning of their infertility treatment, and yet they felt responsible for answers and outcomes they could not control. Nurses were seen more positively for their expression of concern and warmth, which mitigated some anxiety. Yet, their communication was described as lacking with inadequate preparation for procedures, or thoughtless comments to what men or their wives were experiencing. Frustration and anger were common experiences for men.

> M: And when we experienced people who really just behaved less than professionally or behaved insensitively to where we were coming from it made me even more angry. Frankly, we saw a lot of that. That they would be just thoughtless. Just not considering how difficult this was for the people that they were treating and not really going out of their way to try to be comforting or you know, accommodate a little bit, or whatever.

> M: When we started they never ... [got] us together at one time to sit down and say, well here we are, this is the problem you guys are having, and from case studies with other couples, here's what we need to do next. The one thing I wish that probably could have been done, is if they would have gotten us together and explained a little bit.

> M: Then Phyllis and I ... come home, and we talk about what happened. And each of us are asking the other partner a question without the other one really knowing a true answer, so we're just tossing questions back and forth. And we feel a little bit like Kreskin trying to answer a question that we really don't know the answer to, and are not in any medical sort of position to even attempt an answer.

Women echoed their husband's negative relationships and perceptions of physicians. Nevertheless they saw physicians as a source of hope and the answer to their childlessness.

> F: I didn't feel a tremendous amount of support from the physicians we used. We used two different physicians. I wouldn't describe them as having good bedside manner. They were a little brusque, or time concerned, or whatever. I always felt the need to discuss with them, what does this mean, and how hopeful are you. I wanted more there than I got.

> F: So that was frustrating because I didn't know what they were looking for or what their goal was, and they didn't tell me. That would be helpful, if they would tell me the things they would do in order, and how far they can go. Because right now it's like I have no idea what they are going to do next, or if there's anything they can do next.

Wives perceived treatment as disruptive but tolerable, repetitious, and as endless testing. The perception of the unnaturalness of some measures was expressed. Treatment was a sacrifice of their time and lives. They felt it would be worth it, however, if the treatment were successful.

> F: I went through more tests and medication. The treatment was exten-sive. The whole time I thought, it's worth it if it would work out. It's worth it if you become pregnant and there's always a chance, so you try. I wouldn't want to look back and say I didn't try everything I could. I now have the answer.

Diagnosis of infertility helped break women's denial. Knowing what the problems were gave some feeling of control to what had seemed to be an unresolvable situation and relieved feelings of total responsibility for conception.

Marital Functioning

Spousal support was a common experience for males and females (see the box entitled "Marital Functioning"). Both husbands and wives described strategies they would use to be supportive of one another. Mutual com-fort was found in sharing of tears and hope, or in negotiating acceptable solutions to problems. Males' statements tended to focus on the increased tension caused by individual differences in attitudes and coping styles, their desire to be supportive of their wives, and the resulting strain. The "invasion of a private, intimate relationship" of their sexual lives through diagnostic and treatment procedures was commonly described.

> M: It [infertility] brought a lot of stress into our lives. It accentuated dif-ferences when one of us would do something that bothered the other. It was just ... it just made everything much more ready to explode. It was a tremendous strain.

MARITAL FUNCTIONING

Male	Female
Spousal support	Spousal support
Discord	—
Sexual relationship	—
Response to wife	—
—	Perceptions of spouse
—	Protection of spouse
—	Unity

Men's responses to their wives focused around the perception of their wives' pain. A husband's inability to lessen her suffering often resulted in anger, feelings of powerlessness, and failure. Men often recognized the loss of the maternal role for their wives.

M: But I think the main thing that I experience is just feeling bad and seeing the suffering that she experiences sometimes from it. That probably brings up more for me than anything else.

M: Those are the major things, but I think if I were to weight all those demands, the weight of my wife really being at the end of her rope emotionally a lot of the time, needing me to put her back together, or for her to depend on me to make her feel that way is the biggest and most frustrating demand, because it is the one that I am the least equipped to be able to do. There is nothing I can do to make her feel better, and I feel very inadequate.

A comment by one of the oligospermic men reflects a common theme.

M: There's a tremendous challenge for a husband. His wife is going to be dealing with tremendous feelings of incompleteness, of not being a full woman, or not ... of being denied a very rich experience of carrying a child, birthing a child, or nursing a child....

Wives perceived spouses as also grieving. They valued their husbands and recognized they were trying to be supportive. They were, however, sensitive to when their husbands were uncomfortable or stressed, especially as a result of when they had expressed their emotions, such as when crying. Husbands were seen as overwhelmed at times, and having a need to solve an unsolvable problem. Women often protected their spouses by not discussing their feelings, showing their disappointments, or waiting for a time when they believed husbands could handle them.

F: I realize that if I want to be understood by him that I need to space it out so that he's able to listen and not feel overwhelmed. So to get what I want, which is his empathy, or understanding, or thoughts, I know I've got to keep it to myself a big part of the time and use some timing in talking to him.

Women described the conscious decisions the couples had made to not be divided by the infertility experience.

F: My husband and I have recognized that it's a potential wedge not being able to have children, and we've used it in an opposite way to really draw us closer together.

Gender Role

All males tended to see themselves as the protector of their wives from emotional and physical pain. They also saw their spouses as expecting

---

GENDER ROLE

Male	Female
Protector	—
Procreator	Procreator
Comforter	—
—	Mother
—	Nurturer

---

husbands to protect them. Men described some of the things they purposely did to comfort their wives—special outings, listening, being empathetic—but also described support measures as depleting and uncomfortable at times (see the box entitled "Gender Role").

> M: Now if I had no sperm at all, then yes that might have struck me personally much deeper. I haven't really thought about that part of it. I think that there were some times with Monica that, there were some times that I had to just say, God help me because I'm worn out on this. I don't want to talk about it or think about it. I don't want to deal with it. I don't want to cope with it any more. And God would give me the grace to be what Monica needed at those times. Growth experiences are painful, and this must be one heck of a growth experience because there has been an incredible amount of pain and hurt going through it.

> M: It was very draining. It was very consuming. After a night of crying and dealing with the hurt and the pain, I would go to work absolutely drained and wrung out.

The theme of procreator emerged most strongly from the two men with oligospermia, but it was also common for those men for whom there was no medical diagnosis of subfertility. Even though their wives were being treated or also were not diagnosed as infertile, men questioned their role in the couple's childlessness. Self-image was not described as negatively affecting any of the men. Knowing they could still impregnate their wives through artificial insemination by husband (AIH) lessened self-condemnation by those who were subfertile.

Women in this population discussed their roles as mothers, procreators, and as nurturers. They also were protectors, but this theme emerged in their relationships with spouses, family, or others rather than a gender role. Women would respond to uncomfortable questions in ways to keep others from "feeling bad," or would not share emotions or test results so that the hopes of others were kept alive. As previously mentioned, women's gender roles of procreator, mother, and nurturer were closely intertwined with sorrow. Being able to conceive, carry a child, and give birth were desires central to the experience of each female informant. Nurturing included parenting, or as one woman put it, "shaping the essence of another; of being a parent. Being a nurturer, of giving oneself to a child and seeing a child grow."

Self-Perception

This category was unique to the women in this study (see the box entitled "Self-Perception"). A few men referred to their self-perception, but it was not a common experience. Women spoke of how their inability to control their fertility and bear children affected their self-image. Infertility was viewed by most as a failure in their role as a woman, resulting in perceptions of being different from fertile women and couples. Feelings of "abnormality" were common; these feelings were unrelated to whether the husband or the wife had been diagnosed as subfertile. Self-esteem was affected in some women who felt that they were unattractive. Yet others denied that their self-esteem as a woman had decreased. Others described an increase in esteem once they were able to accept their "imperfect bodies." The support of their husband was key to preventing lowered self-esteem.

Recurrent statements described women's perceptions of their bodies as defective, imperfect, and representing a loss. One informant compared her body to the bodies of people with permanent handicaps. Informants saw themselves as healthy women, yet unhealthy.

> F: And I felt like I was a failure as a woman, because here all my other friends were having children, some who didn't want them and some who did. And they had no problems, and here's me.

> F: It [insemination] takes about 2 or 3 minutes, and then you have to lay there for a while. They say normal people have to do that too. [laughter]

> F: With the infertility I felt for a real long time, what are the words that would come to me, "I'm not good enough." I got past that. And when I got past that it no longer was a piece of my self esteem, but more this was just a part of my body, and I had to move to accept that as well as all the other things that are wrong with my body.

SELF-PERCEPTION

Self-image
Self-esteem
Body image

DISCUSSION

The experience of infertility is frustrating and painful for both men and women. Both genders experience the developmental crisis and traumatic situational crisis[21] that accompany their inability to conceive and fulfill a life goal and dream of becoming a parent.[3,22,23] Both experience feelings of isolation from their spouse and others, guilt, powerlessness, and sorrow associated with involuntary childlessness. Despite these similarities, results of this study show that the individual infertility experience is strongly influenced by gender and gender role expectations.

Men in the United States are socialized to be independent, in control, and to suppress or deny their emotions.[24–26] They are expected and expect themselves to provide for and protect their spouses and families. These roles were frequently blocked for male informants by circumstances and situations related to a couple's infertility diagnosis and by the nature of infertility treatment they received. Unfortunately, their experience is not atypical.

Husbands experienced and were cognizant of the physical and emotional pain both spouses were living as a result of diagnosis and treatment. Males perceived their wives as suffering emotionally from the loss of their gender role of childbearing, childbirth, and childrearing. Their reality of being unable to change circumstances or outcomes for themselves or their wives resulted in feelings of guilt, anger, and powerlessness. The husbands' emotions were similar to those of men in related research,[23,27] where the feelings of failure were also intense. As in these studies, however, failure was experienced as the inability to meet marital expectations and of depriving their wives of motherhood, rather than as a sense of personal inadequacy or failure, or role failure. Feelings of personal failure are more characteristic of sterile men who experience more intense feelings of anger, frustration, guilt, and isolation than infertile women.[28,29] These emotions are usually related to feelings of sexual inadequacy or loss of virility. None of the study husbands were diagnosed as sterile, and only two were oligospermic.

Another source for feelings of powerlessness occurred in husbands' interactions with health care providers, particularly physicians. Paternalistic, controlling approaches combined with inefficient communication increased the males' anger, alienation, and dissatisfaction with the health care system. This negative rapport is not an isolated occurrence.[30] At times men felt they and their wives needed protection from the intrusiveness and insensitivity of the people who were supposed to be helping them achieve their goal of a child. Men may feel unable to defend their spouse or lessen the pain associated with treatment, if they wish to accomplish the goal of a child.

Gender differences in emotional expression and seeking of support and intimacy are well documented.[31] Women are more verbally expressive and seek support, especially during times of stress. Men tend to use avoidance, denial, or mute their emotional experience. These gender differences can be accentuated during the infertility experience, possibly increasing marital discord. In this study, husbands viewed their wives' need to verbalize as a demand for them to find solutions to their circumstance, rather than as a coping style. Even when this need was recognized, husbands felt burdened and exhausted in their attempts to be supportive.

Both men and women had a heightened awareness of the menstrual cycle and became invested in the passing of the days. While husbands and wives felt the monthly sorrow when conception did not occur, their first response was to protect their spouse. This reaction was contradictory to other findings, which depict men as uninvolved in their wives' infertility experience.[32,33]

As in other research, these wives experienced infertility as a loss of gender role fulfillment.[24,34-37] This role loss was related to an alteration in self-image and a negative body image. Women's description of their experience reflected more or a different emotional impact than their spouses' did. This finding is not unusual. It might have been influenced, however, by male coping strategies and the number of couples with a female infertility problem.

Women's lack of control over their bodies and lives was frustrating and consuming. They commonly coped through seeking information, attempting to accept their bodies, and verbalizing. Wives identified the positives of their experience, found humor in situations, and deepened their relationship with and faith in God.

Wives were protective of their husbands, perceiving them to be overwhelmed or unable to deal with their wives' emotions. Again, gender differences in coping styles affected the experience of both spouses. When a husband attempted to cope, by seeking "a return to normalcy," or to protect himself or spouse through minimization or avoidance, it may have been misinterpreted by wives as a lack of caring or interest. These factors may have heightened women's feelings of isolation and of "not being understood." Perhaps because women focus on intimacy and support, they reported martial unity as an outcome of their infertility experience more often than the male informants.

Women were frustrated in their relationships with health care providers. While seeking some control through diagnosis and medical intervention, the reality of not being included in treatment goals and plans reinforced feelings of lack of control, dependency, and helplessness.

IMPLICATIONS

Nurses are in primary positions to help infertile couples during their experience of infertility. Of the eight study couples, only one described support from physicians and health care professionals. Rather than focusing on the "cure" of an infant, nurses can support individuals and couples holistically, thereby removing themselves from a potentially adversarial relationship. Being knowledgeable of gender differences in role expectations and coping styles and educating couples to the influence of these differences may ease spousal conflict and miscommunication. Helping the couple identify their individual goals of having a child may uncover differences in the investment spouses have in becoming pregnant. The nurse should assess the meaning of infertility for each spouse and then for the couple. The nurse can then assist spouses to identify individual coping styles, again exploring gender differences that may facilitate understanding of these differences, and help enhance marital support. Couples may be referred to agencies for counseling or to infertility support groups such as RESOLVE.

Nurses and other professionals can empower couples through the establishment of mutual treatment goals and plans. Nurses should provide thorough and meaningful information to deal with the daily decision making these couples face. Helping couples explore treatment options, knowing the inherent risks and expenditures, will increase their feeling of being in control of their lives and facilitate dyadic decision making. Suggesting spousal support measures, particularly at times of monthly loss, can strengthen individual and dyadic functioning. Being knowledgeable of the continued effects diagnosis and treatment may have on the couple's relationship is essential for a holistic approach to care.

REFERENCES

1. Link PW, Darling CA. Couples undergoing treatment for infertility: dimensions of life satisfaction. *Journal of Sex and Marital Therapy* 1986;12:46–59.
2. Butler RR, Koraleski S. Infertility: a crisis with no resolution. *Journal of Mental Health Counseling* 1990;12:151–163.
3. Burns LH. Infertility as boundary ambiguity: one theoretical perspective. *Family Process.* 1987;26:359–372.
4. Committee on Government Operations. *Infertility in America: Why Is the Federal Government Ignoring a Major Health Problem?* 8th report. Washington, DC: US Government Printing Office; 1989.
5. DeCherney AH, Berkowitz GS. Female fecundity as a function of age. *New England Journal of Medicine* 1982;14:75–78.
6. Aral SO, Cates WJ. The increasing concern with infertility. Why now? *JAMA.* 1983;250:2327–2331.
7. Houge CJ, Mollencamp M. The increasing concern with infertility. *JAMA* 1984;252:208. Letter.
8. Sherris JD, Fox G. Infertility and STD: a public health challenge. *Population Reports* 1983;50:114–151.
9. Moore DE, Spandoni LR. Infertility in women. In: Holmes K, Mardl PF, Sparling PF, Wiesner PJ, eds. *Sexually Transmitted Diseases.* New York, NY: McGraw Hill; 1984.
10. Goldsmith MF. "Silent epidemic" of "social disease" makes STD experts raise their voices. *JAMA* 1989;261:3509–3510.

11. US Congress, Office of Technology Assessment. *Infertility: Medical and Social Choices.* Washington, DC: US Government Printing Office; 1988. OTA-BA-358.

12. Allison JR. Roles and role conflict of women in infertile couples. *Psychology of Women Quarterly* 1979;4:97–113.

13. Callan V. The personal and marital adjustment of mothers and of voluntary and involuntary childless wives. *Journal of Marriage and Family Therapy.* 1987;49:847–856.

14. Omery A. Phenomenology: a method for nursing research. *Advances in Nursing Science.* 1983;5:49–63.

15. Oiler C. The phenomenological approach in nursing research. *Nursing Research.* 1982;31:178–181.

16. Reimen DJ. The essential structure of a caring interaction. In: Munhall P, Oiler C, eds. *Nursing Research Methodology.* Norwalk, Conn: Appleton-Century-Crofts; 1986.

17. Spiegelburg H. *The Phenomenological Movement.* The Hague, The Netherlands: Martinees Nijhoff; 1976.

18. Sandelowski M, Pollock C. Women's experience with infertility. *Image: Journal of Nursing Scholarship.* 1986;18:140–144.

19. Seidel J, Kjolseth R, Seymour E. *The Ethnograph.* Littleton, Ore: Qualis Research Associates; 1988.

20. Colaizzi PF. Psychological research as the phenomenologist views it. In: Vails R, King M, eds. *Existential Phenomenological Alternative for Psychology.* New York, NY: Oxford University Press; 1978.

21. Slaikeu KA. *Crisis Intervention: A Handbook for Practice and Research.* Boston, Mass: Allyn & Bacon; 1984.

22. Boyarsky R, Boyarsky S. Psychogenic factors in male infertility: a review. *Medical Aspects of Human Sexuality.* 1983;17:86h–86q.

23. Owens D. The desire to father: reproductive ideologies and involuntarily childless men. In: McKee I, O'Brian M, eds. *The Father Figure.* London, England: Travistock; 1982.

24. Goldberg H. *The Hazards of Being Male: Surviving the Myth of Masculine Privilege.* New York, NY: Nash Publishing; 1976.

25. Pleck JH. *The Myths of Masculinity.* Boston, Mass: MIT; 1981.

26. Harrison JB. Warning: the male sex role may be dangerous to your health. In: Swanson JM, Forrest KA, *Men's Reproductive Health:* Springer Series: Focus Men. 1984;3:11–20.

27. Greil AL, Leitko TA, Porter KL. Infertility: his and her *Gender and Society.* 1988;2:172–199.

28. Bernstein LB, Potts N, Mattox JH. Assessment of psychological dysfunction associated with infertility. *Journal of Obstetrical and Gynecological Nursing.* November-December 1985;(suppl):63–66.

29. Kedem P, Mikulmeir M, Nathanson Y. Psychological aspects of male infertility. *British Journal of Medical Psychology.* 1990;63:73–80.

30. Owens DJ, Read MW. Patients' experience with and assessment of subfertility testing and treatment. *Journal of Reproductive and Infant Psychology.* 1984;2:7–17.

31. Rubin LB. *Intimate Strangers: Men and Women Together.* New York, NY: Harper & Row; 1983.

32. Adler JD, Boxley RL. The psychological reaction infertility: sex roles and coping styles. *Sex Roles* 1985;12:271–279.
33. McEwan KL, Costello CG, Taylor PJ. Adjustment to infertility. *Journal of Abnormal Psychology* 1987;96:108–116.
34. Valentine D. Psychological impact of infertility: identifying issues and needs. *Social Work and Health Care* 1986;11:61–69.
35. Baker MA, Quinkert K. Women's reactions to reproductive problems. *Psychology Reports.* 1983;53:160–166.
36. Mazor MD. Emotional reactions in infertility. In: Mazor MD, Simons HF, eds. *Infertility: Medical, Emotional and Social Consequences.* New York, NY: Human Sciences Press; 1984.
37. Kraft AD, Palombo MA, Mitchell D, Dean C, Meyers S. Schmidt A. The psychological dimensions of infertility *American Journal of Orthopsychiatry.* 1980;50:618–628.

Chapter 5

Ethnographic Research Approach

Social scientists share an interest in and commitment to discovery. Anthropologists as a particular group of social scientists are committed to the discovery of cultural knowledge. Early in the history of social science, individuals interested in culture found that the ways of traditional science were inadequate to discover the nuances of people who live together and share similar experiences. This led to the beginnings of ethnography as a means of studying the life ways or patterns of groups of individuals. Sanday (1983) reports that ethnographic methods are not new. Herodotus, an ancient Greek, was an ethnographer who recorded variations in the cultures to which he was exposed. According to Sanday, Franz Boas's (1948) ethnographic examination of the eskimo culture signaled the contemporary beginning of ethnographic study.

References to the value of ethnographic approaches as a means to study nursing culture can be found as early as the 1970s (Leininger, 1970; Ragucci, 1972). Early nurse ethnographers embraced the methods of anthropology to study phenomena which they perceived were not reducible, quantifiable, or able to be made objective. Leininger (1985) went beyond the borrowing of ethnographic methods to develop what she called ethnonursing research.

This chapter explores the research approach called ethnography. Common elements of ethnographic methodology, its uses, interpretations, and applications are discussed.

WHAT IS ETHNOGRAPHY?

According to Spradley (1980), "ethnography is the work of describing culture" (p. 3). The description of culture or cultural scene must be guided by an intense desire to understand the lives of other individuals so much so that the researcher becomes part of a specific cultural scene. Malinowski (1961) believed that this requires the researcher to learn the "native's point of view" (p. 25). Spradley warned, however, that ethnography is more than the study of the people. He stated that "ethnography means learning from people" (p. 3). "The essential core of ethnography is this concern with the meanings of actions and events to the people [ethnographers] seek to understand" (Spradley, 1980, p. 5).

FUNDAMENTAL CHARACTERISTICS OF ETHNOGRAPHY

There are three characteristics central to ethnographic research: researcher as instrument, fieldwork, and the cyclic nature of data collection and analysis. The study of culture requires an intimacy with the participants who are part of a culture. Ethnography as a method of inquiry provides the opportunity for researchers to conduct studies that attend to the need for intimacy with members of the culture. This is the reason the researcher becomes the instrument. The ethnographer becomes the conduit for information shared by the group.

When anthropologists speak of *researcher as instrument,* they are indicating the significant role ethnographers play in identifying, interpreting, and analyzing the culture under study. The primary way that the researcher becomes the instrument is through observation and recording of cultural data. More than just observing, the researcher often becomes a participant in the cultural scene. Atkinson and Hammersley (1994) stated that "participant observation is not a particular research technique but a mode of being-in-the-world characteristic of researchers" (p. 249).

Participant observation demands complete commitment to the task of understanding. The ethnographer becomes part of the culture being studied in order to feel what it is like for the people in the situation (Sanday, 1983).

Ethnographic researchers, despite becoming part of the cultural scene, will never fully have the insider's view (emic). The emic view is the native's view, which reflects the cultural group's language, beliefs, and experiences. The only way the ethnographer can begin to access the emic view is through collection of the cultural group members' journals, records, or other cultural artifacts.

The strength of participant observation is the opportunity to access information in the outsider's (etic) view. The etic view is the view of the outsider with interpretation. The essence of ethnography is determining what an observed behavior is or what a ritual means in the context of the group studied. Ethnography is the description and interpretation of cultural patterns.

The second fundamental characteristic found in ethnographic research is the location of the conduct of the research. All ethnographic research takes place in the *field*. This means that the researcher goes to the place where the culture of interest is. As an example, Germain (1979) was interested in studying the culture of a cancer unit. She perceived this to be an important subculture of the hospital and believed that studying this culture would provide nurses with significant insights into the care and treatment of cancer patients. Her inquiry was conducted on an oncology unit in a community hospital. She spent one year on the unit collecting data which provided her with insights into the culture of a cancer unit. Physically situating oneself in the environs of the culture under study is a fundamental characteristic in all ethnographic work.

The third essential characteristic is the *cyclic nature of data collection*. In ethnographic research, a question about the differences in human experience found in a foreign culture leads the researcher to question what those differences are. As Agar (1982, 1986) points out, one of the problems for the ethnographer is that there are no clear boundaries between the similarities and differences in human experience. Therefore, the data collected by the ethnographer in the field to describe the differences and similarities lead to still other questions about the culture. Answering those questions leads to still other questions. As pointed out by Spradley (1980) and Spradley and McCurdy (1972), the study ends not because the researcher has answered all of the questions or completely described the culture but rather because time and resources do not allow continuation.

SELECTING THE ETHNOGRAPHIC APPROACH

One of the goals of ethnography is to make explicit what is implicit within a culture (Germain, 1986). Cultural knowledge requires an understanding of the people, what they do, what they say, how they relate to one another, what their customs and beliefs are, and how they derive meaning from their experiences (Goetz & LeCompte, 1984; Spradley & McCurdy, 1972; Spradley, 1980; van Maanen, 1983). With these ideas in mind, nurses interested in exploring cultures or subcultures in nursing or nurse-related cultures have the world available to them for study. Within the profession of nursing, there are many cultures that have not yet been discovered. As an example of a culture within nursing that is implicit, and made explicit through the research of Wolf (1988), is that of nursing rituals. In Wolf's research, she discovered the rituals that nurses use to enable and protect them in their work with patients. Similarly, in Germain's (1979) research on the cancer unit, nurses are provided with a view of another implicit culture being made explicit.

The use of the ethnographic approach provides nurses with the opportunity to explore the holistic nature of society and to ask questions relevant to nursing practice. The naturalistic setting in which ethnographic research is carried out supplies nurses with the view of the world as it is, not as they wish it were. Fundamentally, entrance into the naturalistic setting, the one in which the research participants live without interference from outside sources, is a rich data source for exploring many nursing practice issues.

Nurses conducting ethnographic research must accept reflexivity as part of the research design. Reflexivity, or the position of the researcher as both participant and investigator, provides nurses with the opportunity to explore cultures within the paradigm of nursing that values the affective and subjective nature of human beings. The duality of being both researcher and participant provides opportunities to capitalize on insights derived from datum sources. "'Meaning' is not merely investigated, but is constructed by [researcher] and informant through active and reciprocal relationships and the dialectical processes of interaction" (Anderson, 1991, p. 116). Anderson (1991) states that "field work is inherently dialectical; the researcher affects and is affected by the phenomena (s)he seeks to understand" (p. 117). The reflexivity therefore leads to fuller understanding of the dynamics of particular phenomena and relationships found within cultures.

When choosing ethnography as the approach to study a particular culture or subculture, the nurse should ask several important questions: Do I have the time to conduct this study? Do I have the resources to carry it out? Will the data collected have the potential to bring new insights to the profession? If the answers to these questions are "yes," then the nurse researcher's study has the potential to contribute significantly to the nursing profession.

In addition to answering the questions offered above, nurses interested in ethnography should know the reasons why this approach may be useful. Spradley (1980) identifies four primary reasons for using ethnography to study a particular culture. The first is the documentation of "the existence of alternative realities and to describe these realities in [the terms of the people studied]" (p. 14). Much of what an individual knows about other cultures is interpreted based on the culture from which one comes. This way of thinking promotes the idea of one truth. As discussed in the early chapters of this book, it is limiting to think that one truth and thus one reality exists. For the ethnographer, description of alternate realities provides a rich and varied landscape of human life. Coming "to understand personality, society, individuals, and environments from the perspective of other than professional scientific cultures . . . will lead to a sense of epistemological humility" (Spradley, 1980, p. 15).

A second reason, according to Spradley (1980), for using the ethnographic approach is to discover grounded theories. Through description of the culture, the researcher is able to discover theories that are indigenous to it (Grant & Fine, 1992). Foundational to grounded theorists' research is a belief that the only useful theory is one that comes from or is "grounded" in the beliefs and practices of individuals studied. The principle that research should be based on the beliefs and practices of individuals (cultural groups) studied is also foundational to the work of ethnographers. The major difference between the conduct of an ethnographic and a grounded theory research is that the ethnographer wishing to develop grounded theory will advance the description and interpretation of cultural observations to a level that yields a description of basic social psychological process. For a full discussion of grounded theory the reader is directed to Chapter 7.

A third reason for choosing ethnography is to understand complex societies better. Early in the development of anthropology, it was believed that the method of ethnography was ideally suited to the study of non-Western cultures. Today, anthropologists see the value of using ethnography to study subgroups of larger cultures both Western and non-Western. Examples of this use can be found in nursing in the works of Wolf (1988) and Germain (1979).

The final reason Spradley (1980) offers for using the ethnographic approach is to understand human behavior. Human behavior has meaning and ethnography is one way to discover what the meaning is. This becomes particularly important when nurses look at the health and illness behaviors of patients. Understanding how cultural groups such as Hispanics, the elderly, abused women, or teenagers behave in health and illness situations can assist nurses who care for them to provide better interventions in the hope of potentiating the strategies already in use by the group.

When nurses decide that they will use ethnography to study a culture of interest, a parallel consideration will be whether a macro or micro ethnographic study will be conducted. Leininger (1985) has called these *mini* or *maxi*. Regardless of the terminology, the intent has to do with the scale of the study. A mini or micro ethnography is generally of a smaller scale and very narrow or specific in its focus. Miller's (1991) study of a well group of elderly volunteers who participated in a "southwest Dade County Gray Panther organization" (p. 43) is an example of a mini or micro study. In this study, the researcher interviewed and observed six "essentially healthy" (p. 43) elderly in their homes and during Gray Panther meetings. The number of participants in this study is small and the research is focused on one small faction of a specific social group. Therefore, it is considered a micro ethnography because of the size and period of observation which was limited to six weeks.

A *macro* or *maxi* ethnography is a study that looks at the culture in a broader context, extends over a longer period, and is most often reported in book form. Germain's (1979) and Wolf's (1988) ethnographies are examples of this type of study. Both of these researchers observed a significant number of nurses over the period of one year. The scope is large and the studies were conducted over a considerable period.

Spradley (1980) further delineates the scope of these studies by placing them on a continuum. On the end of micro-ethnography are studies that examine a single social situation (nurses receiving report on one unit), multiple social situations (critical care nurses participating in report on three intensive care units), or a single social institution (the American Cancer Society of Philadelphia). Moving closer to macro-ethnographic studies, Spradley includes multiple social institutions (American Cancer Societies of Northeastern Pennsylvania), single community study (Chinatown in San Francisco), multiple communities (Hispanic communities in East Los Angeles), and complex society (tribal life in Ghana).

INTERPRETATIONS OF THE APPROACH

Ethnographic research methods have been described by a number of individuals. Early ethnographic reports were written by individuals who documented their observations of the cultures they encountered. Many of these individuals were not trained anthropologists but brought rich and vivid accounts of the lives of the people they met. Sanday (1983) states that these recorders were not participants in paradigmatic ethnography. Paradigmatic ethnography consist of the range of activities completed by a trained ethnographer including observation, recording, participation, analyzing, reporting, and publishing experiences with a particular cultural group. Sanday offers three traditions within paradigmatic ethnography: holistic, semiotic, and behavioristic.

The *holistic* ethnographic interpretation is the oldest. The commitment of researchers in this tradition is to "the study of culture as an integrated whole" (Sanday, 1983, p. 23). According to Sanday, the ethnographers who ascribed to this approach included Benedict (1934), Malinowski (1961), Mead (1949), and Radcliffe-Brown (1952). Although all four varied in their focus, the underlying commitment was to describe as fully as possible the particular culture of interest within the context of the whole. For instance, "Mead and Benedict were interested in describing and interpreting the whole, not in explaining its origin beyond the effect of the individual on it" (Sanday, 1983, p. 25). Radcliffe-Brown and Malinowski were not committed to the "characterization of the cultural whole but to how each trait functions in the total cultural complex of which it is part" (Sanday, 1983, p. 25). Although the focus of both sets of ethnographers is different, the underlying commitment to viewing the culture as a whole is preserved.

The *semiotic* interpretation is focused on gaining access to the native's point of view. Like the holistic interpretation, the major anthropologists in this tradition did not share epistemologies. The two major followers of this tradition are Geertz (1973) and Goodenough (1970, 1971). According to Sanday (1983), Geertz sees the study of culture not as a means to defining laws but rather as an interpretative enterprise focused on searching for meaning. Further, Geertz believes that the only way to achieve cultural understanding is through thick descriptions. Thick descriptions can be best described as large amounts of data (descriptions of the culture) collected over extensive periods. According to Geertz, the analysis and conclusions offered by ethnographers represent fictions developed to explain rather than to understand a culture.

Goodenough (1970, 1971) is an ethnographer who embraces the semiotic tradition. He does so through what has been described as *ethnoscience*. Ethnoscience is defined as "a rigorous and systematic way of studying and classify emic (local or inside) data of a cultural group's own perceptions, knowledge, and language in terms of how people perceive and interpret their universe" (Leininger, 1970, pp. 168-169).

According to Sanday (1983), Geertz's commitment is to the "notion that culture is located in the minds and hearts of men" (p. 30). The way that culture is described is through writing out of systematic rules, of formulating ethnographic algorithms, which make it possible to produce acceptable actions much as the "writing out of linguistic rules makes it possible to produce acceptable utterances" (Sanday, 1983, p. 30).

"The differences between Geertz and Goodenough are not in aim but in the method, focus, and mode of reporting" (Sanday, 1983, p. 30). Both ethnographers are committed to the careful description of culture. Geertz's method and reporting are seen more as an art form as opposed to Goodenough's where the focus is on rigorous, systematic methods of collecting data and reporting findings.

The third interpretation is the *behaviorist* approach. In this approach, the ethnographer is most interested in the behavior of members of a culture. The main goal "is to uncover covarying patterns in observed behavior" (Sanday, 1983, pp. 33-34). This approach is deductive. The ethnographer subscribing to this interpretation looks specifically for cultural situations that substantiate preselected categories of data. The use of this interpretation deviates radically from the intent of the other two interpretations which rely solely on induction.

Leininger (1978, 1985), a nurse anthropologist, developed her own interpretation of ethnography. This approach she called *ethnonursing*. Ethnonursing, according to Leininger, is "the study and analysis of the local or indigenous people's viewpoints, beliefs, and practices about nursing care behavior and processes of designated cultures" (Leininger, 1978, p. 15). The goal of ethnonursing is to "discover nursing knowledge as known, perceived and experienced by nurses and consumers of nursing and health services" (Leininger, 1985, p. 38). The primary function of Leininger's approach to ethnography is its focus on nursing and related health phenomena. This has been an important contribution to the field of nursing. Many nurse ethnographers subscribe to Leininger's philosophy and apply the methods of inquiry she proposed.

APPLICATION OF THE APPROACH

When individuals choose to conduct an ethnographic research study, usually they have decided that there is some shared cultural knowledge which they would like to have access to. The way individuals access cultural knowledge is through making cultural inferences. Cultural inferences are observer's (researcher's) conclusions based on what is seen or heard while studying another culture. Making inferences is the way that individuals learn many of their own group's cultural norms or values. For instance, if a child observes another child being scolded for talking in class, without being told, the observer concludes that talking in class can lead to an unpleasant outcome. Therefore, the child learns through cultural inference that talking in class is not acceptable. This same process is employed by ethnographers in their observations of cultural groups.

According to Spradley (1980), generally three types of information are used to generate cultural inferences: cultural behavior (what people do), cultural artifacts (the things people make and use), and speech messages (what people say).

A significant part of culture is not readily available. This information is called *tacit* knowledge. It consists of the information members of a culture know but that they do not talk about or express directly (Hammersley & Atkinson, 1983; Spradley, 1980). In addition to accessing explicit or easily observed cultural knowledge, the ethnographer has the responsibility of describing tacit knowledge as well.

ROLE OF THE RESEARCHER

To access explicit and tacit knowledge, researchers must understand the role they will play in the discovery of cultural knowledge. Because the researcher becomes the instrument, he or she must be cognizant of what the role of instrument entails. As stated earlier in this chapter, the role of instrument requires the ethnographer to participate in the culture, observe the participants, document observations, collect artifacts, interview members of the cultural group, analyze the findings, and report them. This requires a significant commitment to the research, one that should not be taken lightly.

Spradley (1980) has identified 11 steps in the conduct of ethnographic research. Table 5.1 summarizes these steps. The processes for data generation, treatment, analysis, and interpretation will be discussed within the framework of the steps identified.

Data Generation and Treatment

Gaining Access

As stated earlier, one of the first considerations when initiating an ethnographic study is to decide on the focus. Based on the focus of the inquiry, the researcher can decide the scope of the project. Will the focus be micro or mini ethnography; a single social situation (nurses receiving report on one unit), multiple social situations (critical care nurses participating in report on three intensive care units), a single social institution (the American Cancer Society of Philadelphia), or will it be maxi or macro ethnography; multiple social institutions (American Cancer Societies of Northeastern Pennsylvania), a single community study (Chinatown in New York City), multiple communities (Hispanic neighborhoods in East Los Angeles), complex societies (tribal life in Ghana)?

Once the scope of the project has been decided, the next step is to gain access to the culture. Since ethnography requires the study of peo-

---

TABLE 5.1 STEPS FOR CONDUCTING ETHNOGRAPHIC RESEARCH

Doing participant observation

Making an ethnographic record

Making descriptive observations

Making a domain analysis

Making focused observation

Making a taxonomic analysis

Making selected observations

Making a componential analysis

Discovering cultural themes

Taking a cultural inventory

Writing an ethnography

ple, the activities they are involved in and the places in which they live, in order to conduct the study, the researcher will need to gain access. This may be the most difficult part of the study. Because the researcher is not usually a member of the group studied, individuals situated in the culture of interest may be unwilling or unable to provide the access required. In still other instances, there may be some *social situations* that can be studied without permission of the group. For instance, if one is interested in the culture of individuals who come to the local pharmacy to obtain their medications, permission may not be required. However, if one is interested in studying the culture of health professionals in an outpatient clinic, permission will be necessary.

Access will be easiest when the purpose of the study is clearly stated and information is shared regarding protection of confidentiality of participants. In addition, offering to participate in the setting may enhance the ability to gain entry to the social situation. If for example, the researcher wishes to study the culture of health professionals working in an outpatient clinic, willingness to participate by offering "volunteer" services while in the setting may improve the chances of obtaining admission. As a "volunteer" the researcher not only has the opportunity to make observations but will become part of the culture after remaining on the scene for an extended period of time.

Participant Observation

Actual field work begins when the researcher starts asking questions of the culture chosen. Initially the ethnographer asks broad questions. With the clinic as an example, broad questions such as the following are asked: Who works in the clinic? Who comes to the clinic for care? What is the physical set-up of the clinic? Who provides the care to clients who come to the clinic? In addition to asking questions, the researcher will begin to make observations. Three types of observations can occur: descriptive, focused, and selective (Spradley, 1980). *Descriptive observations* start when the researcher enters the social situation. What the ethnographer is trying to do is to begin to describe the social situation, to get an overview of the situation and determine what is going on. After this type of observation is complete, more focused descriptive observations will be conducted. These observations are generated from questions asked during the initial descriptive phase. For example, while in the clinic one discover that nurses are responsible for health teaching. A *focused observation* is required to look specifically at the types of health teaching done by the nurses in the setting. Based on this focused observation, the researcher conducts a more *selective observation*. As an example, the researcher observers that only two out of the seven nurses in the clinic conduct any health teaching with AIDS clients. A selective interview or observation including these two nurses will address additional questions about why the clinic staff members behave as they do. The neophyte ethnographer should not be led to believe that observations and interviews are conducted in the linear manner described above. Broad questions can arise out of any observation as can focused or selective questions.

Another important distinction to be made based on the above description is that an observation is not intended to mean merely a "looking at" on the part of the researcher. An observation entails looking, listening, asking questions, and collecting artifacts.

At any given time, the ethnographer may be more or less involved in the social situation. There may be times such as when the clinic is very busy, that as a "volunteer" the researcher is very involved in participating in the culture. At times of lesser traffic, more observation may take place. Explicit rules for when to participate and when to observe are not available. The degree of participation in the social situation needs to be determined by the researcher, the *actors* and the activity. The term *actors* refers to the members of the culture under study.

Making the Ethnographic Record

With the completion of each observation, the ethnographer is responsible for documenting the experience. The documents generated from the observations are called *field notes*. Field notes can be managed by hand writing notes and storing them manually or by using computer programs to store and categorize data. The most popular computer program used by ethnographers is *Ethnograph* (Seidel, Kjolseth, & Seymour, 1988). This program can be used to organize data. If an individual does not have a computer available or is more comfortable documenting in writing, notes can be used and organized in file boxes that chronicle what is seen, what is heard, answers to questions asked, and created or collected artifacts.

In the clinic, for example, the researcher may observe the physical layout. Based on the observation, questions may be asked related to what happens in each room. A floor plan (artifact) may become part of the record. Pictures also may be taken to document the colors of the clinic or the decorations used. These artifacts may offer important insights as the study goes on.

It is important throughout the study, but especially in the beginning, not to focus too soon and also not to assume that any comment, artifact, or interaction is incidental. Experiences should be documented to create a thick or rich description of the culture. As illustrated above, the researcher should document the colors of the clinic. This may seem incidental; however, if a staff member later states that it is important to maintain a calm atmosphere in the clinic because of the types of patients seen, then the choice of the color blue for the walls may be an artifact that supports this belief system.

In addition to recording explicit details of a situation, the ethnographer also will record personal insights. The wide-angle view of the situation will provide the opportunity not only to detail what is said but also to share what may be implicit in the situation. Using a wide-angle lens to view a situation provides the ethnographer with a larger view of what is actually occurring in a social situation. For example, if an ethnographer is interested in observing change of shift report and attends the report with the purpose of investigating the nurses interactions, the researcher may miss valuable information regarding the report. With a wide-angle approach, the ethnographer would observe all individuals, activities, and artifacts that are part of the social situation, not merely focus on the interactions between the nurses in the report. Attention to all parts of the social situation will contribute to a richer description of the cultural scene.

Spradley (1980) offered three principles to be kept in mind during documentation of the observation: "the language identification principle, the verbatim principle, and the concrete principle" (p. 65).

The first principle is *language identification*. This principle requires that the ethnographer identify in whose language the text is written. Spradley (1980) shared that the most frequently recorded language is the amalgamated language (Example 5.1). This is the use of the ethnographer's language as well as that of informants. As a nurse ethnographer recording the observation of a clinic day, one might choose to mix the answers to questions with personal observations. This becomes difficult when data analysis begins because the researcher can lose sight of the cultural meaning of the observation. To minimize the potential of this happening, entries should identify the person making the remarks. Example 5.1 illustrates the correct way to record field notes. In Example 5.2, the record does not describe how specific information was obtained. It is dif-

---

Example 5.1

Field note Entry #1: March 16, 1994

ETHNOGRAPHER	Today when I visited the clinic, I noticed that the walls were painted blue. I asked the receptionist who had done the decorating.
RECEPTIONIST	"We had several meetings with the decorator."

ficult to decipher whether these are the researcher's interpretations or whether the information was obtained directly from the informants.

Although Example 5.1 is a limited notation, the reader can get a sense of how field notes should be reported to facilitate analysis. In this example, the response by the receptionist gives the ethnographer clear information about the decorating. The fact that the receptionist used the word "we" in Example 5.1 gives the researcher insight into the interactions that take place among members of the staff. Although Example 5.2 offers significant information, after long months of data collection, it will be very difficult to return to this note and identify the researcher's insights from factual information obtained from the informants.

The reporting of the receptionist's comments in Example 5.1 reflects the second principle: the *verbatim principle*. This principle requires the ethnographer to use the exact words of the speaker. This principle can be adhered to through the use of audiotaping. Audiotaping not only provides the ethnographer with verbatim accounts of conversation but it also affords the researcher an extensive accounting of an interaction that provides the material for intensive analysis.

Documenting verbatim statements also provides the researcher with a view of native expressions. In the exemplar, the use of verbatim documentation allows the researcher to gain insight into the language. In this example, the receptionist used the word "we" to describe the activities with the decorator. The use of the word "we" may provide valuable insights into the culture of the clinic.

The *concrete principle* is the third precept discussed by Spradley (1980). This principle requires that the ethnographer document what is seen and heard without interpretation. Generalizations and interpretations may limit access to valuable cultural insights. To reduce interpretation, the researcher should document observations with as much detail as possible. Example 5.3 offers an example of the concrete principle.

Example 5.2

Field note entry #1: March 16, 1994

Today I observed the clinic waiting area. The area is painted in a pale blue. The chairs are wood and fabric. The fabric is a white and blue print which contrasts with the wall paper. The waiting area is very busy. The colors have an effect on the patients. They come in looking very harassed then they fall asleep. A decorator helped with the colors.

Example 5.3

The clinic waiting area is painted ocean blue. The ladderback chairs are light brown wood with upholstered seats. The fabric on the seats is an ocean blue and white checkered pattern. There are two small two foot by three foot by two and one half foot brown wooden tables between the six chairs in the waiting room. There are two chairs along one wall with a table in the corner. Then, two chairs along the second wall with another table in the corner. The third wall has the two remaining chairs. The room is an eight by nine rectangle. Each table has a ginger jar lamp. The lamp base and shade are white. The fourth wall has a door and window on it. The draperies on the window are floor length and match the pattern on the chairs.

Individuals enter the clinic state their names to the receptionist, sit in the chairs and close their eyes. Some patients snore.

ETHNOGRAPHER   "The colors in this room are great. Everything seems to go together so well. Who did the decorating?"

RECEPTIONIST   "We had several meetings with the decorator."

In this example, all documentation is clear. Facts are recorded as facts and conversation is recorded verbatim as conversation. This type of concrete documentation illustrates recording without interpretation or generalization.

Making Descriptive Observations

Every time the ethnographer is in a social situation, descriptive observations will be made. Descriptive observations generally are not made with specific questions in mind. General questions guide this type of observation. These questions have been called *grand tour* questions. An example of a grand tour question that could initiate a study of a particular clinic might be as follows: "How do people who live in this neighborhood receive health care?" Remembering that the three primary foci of all observations include the actors, the activities, and the artifacts will assist in the development of grand tour questions.

Spradley (1980) stated that there are nine major dimensions to any social situation: space, actor, activity, object, act, event, time, goal, and feeling.

Space identifies the physical place or places where the culture of interest carries out its social interactions. In the clinic example used throughout this chapter, space would include the physical layout of the care delivery site.

Actors are people who are part of the culture under investigation. The nurses, patients, physicians, maintenance workers, secretarial/receptionist staff, and family members of patients in the clinic would all be included based on this example.

The *activities* are the third dimension. Activities are the actions carried out by members of the culture. They include activities such as the treatments provided to patients and conversations between members of the cultural group.

The fourth dimension, *object,* would include artifacts such as implements used for care, pamphlets read by patients, records made by the staff, and meeting minutes. Any inanimate object included in the space under study may give insight into the culture.

Single actions carried out by members of the group are the fifth dimension described by Spradley (1980) as *act.* An example of an act observed in the clinic would be locking of the medicine cabinet.

An *event* is a set of related activities carried out by members of the culture. One day in the clinic, the ethnographer may observe the staff giving a birthday party for a long-time patient.

It is very important to document the *time* that observations are made and what activities take place during those times. In addition to recording time, the researcher must relate the effect time has on all nine dimensions of social situations.

Goal is the eighth dimension described by Spradley (1980). This relates specifically to what members of the group hope to achieve. For instance, in painting the clinic blue, the staff may relate that their intention was to have a calming effect on patients who often must wait for long periods.

Feelings should also be recorded for each social situation. What emotions are expressed or observed? In regard to the birthday party in the clinic, the ethnographer might observe tears from the recipient of the party, cheers by the staff, and anger by the family member. Recording feelings provides a rich framework from which to make cultural inferences.

These nine dimensions can be useful in guiding observations and questions that will be made of social situations. It is beneficial to plot the nine dimensions in a matrix (Spradley, 1980). This will insure the contrast of all nine dimensions to each other. For example in addition to describing the space where the culture carries out its interactions, space should be related to object, act, activity, event, time, actor, goal, and feelings. What does the space look like?

What are all the ways space is organized by objects?; what are all the ways space is organized by acts?; what are all the ways space is organized by activities?, what are all the ways space is organized by events?; what spatial changes occur over time?; what are all the ways space is used by actors?; what are all the ways space is related to goals?; what places are associated with feelings?" (Spradley, 1980, pp. 82–83).

Once data are collected on all nine dimensions and they are related to each other, the researcher can begin to focus further observations.

Making a Domain Analysis

During the conduct of an ethnographic study, the researcher is required to analyze data throughout the study. Analyzing data during the fieldwork helps to structure latter encounters with the social group of interest. Ethnographic data "analysis is a search for patterns" (Spradley, 1980, p. 85). These patterns make up the culture.

To begin to understand cultural meaning, ethnographers must analyze social situations that they observe. A social situation is not the same as the concept of culture. "A social situation refers to the stream of behavior (activities) carried out by people (actors) in a particular location (place)" (Spradley, 1980, p. 86). Analysis of the social situation will lead to discovery of the *cultural scene*. Cultural scene is an ethnographic term which refers to the culture under study (Spradley, 1980).

The first step in analysis is *domain analysis*. To do a domain analysis, the ethnographer focuses on a particular situation. The outpatient clinic will serve as a reference point for this discussion.

The category, people in the clinic, is the first domain to be analyzed. The question to be asked is, "Who are the people who are in the clinic?" Looking at the field notes, the people in the clinic should be easy to identify. (See Fig. 5.1.)

Spradley (1980) suggests that it is important to identify the semantic relationships in the observations made. For example, *x* is a kind of *y*. Nurses are kinds of people in the clinic. Further, another analysis can be done to explore the types of nurses who work in the clinic.

Hammersley and Atkinson (1983) approach analysis somewhat differently. They recommend the generation of concept categories followed by further refinement into subcategories. Regardless of the method used, it is essential that the researcher work to discover the cultural meaning for people, places, artifacts, and activities. Creating as extensive a list as possible of categories will assist in discovery. To maintain inclusiveness, return to the nine dimensions (p. 141) recommended by Spradley (1980). Generating domain analyses leads the ethnographer to ask additional questions and make further observations to explore the roles and relationships of the members of the cultural group.

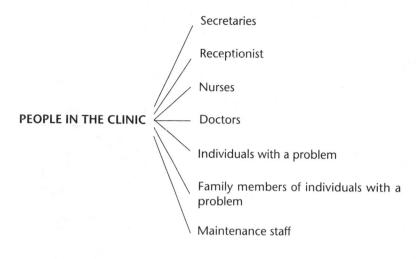

Fig. 5.1

Making Focused Observations

Based on the domain analysis completed by the ethnographer, new observations will need to be made and additional material collected. The domain analysis should be the trigger for the next round of observations. The researcher identifies the domain categories that need development and then returns to the research site.

For example, based on the identification of different types of nurses in the clinic, the ethnographer will want to focus on the different types of nurses and discover their specific roles and activities. This can provide important insight into the culture of the situation.

Making a Taxonomic Analysis

The taxonomic analysis is a more in-depth analysis of the domains chosen earlier. What the researcher is searching for is larger categories to which the domain may belong. For example, nurses in the clinic is a category identified in the domain analysis. Nurses are a type of people in the clinic. Additionally, there are types of nurses. One of the ways nurses can be categorized is based on their educational backgrounds: licensed practical nurses (LPNs), registered nurses (RNs), nurse practitioners (NPs), and clinical nurse specialists (CNSs). These can further be broken down based on the focus of patients they care for in the particular culture under study. (See Fig. 5.2.)

Once this analysis is completed, the ethnographer will look for relationships among the parts or relationships to the whole. Based on these

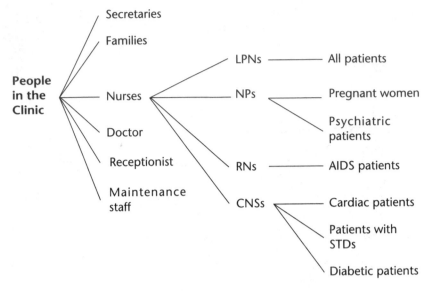

Fig. 5.2

new categories, additional observations will be made and additional questions asked. For instance, Why do the registered nurses have the primary responsibility for care of the patients with AIDS and sexually transmitted diseases? Are there different types of AIDS patients and are they cared for by specific registered nurses? Are AIDS patients treated differently from the patients with sexually transmitted diseases? Are other nurses consulted regarding the care of these two groups of patients? Are the nurses able to select the types of patients they care for?

As can be seen, a number of questions have been generated from this taxonomic analysis of the concept nurse. In addition to using a reductive exercise, the ethnographer should be trying to discover whether there are larger categories that have not been accounted for. For example, are the people in the clinic a part of a larger system? If the clinic is affiliated with a hospital, or public or private organization, then the answer is yes. Questions then will be generated based on this association. Focused interviews will need to be conducted to validate whether the larger or smaller categorizations as derived by the nurse ethnographer are accurate.

Making Selected Observations

Described earlier is the need to further refine the data that have been collected. This requires selective observations. These selective observations will help to identify the "dimensions of contrast" (Spradley, 1980, p. 128).

Spradley offered several types of questions that will help to discern the differences in the dimensions of contrast. The first is the *dyadic* question. This question seeks to identify the differences between two domains. The question asked is, "In what way are these two things different?" To illustrate the point, the example described earlier will be used. One of the questions the researcher should ask is, "In what ways are nurse practitioners and clinical nurse specialists different?"

Triadic contrast questions comprise the second category. These questions seek to identify how three categories related to each other: "Of the three, nurse practitioners, clinical nurse specialist, and registered nurses, which two are more alike than the third?"

Card sorting contrast questions are the third category. When using this method, the ethnographer places the domains on cards and sorts them into piles based on their similarities. By identifying the similarities, the contrasts become easily recognizable. Asking these questions of data already available will lead the ethnographer back to the setting to ask still other questions.

Componential Analysis

"Componential analysis is the systematic search for attributes associated with cultural categories" (Spradley, 1980, p. 131). During this stage of analysis, the researcher is looking for units of meaning. Each unit of meaning is considered an attribute of the culture. Again, the researcher is searching for missing data. During componential analysis, each domain is examined for its component parts. Questions of contrast are once again asked. Based on the identification of missing data, selected observations will occur. Table 5.2 is an example of simple componential analysis that illustrates dimensions of contrast based on sorting of people who work in the clinic. The purpose of using this process is to search for contrasts,

TABLE 5.2   DIMENSIONS OF CONTRAST

Domain	Licensed	Supervised Personnel	Health Care Provider
Doctors	yes	no	yes
Nurses	yes	yes	yes
Sec.	no	yes	no
Recept.	no	yes	no
Maint.	no	yes	no

sort them out, and then group them based on similarities and differences. This activity will provide the ethnographer with important information regarding the culture under study.

Reviewing the example, the ethnographer is able to determine that unlicensed personnel do not provide health care. Also, this analysis helps to begin to identify a hierarchial structure. Both hypotheses must be validated through selective interviews and observations.

To carry out a full componential analysis, the ethnographer should move through the process in a sequential manner. The steps of the procedure are as follows: (1) select a domain for analysis (people who work in the clinic); (2) inventory previously discovered contrasts (some members are licensed, have supervisors whom they report to and provide health care); (3) prepare the work sheet, which is called a paradigm; (4) classify dimensions of contrast that have binary values (licensed, yes or no); (5) combine related dimensions of contrast into ones that have multiple values (doctors and nurses are licensed personnel who provide health care); (6) prepare contrast questions for missing attributes (Are doctors the owners of the clinic since they appear not to have a reporting relationship?); (7) conduct selective observations and interviews to discover missing data and confirm or discard hypotheses; (8) prepare a complete paradigm (Spradley, 1980). "The final paradigm can be used as a chart in [the] ethnography" (Spradley, 1980, p. 139). Although every attribute will not be discussed on the chart, important ones can be. This allows the ethnographer to present a large amount of information in a concise and clear manner (Spradley, 1980).

Data Analysis

Although data analysis takes place throughout data collection, the next two stages concentrate solely on data analysis. These two stages will be discussed separately.

Discovering Cultural Themes

The discovery of cultural themes requires the ethnographer to look carefully over the data collected and identify recurrent patterns. These patterns, whether tacit or explicit, constitute the culture.

To complete the theme analysis, the researcher must become immersed in the data. This requires focused concentration over an extended period of time. The purpose of immersion is to identify patterns that have not become apparent to this point in the study or to explore patterns that may have been generated previously to assure their soundness. Spradley (1980) identifies six universal themes that may be helpful during this stage of data analysis. These themes are not meant to explain all patterns, but they do provide a place to begin. The universal themes are as follows: Social conflict—what types of conflicts are occurring between people in social situations? Cultural contradiction—is there information derived from the cultural group that appears contradictory? Informal techniques of social control—are there informal patterns of behavior that result in social control? Managing interpersonal relationships—how do members of the group conduct their interpersonal relationships? In addition, there are the themes of acquiring and maintaining status and solving problems. Finally, writing an overview summary of the cultural scene will help to identify themes that have not been discovered.

Taking a Cultural Inventory

Completing a cultural inventory is the first stage in writing an ethnography. A cultural inventory provides the opportunity to organize collected data. The inventory consists of the following: (1) listing cultural domains; (2) listing analyzed domains; (3) collecting sketch maps, which are drawings of places or activities; (4) listing themes; (5) completing an inventory of examples; (6) identifying organizing domains; (7) completing an index or table of contents; (8) completing an inventory of miscellaneous data; and (9) suggesting areas for future study (Spradley, 1980). Once the inventory is completed, the researcher is ready to write the ethnography.

Interpreting the Findings

The purpose of an ethnographic study is to describe the culture. It is important to remember that there are probably no two researchers who would describe the culture in the same way. This is related to issues of the culture of the researcher, the time period in which the study is conducted, and also the information gathered by the researcher. Some would argue that these are exactly the reasons why qualitative methods and in particular ethnography can never be viewed as science. On the contrary, these are precisely the reasons why ethnography and other qualitative methods are science. What most qualitative methods of research seek to do is share a context-bound view of phenomena; in this case, the phenomenon is the culture of a group.

Because culture is ever changing and dynamic, the discoveries of today are applicable in context. These discoveries bring important insights; they do not pretend to bring forward "the truth," but rather a truth. So, as the ethnographer begins to write the findings of the study, it is important to remember that if appropriate rigorous methods were used to collect and analyze data, then the product is one view of a truth.

Writing the Ethnography

The purpose of writing an ethnography is to share with people what has been learned and to attempt to make sense out of the cultural patterns that present themselves. To do so, an ethnographer must ask the question, "For whom am I writing?" Based on the answer to this question, the document will look very different. If writing for a scholarly community, detail will be important. If writing for the popular press, insights with exemplars will be most useful. If writing for an organization in the form of a formal report, attention must be paid to those details that reflect the concerns that directed the inquiry.

One of the best ways to know what to write is to look for examples of what has been written. An ethnographer may choose to report in a natural history, chronological or spacial, or choose to organize information based on significant themes (Omery, 1988). Reviewing published texts that chronicle macro-ethnographies, or scholarly journals that have published micro-ethnographies will provide good examples of how to organize the final ethnographic report. Every detail or idea may not be collapsible into one journal article or one book. Focusing on aspects of the research for several books or articles may be the only feasible way to report the findings of an ethnographic study.

Several drafts may be needed until the document reflects the study. Colleagues can be recruited to critique the work. They can help the neophyte researcher discover whether the topic has been covered appropriately.

ETHICAL CONSIDERATIONS

In Chapter 13 a complete discussion of the ethics of qualitative research is offered. However, the general considerations that ethnographers must incorporate into the conduct of their work should be noted . Germain (1986) offered five ethical considerations:

1. Informed consent.
2. The protection of privacy, anonymity, and confidentiality of members of the subculture during the period of data collection and at the the time of publication of the report vis-a-vis scientific integrity of the report.
3. Potential use of findings and power relationships among various levels of the study population.
4. Objectivity versus subjectivity with regard to selection, recording, and reporting phenomena.
5. Intervention versus nonintervention in the activities of the subculture (pp. 150–151).

These considerations should serve as the ethical framework for the conduct of ethnographic research.

SUMMARY

In this chapter, the ethnographic approach to research has been discussed. Issues related to selection of the method, interpretations of the approach, application of the approach, and interpretation of the findings have been presented. A thorough explanation of conduct of ethnographic research has been shared in the hope that it will provide a framework from which to conduct the first ethnographic inquiry.

Ethnography offers a significant research approach to the individual who is interested in learning about culture, willing and able to report data in narrative format, comfortable with ambiguity, able to build trusting relationships, and comfortable working alone (Germain, 1986). The study of culture, whether in a nursing unit well known or a country whose health practices are unknown, offers exciting discovery opportunities. Nurse researchers who choose to employ this approach will find that the focus of the study will become an intimate part of their daily existence until it has been fully explored, described, and interpreted.

In the next chapter, a review of research using the approach will be addressed. It is hoped that this review will further assist those interested in the approach to understand the method and provide concrete criteria from which to judge the merits of published reports.

REFERENCES

Agar, M. H. (1982). Toward an ethnographic language. *American Anthropologist, 84*(4), 779–795.

Agar, M. H. (1986). *Speaking of ethnography*. Beverly Hills, CA: Sage.

Anderson, J. M. (1991). Reflexivity in fieldwork: Toward a feminist epistemology. *Image: Journal of Nursing Scholarship, 23*(2), 115–118.

Atkinson, P., & Hammersley, M. (1994). Ethnography and participant observation. In N. K. Denzin & Y. S. Lincoln, (Eds.), *Handbook of qualitative research* (pp. 248–261). Thousand Oaks, CA: Sage.

Benedict, R. (1934). *Patterns of culture*. New York: Houghton Mifflin.

Boas, F. (1948). *Race, language and culture*. New York: Macmillan.

Geertz, C. (1973). *The interpretations of culture*. New York: Basic Books.

Germain, C. P. (1979). *The cancer unit: An ethnography*. Wakefield, MA: Nursing Resources.

Germain, C. P. (1986). Ethnography: The method. In P. L. Munhall & C. J. Oiler (Eds.), *Nursing research: A qualitative perspective* (pp. 147–162). Norwalk, CT: Appleton-Century-Crofts.

Goetz, J. P., & LeCompte, M. D. (1984). *Ethnography and qualitative design in educational research.* Orlando: Academic Press.

Goodenough, W. (1970). *Description and comparison in cultural anthropology.* Chicago: Aldine.

Goodenough, W. (1971). *Culture, language and society.* Reading, MA: Addison-Wesley.

Grant, L., & Fine, G. A. (1992). Sociology unleashed: Creative directions in classical ethnography. In M. D. LeCompte, W. L. Milroy, & J. Preissle (Eds.), *The handbook of qualitative research in education* (pp. 405–446). San Diego: Academic Press, Inc.

Hammersley, M., & Atkinson, P. (1983). *Ethnography: Principles in practice.* London: Tavistock Publications.

Leininger, M. (1970). *Nursing and anthropology: Two worlds to blend.* New York: Wiley.

Leininger, M. (1978). *Transcultural nursing: Concepts, theories and practices.* New York: Wiley.

Leininger, M. (1985). Ethnography and ethnonursing: Models and modes of qualitative data analysis. In M. Leininger (Ed.), *Qualitative research methods in nursing* (pp. 33–71). Orlando: Grune & Stratton.

Malinowski, B. (1961). *Argonauts of the Western Pacific.* New York: Dutton.

Mead, M. (1949). *Coming of age in Samoa.* New York: New American Library, Mentor Books.

Miller, M. P. (1991). Factors promoting wellness in the aged person: An ethnographic study. *Advances in Nursing Science, 13*(4), 38–51.

Omery, A. (1988). Ethnography. In B. Sarter (Ed.), *Paths to knowledge: Innovative research methods for nursing* (pp. 17–31). New York: National League for Nursing.

Radcliffe-Brown, A. R. (1952). *Structure and function in primitive society.* London: Oxford University Press.

Ragucci, A. T. (1972). The ethnographic approach and nursing research, *Nursing Research, 21*(6), 485–490.

Sanday, P. R. (1983). The ethnographic paradigm(s). In J. van Maanen (Ed.), *Qualitative methodology.* (pp. 19–36). Beverly Hills, CA: Sage.

Seidel, J., Kjolseth, R., & Seymour, E. (1988). *The ethnograph.* Littleton, OR: Qualis Research Associates.

Spradley, J. P. (1980). *Participant observation.* New York: Holt, Rinehart & Winston.

Spradley, J. P., & McCurdy, D. W. (1972). *The cultural experience: Ethnography in complex society.* Prospect Heights, IL: Waveland Press.

van Maanen, J. (1983). The fact of fiction in organizational ethnography. In van Maanen (Ed.), *Qualitative methodology* (pp. 36–55). Beverly Hills, CA: Sage.

Wolf, Z. R. (1988). *Nurses' work, the sacred and the profane.* Philadelphia: University of Pennsylvania Press.

Chapter 6

Application of Ethnographic Research in Nursing Education, Practice, and Administration

Ethnography, as a means of studying nursing and the cultural practices imbedded within it, creates unlimited opportunities for nurses interested in using this approach. The study of patterns within a culture provides an excellent opportunity to describe the practices of the people nurses care for, to understand the health-related phenomena of persons of varying cultures, and to examine nursing's own unique culture. Ethnography provides the opportunity to explore not just the clinical aspects of nursing but also its administrative and educative patterns and life ways.

In this chapter, an overview of ethnographic studies exploring cultures of interest to nursing will be provided. In addition, micro-ethnographic studies reflecting the areas of clinical nursing practice, nursing education, and nursing administration will be critiqued to provide the reader with examples of published work and the contributions they have made to the field. At the end of the chapter, the reader will find Appendix 6.1 which summarizes a series of ethnographic studies representing the areas of nursing education, administration, and practice.

The studies examined in the chapter will be critiqued using the "Critiquing Guidelines for Qualitative Research" presented earlier in Table 4.1. A reprint of the Mackenzie article can be found at the end of this chapter to assist the reader in understanding the critiquing process.

Qualitative Research in Nursing: Advancing the Humanistic Imperative by Helen J. Streubert and Dona R. Carpenter. Copyright © 1995 by J. B. Lippincott Company.

ETHNOGRAPHIC APPROACH APPLIED TO NURSING PRACTICE

Ethnographic research methodology provides an exceptional opportunity for nurses interested in examining clinical practice issues. Whether the interest is in studying the rituals inherent in nursing practice (Wolf, 1988) or the wellness in aging populations (Miller, 1991), ethnographic research provides the framework for exploring the richness of nursing and nursing-related phenomena.

Two studies will be examined in this section: "Factors Promoting Wellness in the Aged Person: An Ethnographic Study" (Miller, 1991) and "Nursing Perceptions of Collaboration with Indigenous Healers in Swaziland" (Upvall, 1992). These studies were chosen because of their differences in focus. Upvall's study represents a traditional perspective on ethnography, which is the ethnographer's living among the people of a foreign culture, whereas Miller's study illustrates the value of studying specific cultural practices among known populations, such as the aged.

Miller (1991) identifies the *aim* of her study as the understanding of "wellness in aging from the perspective of the aging person and to highlight factors contributing to wellness and aging" (p. 43). Upvall (1992) states that the purpose of her study is to answer the question "How do nurses from various health care settings perceive collaboration between indigenous and cosmopolitan health care systems?" (p. 27). In both studies, the authors are interested in looking specifically at an element of a culture. For this reason, both represent micro-ethnographic research studies because their focus is limited to a particular aspect of a culture and not the culture itself.

Upvall (1992) asks a grand tour question to begin her study which reflects the common practice of most ethnographers: "How do nurses from various health care settings (government, private, mission, industrial, and non-governmental organizations) perceive the articulation of indigenous and cosmopolitan health care systems?" (p .28). From this question, other questions can be asked as the participants in the study led the researcher toward a full understanding of the culture.

Both authors clearly state why they chose to use an ethnographic approach to study their particular area of interest. In Miller's (1991) study of wellness in the aged, she stated that the ethnographic approach will "ferret out the meaning from the perspective of those living [the experience]" (p. 43). Upvall (1992) used ethnography because it enabled her to be involved in "listening, observing behavior, participating in activities, and questioning" (p. 29) the culture of her interest. Both of these represent sound reasons for utilization of this approach. Philosophically, both researchers are focused on the systematic process of observing, detailing, describing, documenting, and analyzing the life ways or particular patterns of a culture (or subculture) in order to grasp the life ways or patterns of the people in their familiar environment (Leininger, 1985, p. 35).

The choice of ethnography by both researchers is appropriate to answer the questions being asked.

Upvall (1992) described the *sample* for her inquiry as 65 nurses practicing in Swaziland. These individuals work in "urban, peri-urban and rural areas" (p. 31) of the country. In addition to nurses, Upvall interviewed officials from the Ministry of Health to get their perceptions of collaboration between the nurses and the indigenous health workers.

Six members of the Gray Panthers organization living in southwest Dade County, Florida, comprised the participants in Miller's (1991) study. The sample was equally distributed by gender. The ages of the group ranged from 70 to 81 years. The informants were all in "essentially good health" (p. 43) despite their suffering from chronic diseases such as arthritis and diabetes. None of the chronic conditions created incapacitation. Miller also pointed out that her participants were members of middle and upper income groups. This is an important piece of demographic information. Specifically, it tells the potential utilizer of the findings who the well, aged informants were. Findings from this study may be extrapolated to similar population groups only after determination of the similarities between groups has been identified. However, the findings should only be considered transferrable based on the specifics of the group and after validation of the commonalities.

In both cases, the individuals chosen to inform the inquiry are appropriate. They are both members of the culture of interest and have intimate knowledge of the focus of the inquiry.

The focus in both studies is on collection of data that will inform the nursing community about human experience. The strategies used by both researchers are varied. Upvall (1992), in conducting her research in Swaziland, utilized participant observation, formal and informal interviewing and review of artifacts. She described the type of participant observation conducted as moderate participation as defined by Spradley (1980). This type of participation provided her with the opportunity to be limitedly involved in the activities of the nurses in the field, thereby providing her with rich opportunities for interviewing participants in an informal way. This type of participation often provides the researcher with opportunities not available when observation only is used.

The artifacts reviewed by Upvall (1992) included reports regarding research completed by other researchers that are not available in the United States. Review of artifacts provides ethnographers with opportunities to view aspects of culture often not available through interviewing or participant observation (Spradley & McCurdy, 1972).

Miller (1991) identified her *data collection strategies* as semi-structured interviews and participant observation with the aged participants.

From the author's account of the study, it is difficult to ascertain exactly what her participation was. It is clear that she observed the seniors in particular activities; however, there is no description of what her part in these activities was.

There are two aspects of data collection not described by either researcher: saturation of the data and protection of human subjects. Upvall (1992) spent 12 months in the field with her participants. Although it is not stated, saturation of data is likely to have occurred given the prolonged period of time the researcher spent in the field. In the case of Miller's (1991) research, saturation is not addressed. However, she stated that she spent approximately six weeks with the participants in weekly interviews. Although saturation of the data could have occurred during the six-week period, it is difficult to determine given her reporting of the study. Longevity in the field is not necessarily a predictor or determinant of saturation. However, with a very focused study, it is assumed that a longer period of time in the field would achieve saturation.

Neither author discusses protection of human subjects. As Germain (1986) points out, this is an extremely important part of ethnographic field studies and needs to be specifically dealt with given the intimacy of contact with participants over a prolonged period.

Upvall (1992) conducted her analysis using three very traditional methods of ethnographic data analysis: "rewriting, coding and comparison" (Pfaffenberger, 1988, cited in Upvall, 1992, p. 31). Rewriting requires rewriting the field notes and transcribing the tape-recorded interviews. Comparison "was accomplished through the use of THE ETHNOGRAPH computer program" (p. 31). In Miller's (1991) study, she stated that she used content analysis to analyze her data. No specifics were included.

It is not unusual that the details of both researchers' data analyses are not included. The amount of detail reported in an ethnographic account is largely related to the audience for which it is intended (Wolcott, 1990). In a nursing research journal, it would be very difficult to include the details of data analysis given the limitations on article lengths advised by the publishers.

The *findings* of both researchers' studies are reported as themes. These are illustrated by specific quotes made by the participants in the study. Using quotes to illustrate themes helps the reader appreciate the richness of the data.

Any qualitative study should demonstrate *rigor*. The measure of rigor in qualitative research is the assessment of credibility, auditability, fittingness, and confirmability of the data (Yonge & Stewin, 1988).

Credibility is the measure of whether the participants recognize the experience to be their own based on their reading of the data. Neither researcher reported this information; therefore, the reader has no way of determining whether the participants recognized the experience as their own.

The *auditability* of the two studies is limitedly addressed based on discussions of the research process used. As reported earlier, the paper trail that should accompany any qualitative study is limited in journal articles. It would be difficult, based on the reports of these studies, to decide whether the auditability criterion has been met.

The *fittingness* of the data in both studies is based on whether the findings can fit or find meaning outside of the study situation. Miller's (1991) findings related to wellness in aged populations have meaning outside of the study situation as documented by her references to Erickson's (1964) work cited in her report. She illustrated for readers the relationship between her work and that done by other researchers. Upvall (1992) reported that her findings would be useful to other African cultures that support both indigenous and cosmopolitan health models. Both studies, therefore, have utility or fit outside of the study situation.

A major strength of both studies is that they are presented in the context of what is known and what is offered in the voices of the participants. The reader is able to grasp the importance of the work and the essences of subcultures described in both cases. Miller (1991) and Upvall (1992) shared with readers the literature related to both studies to further illustrate the context of the studies and usefulness of their findings.

The *conclusions, implications, and recommendations* are appropriately stated. Miller (1991) offered the importance of the knowledge gained from this study and recommended that research continue with well elderly to help nurses more fully understand the aging process.

Upvall (1992) provided suggestions for integrating indigenous health care with cosmopolitan care based on the findings of her study. She did not offer suggestions for future research.

The studies completed by Miller (1991) and Upvall (1992) are two excellent examples of the utilization of ethnographic research in clinical practice. In Miller's study the reader learns about wellness as a group of well elderly experience it. In Upvall's study insight is gained into the culture of Swaziland nurses and how they see collaboration between indigenous health care workers and the cosmopolitan health care system. The value of both of these studies is found in rich descriptions of these subcultures. Deeper knowledge and understanding will lead the way to improved health care for particular groups (cultures) by nursing professionals.

ETHNOGRAPHIC APPROACH APPLIED TO NURSING EDUCATION

Nursing education presents another context for nurse researchers to conduct ethnographic studies. The nature of students and faculty coming together for the purpose of an educational opportunity creates its own culture. Few studies have been published that illustrate the life ways of

students and faculty. This provides rich opportunities for nurses interested in nursing education research using the ethnographic approach.

Mackenzie (1992) is a nurse researcher who chose to study nursing education using the ethnographic approach. Her study, entitled
"Learning from Experience in Community: An Ethnographic Study of District Nursing Students," provides nurses interested in this method with an
example of how to apply it in nursing education.

The culture of interest to Mackenzie (1992) is composed of district
nursing students experiencing a community rotation. The reason given for
studying this phenomenon using ethnography is to gain an understanding of these students' learning experiences while functioning in community settings. Further, Mackenzie stated that she conducted the study using
ethnography because she believed that there are different interpretations
of experiences in natural settings and also because there has been very
little research conducted with students outside of the hospital setting
specifically as it relates to learning. In addition, Mackenzie included in this
report the philosophical assumptions for conducting an ethnographic
study to examine the culture of interest.

The purpose of Mackenzie's (1992) study is clear. She is interested
in describing and understanding district nursing students learning in community settings. The significance of this study is documented specifically
as it relates to initiatives in the United Kingdom appertaining to community-based health care and implications for nursing educators in settings
that do not afford direct supervision of students.

Mackenzie (1992) reported that she used the ethnographic approach
to conduct her study. This method afforded her the opportunity to conduct
her study in a flexible way "allowing change in direction as the research
question is refined and re-defined and theory is developed" (p. 684).

The individuals who informed this inquiry were district nursing students with different amounts of experience in the setting. These informants were practicing in 14 health authorities located in both urban and
rural settings. Given that these students were active participants in the
culture of interest, they appropriately represent the culture studied.

Data were collected through participant observation and informal
and unstructured interviews. Mackenzie (1992) traveled with some of the
students as they visited clients in the community. During these visits, she
observed students' behaviors. In addition, interviews were conducted with
students over the two-year period of the study to assist the researcher in
more clearly understanding the culture of learning in the community setting. All observations and interviews were recorded in field notes developed during the observations and interviews, or immediately following
encounters. Adequate description of data collection methods assists readers to determine whether the researcher met the audibility criterion.

Saturation of data and protection of human subjects is not addressed in the report. As stated earlier, length of time in the setting can be used as a measure of data saturation in an ethnographic study. In this case, a two-year data collection period on a focused topic should allow for saturation.

Mackenzie (1992) reported that her data collection and data analysis occurred in an cyclical manner. She combined the processes of "reflection, imaginative thinking and systematic sifting and analysis of evidence from the data as outlined by Hammersley and Atkinson" (p. 685). This led to identification of conceptual categories. The reporting of the cyclic nature of data collection and data analysis represents an essential characteristic of ethnographic research.

Mackenzie (1992) reported, in addition, that she was unable to fully report the findings of the study in the published report. She informed the reader which parts of the study were included.

Information reflecting how she came to her conclusions regarding conceptual categories was not specifically reported. This leads the reader to accept at face value the categories offered by the researcher. Further, there is no discussion of validation of the findings with the participants or any other outside judge. This could be viewed as a weakness. It is essential that ethnographers report the validation of their findings.

The findings of this study can be applied outside the study setting. Mackenzie (1992) clearly stated how nurse educators can use the findings of her work. She also related her findings to other reported studies in similar areas demonstrating fittingness of the data.

The findings of this study are presented in context. The researcher keeps her recommendations within the parameters of similar groups of participants. A limitation in the reporting of the findings is the superficial accounting of the data. The richness of her encounters among the students is not present in this report. The intent to cover three major categories of data should have assisted the researcher in her reporting; however, this is not the case. The reader does not get an in-depth understanding of the students' learning experiences. The conceptual categories of "fitting in" and "trying and testing out" are more fully described than is the category of "reality of practice." Whenever an ethnographer chooses to report an ethnographic study in the form of a published article with specific page limitations, the risk of producing a document limited in its richness usually is inevitable.

The conclusions of Mackenzie's (1992) work are clear. At times, there is some overstatement of the implications; however, this is related, most probably, to her knowledge of the complete study.

Mackenzie's (1992) work is important because it provides the reader with the opportunity to begin to understand the learning experience of students in the community setting. As nurse educators in the United States move to meet the health care initiatives that appear to be leading to more community-based nursing practice, studies such as Mackenzie's will need to be replicated to understand fully the impact of learning and practicing in community settings.

ETHNOGRAPHIC APPROACH APPLIED TO NURSING ADMINISTRATION

Nursing administration has its own cultures. Nurses who come to an administrative role view their function differently than individuals who are educated to be business administrators. For this reason, it appears that there are rich opportunities to use the ethnographic research approach to study the culture of nursing administration.

In this section, Everson-Bates' (1992) article, "First-line Managers in the Expanded Role: An Ethnographic Analysis," will be examined. The focus as identified by the author is to study the

> beliefs, values, and behaviors of nurse managers considered to be effective and successful in their practice and the implications of these characteristics for manager selection and development (p. 32).

Everson-Bates (1992) clearly defined the term *expanded role* as assisting the reader in understanding the intent of the study. The researcher shares that the reason she chose ethnography is because so little is known about the phenomenon. First-line nurse managers can be viewed as subculture in nursing and as such represent an appropriate phenomenon of study. The philosophical underpinnings of this study are not shared by Everson-Bates. As her reason for using ethnography, she informed the reader only that there has been limited study in this area.

Everson-Bates (1992) implied that the importance of conducting the study is to enhance recruitment of effective nurse managers. This is not clearly stated. Her purpose is to use ethnographic field methods of observation and interview to capture the "beliefs, values, and behaviors" (p. 32) of first-line managers.

The participants in this study consisted of "16 inpatient nurse managers who were identified as effective in their role by their immediate supervisor, the director of nursing" (Everson Bates, 1992, pp. 32-33). It appears, based on the researcher's provision of a definition of effective, that these individuals were capable of informing the inquiry.

In addition to interviews with the 16 inpatient nurse managers, one manager was observed intensively for two months to provide the data for development of the semi-structured interview guide used with the 16 participants. Using observation of one individual to provide data for the interview guide is not a typical way of conducting an ethnographic study.

Generally, ethnographers move from observation to interview and back to observation in a cyclical manner based on cues they receive from participants. Everson-Bates (1992) also conducted interviews with four directors of nursing and two vice presidents for patient services "to explore their expectations for the role of manager" (p. 33). The lack of description of data collection strategies is a limitation of this study. The length of time the interviews were conducted is reported. In addition, Everson-Bates (1992) stated that she analyzed the tapes of her interviews with numerous documents and observations of management processes and meeting. No specifics were offered regarding the data analysis other than these references. In addition, there was no discussion of protection of human subjects.

Everson-Bates (1992) did not explain how she arrived at her conclusions. She did report her findings as major themes and shares the context of conversations to explicate the themes; however, the reader is uncertain as to how she treated the data.

The themes represent snapshots of the role of nurse managers. These included "one part task-the tracking of bureaucratic systems. . .and four parts process: 1) social control; 2) 'resourcing'; 3) translating/interpreting/negotiating; and 4) facilitating" (p. 33). The reporting of data would be enhanced by additional references to the subjective comments shared by the participants.

The credibility and auditability of the findings were not described. The author did not tell the reader whether the nurse managers were aware of her findings. Because of the very limited description of the method it would be extremely difficult to determine whether the auditability criterion was met. As stated earlier, it is not unusual for the auditability criterion not to be met in the published report based on the intended readership of the document and page limitations.

Everson-Bates (1992) did make a significant effort to place the study in the context of what is already known about nurse managers; for this reason, she demonstrated the "fit" of her findings. Whether her results were meaningful to the participants in the study is unknown.

The findings of the study are presented in context; however, Everson-Bates (1992) stated:

> Although ethnographic methodology is not designed to generalize findings beyond the study participants, there are striking parallels to be drawn within nursing, management and the lay literature" (p. 36).

Because the discussion of themes occurred primarily in the words of the researcher, it is difficult to get a sense of the values, beliefs,and behaviors from the emic point of view.

Everson-Bates' (1992) conclusions relate to the data she reported in the study. Recommendations were made based on her interpretation of the data. Specific recommendations for future study were not offered.

This study represents one of the few nursing administration studies conducted and published in the United States using ethnographic methodology. In light of the limited number of studies published on nursing administration using the ethnographic approach, tremendous opportunities exist for nurse researchers interested in this content area and ethnographic methodology.

SUMMARY

In this chapter, samples of ethnographic research have been reviewed as they have been published in the areas of nursing education, nursing research, and nursing practice. Each critique presents the strengths and limitations of reporting ethnographic research. Each reviewed author has contributed to the literature and has provided the reader with an opportunity to become part of the culture or subculture they studied.

Ethnographic research and the studies published that utilize it add to the richness and diversity of the human experience by allowing its readers to share in the lives of the people studied. As nurse researchers become more comfortable with multiple ways of knowing and multiple realities, all nurses will benefit by participating in the creation and dissemination of the knowledge imbedded in cultural realities; the cultural realities that enrich each person's life.

REFERENCES

Barton, J. A. (1991). Parental adaptation to adolescent drug abuse: An ethnographic study of role formulation in response to courtesy stigma. *Public Health Nursing, 8* (1), 39–45.

Buckley, B. P. R. (1990). *The teaching-learning process in selected clinical nursing practice contexts.* Doctoral dissertation, University of Toledo, 1990. (University Microfilms No. PUZ9023876).

Chubon, S. J. (1992). Home care during the aftermath of Hurricane Hugo. *Public Health Nursing, 9*(2), 92–102.

Clarridge, A., Couchman, W. A., & Holloway, I. M. (1991). Interaction in the classroom: District nurse students and their teachers. *Nurse Education Today, 12,* 200–206.

Connelly, L. M., Keele, B. S., Kleinbeck, S. V. M., Schneider, J. K., & Cobb, A. K. (1993). A place to be yourself: Empowerment from the client's perspective. *Image: Journal of Nursing Scholarship, 25*(4), 297–303.

Denyes, M. J., Neuman, B. M., & Villarruel, A. M. (1991). Nursing actions to prevent and alleviate pain in hospitalized. *Issues in Comprehensive Pediatric Nursing, 14,* 31–48.

Doolittle, N. D. (1991). Clinical ethnography of lacunar stroke: Implications for acute care. *Journal of Neuroscience Nursing, 23*(4), 235–240.

Erickson, E. H. (1964). *Childhood and society* (2nd ed.). New York: Norton.

Everson-Bates, S. (1992). First-line nurse managers in the expanded role: An ethnographic analysis. *Journal of Nursing Administration, 22*(3), 32–37.

Field, P. A. (1983). An ethnography: Four public health nurses' perspectives of nursing. *Journal of Advanced Nursing, 8,* 3–12.

Gagliardi, B. A. (1991). Families experiencing of living with a child with Duchennes Muscular Dystrophy. *Applied Nursing Research, 4*(4), 159–164.

Germain, C. (1984). Sheltering abused women: A nursing perspective. *Journal of Psychosocial Nursing, 22*(9), 24–31.

Germain, C. (1986). Ethnography: The method. In P.L. Munhall & C.J. Oiler (Eds.), *Nursing research. A qualitative perspective* (pp.147–162). Norwalk, CT: Appleton-Century-Crofts.

Leininger, M. M. (1985). Ethnography and ethnonursing: Models and modes of qualitative data analysis. In M. M. Leininger (Ed.), *Qualitative research methods in nursing.* Orlando, FL: Grune & Stratton.

MacGuire, J. M., & Botting, D. (1990). The use of ethnographic programs to identify perceptions of nursing staff following introduction of primary nursing in an acute medical ward for elderly people. *Journal of Advanced Nursing, 15,* 1120–1127.

Mackenzie, A. E. (1992). Learning from experience in the community: An ethnographic study of district nurse students. *Journal of Advanced Nursing, 17,* 682–691.

Magilvy, J. K., McMahon, M., Bachman, M., Roark, S., & Evenson, C. (1987). The health of teenagers: A focused ethnographic study. *Public Health Nursing, 4*(1), 35–42.

Marsden, C. (1988). Care giver fidelity in a pediatric bone marrow transplant team. *Heart & Lung, 17*(6), 617–625.

McCormack, B. (1992). A case study identifying nursing staffs' perception of the delivery method of nursing care in practice on a particular ward. *Journal of Advanced Nursing, 17,* 187–197.

Miller, M. P. (1991). Factors promoting wellness in the aged person: An ethnographic study. *Advances in Nursing Science, 13*(4), 38–51.

Montbriand, M. J., & Laing, G. P. (1991). Alternative health care as a control strategy. *Journal of Advanced Nursing, 16,* 325–332.

Nikkonen, M. (1992). Caring in the preparation of long-term psychiatric patients for non-institutional care: Ethnonursing study. *Journal of Advanced Nursing, 17,* 1088–1094.

Paterson, B. L. (1991). *The juggling act: An ethnographic analysis of clinical teaching in nursing education.* Unpublished doctoral dissertation, The University of Manitoba, Canada.

Spradley, J. P. (1980). *Participant observation.* New York: Holt, Rinehart and Winston.

Spradley, J. P., & McCurdy, D. W. (1972). *The cultural experience: Ethnography in complex society.* Prospect Heights, IL: Waveland Press.

Upvall, M. J. (1992). Nursing perceptions of collaboration with indigenous healers in Swaziland. *International Journal of Nursing Studies, 26*(1), 27–36.

Villarruel, A. M., & de Montellano, B. O. (1992). Culture and pain: A Mesoameri-
can perspective. *Advanced Nursing Science, 15*(1), 21–32.
Wolcott, H. F. (1990). Making a study "more ethnographic." *Journal of Contemporary Ethnography, 19*(1), 44–72.
Wolf, Z. R. (1988). *Nurses' work, the sacred and the profane.* Philadelphia: University of Pennsylvania Press.
Yonge, O., & Stewin, L. (1988). Reliability and validity: Misnomers for qualitative
research. *Canadian Journal of Nursing Research, 20*(2), 61–67.

APPENDIX 6.1 EXAMPLES OF MICRO-ETHNOGRAPHIC STUDIES

Author	Domain	Culture	Focus	Data Dollection	Data Analysis
Barton, J .A. (1991)	Practice	Parents of drug abusing teens	Parental response	Journals, observations interviews	Ethnography, conceptual and theoretical coding
Chubon, S. J. (1992)	Practice	Home care nurses	Job stress following disaster	Interview/participant observation	Not reported
Connelly, L. M., Keele, B. S., Kleinbeck, S. V. M., Schneider, J. K., & Cobb, A. K. (1993)	Practice	Chronic mental health patients	Empowerment	Participant observation/interview/ document review	Spradley's developmental research sequence
Denyes, M. T., Neuman, B., & Villarruel, A. M. (1991)	Practice	Pediatric nurses	Pain relief measures	Interview	Leininger's thematic & pattern analysis
Doolittle, N. D. (1991)	Practice	Stroke patients	Recovery experience	Focused interview	"Interperative"
Field, P. A. (1983)	Practice	Nurses	Public health nursing	Participant/observation interview artifacts	Not reported

(cont'd.)

Author	Domain	Culture	Focus	Data Dollection	Data Analysis
Gagliardi, B. A. (1991)	Practice	Families with children with Duchenne's muscular dystrophy	Family experience	Participant/observation	Constant comparative
Germain, C. P. (1984)	Practice	Abused women's shelter	Health concerns of occupants	Participant/observation interview	Not reported
Magilvy, J. K., McMahon, M., Bachman, M., Roark, S., & Evenson, C. (1987)	Practice	Teenagers	Health needs	Interview participant/ observation	Not reported
Marsden, C. (1988)	Practice	Bone marrow transplant team	Fidelity	Observation	Content analysis
Montebriand, M. J., & Lang, G. P. (1991)	Practice	Public health nurses	Alternative health care as a control strategy	Interviews	Ethnography conceptual and theoretical coding
Villarruel, A. M., & deMontellano, B. O. (1992)	Practice	Meso-Americans	Pain	Artifacts	Ethnohistoric methods

Author (Year)	Category	Setting	Phenomenon	Data collection	Analysis
MacGuire, J. M., & Botting, D. A. (1990)	Administration	Nursing unit	Primary nursing	Interview	Ethnography
McCormack, B. (1992)	Administration	Nursing unit	Care delivery method	Interview diaries	Latent content analysis
Nikkonen, M. (1992)	Administration	Nurses practicing in long-term psychiatric facility	Caring practices in preparation for discharge	Interview, observations, artifacts	Ethnonursing
Buckley, B. P. R. (1990)	Education	Student clinical sites	Teaching/learning process	Participants/observation	Not reported
Clarridge, A., Couchman, W.A., & Holloway, I. M. (1991)	Education	Nursing classroom	Student/faculty interaction	Observation (video camera)	Constant comparative
Paterson, B. L. (1991)	Education	Teaching faculty	Teaching faculty	Participant/observation interviews, artifact	Constant comparative

Learning from Experience in the Community: An Ethnographic Study of District Nurse Students

Ann E. Mackenzie, PhD, MA, RNT, DN, RGN

This study seeks to gain an understanding of the learning experiences of district nurse students in the learning environment of the community, and to examine learning in the practice setting from the perspective of the student. Since the research depends upon the changing and differing interpretations of the individuals involved in the natural setting of the community, an ethnographic approach has been adopted. The experiences of students are monitored throughout the taught practice element of the district nurse course in both inner city and rural/urban locations. Data, collected through interview and observations, are analysed in the context of theory relating to adult learning and learning from experience. Three major categories are identified. Examples from these categories are identified and discussed. The categories are sequential and represent the learning process experienced by the students in the practice setting as they learn to fit into a new environment, test out their own ideas and compare the unreality of college with the reality of practice. Attention is drawn to the difficulties for students of fitting into new settings and trying out change, to the detrimental effect on learning of rigid practice routines and to the powerlessness of community practice teachers to exert a major influence on the learning environment. These issues are discussed in the context of changes in nurse education and evaluation of the community learning environment.

ANN E. MACKENZIE: Lecturer in Nursing, Department of Nursing Studies, King's College London, Cornwall House Annex, Waterloo Road, London SE1 8TX, England

Reprinted from Mackenzie, A. E., Learning from experience in the community: An ethnographic study of district nurse students, *Journal of Advanced Nursing, 17,* pp. 682–691, with permission of Blackwell Scientific Publications Ltd., © 1992.

INTRODUCTION

The research is set against the background of substantial changes in nurse education in the form of Project 2000 (UKCC 1986). A re-orientation towards the community has implications for the education of nurses in hospital and community settings and for the learning experiences of students undertaking pre-registration and post-registration courses (UKCC 1990). During the post-registration preparation of practitioners such as district nurses for specialisms in primary health care, the location and main area of experience for learning advanced clinical practices will be in the community. This setting outside hospital and large institutions is largely unexamined as a learning environment, but is a very varied, and potentially, a very rich environment for learning.

Hospital research studies have been very influential in bringing the problems of learning in the clinical setting to the fore (Pembrey 1980, Orton 1981, Fretwell 1982, Melia 1987). Research has highlighted that students' learning is affected by the varying teaching and management abilities of the ward sister to influence the learning climate (Lathlean 1988). These studies provided strong evidence for some of the deficiencies in the education system of nurses in hospital settings, particularly the influence of service demands and the lack of meaningful integration between school-based teaching and ward-based experience. Both have led to changes (UKCC 1986) which will be implemented by Project 2000 programmes in the form of super-numerary status and training for qualified ward staff in teaching and assessing students.

While the hospital-based studies have alerted nurse educators to the difficulties of learning from the ward setting, they have done little to examine how students learn in relation to adult learning theory, concentrating more on sociological and organizational theories as their framework. There has been some recognition that learning theory is important in relation to the 'theory practice gap' (Alexander 1983) and in identification of attributes of good teachers (Marson 1982). However, it would seem important at this stage that nurse education does not accept uncritically the adult learning theorists with close evaluation of their contribution to the curriculum. Already adult learning theory is influencing curriculum methods. For instance, the use of mentors or preceptors for learners in the practice setting is causing a degree of confusion (Morle 1990), mainly because the aims of this innovation have not been made clear (Parry 1990).

If nurse educators are to benefit from examining some of these issues concerning learning in practice settings, then the issues need to be examined within an educational context. Adult learning theory has been utilized in a fairly *ad hoc* way by nurse teachers and it therefore seems appropriate that it should provide a framework for further studies in the practice setting of the community which will, in future, provide the starting point for nurse students and will be the learning context for advanced practice in community nursing (UKCC 1990).

THE STUDY

The study examines the experiences of district nurse students in the learning environment of the community. The community learning environment is defined as all the opportunities that are available to the students while they are placed in the practice setting.

The aim of the research is to gain an understanding of the learning experiences of district nurses from the perspective of the students.

ADULT LEARNING

As identified above, adult learning theory arising from the practices and methods of adult education and drawn from the humanistic philosophy of education, is evident in current texts in nurse education (Allan & Jolley 1987, Bradshaw 1989, Kenworthy & Nicklin 1989). These texts are part of the implementation of the greatest change in nurse education since the new syllabus for general nurse training was introduced in 1952. They demonstrate the different and often contradictory epistemological approaches that are prevalent in nurse education and which lead writers in curriculum to advocate an eclectic approach (Beattie 1987). To some extent, adult learning theory has not helped to clarify the situation as it is itself engaged in epistemological debate (Bright 1989).

A concern for the learner is the prevailing and common theme in most adult education. It draws strongly on the democratic ideals expounded by writers such as Dewey (1916) and is based on the humanistic principles that conceive the learner to be self-directing, autonomous and independent (Brookfield 1987, Boud 1988). Dewey, who has had a prevailing influence on adult education, identified experience as an important aspect of learning—the various parts of experience being connected by reflective activity. This dynamic and cyclical process has since been explored and expanded (FEU 1981, Kolb 1984, Baud et al. 1985, Mezirow 1981, Schön 1987, Jarvis 1987). Experience is the total response of a person to a situation or event—'what he thinks, feels, does and concludes at the time or thereafter' (Boud et al. 1985). Reflective activity involves recapturing experience, thinking about it, mulling it over and evaluating it.

The crucial question about the relationships between learning, reflection, experience and professional competence is still to be addressed. There is a danger, however, that the individualistic nature of the focus on reflection and experience will be examined without recognition of its social and political context and the constraints or influences that these contexts have on learning (Kemmis 1985). In nurse education, where learning experiences straddle both college and practice settings, the influences on the learning environment will be diverse and may be more apparent and obvious to the learner than to the teacher.

Community Learning Environment

This study concentrates on the student's perceptions of the learning environment in the practice setting of the community. Here, nurses practise in a patient-controlled environment where immediate decisions have to be made without recourse to consultation with either nursing or medical colleagues. Apart from these basic differences for any nurse working in the community, there are differences for those who are aspiring to be district nurses now (Mackenzie 1989) and in the future (UKCC 1990). These differences will be further enhanced by policy changes in community care (Ross 1990) and by what Beardshaw & Robinson (1990) call the challenges in community of the 'new nursing'. The issues to be addressed here are those that arise from the processes of learning and from the students' experiences of learning in the complex and uncertain environment of the community.

Ethnography

In the absence of any parallel work in nurse education, the work of ethnographers in the sociology of education, encapsulated by the approach of Hammersley & Atkinson (1983), provides a useful framework for the method used in this study.

The underlying assumptions of the ethnographic method described by Hilton (1987) provided the starting point for this research and determined the appropriateness of this method, representing a particular epistemological stance within the broad qualitative approach. Such assumptions can be regarded as a set of orientations which guide ethnographic researchers in their research strategies and design (Atkinson 1979). They underpin methodological principles—the distinctive methodological ideas that feed into the ethnographic method. The ethnographer then is concerned with meaning and understanding, recognizing that individuals interpret situations and act in accordance with their interpretation and understanding of each situation. As situations change so do the interpretations of the individuals involved.

Negotiating roles and changing perspectives are part of a process of interaction and can only be fully understood by investigation in the natural setting or social context. A holistic approach provides a view of people within their social group or environment. There will be different perspectives in each situation. The ethnographer will try to comprehend these perspectives and perhaps hypothesize about differences and similarities without determining whether or not there is a correct one (Hammersley 1984, Hilton 1987).

RESEARCH DESIGN

The design of research using the ethnographic approach cannot be totally pre-determined. However, this does not mean that there is no pre-planning, nor that ethnographic research is a haphazard activity (Hammersley & Atkinson 1983). Whilst there is flexibility in the study design allowing change in direction as the research question is refined and re-defined and theory is developed, there is also a need to identify and select the area for study and the broad setting in which it will take place, and to treat data collection and analysis in a systematic way. The author's own experience in carrying out this ethnographic research has shown that compromises in small-scale studies lead to a demand for pre-planning and less scope for changes in direction, although the refinement of the research questions and theory development still remain an integral part of the process.

The starting point for this research was a set of questions about the learning of student district nurses in practice settings in the community. The questions raised originated from the author's experiences in practice and in teaching, particularly in district nursing, and were stimulated by the research studies in the hospital settings (Orton 1981, Fretwell 1982, Ogier 1982) and in district nursing (Battle & Salter 1985). The questions have been considered in the light of significant theoretical ideas from the literature of adult learning and district nurse education.

In Malinowski's (1922) terms, these questions or 'fore-shadowed problems' are the starting point for fieldwork rather than a set of 'pre-conceived ideas' to be proved. Early fieldwork drew attention to the difficulties and complexities of trying to identify characteristics of 'good' and 'bad' learning environments in the community. Asking outright questions about what helped students to learn quickly exhausted topics of conversation simply because students were not able to describe what helps them to learn. It is through the students' descriptions of what they have done that instances of learning and their possible starting points or deterrents are identified.

Sampling: Selecting of Settings and Cases

The geographical location of the placement was the initial determining factor for the setting and subsequently for the sample cases within the settings. Two education institutions were chosen for their ability to provide, on the one hand, placement settings from inner-city locations and, on the other, placement settings from urban and rural locations. In total, 14 health authorities were involved; eight in the first year providing inner city locations and six in the second providing urban and rural locations.

The setting is the placement in which the students undertake their experience during the taught practice element of the course alongside a community practice teacher who has responsibility for managing the learning environment and for teaching and assessing the practice of district nursing. The placement covers the geographical area in which the community practice teacher is based and from which the caseload is drawn. The cases for study were the individual students chosen who are placed in the setting. Three of the students in each year had less than 1 month's community experience and were therefore regarded as direct entry, the remaining students had varying lengths of experience up to a maximum of 5 years.

Fieldwork Procedures

Methods of data collection were informal or unstructured interviews and observations. One interview was carried out with each student following the first placement and two further interviews with each student during their placements. At this time, interviews were carried out with each community practice teacher. There was therefore a potential total of 80 interviews over 2 years. A group interview with students was also undertaken at the end of the first year, but was not possible in the second year. Interviews were tape recorded and then transcribed.

Observations were made at each placement visit including, in the third placement, accompanying students wherever possible on their normal routine. Each visit to the placement then could be regarded as participant observation of which interviews were a part.

Observations were recorded in field notes and were open to the students' scrutiny but none took the opportunity to read them. However, they were used as a reference point at the interviews in an attempt to validate the author's interpretation of the meaning of the behaviour she had observed.

Analysis

The process of analysis, although described as if subsequent to the data collection, is part of it and not a distinct stage. The combined process of reflection, imaginative thinking and systematic sifting and analysis of evidence from the data, as outlined by Hammersley & Atkinson (1983), underpins much of ethnographic research in education and provides the framework for this study.

The end point of analysis is the identification of conceptual categories, that is concepts linked together logically in terms of adult learning theory. The three categories emerge in the first place from an analysis of the transcripts of the students' interviews. Further evidence is drawn from the observations with students and the interviews with community practice teachers. This variety of evidence provides a range of different perspectives on the students' learning process.

There is a sequence to the evidence as it emerges from the data that closely follows the learning process being experienced by the student. The sequence is evident across the categories and it is around this process that the integration of categories has been developed. The overlaps are confirmatory rather than contradictory. Only a selective description of the categories is possible here to demonstrate the process of 'fitting in', 'trying and testing out' and 'reality of practice', of which a more detailed account can be found elsewhere (Mackenzie 1990).

FITTING IN

The learning process involved in becoming a district nurse is character-ized by as much uncertainty as the community itself portrays. One of the first challenges is fitting into the learning environment—not so much a physical environment such as a health centre or general practitioner's (GP) surgery, but a social environment of colleagues and patients and routines and accepted practices. It is as much to do with being accepted into the group, of which patients and professional carers play almost equal parts, as about learning what district nurses do.

Fitting in with Colleagues

Finding one's way round a maze of streets, tower blocks or housing estates in some areas of the city or town where violence is not unknown can be disconcerting and different from finding one's way round an insti-tution. However, fitting into the routines and practices of the group was much more of an unknown quantity and is something akin to the expe-rience of a stranger entering a new group (Schutz 1964). The lack of expe-rience gives students both direct entry and non-direct entry, the feeling of 'a man with no history' (Schutz 1964).

How well this early fitting in worked has much to do with learning needs: how they were identified; how they were interpreted; and what impact this had on the learning opportunities for the student.

Assessing students' needs is an espoused theory of community prac-tice teachers who all adhere to this way of identifying what students need to be taught and in what order. Having said this, it appears that commu-nity practice teachers already have a sequence of events in their head—that is, moving from task-orientated techniques to management as if in a hierarchy of learning. The learning needs of the student merely amend that sequence but do not reorder it. Identifying learning needs is normally a joint effort between student and community practice teachers. Conces-sions can be gained by the student in small ways such as not carrying out evening visits if the student has already worked on the evening ser-vice. This type of negotiation is regarded as showing respect and is linked with being accepted and with increased confidence.

However competent students feel they are at some activities such as dressing techniques, they still have to go through the routine of demon-strating that competence to the community practice teacher. At least half the students found this difficult:

> I find being watched all the time fairly hassling, I don't like it at all ... I
> must admit I feel resentful that after so many years I am having someone
> see that I can do a dressing properly.
>
> (Student)

One of the problems seemed to be that the techniques that students might want updating or adapting were not dealt with separately. For the student, relevance is not just competency-based but has to do with acceptance by the group including the patient and, until this is demonstrated in some form, learning seems to be postponed.

Fitting in with Patients

Acceptance by patients is linked with the status of being a student and of feeling part of the district nursing team. Doing the work means working with patients. Contact with patients is the *raison d'être* for being a district nurse. Five of the direct entry students said they moved out of hospital to 'get back to the patient'. Students wanted to be well known by patients and to be involved in making decisions about care which demonstrated a recognition of their expertise and their acceptance as another colleague. Having described feeling very much 'on the margins', this student now describes the move towards acceptance.

> But now they ask my opinion—you know, you've done a lot of orthopaedics, what do you think to this—because we had a hip replacement that had got a hip problem. So I felt part and parcel of it although I was still standing on the sidelines looking in. I didn't feel so much like a spare part.
>
> (Student)

Strategies for Fitting in

Every student made reference to strategies used to gain acceptance and to maintain their place in the group. The fact that students preferred not to make comment or to ask challenging questions and keep a low profile were common. Also, trying to act like an interested and positive learner was seen as appropriate to the student role and being 'non-threatening'.

> So to start with, we were on slightly iffy ground. I think she thought I might pretend I knew everything.
> How did you cope with that?
> By not being deliberately ignorant but by asking lots of questions.
>
> (Student)

> I have learned actually to abolish my responsibilities [as a nurse]. I have purposely kept a low profile unless she has specifically asked my opinion and then I give it.
>
> (Student)

Fitting in with colleagues and patients takes up time and energy but is an important part of the learning process both from the students' and the community practice teachers' perspectives. Students quickly learn what they are expected to do and try to conform in varying degrees to these expectations. Even where there were good and trusting relationships with community practice teachers, there was a reluctance to challenge funda-

mental ideas about practice, such as how work is organized and dele-
gated, and the justification of decision making.

Querying treatments was a fairly easy thing to do and bringing new
ideas from college was usually welcomed. In some instances, discussion
about the sensitive areas of why unnecessary visits were made or relationships with GPs with respect to dominance and to teamwork was not
initiated if it was thought it would upset the balance of fitting in. For the
sake of maintaining this balance, opportunities were at best postponed
until after the course and at worst lost.

It would seem that an effective learning environment is established
by attention to this fitting in process and is linked to the extent to which
students can utilize the learning strategies described in the next category.

TRYING AND TESTING OUT

One of the prevalent activities in district nursing is, not unexpectedly,
visiting patients. It is in this respect where the 'trying and testing out' category is most apparent. From the beginning of the first placement the
student is inducted into the role of the district nurse by observing the specific routines of the community practice teacher. Learning by doing is crucial to the student; several students talk of itching to be involved and
learning more by themselves. They seek increasing independence from
their community practice teacher to test out their future role alone in the
patient context and to be more self-directing in their work and their learning. The students make use of their past experience by comparison and
by extending their experience. However, learning through self-direction
is dependent on continued access to the community practice teacher otherwise learning becomes repetitive and demotivating.

Students talk about checking up, discussing problems, trying things
out and linking this with greater responsibility. Self-direction is only useful when it is purposeful and when students know what they are to learn.
Sometimes self-direction was not useful and it occurred when community
practice teachers did not give enough guidance about district nursing
practice or when they were not accessible enough to talk about some of
the events students had experienced, as demonstrated here.

> I just feel at the moment I'm being used as a pair of hands. Q has been doing
> clinics and if I've any problems I've really just had to figure it out myself
> without being able to ask. I don't like having to feel like this. Whereas before
> we perhaps met at the patient's and I could chat to her in the car.
>
>   (Student)

This changed state of affairs was due to staff illness and holidays. The
student here was carrying out the same routines that she had been carrying out in her previous post as a community staff nurse. The community practice teacher appeared powerless to bring about any organizational change and the student suffered. Trying and testing out was a

constant feature of the author's observations and was part of getting a feel for district nursing and coming to know of its complexities:

> I'm becoming very much aware of the differences in the position that you are in ... it doesn't matter how strongly I think something, I've got to be absolutely sure that it's what the person in the home wants, if possible, to get them to make the moves ... to actually say I want it.
>
> (Student)

However, this student goes on to discuss the time consuming nature of such an approach to care:

> It's different on the timing, you're thinking all the time, how much time have I got, how much time am I going to use, what am I going to do next? That's a strange feeling, I'm still coming to terms with it. How much time to spend on each one (patient visit), and yet give good quality care? I thought of it even more today with Mrs D. I understood how it's much easier to go in and out the house quite fast, because you've got this ongoing thing of the next visit that you spend more on one visit with one person and less the next visit.
>
> (Student)

Trying and testing out in the reality of the patient's home, although within the given parameters of a caseload controlled by others, provides good learning opportunities within the patient context of individual care. Increasing responsibilities for patient care moves the student on to managerial aspects of the role and decisions about delegation, referral and change. However, there are limits to this sort of activity demonstrated when students want to make changes. They are limited by the fact that they do not have control of the caseload and they come up against attitudes that do not easily accommodate change. So although the students become independent of the community practice teacher, they are not able to utilize their trying and testing out strategy to its full potential and, for some, the placement becomes boring. It reinforced the worst of practice and students who were keen to be innovative became disillusioned to the point of wanting to leave district nursing.

Learning Opportunities

To some extent it seems that community practice teachers are unable to control the learning opportunities that students might take advantage of. They were not able to control high fluctuations in workloads and they were not able to provide an environment conducive to trying out change. The strategy of trying and testing out was dependent, for the most part, on the routines of practice and what the caseload offered. It certainly is not a deliberate ploy on the part of the community practice teacher to give poor experience and, indeed, for most it was a source of anxiety. However, it curtails the pace of progress for those students who quickly become skilled in individualized care in the home. All students, despite their qualified status, have a need to learn about caseload management and the management of change in primary health care.

It perhaps adds another dimension to the findings of Battle & Salter (1985) that newly qualified district nurses have not been given the chance to try out change in the placements and are therefore ill prepared to cope with such strategies in the reality of practice. Risk taking for students in both years was mainly confined to visiting new patients, which to some extent is an unknown situation, but the consequences of how often people are visited and who gets visited are also important in future practice (Badger et al. 1989). However, it is not easy to arrange such opportunities as changes in caseload management have implications for other team members who may feel the repercussions if things go wrong.

Students became very resilient about their variable opportunities of learning and this is clearly demonstrated in the next category.

REALITY OF PRACTICE

The reality of practice is highly valued as a learning resource. The student moves between what is regarded as the reality of practice and the ideal of college. Students are critical of both college and practice in their respective attempts to portray and teach district nursing. However, students do not seem daunted by the differences and indeed live with each different perspective without obvious difficulty. Overcoming the differences seems to be more of a stumbling block for course planners and teachers than for the students.

It would be too simple to say that this category is merely a difference between college and practice. Within practice there are differences: on the one hand, the students' ideas of what district nursing should be about, presumably influenced in part by college teaching and, on the other hand, what practitioners think district nursing is about as demonstrated by their practice. The gap between college and practice is much talked about in nursing in terms of the theory practice gap, but the gap within practice is equally important to these students. Both student interviews and observations provide evidence for these differences:

> I still think theory is idealogic, the practice is realistic. I'm looking at what they [college lecturers] are telling me down here [hands describe a path] and I'm looking at what I can actually put into practice down here [hands describe a path]. What theory there is, is there and I think to myself that I will remember for the exam situation, this is what can really happen.

> (Student)

No Easy Answers to Problems

Students also begin to realize there is no easy answer to the problems of practice. An extract from the field notes describes such a situation. The student works on a large estate where some of the tower blocks are notorious for violence:

> Driving round the estate, Mary [student] describes Gary [patient] who is in his 30s and has bilateral amputation following a motor bike accident.
> We enter a small ground floor flat. Sparsely furnished and cold. As we enter, Mary says the electricity has been cut off. We are let in by Gary's wife.
> Mary goes into the bedroom. I follow and stand near the wall.
> Gary is in bed. Mary says, 'are you getting up today?' No answer from Gary who turns his face to the wall. He is arguing with his wife about when she should go shopping. She is sitting on a chair at the bottom of the bed. Wife says, 'he lies in bed all day'.
> Mary offers to help Gary to get up. No answer. Mary then asks about the social services and the electricity bill. Gary says they have not done anything. Mary says she will contact them again and speak to Katy [community practice teacher].
> Mary asks, 'how is your son?' The wife says he comes home from school [residential special school] for the weekend.

On returning to the surgery the student discussed this visit with the community practice teacher who sympathized with the student's feeling of frustration and attempted to set it within the context of the estate where many such social problems prevail. This example is one of many where reality can be overwhelming and painful. Previous experience has not provided a 'stock of knowledge' (Jarvis 1987) to use in this situation and the community practice teacher becomes an important resource. Although there is evidence that community practice teachers discuss situations before and after visiting, it is not clear whether this discussion is of a reflective nature: returning to experience, attending to feelings, re-evaluating experience (Boud *et al.* 1985), which is more appropriate in this situation than looking for theoretical answers to fit the 'messy problems' (Schön 1983) of practice.

There are other instances such as nursing models or delegation where there are differences and contradictions which do not curtail learning but provoke discussion about practice. It engages the student in thinking about the difficulties and, as such, is relating the two areas of learning but not in the sense of application of knowledge to practice—the technical rationality model (Schön 1983)—but through experience which provides the impetus for linking the two. Clearly, the role of the community practice teacher is extremely important here. This coming to an understanding of district nursing practice is not an end point. All students recognize that they will continue learning and that the course is the starting point for competency as a district nurse, what one student called 'a discovering practitioner'.

CONCLUSIONS

As all the categories show, there are barriers to the students' learning, not least the practice regimes that direct and, in some instances, restrict the students' opportunities for reflection. Learning resources are often reliant on the vagaries of the workload in district nursing practice. The practice setting is where students experience directly the pressures and stresses of the uncertain world of district nursing. It is in this environment of meeting everyday problems that there is the opportunity to reflect on the problems of practice such as are described by Schön (1983) in his much-used phrase of 'reflection-in-action', a sort of thinking on your feet which is familiar to many professionals. However, the extent to which this is exploited as a learning strategy by the community practice teacher is questionable in Schön's terms of reframing the problem and encouraging action in uncertainty. For students this presented a difficulty as the action they may consider appropriate could be different from that favoured by the district nurse who has responsibility for the caseload. The dilemma is well stated by one student: 'you have to know which sister is looking after the patient to know what you have to do'. This does not mean that students do not have their own ideas, but they develop ways of putting forward these ideas in an acceptable way.

The concept of reflection-in-action, and the place of practical knowledge as a legitimate and central type of knowledge for practitioners, has been examined in a British context in teacher education (Fish 1989) and nursing (Powell 1989). The difficulty for district nurse students is that there is no obvious stock of practical district nursing knowledge for them to apply. However, there is a consensus of opinion from community practice teachers about what should be taught, based on the objectives from the college. The students do not always share this view but are not always able to discuss the different perspectives freely.

A similar situation is described for health visiting students by Twinn (1989). This questions the feasibility of developing the intuitive judgement of 'knowing-in-practice' (Schön 1983), necessary to advanced practitioners, where knowledge is generated from practice and where the artistry of practice is observable; the reality of practice can be very contradictory and difficult to unravel. However, this contradiction is a potential for learning with teachers who can help students to learn from reflecting on their experience, not just in the protected situation of a practicum 'free of pressures, distractions, and risks' (Schön 1987), but where the real problems are experienced—a modified practicum. Here community practice teachers would also be required to make explicit their personal theories of practice (Fish 1989), that is their assumptions, values and beliefs about district nursing practice, and share them to some purpose with the student thereby balancing the skills-based model of teaching which seems to prevail.

Learning Environment

The learning environment is much more about the practitioners, their ways of working and their attitudes to students and to learning than about physical characteristics such as health centres, teaching rooms and offices (ENB 1991). Learning from experience in practice is about facilitation of learning; about controlling some of the experiences and about being able to identify and formulate a theory from practice. The application of theory to practice model raises difficulties for students within practice where there are contradictions between practitioners and between college and practice—where curriculum does not portray the reality of district nursing practice. The skills model of practice presented by the objectives model of the district nurse curriculum is contradictory to the humanistic model of adult learning taught on community practice teacher courses. Furthermore, the individualistic approach to practice espoused by district nurses is at odds with the task-orientated and work-driven practice experienced by the students.

Community practice teachers express their own frustrations at not being able to give students what they feel is a good deal. There is conflict between their aims for learning and what is achievable. It is not that they are insensitive to the problems of students or that they are unaware of the shortcomings of practice. It is rather that their own aspirations for teaching cannot be achieved and raises questions about their preparation and continuing education (Maggs & Purr 1989).

Issues in Learning

The opportunities to experience many aspects of practice are clearly available. However, the opportunities to realize the learning potential of practice and to conceptualize it as the focus for developing district nursing practice raise issues that future education for district nurses needs to consider (UKCC 1990). This will involve the development of a sensitive and comprehensive criterion for measuring and evaluating the community learning environment that recognizes the complex range of issues involved in learning in practice at an advanced level, namely:

1. the amount and level of influence of the community practice teacher on the opportunities for learning in the practice setting,
2. the awareness of staff within the setting about the learning needs of district nurse students who will be practising at an advanced level,
3. the attitudes of all staff to change and innovation,
4. the level and amount of control of the community practice teacher over workloads,
5. the ability of the community practice teacher to develop strategies for helping students to learn from reflection on experience and to make available their own ideas of practice,
6. the assessment of prior learning and its relationship to competence and the identification of learning needs,
7. a clarification of the epistemological stance of the college and the practice setting as environments for learning.

While the quantifiable things such as numbers of staff, numbers on caseloads, rooms for study are important, a more comprehensive package of evaluation is required. Related to the evaluation of the learning environment is the specific development of community practice teachers' skills. Action research, involving both community practice teachers and students, to develop teaching strategies based on experience and reflection would be a further way forward.

References

Alexander M.F. (1983) *Learning to Nurse. Integrating Theory and Practice.* Churchill Livingstone, Edinburgh.

Allan P. & Jolley M. (1987) *The Curriculum in Nursing Education.* Croom Helm, London.

Atkinson P. (1979) *Research Methods in Education and the Social Sciences. Block 3 Research Design—Part 5—Research Design in Ethnography.* Open University Press, Milton Keynes.

Badger F., Cameron E. & Evers H. (1989) District nurses' patients—issues of caseload management. *Journal of Advanced Nursing 14*(7), 518–527.

Battle S. & Salter B. (1985) *The District Nurse's Changing Role.* University of Surrey, Guildford.

Beattie A. (1987) Making curriculum work. In *The Curriculum in Nursing Education* (Allan P. & Jolley M. eds), Croom Helm, London.

Beardshaw V. & Robinson R. (1990) *New for Old? Prospects for Nursing in the 1990's.* Research Report 8. King's Fund Institute, London.

Boud D. (ed.) (1988) *Developing Student Autonomy in Learning* 2nd edn. Kogan Page, London.

Boud D., Keogh R. & Walker D. (1985) *Reflection: Turning Experience into Learning.* Kogan Page, London.

Bradshaw P.L. (1989) *Teaching and Assessing in Clinical Practice.* Prentice Hall, London.

Bright B.P. (1989) *Theory and Practice in the Study of Adult Education. The Epistemological Debate.* Routledge, London.

Brookfield S.D. (1987) *Developing Critical Thinkers. Challenging Adults to Explore Alternative Ways of Thinking and Acting.* Open University Press, Milton Keynes.

Dewey J. (1916) *Democracy and Education: An Introduction to the Philosophy of Education.* The Free Press, New York.

ENB (1991) *Criteria and Guidelines for Taught Practice Placements for District Nurse Students.* Circular 1991/05/MB. English National Board for Nurses, Midwives and Health Visitors, London.

FEU (1981) *Experience, Reflection, Learning.* Department of Education and Science, Further Education and Development Unit, London.

Fish D. (1989) *Learning Through Practice in Initial Teacher Training.* Kogan Page, London.

Fretwell J.E. (1982) *Ward Teaching and Learning.* Royal College of Nursing, London.

Hammersley M. (1984) *Ethnography Methods and Data. Research Methods in Education and the Social Sciences DE304, Block 3 Unit 16.* Open University Press, Milton Keynes.

Hammersley M. & Atkinson P. (1983) *Ethnography Principles in Practice*. Tavistock Publishers, London.

Hilton A. (1987) *The Ethnographic Perspective Module 7. Research Awareness*. Distance Learning Centre, South Bank Polytechnic, London.

Jarvis P. (1987) *Adult Learning in the Social Context*. Croom Helm, London.

Kemmis S. (1985) Action research and politics of action. In *Reflection: Turning Experience into Learning* (Boud D. *et al.* eds), Kogan Page, London.

Kenworthy N. & Nicklin P.J. (1989) *Teaching and Assessing in Nursing Practice. An Experimental Approach*. Scutari Press, London.

Kolb D.A. (1984) *Experimental Learning. Experience as the Source of Learning and Development*. Prentice-Hall, New York.

Lathlean J. (ed.) (1988) *Research in Action. Developing the Role of the Ward Sister*. King's Fund Centre, London.

Mackenzie A.E. (1989) *The District Nurse Within the Community Context. Key Issues in District Nursing—Paper One*. District Nursing Association, Edinburgh.

Mackenzie A.E. (1990) Learning from experience in the community: an ethnographic study of district nurse students. Unpublished PhD thesis. University of Surrey, Guildford.

Maggs C. & Purr B. (1989) *An Evaluation of the Education and Preparation of Fieldwork and Practical Work Teachers in England*. Ashdale Press, Oxford.

Malinowski B. (1922) *Argonauts of the Western Pacific*. Routledge and Kegan Paul, London.

Marson S.N. (1982) Ward sister—teacher or facilitator? An investigation into the behavioral characteristics of effective ward teachers. *Journal of Advanced Nursing 7*, 347–357.

Melia K.M. (1987) *Learning and Working*. Tavistock Publishers, London.

Mezirow J. (1981) A critical theory of adult learning and education. *Adult Education 3*(1), 3–24.

Morle K.M.F. (1990) Mentorship—is it a case of the emperor's new clothes or a rose by any other name? *Nurse Education Today 101*,66, 69.

Ogier M.E. (1982) *An Ideal Sister*. Royal College of Nursing, London.

Orton H.D. (1981) *Ward Learning Climate*. Royal College of Nursing, London.

Parry A. (1990) Preparation for mentorship. Unpublished BSc Dissertation. King's College, London.

Pembrey S.E.M. (1980) *The Ward Sister—Key to Nursing*. Royal College of Nursing, London.

Powell J.H. (1989) A reflective practitioner in nursing. *Journal of Advanced Nursing 14*, 824–832.

Ross F.M. (1980) *New Horizons in Community Care: Policy Perspectives for District Nursing. Key Issues in District Nursing—Paper Two*. District Nursing Association, Edinburgh.

Schön D.A. (1983) *The Reflective Practitioner. How Professionals Think in Action*. Basic Books, New York.

Schön D.A. (1987) *Educating the Reflective Practitioner*. Jossey Bass, San Francisco.

Schutz A. (1964) *The Stranger. Collected Papers II. Studies in Social Theory*. Martinus Nijhoff, The Hague, pp. 91–105.

Twinn S.F. (1989) Change and conflict in health visiting practice: dilemmas in assessing the professional competence of student health visitors. Unpublished

PhD thesis. Institute of Education, University of London, London.

UKCC (1986) *Project 2000. A New Preparation for Practice*. United Kingdom Central Council for Nurses, Midwives and Health Visitors, London.

UKCC (1990) *The Report of the Post-Registration Education and Practice Project*. United Kingdom Central Council for Nurses, Midwives and Health Visitors, London.

Chapter **7**

Grounded Theory Research Approach

Grounded theory is a qualitative research approach used to explore the social processes that present within human interactions. Application of the approach develops explanations of key social processes or structures that are derived from or grounded in empirical data (Hutchinson, 1993a). "Grounded theorists base their research on the assumption that each group shares a specific social psychological problem that is not necessarily articulated" (Hutchinson, 1993a, p. 185). Glaser and Strauss (1967) developed the method and published the first text addressing method issues entitled *The Discovery of Grounded Theory.* Nursing has used the method to describe phenomena important to professional nursing (Benoliel, 1967; Hutchinson, 1992, 1993b; Stern, 1981; Wilson 1977, 1986).

As a qualitative research method, grounded theory has been used extensively in the discipline of sociology. The significance of grounded theory, as a method to investigate phenomena important to nursing, has been widely recognized by nurse researchers and has resulted in its continued application as a qualitative research approach.

Grounded theory is an important research method for the study of nursing phenomena. The method explores the richness and diversity of human experience and contributes to the development of middle-range theories in nursing. This chapter reviews fundamental themes of grounded theory and addresses methodological issues specific to engaging in this qualitative research approach. The discussion of method issues that follows is designed to peak the curiosity of the researcher interested in conducting grounded theory investigations and lead to additional reading of primary sources which is necessary to grasp fully the method in a comprehensive manner.

Qualitative Research in Nursing: Advancing the Humanistic Imperative by Helen J. Streubert and Dona R. Carpenter. Copyright © 1995 by J. B. Lippincott Company.

WHAT IS GROUNDED THEORY?

Grounded theory, as a method of qualitative research, is a form of field research. Field research refers to qualitative research approaches that explore and describe phenomena in naturalistic settings such as hospitals, outpatient clinics, or nursing homes. "The purpose of field studies is to examine in an in-depth fashion the practices, behaviors, beliefs, and attitudes of individual or groups as they normally function in real life" (Polit & Hungler, 1991, p. 195). The method systematically applies specific procedural steps to ultimately develop a grounded theory, or theoretically complete explanation about a particular phenomenon (Stern, 1980; Strauss & Corbin, 1990); Strauss and Corbin (1990) explain:

> A grounded theory is one that is inductively derived from the study of the phenomenon it represents. That is, it is discovered, developed, and provisionally verified through systematic data collection and analysis of data pertaining to that phenomenon. Therefore, data collection, analysis, and theory stand in reciprocal relationship with each other. One does not begin with a theory, then prove it. Rather, one begins with an area of study and what is relevant to that area is allowed to emerge (p. 23).

The goal of grounded theory investigations is discovery of theoretically complete explanations about particular phenomenon. According to Strauss and Corbin (1990), grounded theory involves:

> Systematic techniques and procedures of analysis that enable the researcher to develop a substantive theory that meets the criteria for doing "good" science: significance, theory-observation compatibility, generalizability, reproducibility, precision, rigor, and verification (p. 31).

The systematic techniques and procedures of analysis that are critical to grounded theory investigations are reviewed in this chapter. Through an inductive approach, the researcher using the method generates theory that can be either formal or substantive. Glaser and Strauss (1967) explain *substantive theory* as that which is developed for a substantive, or empirical area of inquiry. Examples pertinent to nursing might include patient care, hope for patients undergoing bone marrow transplantations (Ersek, 1992), or therapeutic touch (Heidt, 1990).

Formal theory is developed for a formal or conceptual area of inquiry (Glaser & Strauss, 1967). Examples might include socialization to professional nursing or authority and power in nursing practice. *Substantive* and *formal theory* are considered to be *middle-range theories* in that both types of theory fall between the working hypotheses and the all-inclusive grand theories (Glaser & Strauss, 1967).

Middle-range theories have a narrower scope than grand theories, and encompass limited concepts and aspects of the real world (Fawcett,1989). Middle-range theories have been purported to be most useful since they can be empirically tested in a direct manner (Merton, 1957).

Other ranges of theory include *grand theories* and *micro* or *partial* theories. Grand theories are complex, attempting to explain broad areas within a discipline as opposed to middle-range theory, composed primarily of relational concepts (Marriner-Tomey, 1989). Grand theories are broadest in scope, frequently lack operationally defined concepts, and are not suitable to direct empirical testing (Fawcett, 1989). Partial theories are the most limited in scope and utility, comprising summary statements of isolated observation within a very narrow range of phenomena. Some partial or micro theories may be developed into middle-range theories with additional research (Fawcett, 1989).

An important concept for the new grounded theorist to recognize is that the researcher does not begin with theory. Instead, the researcher identifies essential constructs from generated data and from these data theory emerges. Procedural steps in grounded theory are specific and occur simultaneously (see Figure 7.1). Since the information that is pertinent to the emerging theory comes directly from the data, the generated theory remains connected to or grounded in the data (Glaser & Strauss, 1967; Stern,1980; Strauss & Corbin,1990).

Stern (1980) differentiated grounded theory from other qualitative methodologies. She isolated five basic differences of grounded theory that include the following:

1. The *conceptual framework is generated from the data* rather than from previous studies;
2. The researcher attempts to *discover dominant processes in the social scene* rather than describing the unit under investigation;
3. *Every piece of data is compared with every other piece* of data;
4. The *collection of data may be modified* according to the advancing theory; that is false leads are dropped, or more penetrating questions are asked as needed;
5. *The investigator examines data as they arrive,* and begins to code, categorize, conceptualize, and to write the first few thoughts concerning the research report almost from the beginning of the study (p. 21).

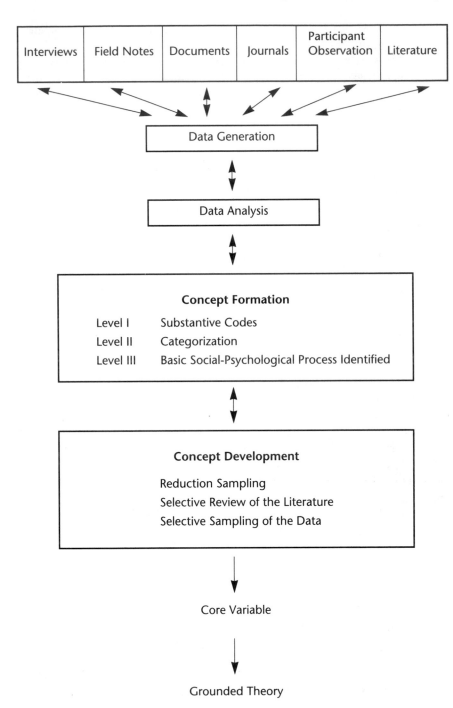

Figure 7.1. *Grounded theory and connections between data generation, treatment, and analysis.*

FUNDAMENTAL CHARACTERISTICS OF GROUNDED THEORY METHOD

Since Glaser and Strauss (1967) were the first to address grounded theory as a research method, they are consequently credited with the development and refinement of the method. Stern (1980) has written about the use of grounded theory in nursing and the importance of its use as a rigorous research method. She described five steps in the process of grounded theory research that comprise fundamental components of the method. They include: (1) collection of empirical data; (2) concept formation; (3) concept development; (4) concept modification and integration; and (5) production of the research report.

As noted earlier, grounded theory explores basic social processes. The theory of symbolic interactionism, described by George Herbert Mead (1964) and Herbert Blumer (1969), is directly related to grounded theory method. In symbolic interactionism theory it is believed that people behave and interact based on how they interpret or give meaning to specific symbols in their lives. These symbols can include a style of dress, or verbal and nonverbal expressions. For example, the nurse's cap, which is seen less and less frequently, was a style of dress that gave meaning to some patients. This can be interpreted from statements such as "How do I know you are my nurse if you do not wear your cap?" or "I liked it better when nurses wore caps; they looked more professional." Language can also have different meaning for different people. A common statement made by many nurses is "I'm working on the floor today." Individuals familiar with the health care environment are likely to interpret that statement to mean that the nurse has been assigned to a specific unit in the hospital where she/he is providing nursing care to patients. This statement may be understood differently by someone who is not familiar with the hospital setting or by someone from a different culture. "I'm working on the floor today" may be interpreted as cleaning or repairing the floor. Stern, Allen, and Moxley (1982) emphasized:

> It is also through the meaning and value of which these symbols have for us that we try to interpret our world and the actors who interact with us. In this way, we try to read minds, and to act accordingly. Learning the meaning and value of interactional symbols is everyone's lifetime study, and no easy task (p. 203).

The study and exploration of the social processes that present within human interaction, which is grounded theory, is linked directly to symbolic interactionism.

Grounded theory methodology combines both inductive and deductive research methods (Glaser & Strauss, 1967; Stern, 1980; Strauss &

Corbin, 1990). From an inductive perspective, theory emerges from specific observations and generated data. The theory can then be tested empirically to develop predictions from general principles, that is, the deductive research method.

Hutchinson (1993a) addressed an important difference between verificational research and grounded theory research. Her explanation is very helpful in clarifying the inductive nature of grounded theory. She explained:

> In verificational research, the researcher chooses an existing theory or conceptual framework and formulates hypotheses, which are then tested in a specific population. Verificational research is linear; the researcher delineates a problem, selects a theoretical framework, develops hypotheses, collects data, tests the hypotheses, and interprets the results. On a continuum, verificational research is more deductive whereas grounded theory research is more inductive. Verificational research moves from a general theory to a specific situation, whereas grounded theorists aim for the development of a more inclusive, general theory through the analysis of specific social phenomena (Hutchinson, 1993a, p. 183).

Constant comparative analysis is another fundamental characteristic that guides the generation and treatment of data. Comparative analysis of qualitative data combines an analytic procedure of constant comparison with an explicit coding procedure for generated data. "The constant comparative method is concerned with generating and plausibly suggesting many categories, properties, and hypotheses about general problems" (Glaser & Strauss, 1967). *Core variables* that are broad in scope interrelate concepts and hypotheses that emerge during data analysis. *Basic social psychological processes* illustrate the social processes that emerge from the data analysis. These fundamental characteristics are explained in greater detail in the section of this chapter that deals with application of grounded theory method.

SELECTING THE GROUNDED THEORY APPROACH

The need for more middle-range theories in nursing that can be empirically tested is one reason for using grounded theory to conduct scientific investigations of phenomena important to nursing. Stern, Allen, and Moxley (1982) further articulated the link between grounded theory and nursing. Factors linking grounded theory to nursing are that nursing occurs in a natural rather than controlled setting, and that nursing process requires "constant comparison of collected and coded data, hypothesis generation, use of the literature as data, and collection of additional data to verify or reject hypotheses" (Stern, Allen, & Moxley, 1982, p. 201).

Grounded theorists embarking on a new investigation should ask themselves these questions: "Has enough attention been paid to this particular phenomenon in terms of the individual's point of view? Has empirical research and published literature offered what seems to be an over simplification of the concepts relevant to the phenomenon under investigation? Is there a need for a deeper understanding of specific characteristics related to a particular phenomenon? Has the phenomenon been previously investigated?" Positive answers to these or similar questions can validate for the grounded theorist that method choice is appropriate. Finally, as in any type of research, the grounded theorist must consider the issues of available resources, time frame, and personal commitment to the investigation.

Application of the Approach

Application of grounded theory research techniques to the investigation of phenomena important to nursing education, practice, and administration involves several processes. A discussion regarding the development and refinement of the research question, sampling, literature review, and role of the researcher in grounded theory investigations is followed by data generation, treatment, and analysis.

The Research Question

As stated earlier, the main purpose of using the grounded theory approach is to explore social processes with the goal of developing theory. The research question in a grounded theory investigation identifies the phenomenon to be studied. More specifically the question lends focus and clarity regarding what the phenomenon of interest is (Strauss & Corbin 1990). Further:

> We need a research question or questions that will give us the flexibility and freedom to explore a phenomenon in depth. Also underlying this approach to qualitative research is the assumption that all of the concepts pertaining to a given phenomenon have not yet been identified, at least not in this population or place; or if so, then the relationships between the concepts are poorly understood or conceptually undeveloped (Strauss & Corbin, 1990, p. 37).

The nature of grounded theory methodology requires that the research question be refined as data are generated and analyzed in the study. Because the study's focus may change depending on the data generated, the original question merely lends focus to the study. A truly accurate research question is impossible to ask prior to any grounded theory study (Hutchinson, 1986).

One example of how a grounded theory question can be asked to begin an investigation and lend focus to the study is: How do nursing faculty address skill performance by nursing students that is unsafe? The question is very broad, but adds focus to the investigation by clarifying that the study will explore faculty evaluation and feedback techniques, when student performance is unsafe. As data collection and analysis proceed, the focus of the study may change, given the emerging theory. The focus of the study could hypothetically change to "What is unsafe skill performance?" Most importantly, the researcher must begin with a question that is very broad but that provides focus, and expect that the question will be refined throughout the research process.

Sample

Just as it is impossible to finalize the research question prior to a grounded theory investigation, it is equally impossible to know how many subjects will be involved. The sample size is determined by the data that are generated and the analysis of those data. The grounded theorist continues to collect data until saturation is achieved. In terms of grounded theory,

> saturation refers to the completeness of all levels of codes when no new conceptual information is available to indicate new codes or the expansion of existing ones. The researcher, by repeatedly checking and asking questions of the data, ultimately achieves a sense of closure (Hutchinson, 1986, p. 125).

Role of the Researcher

Stern (1980) emphasized that in a naturalistic setting, as opposed to a laboratory, it is impossible to control for the presence of the researcher. The investigator brings personal experience to the study to enhance understanding of the problem. According to Stern, Allen, and Moxley (1982), in the conduct of naturalistic research one does not attempt to remove oneself from the study. Rather, researchers openly recognize that they have a role in the investigation. Stern, Allen, and Moxley (1982) further delineate the role of the grounded theorist as follows:

> The grounded theory researcher works within a matrix where several processes go on at once rather than following a series of linear steps. The investigator examines data as they arrive, and begins to code, categorize, conceptualize, and to write the first few thoughts concerning the research report almost from the beginning of the study (p. 205).

The researcher is an integral part of the investigation, and because of this, the researcher must recognize his or her intimate role and include the implications of that role in the actual investigation and interpretation of the data.

Strauss and Corbin (1990) identified skills needed for doing qualitative research. They include the ability "to step back and critically analyze situations, to recognize and avoid bias, to obtain valid and reliable data, and to think abstractly" (p.18). Further,

> a qualitative researcher requires theoretical and social sensitivity, the ability to maintain analytical distance while at the same time drawing upon past experience and theoretical knowledge to interpret what is seen, astute powers of observation, and good interactional skills (Strauss & Corbin, 1990, p. 18).

To conduct a grounded theory investigation the researcher must possess excellent interpersonal skills, observational skills, and writing ability that puts into words with a high degree of accuracy what has been learned.

Ethical Considerations

The researcher must also give consideration to the ethical implications of conducting a grounded theory investigation or, for that matter, any qualitative investigation. Informed consent, maintaining confidentiality, and the handling of sensitive information are just a few examples of ethical consideration that must be addressed. Since it is impossible to anticipate what sensitive issues might emerge during data collection in a grounded theory investigation, the researcher must be prepared for unexpected concerns. Chapter 13 provides additional discussion of ethical considerations pertinent to a qualitative investigation.

Data Generation

Data for a grounded theory study may be collected from interview, observation, or documents, or from a combination of these sources (Stern, 1980). Daily journals, participant observation, formal or semi-structured interviews, and informal interviewing are valid means of data generation.

An example of data generation is provided by Hutchinson (1992) in her article entitled "Nurses Who Violate the Nurse Practice Act: Transformation of Professional Identity." Hutchinson (1992) described her data generation techniques as follows:

> data were gathered from phone and face-to-face in-depth interviews with a purposive volunteer sample of 30 nurses who went before the Florida Board of Nursing (BON), one attorney who worked with the BON, three members of the BON and the executive director, one mem-

ber of the Probable Cause Panel and two nurse investigators who
worked with the Department of Professional Regulation (DPR). Nurses
ranged in age from 21–63, were Caucasian, Afro-American, Hispanic and
Filipino; male and female. Their education ranged from the associate
degree to the baccalaureate degree; some were trained as nurse practitioners, nurse anesthetists and certified nurse midwives. Interview questions for the nurses were: 1. Tell me about your alleged "violation" of
the Nurse Practice Act. What was the "problem?" How did it occur? How
did you get reported to the DPR? After you were reported to the DPR
what happened? 2. What was it like to go before the BON? Best/Worst
things? 3. How could the BON experience be better? 4. What would you
tell other nurses who have to go before the BON? 5. Where do you go
from here? (p. 134).

Hutchinson (1992) further explained that her data collection included participant observation at six BON meetings and three administrative hear-
ings as well as document analysis that involved reading files on nurses
that had gone before the BON. This example should give the reader a
good sense of the many methods that are used in data generation in a
grounded theory investigation.

    Data gathered using field techniques, observational methods, and
documents and publications are then examined and analyzed through a
system of constant comparison until the investigation generates a number
of hypotheses. As the investigator develops hypotheses, he or she con-
sults the literature for previously developed theories that relate to the
emerging hypotheses of the study in progress. The developed theory,
consisting of related factors or variables, should be suitable for testing
(Hutchinson, 1986; Stern, 1980; Strauss & Corbin, 1990).

Data Treatment

The choice of data treatment and collection methods is influenced primarily by the researcher's preference. Interviews are generally tape
recorded and transcribed verbatim. Field notes should be transcribed
immediately and typed double spaced. It is also helpful to leave at least
a two-inch margin on one side of the transcribed data sheets for coding
purposes. Table 7.1 provides the reader with an example of a field note
and level 1 coding.

Data Analysis—Generating Theory

The discovery of a core variable is the goal of grounded theory. "The
researcher undertakes the quest for this essential element of the theory,
which illuminates the main theme of the actors in the setting, and expli-
cates what is going on in the data" (Glaser, 1978, p. 94). The core variable

TABLE 7.1   SAMPLE OF A FIELD NOTE

Field Note	Level I Codes
2/18/94	

There are seven students, one faculty member, and three staff members to care for 35 orthopedic patients. Each student has been assigned one patient. The students are juniors in a baccalaureate nursing program. This is their *first clinical experience* and their fourth week on the unit. The instructor is working with a student as she prepares an intramuscular injection. *The student's hands are trembling.* She — **Fear**

drops the uncapped syringe on the floor, bends down, picks up the syringe and prepares to use the contaminated syringe to prepare the injection. *The instructor asks her what is wrong with the way she is* — **Questioning**
proceeding. The student does not know. Tears are — **Overwhelming**
welling up in the student's eyes. The instructor's face is — **Frustration**
flushed and she seems frustrated. The instructor

explains what is wrong, *tells* the student she is unpre- — **Telling**
pared for the experience, and *asks* a staff member to — **Asking**
give the injection. The staff member comments she doesn't have time. *The student leaves the medication room crying. The instructor takes her to a conference* — **Privacy**
room to discuss the incident.

---

serves as the foundational concept for theory generation and "the integration and density of the theory are dependent on the discovery of a significant core variable" (Hutchinson, 1993, p. 193). The core variable has six essential characteristics:

1. It recurs frequently in the data;
2. It links the various data together;
3. Because it is central, it explains much of the variation in all the data;
4. It has implications for a more general or formal theory;
5. As it becomes more detailed, the theory moves forward;
6. It permits maximum variation and analyses (Strauss, 1987, p. 36).

Basic social psychological processes (BSPs) are core variables that illustrate social processes as they continue over time, regardless of varying conditions (Glaser, 1978, p. 100). For example, in the article by Hutchinson (1992), "Nurses Who Violate the Nurse Practice Act: Transformation of Professional Identity." the basic social process is the "transformation of professional identity that involves alterations in their ways of viewing themselves, their work and the profession of nursing" (p. 135).

Concept Formation

Grounded theory requires that the researcher collect, code, and analyze data from the beginning of the study. "The method is circular, allowing the researcher to change focus and pursue leads revealed by the ongoing data analysis" (Hutchinson, 1986, p. 119). Figure 7.1 illustrates the circular nature of data analysis in grounded theory.

Coding

During the conduct of a grounded theory investigation, the processes of data collection, coding, and analysis are occurring simultaneously. As data are collected through interviews, participant observation, field notes, and so on, the researcher begins to code the data. Data are examined line by line, processes are identified, and underlying patterns conceptualized. Coding occurs at three levels, explanations of which follow.

Level I Coding

Level I coding requires that the grounded theorist look for process. As data are received, the investigator applies a system of open coding. This means examining the data line by line and identifying the processes in the data. The coding of each sentence and each incident into as many codes as possible to ensure a thorough examination of the data is critical. Code words are written in the wide margins of the field notes for easy identification.

In *Level I coding* the codes are called substantive codes because they codify the substance of the data and often use the very words used by the participants themselves (Stern, 1980, p. 21). Substantive codes are of two kinds: (1) those that are taken from the language of the people who were observed or interviewed, and (2) implicit codes that are constructed by the researcher based on concepts obtained from the data (Mullen & Reynolds, 1978).

From the very beginning of the study the grounded theorist attempts to discover as many categories as possible and compare them with new indicators to uncover characteristics and relationships. Early codes are discarded if they lack foundation in the data and more may be added as data gathering progresses (Mullen & Reynolds, 1978).

Level II Coding

Level II codes or categorizing requires use of the constant comparative method in the treatment of data. Data are coded, compared with other data, and assigned to clusters or categories according to obvious fit. Categories are simply coded data that seem to cluster together and may result from the condensing of level I codes (Hutchinson, 1986; Stern, 1980). Deciding on specific categories is facilitated by questioning what each level 1 code might indicate and then comparing each level 1 code with all other level 1 codes. This enables the researcher to determine what particular category would be appropriate for the grouping of similar level 1 codes. Each category is then compared with every other category to ensure that they are mutually exclusive.

Level III Coding

Level III codes describe the basic social psychological process (BSP). BSPs are a type of core variable that illustrate social processes as they continue over time, regardless of varying conditions (Glaser, 1978, p. 100). BSPs are essentially the title given to the central themes that emerge from the data.

Questions suggested by Glaser and Strauss (1967) to describe the BSP include: "What is going on in the data? What is the focus of the study and the relationship of the data to the study? What is the problem that is being dealt with by the participants?" Finally, "What processes are helping the participants cope with the problem?"

For example, in a study by Heidt (1990) entitled "Openness: A Qualitative Analysis of Nurses' and Patients' Experiences of Therapeutic Touch" published in *Image: Journal of Nursing Scholarship,* the author offered the following response to questions raised in the preceding paragraph by Glaser and Strauss (1967), saying:

> They were sick and wanted the help of the nurses to relieve their pain and or anxiety as well as to find ways to cope with their illness. Their energy fields could be characterized as being "closed" or depleted as a result of their illnesses. The nurses intentionally opened themselves to a healing energy that was within them and in the universe, and they acted as a "link" for the flow of this energy to their patients. Through this helping relationship, the patients' field of energy opened, and their inner resources for healing were stimulated (Heidt, 1990, p. 181).

Concept Development

Three major steps expand and densify the emerging theory: reduction, selective sampling of the literature, and selective sampling of data. Through these processes the core variable emerges (Stern, Moxley, & Allen, 1982, p. 207).

Reduction

During data analysis an overwhelming number of categories emerge that need to be reduced in number. Comparing categories with one another allows the researcher to see how they cluster or connect and can be fit under another broader category (Stern, Allen, & Moxley, 1982, p. 207). Category reduction is an essential component ascertaining the primary social processes or core variables that trace the action in the social scene being investigated. The result of this reduction is a clustering of categories that, when combined, form a category of broader scope.

Selective Sampling of the Literature

Stern (1980) suggests that attempting a literature search before the study begins is unnecessary and perhaps may even be detrimental to the study. Reviewing the literature may lead to prejudgments and effect premature closure of ideas; the direction may be wrong; and available data or materials may be inaccurate (Stern, 1980).

Selective sampling of the literature is suggested and generally follows or occurs simultaneously with data analysis. The literature review serves to help the researcher become familiar with what has been published about the concepts under study and to fill in the missing pieces in the emerging theory. Referring back to the example illustrating development of the research question, the investigator may look at the literature that has been published on teaching clinical skills, evaluation of those skills, or perhaps literature on what constitutes unsafe performance. Depending on what additional data emerge, the researcher will also need to review literature pertinent to those new concepts.

As theory begins to develop, the literature review is conducted with the purpose of learning what has been previously published about the emerging concepts. The existing literature is used as data, and woven into a matrix consisting of data, category, and conceptualization. Literature, carefully scrutinized, helps expand the theory and relate it to other theories (Stern, Allen, & Moxley, 1982). In other words, the literature can fill in gaps in the emerging theory and add completeness to the theoretical description.

Selective Sampling of the Data

As the main concepts or variables become apparent, comparison with the data determines under which conditions they occur and if they seem central to the emerging theory. Additional data may be collected in a selective manner for the specific purpose of developing the hypotheses and identifying the properties of the main categories. Through selective sampling, saturation of the categories occurs (Stern, Allen, & Moxley, 1982, p. 208).

Emergence of the Core Variable

Through the process of reduction and comparison, the core variable for the investigation emerges. "The concept of core variable refers to a category which accounts for most of the variation in a pattern of behavior and which helps to integrate other categories that have been discovered in the data" (Mullen & Reynolds, 1978, p. 282).

Heidt (1990) identified the core variable of her grounded theory investigation as opening. "Opening was defined as the core variable linking the experiences of nurses and patients in the process of giving and receiving therapeutic touch" (pp.181–182).

After the emergence of the core variable, the researcher begins the steps of concept modification and integration. Through the use of theoretical codes, the conceptual framework moves from a descriptive to a theoretical level.

Concept Modification and Integration

Theoretical Coding

Theoretical codes give direction to the process of examining data in theoretical rather than descriptive terms (Stern, 1980). According to Stern (1980), this means applying a variety of analytical schemes to data to enhance their abstraction. Moving from descriptive to theoretical explanations, the researcher examines all the variables that may impact on data analysis and findings (Stern, 1980). During concept modification and integration, memoing is used to maintain the researcher's ideas pertinent to the emerging theory.

Memoing

Memoing preserves emerging hypotheses, analytical schemes, hunches, and abstractions. Memos must be sorted into cluster concepts. Sorting allows the researcher to tie up loose ends or cut them off. During the process it becomes clear how concepts fully integrate with one another, and which analytical journey extends beyond the focus of the research report. Memos that do not fit are set aside until the time when another focus of the study is written. Sorted memos become the basis for the research report (Stern, 1980). Memos can be written on file cards or paper.

PRODUCTION OF THE RESEARCH REPORT

The research report for a grounded theory investigation presents the theory, substantiated by supporting data from field notes. The report should give the reader an idea of where the data came from, how they were rendered, and how the concepts were integrated. A good report reflects the theory in ways that allow the outsider to grasp its meaning and apply its concepts.

EVALUATION OF GROUNDED THEORIES

Strauss and Corbin (1990]) identified four criteria for judging the applicability of theory to a phenomenon: fit, understanding, generality, and control. If theory is faithful to the everyday reality of the substantive area and is carefully induced from diverse data, then it should *fit* that substantive area. If insufficient data were collected and closure attempted too soon, then it is not possible to meet this criterion. Because it represents a reality, it should also be comprehensible and make sense to both the persons who were studied and to those practicing in that area. In other words, the grounded theory derived should be immediately recognizable to a practitioner with experience in the area studied, therefore meeting the criteria of *understanding*. If the data upon which it is based are comprehensive and the interpretations conceptual and broad, then that theory should be abstract enough and include sufficient variation to make it applicable to a variety of contexts related to the phenomenon under study, thus meeting the criteria of *generality*. Finally, the theory should provide *control* with regard to action toward the phenomenon (Strauss & Corbin, 1990).

SUMMARY

Grounded theory plays a significant role in the conduct of qualitative research. The fundamental characteristics and application of the approach have been reviewed and include issues related to refinement of the research question, sampling, data generation, treatment, and analysis. Applied to the profession of nursing, grounded theory can increase middle-range substantive theories and help explain theoretical gaps between theory, research, and practice. Chapter 8 continues with the grounded theory method as it has been applied in nursing education, practice, and administration.

REFERENCES

Benoliel, J. Q. (1967). *The nurse and the dying patient.* New York: The Macmillan Co.
Blumer, H. (1969). *Symbolic intervention, perspective and method.* Englewood Cliffs, NJ: Prentice–Hall, Inc.
Ersek, M. (1992). The process of maintaining hope in adults undergoing bone marrow transplantation for leukemia. *Oncology Nursing Forum, 19*(6), 883–889.
Fawcett, J. (1989). *Analysis and evaluation of conceptual models of nursing,* 2nd. ed. Philadelphia: F.A. Davis Co.
Glaser, B. (1978). *Theoretical sensitivity.* Mill Valley, CA: Sociology Press.
Glaser, B., & Strauss, A. (1967) *The discovery of grounded theory.* Chicago: Aldine.

Heidt, P. R. (1990). Openness: A qualitative analysis of nurses' and patients' experiences of therapeutic touch. *Image: Journal of Nursing Scholarship, 22* (3), 180–186.

Hutchinson, S. (1986). *Grounded theory: The method.* In P. L. Munhall & C. J. Oiler (Eds.), *Nursing research: A qualitative perspective* (pp. 111–130). Norwalk, CT: Appleton-Century-Crofts.

Hutchinson, S. A. (1992). Nurses who violate the nurse practice act: Transformation of professional identity. *Image: The Journal of Nursing Scholarship, 24*(2), 133–139.

Hutchinson, S. A. (1993a). Grounded theory: The method. In P. L. Munhall & C. O. Boyd (Eds.), *Nursing research: A qualitative perspective* (pp. 180–212). New York: National League for Nursing Press, Pub. No. 19–2535.

Hutchinson, S. A. (1993b). People with bipolar disorders quest for equanimity: Doing grounded theory. In P. L Munhall & C. O. Boyd (Eds.), *Nursing research: A qualitative perspective* (pp. 213–236). New York: National League for Nursing Press, Pub. No. 19–2535.

Marriner-Tomey, A. (1989). *Nursing theorists and their work,* 2nd ed. Philadelphia: C. V. Mosby Co.

Mead, G. H. (1964). *George Herbert Mead on social psychology.* Chicago: University of Chicago Press.

Merton, R.K. (1957). *Sociological theory: Uses and unities.* New York: Free Press

Mullen, P. D., & Reynolds, R. (1978). The potential of grounded theory for health education research: Linking theory and practice. *Health Education Monographs, 6*(3), 280–294.

Polit, D. F., & Hungler, B. P. (1991). *Nursing research: Principles and methods,* 4th ed. Philadelphia: J. B. Lippincott Co.

Stern, P. N. (1980). Grounded theory methodology. Its uses and processes. *Image, 12*(7), 20–23.

Stern, P. N. (1981). Solving problems of cross-cultural health teaching: The Filipino childbearing family. *Image, 13*(2), 47–50.

Stern, P. N., Allen, L. M., & Moxley, P. A. (1982). The nurse as grounded theorist: History, processes, and uses. *Review Journal of Philosophy and Social Science, 7*(1&2), 200–215.

Strauss, A. (1987). *Qualitative analysis for social scientists.* New York: Cambridge University Press.

Strauss, A., & Corbin, J. (1990). *Basics of qualitative research.* Newbury Park, CA: Sage.

Wilson, H. S. (1977). Limiting intrusion—Social control of outsiders in a healing community. *Nursing Research, 26*(2),103–111.

Wilson, H. S. (1986). Presencing—Social control of schizophrenics in an antipsychiatric community: Doing grounded theory. In P. L. Munhall & C. J. Oiler (Eds.), *Nursing research: A qualitative perspective* (pp. 131–144). Norwalk, CT: Appleton-Century-Crofts.

Grounded Theory Research Approach Applied to Nursing Education, Practice, and Administration

Method issues addressed in Chapter 7 that pertain to grounded theory investigations will be addressed in this chapter in relation to studies that have been published in the areas of nursing practice, education, and administration. Two important questions guiding the direction of this chapter are: When should grounded theory be used? and How has the method been used to study issues in nursing education, administration, and practice? Three published studies are reviewed using the guidelines for evaluating completed grounded theory research outlined in Table 8.1. Chapter 8 also provides the reader with an overview of selected studies that highlight how nurse researchers have used grounded theory in nursing practice, education, and administration (see Table 8.2). A reprint of the Bright (1992) article can be found at the end of this chapter to assist the reader in understanding the critiquing process.

CRITIQUING GROUNDED THEORY INVESTIGATIONS

Strauss and Corbin (1990) state that "a qualitative study can be evaluated accurately only if its procedures are sufficiently explicit so that readers of the resulting publication can assess their appropriateness" (p. 249). "If a grounded theory researcher provides this information, readers can use these criteria to assess the adequacy of the researcher's complex coding procedure. Detail given in this way would be supplemented with cues that could in longer publications, at least be read as pointing to extremely careful and thorough tracking of findings of conscientious and imaginative theoretical sampling" (Strauss & Corbin, 1990, pp. 253–254).

(Text continues on p. 169)

Qualitative Research in Nursing: Advancing the Humanistic Imperative by Helen J. Streubert and Dona R. Carpenter. Copyright © 1995 by J. B. Lippincott Company.

TABLE 8.1 GUIDELINES FOR CRITIQUING RESEARCH USING GROUNDED THEORY METHOD

Statement of the Phenomenon of Interest
1. Is the phenomenon of interest clearly identified?
2. Has the researcher identified why the phenomenon requires a qualitative format?

Purpose
1. Is the purpose for conducting the research made explicit?
2. Does the researcher describe the projected significance of the work to nursing?

Method
1. Is the method used to collect data compatible with the purpose of the research?

Sampling
1. Does the researcher describe the selection of participants?
2. What major categories emerged?
3. What were some of the events, incidents, and/or actions that pointed to some of these major categories?
4. What were the categories that led to theoretical sampling?
5. After the theoretical sampling was done, how representative did the categories prove to be?

Date Generation
1. Does the researcher describe data collection strategies?
2. How did theoretical formulations guide data collection?

Data Analysis
1. Does the researcher describe the strategies used to analyze the data?
2. Does the researcher address the credibility, auditability, and fittingness of the data?
3. Does the researcher clearly describe how and why the core category was selected?

Empirical Grounding of the Study—Findings
1. Are concepts grounded in the data?
2. Are the concepts systematically related?
3. Are conceptual linkages described and are the categories well developed? Do they have conceptual density?
4. Are the theoretical findings significant and to what extent?
5. Was data collection comprehensive and analytical interpretations conceptual and broad?
6. Is there sufficient variation to allow for applicability in a variety of contexts related to the phenomenon investigated?

Conclusions, Implications, and Recommendations
1. Do the conclusions, implications, and recommendations give the reader a context in which to use the findings?
2. Do the conclusions reflect the findings of the study?
3. Are recommendations for future study offered?
4. Is the significance of the study to nursing made explicit?

Adapted from: Streubert, H. (1994). Evaluating the qualitative research report. In G. W. LoBiondo & J. Haber (Eds.), *Nursing research: Methods, critical appraisal, and utilization*, 3rd ed.(pp. 481–499). St. Louis: Mosby; and Strauss, A., & Corbin, J. (1990). *Basics of qualitative research: Grounded theory procedures and techniques*. Newbury Park, CA: Sage Publications.

TABLE 8.2   SELECTED REVIEW OF GROUNDED THEORY INVESTIGATIONS

Author	Domain	Purpose	Sample	Data Generation Methods	Results
Baker, C., & Stern, P. N. (1993)	Practice	To investigate the evolution of readiness to self-manage a non-fatal chronic illness	Purposive sample of 12 individuals with a non-fatal chronic illness and the primary nurse caring for these individuals	Interviews	The findings indicated that the key process in self-care readiness was finding meaning in chronic illness.
Beck, C. T. (1993)	Practice	To investigate the nature of the specific social psychological process used to resolve post partum depression	Purposive sample of 12 mothers	Participant observation and indepth taped interviews	Loss of control was identified as the basic social psychological problem. Women attempted to cope through a four-stage process of teetering on the edge which included encountering terror, dying of self, struggling to survive, and regaining control.
Biley, F. C. (1992)	Practice	To determine patients' feelings about participating in decision making about nursing care	8 patients	Informal interviewing	Category saturation was not achieved. Data suggest three categories that describe situations that effect patient choice and participation in decision making and include: 1. If I am well enough. . . 2. If I know enough. . . 3. If I can. . .
Diepeveen-Speekenbrink, J. C. (1992)	Education	To discover the views of Dutch administrators of intramural health care institutions on the need for graduate nursing education and nursing research in the Netherlands.	13 administrators	Semi-structure interviews that were tape recorded and transcribed verbatim	Three major themes emerged from data analysis and included change, problems, and solutions.

Author (Year)		Purpose	Sample	Data collection	Findings
Dobos, C. (1992)	Practice	To define risk as it pertains to clinical practice	Three registered nurses in clinical roles	Interviews	Risk in clinical practice was defined as uncomfortable and unavoidable role-related situations characterized by high unpredictability and negative or hostile overtones, dependency on others, high performance expectations, and health threats that extend beyond work hours. Findings refute the notion that nurses avoid risk and that risk requires strategies to minimize its negative impact.
Ersek, M. (1992)	Practice	Exploration of the processes of hoping in adults undergoing bone marrow transplantation	Purposive sampling. 10 men and 10 women aged 20 to 58 who had undergone bone marrow transplant	Audiotaped interviews transcribed verbatim. Total of three interviews, once during pre-admission; between days 9 and 12; and 25–28 days post-transplant.	Core categories were: Dealing with it and keeping it in its place. The relation between the two categories is explained by the dialectic of maintaining hope.

(cont'd.)

TABLE 8.2 (CONT'D.)

Author	Domain	Purpose	Sample	Data Generation Methods	Results
Estabrooks, C. A., & Morse, J. A. (1992)	Practice	How do intensive care nurses perceive touch and the process of touching? How do intensive care nurses learn to touch?	8 experienced intensive care nurses	Interviews	Two substantive processes were revealed: the touching process and acquiring a touching style. The core variable was cueing and is defined as: "the process by which, through symbolic interaction with others, one determines the need for and the appropriateness of touch" (p. 452).
Flaming, D., & Morse, J. M. (1991)	Practice	To examine what boys experience emotionally as they go through the physical changes of puberty	22 male participants	Open-ended questioning, tape recorded and transcribed verbatim	A basic social psychological process emerged and was labeled "minimizing embarrassment," with four stages: waiting for the change, noticing the change, dealing with the change, and feeling comfortable with the change.
Heidt, P. R. (1990)	Practice	Exploration and description of experiences of nurses and patients in the process of giving and receiving therapeutic touch	14 nurses who had practiced therapeutic touch for a minimum of three years	Interviews and observations of one treatment session	The primary experience of therapeutic touch is opening to the flow of the universal life energy. This includes three major categories of experience: opening intent, opening sensitivity, and opening communication.

Author (Year)		Purpose	Sample	Method	Findings
Hutchinson, S. A. (1992)	Practice	To explore and describe experiences of nurses who had been accused of violating the Nurse Practice Act	Purposive volunteer sample of 30 nurses	Indepth interviews, participant observation	The nurses experienced a transformation of professional identity which involved five phases - being confronted, assuming a stance, going through it, living the consequences and re-visions.
Lewis, T. (1990)	Practice	To explore ward sisters'/charge nurses' perceptions of their responsibilities	10 hospital sisters from two large hospitals in the south of England	Semi-structured interviews	From the data analysis, substantive theory was developed that ward sisters act to gatekeep the professional function of the nurse.
May, R. A. (1980)	Practice	To explore the experience of first-time expectant fathers	20 couples	Open-ended interviewing, field notes	The phenomenon of expectant fatherhood include that the man has a choice about how the pregnancy experience is structured, detachment or involvement is difficult to measure objectively and three distinct styles of detachment/involvement were identified and include observer styles, expressive styles and instrumental styles.

(cont'd.)

TABLE 8.2 (CONT'D.)

Author	Domain	Purpose	Sample	Data Generation Methods	Results
Swanson, J. M. (1988)	Practice	To describe the interactive process of learning to use and manage contraception	60 participants	Unstructured formal interviews	Prioritized discovery describes the process of finding out something previously unknown and is influenced by the following processes: identifying; tailoring/retailing; coordinating.
Turner, M. A., Tomlinson, P. S., & Harbaugh, B. L. (1990)	Practice	Exploration of the dimensions of uncertainty of parents whose child was hospitalized in a pediatric intensive care unit	Convenience sample of 13 parents of 8 critically ill children	1 to 1½ hour interviews of parents within 2–4 days after admission of a child to a pediatric ICU	A model of PICU uncertainty was derived which identified four areas in which ambiguity, conflicting information, or perceived inefficiency gave rise to uncertainty.

Further, Strauss and Corbin (1990) note that in reality "there may be no way that readers can accurately judge how the researcher carried out the analysis" (p. 253). Therefore, some guiding criteria for evaluating grounded theory investigations are provided for the reader. The criteria can assist reviewers of grounded theory studies to search out the critical elements of the method. It is important to recognize that when critiquing any published investigation, that journal restrictions, page limitations, or other external forces beyond the control of the author may require that certain material be deleted, resulting in a limited critique of the research. As noted earlier in this text, readers interested in a fuller discussion of method in a published study should contact the author.

GROUNDED THEORY APPROACH APPLIED TO NURSING PRACTICE

One excellent example of grounded theory research related to the practice arena is the study "Making Place: The First Birth in an Intergenerational Family Context" (Bright, 1992). This research report is reviewed as an example of the use of grounded theory for the investigation of phenomena important to nursing practice. Very often in published research, methodology is merely highlighted. Bright's article is an excellent example of the intensity and rigor of grounded theory method and offers the reader a clear example of use of the constant comparative method.

Interaction among parents, grandparents, and firstborn infants is the *phenomenon of interest* for Bright's (1992) grounded theory investigation. Because the author was interested in generating new knowledge of intergenerational family processes related to the birth of a first child, grounded theory method suited the investigation. According to Bright (1992), "The grounded theory method of research was used to generate new knowledge of intergenerational family processes related to the birth of the first child" (p. 78).

Early in the report, Bright (1992) explicitly identified the *purpose* of her investigation as the discovery of "how new expectant parents and grandparents prepare for and respond to the arrival of the firstborn child-grandchild" (p. 76). More specifically, Bright articulated objectives for her study which included the following:

> to expand the scope of knowledge about the birth of the first child as an intergenerational experience and, second to discover the basic social process associated with the family event and to generate theory on normative family processes (p. 76).

Her clear and concise explanation of purpose assists the reader in com-
prehending the goals of her work and lends focus to the remainder of
the study. Bright further described the projected significance of her work
to nursing in the literature review provided.

Original selection of the *sample* by Bright (1992) included

> three families which consisted of three infants, their parents, and 6 sets
> of grandparents. Each family participated in the study for a period of
> 15 months, beginning with the last trimester of their first pregnancy and
> ending on the child's first birthday. In each family, the expected baby
> was the couple's first child and the first grandchild of at least one set of
> grandparents (p. 79).

Bright (1992) also provided some additional descriptive data about
her sample, noting that they were healthy and employed. Additional data
related to ethnic background were also provided. Since participant selection is directly related to the outcome of the study, it is very important that
participants are capable of informing the study. Bright discussed in depth
the *ethical considerations* guiding her sample selection which included
interest of the participants, informed consent, assurance of confidentiality, anonymity in all oral and written research reports, and respect on the
part of the researcher for "their right to choose what information to
divulge in the study, and that they could discontinue participation in the
study at any time without penalty" (p. 80). Ethical considerations in qualitative research in many ways are unique. It is helpful to the reader and
to researchers new to grounded theory method to have a sense of what
ethical considerations were taken by the researcher conducting a particular study. Bright's discussion of ethical considerations adds to the understanding of the actual implementation of the method.

Bright (1992) clearly described her *data generation strategies*. These
strategies included beginning the data collection process with an initial interview. An early theme that emerged during the initial interviews was that of
anticipatory preparation for the baby. Bright (1992) provided examples of
direct quotes leading to this theme. *Theoretical sampling* was used based on
the discovery of a variable that had the potential to influence Bright's data
analysis. The variable of concern was whether a pregnancy had been planned
and how an unplanned pregnancy might affect the family's experience. Bright
(1992) noted this change in the sampling and was able to conclude the following: "Although this family struggled with in-law conflicts related to the
precipitous marriage, both parents and all grandparents were eagerly and
happily anticipating the birth of the unexpected child" (pp. 82–83).

The detailed description of Bright's data collection strategies and
how theoretical formulations guided data collection are illustrated in the
following example:

Initial interviews prior to the baby's birth included both parent and grandparent generations together which allowed the researcher to observe interactional patterns among children, parents, and in-laws as well as to learn about family beliefs, traditions, expectations, and past experiences related to the anticipated birth event. After the baby's birth, family members were interviewed individually, in dyads, and in small groups as the developing hypotheses indicated need. Thus data were collected through theoretical sampling (Bright, 1992, p. 80).

In addition to interviews, Bright also used participant observation and semistructured telephone interviews to "clarify data and to check the validity of the researcher's developing hypotheses so that the emerging theory reflected the lived experience of the families" (p. 81).

Given the amount of data generated in a grounded theory study, clearly presenting the process can be cumbersome. Bright (1992) described the strategies she used for *data analysis* very clearly, a major strength of the report. The reader can understand how she proceeded through the process of constant comparative analysis through concise clear examples. Bright (1992) explained:

Analysis of data was conducted as a continuous, ongoing process which was integrated with data collection and coding. Interviews were audio-taped, transcribed, and coded line by line. Kinship genograms were drawn for each family to obtain both historical and intergenerational relational data. One three-generation family interaction was videotaped to provide recorded nonverbal as well as verbal data for coding. Field notes from participant observation were included in the coded data. Coded data were clustered into related categories and were compared with one another and with new data to discover the relationships among the data. Specific questions helped to focus the process of constant comparative analysis (p. 84).

Bright (1992) also addressed procedures for ensuring *credibility, auditability,* and *fittingness* of the data under reliability and validity. Reliability was enhanced by ensuring that theoretical observations were grounded in the data. She also established interrater reliability by "concurrent data categorization performed by a family therapist, who coded initial interview data and achieved 90% agreement with the researcher's coding" (p. 85). Finally, "three parent and three grandparent couples corroborated the validity of the emergent theory in their post study review of the research report" (p. 85).

When writing the theory, Bright (1992) conducted memo writing concurrently with coding and categorizing procedures. "Making place" (p. 86) was identified by Bright (1992) as the *core category*. The two major domains of "making place" included making a physical place and making a social place. The emergence of the core variable is described for the reader.

From an empirical standpoint, and given the extent to which Bright (1992) shared the process of data collection and analysis, the concepts that emerged seemed grounded in the data. Bright (1992) carefully varied her data collection to provide for sufficient examples allowing for applicability of her findings in a variety of settings. The findings are significant to family nursing research and are easily understood by the reader.

There are many *conceptual linkages* and the categories are well developed, providing *conceptual density*. Bright (1992) addressed the limitations of the study and emphasized:

> This study included data from a small group of families who were maritally intact, relatively financially stable, and whose extended family was geographically intact. Theoretical sampling among more families with ethnic, socioeconomic, and membership variability is needed to further saturate and densify the theory of making place (p. 93).

Bright's (1992) *conclusions, implications,* and *recommendations* can be used in family nursing research. Bright noted "the concept of making place offers a useful focus for family nursing, namely, the importance of the relational context of family health" (p. 94). Bright suggested that "the nurse's awareness of the importance of the entire family's response to the first child's birth will assist in the identification of problems related to making place" (p. 95). One recommendation for future study included "identifying the process of making place in various family configurations" (p. 95). Bright's study provided valuable insights for family nursing practice and emphasized the importance of grounded theory research methods to the generation of middle range theories important to nursing practice.

GROUNDED THEORY APPROACH APPLIED TO NURSING EDUCATION

An example of grounded theory research related to education is a study by Burnard (1992) entitled "Students Nurses' Perceptions of Experiential Learning," published in *Nurse Education Today*. This research report is reviewed as an example of a grounded theory investigation applied to nursing education.

Burnard's (1992) study is a good example of presentation of the findings from a grounded theory investigation. There is less discussion of specific method issues in this work, and the author notes this as being related to space issues and requirements for the paper. As noted earlier, often limitations provided by journal publishers prevent detailed discussion of method issues in qualitative research reports. This study provides the reader with an excellent example of the important contribution grounded theory can make to the education of nurses.

The *purpose* of Burnard's (1992) study was to identify the perceptions of student nurses toward experiential learning. He identified the need for a qualitative format as being related to exploration and clarification issues surrounding his topic. Burnard described the projected significance of the work to nursing as being related to the recommendation of experiential learning in nursing literature, particularly in the fields of psychiatric nursing and interpersonal skills training.

Burnard (1992) used a *convenience sample* which included 12 student nurses in different parts of the United Kingdom. Data collection strategies included in-depth interviews. Theoretical sampling was not addressed. This may be due to journal limitations placed on method discussion.

A variety of categories emerged during data analysis, and this section formed the heart of the report provided by Burnard (1992). Students found experiential learning to be something more than "just being taught" (p. 164), and they stated that they learned the most about nursing from working in a clinical setting. Classroom learning, although valued, was viewed as less valuable than clinical learning. Burnard provided the following examples of students insights regarding the range of activities identified as contributing to experiential learning:

> We have had role play, small group exercises, empathy exercises, ice-breakers, games, those sorts of things. We have done other things like being blindfolded and tied up and so forth and we've done role play and psychodrama. We've done psychodrama and lots of exercises (p. 170).

Data collection appeared comprehensive given the presentation of the findings. Saturation was not addressed, making a determination regarding conceptual density of the findings difficult. Theoretical sampling, emergence of major categories, and selection of a core category were not addressed in the article.

Burnard (1992) reported that data analysis occurred in two ways: simple content analysis of themes and a modified grounded theory approach. Bernard noted:

> There is not space in this paper to describe, in detail, the processes involved in analyzing the data. Suffice to say that a rigorous method of working through the interview transcripts was devised as were methods of coding and categorizing the data. Validity checks were maintained throughout the analysis by checking and rechecking the emerging categories with the respondents. The validity of the analysis method was also checked by having two disinterested research colleagues develop their own category

systems from the data. In this sense, the category system was negotiated, although in the end (as with any method of analysis) the researcher has to take responsibility for the overall system of analysis (p. 163).

The *findings* of the study have implications for nursing education specifically related to educators. How nurse educators plan and use this type of learning in nursing education settings is important to educational outcomes. Experiential learning was highly valued by students and provided opportunity for making connections between theory and practice. Although recommendations for future study were not offered, Burnard (1992) concluded:

> These reviews of experiential learning offer a different perspective to the one traditionally offered in the literature on experiential learning. They have implications for the use and planning of experiential learning sessions in all branches of nursing. Nurse educators need to be clear about what they mean by the term 'experiential learning' and also need to ensure that students are adequately prepared for any new learning situations that they bring to the learning arena (p. 172).

GROUNDED THEORY APPROACH APPLIED TO NURSING ADMINISTRATION

Porter's (1987) work offers an example of grounded theory applied to nursing administration in her article entitled "Administrative Diagnosis— Implications for the Public's Health." This research report is reviewed as an example of the grounded theory approach applied to nursing administration.

Porter (1987) described the *purpose* of her study as "describing the diagnostic reasoning of community nurse-administrators so as to enable the development of a factor-isolating theory of population group diagnosis using the grounded-theory method" (p. 247).

Porter (1987) grounds the importance of her work in a comprehensive review of the literature and sound rationale. Porter (1987) emphasized:

> The nursing process specific to community health states has received limited attention by the profession, possibly because of the conceptual problems inherent in community diagnosis. While public health science is an essential element of community nursing, it cannot be relied on as the exclusive source of nursing diagnoses (p. 247).

Porter suggested that "perhaps the theoretical and practical problems associated with community diagnosis could be avoided by analyzing health states of the interacting populations that comprise the community" (p. 247).

Porter identified the rationale for using a qualitative format as the following:

> An inductive study was thus warranted to isolate the fundamental concepts of the diagnostic reasoning process of community nurse-administrators. A grounded theory or constant comparative method was chosen to enable the development of a factor-isolating theory of population group diagnosis (p. 248).

Porter (1987) reported using a *convenience sample* of 31 nurse-administrators of city and county health departments from one state. Data collection involved the use of an open-ended questionnaire and follow-up telephone interviews with each subject.

"The author and two nurses with experience in grounded theory served as independent data coders" (p. 248). Initial categories were listed for the reader in table format. Porter (1987) used table format to illustrate for the reader how the initial categories emerged and how they were revised. This was helpful as an illustration of how the constant comparative method was used in *data analysis*. Figure 1 in the article provided the reader with an example of the process of data analysis, addressing how categories were revised as new data emerged. The final column in Figure 1 outlined the factor isolating theory of community nurse-administrators diagnosis. The appendix provided by Porter (1987) gave examples of data showing congruence with factor-isolating theory of community nurse-administrator diagnosis. This information is very helpful in following the line of thinking of the researcher during the process of data analysis.

Porter (1987) addressed issues of *credibility, auditability,* and *fittingness.* She noted:

> The author and two nurses with experience in grounded theory research served as independent data coders. The questionnaire and interview data were first coded into as many of the information categories as pertained and then into one of the service change categories. Complete agreement among the coders was reached for 68 percent of the datum incidents, and two coders agreed on the other 32 percent for a satisfactory level of agreement (p. 248).

Porter (1987) offered many conceptual linkages in her report, and categories were well developed, providing *conceptual density.* She provided sufficient variation in her sampling and analysis to allow for applicability of the findings in a variety of contexts. The five concepts of Porter's factor isolating theory that emerged were "need-related cue processing, population group diagnosis, diagnostic staging, health care system diagnosis, and diagnosis-based management" (p. 252). The factor-isolating theory of community nurse-administrator diagnosis described by Porter were:

> Community nurse-administrators make a series of two diagnoses prior to proposing change in agency services; the first diagnosis relates to the specific health status of the population group and the second diagnosis relates to the match or mismatch between the group's need and health services (p. 252).

The *conclusions, implications,* and *recommendations* give the reader a context in which to use the findings. Porter's *conclusions* reflect the findings of her study. Porter's study has implications for the public's health which she noted in the concluding section of her paper. She noted that "it is essential that the nurse take the initiative in determining the factors that could potentially lead to vulnerable or at-risk status for a group" (p. 253). She also noted that "the theory can serve as a frame-work for describing the nurse's health planning role to population group representatives and decision makers" (p. 255). Finally, Porter recommended areas for future study.

SUMMARY

Grounded theory as a qualitative research approach provides an excellent method of investigation for phenomena important to nursing. Application of the method to areas important to nursing practice, education, and administration are reviewed. This chapter offers the new grounded theorist examples of research that apply the method described in Chapter 7. Recognizing the need for middle-range theory development in nursing, investigators should continue to apply this rigorous qualitative method to the investigation of phenomena important to nursing practice, education, and administration.

REFERENCES

Baker, C., & Stern, P. N. (1993). Finding meaning in chronic illness as the key to self care. *Canadian Journal of Nursing Research, 25*(2), 23–36.

Beck, C. T. (1993). Teetering on the edge: A substantive theory of postpartum depression. *Nursing Research, 42*(1), 42–48.

Biley, F. C. (1992). Some determinants that effect patient participation in decision-making about nursing care. *Journal of Advanced Nursing, 17,*.414–421.

Bright, M. A. (1992). Making place: The first birth in an intergenerational family context. *Qualitative Health Research, 2*(1), 75–98.

Burnard, P. (1992). Student nurses' perceptions of experiential learning. *Nurse Education Today, 12,* 162–173.

Diepeveen-Speekenbrink, J. C. (1992). The need for graduate nursing education and nursing research in the Netherlands: An exploratory study. *International Journal of Nursing Studies, 29*(4), 393–410.

Dobos, C. (1992). Defining risk from the perspective of nurses in clinical roles. *Journal of Advanced Nursing, 17*(11), 1303–1309.

Ersek, M. (1992). The process of maintaining hope in adults undergoing bone marrow transplantation for leukemia. *Oncology Nursing Forum, 19*(6), 883–889.

Estabrooks, C. A., & Morse, J. M. (1992). Toward a theory of touch: The touching process and acquiring a touching style. *Journal of Advanced Nursing, 17*, 448–456.

Flaming, D., & Morse, J. M. (1991). Minimizing embarrassment: Boys' experiences of pubertal changes. *Issues in Comprehensive Pediatric Nursing, 14*, 211–230.

Heidt, P. R. (1990). Openness: A qualitative analysis of nurses' and patients' experiences of therapeutic touch. *Image: Journal of Nursing Scholarship, 22*(2),180–186.

Hutchinson, S. A. (1992). Nurses who violate the nurse practice act: Transformation of professional identity. *Image: Journal of Nursing Scholarship, 24*(2), 133–139.

Lewis, T. (1990). The hospital ward sister: Professional gatekeeper. *Journal of Advanced Nursing, 15*(7),808–818.

May, K. A. (1980). A typology of detachment/involvement styles adopted during pregnancy by first time expectant fathers. *Western Journal of Nursing Research, 2*(2), 445–461.

Porter, E. J. (1987). Administrative diagnosis—Implications for the public's health. *Public Health Nursing, 4*(40), 247–256.

Strauss, A., & Corbin, J. (1990). *Basics of qualitative research: Grounded theory procedures and techniques.* Newbury Park, CA: Sage Publications.

Streubert, H. J. (1994) Evaluating the qualitative research report. In G. W. LoBiondo & J. Haber (Eds.), *Nursing research: Methods, critical appraisal, and utilization,* 3rd ed. (pp. 481–499). St. Louis: Mosby.

Swanson, J. M. (1988). The process of finding contraceptive options. *Western Journal of Nursing Research, 10*(4), 492–503.

Turner, M. A., Tomlinson, P. S., & Harbaugh, B. L. (1990). Parental uncertainty in critical care hospitalization of children. *Maternal Child Nursing Journal, 19*(1) 45–62.

Making Place: The First Birth in an Intergenerational Family Context

Mary Anne Bright

*Interaction among parents, grandparents, and firstborn infants was
studied in three healthy families over a period of 15 months, beginning
in the last trimester of pregnancy and ending on the infant's first birthday. The grounded theory research method of constant comparative
analysis resulted in the identification of an evolutionary family process
that reflected reorganized interpersonal patterns and expanded the
three-generational intrafamilial boundaries. Making place is defined as
the process occurring in a family through which a newborn individual
receives recognition as a member of that family. It is an integrative process in that it facilitates the creation of new relational connections
within the family as well as giving new meaning to already existing
ones. The concept of making place offers a useful focus for family nursing, namely, the importance of the relational context of family health.*

The birth of the first child precipitates a major transition in the life of a
family. Hill (1964) observed that the arrival of the first child marks a profound change in family reorganization because the oldest child's development presents new and different problems not yet encountered by the family. Duvall (1974) acknowledged the significance of the birth of the first child
as a stimulant of a new developmental level for the family, during which the
new parents not only create new roles vis-à-vis the baby but develop new
ways of relating to the parents and with the extended family.

AUTHOR'S NOTE: The author gratefully acknowledges the critical contributions of Janine
McGill Roberts, Doris E. Chaves, and Alvin E. Winder. Correspondence or requests for
reprints should be addressed to Mary Anne Bright, Assistant Professor, School of Nursing, 325 Arnold House, University of Massachusetts, Amherst, MA 01003.

Reprinted from Bright, A. O., Making place: The first birth in an intergenerational family
context, *Qualitative Health Research, 2:1,* pp. 75–98, with permission of Sage Publications, Inc. © 1992.

The general purpose of this study was to discover how new expectant parents and grandparents prepare for and respond to the arrival of the firstborn child-grandchild. The specific objectives of the study were, first, to expand the scope of knowledge about the birth of the first child as an intergenerational experience and, second, to discover the basic social process associated with this family event and to generate theory on normative family processes.

LITERATURE REVIEW

Carter and McGoldrick (1980) defined the family as "an emotional system of at least three generations, which is the operative emotional field at any given moment" (p. 9). They asserted the importance of studying interlocking tasks, problems, and relationships of the three-generational family system as it encountered both "normative" and "transgenerational" stress.

The birth of the first child has been researched in light of its associated stresses and has been examined as a family developmental crisis. Cowan, Cowan, Cole, and Cole (1978) studied 8 first birth families and observed that this event predisposes family members to disequilibrium within the complex process of changing identities, role behaviors, and communication patterns among the three generations. LeMasters (1975) reported that 83% of 46 couples experiencing the birth of the first child described extensive or severe crisis in the postpartum period. Larsen (1966) studied the stresses of the childbearing year as perceived by 130 women, who reported that their stress was increased by the interference of relatives and neighbors. Russell (1974) interviewed 511 couples after the birth of their first babies and found that their stress was related to fatigue, maternal loss of figure, money, and difficulties with in-laws.

The birth of the first child has been studied within the conceptual framework of individual developmental tasks of the new parents. Rubin (1975) identified the maternal tasks of pregnancy, which included identity reformulation, reordering interpersonal relationships and interpersonal space, and personality maturation. Barnhill, Rubenstein, and Rocklin (1979) postulated that among the expectant father's developmental tasks is the need to establish the nuclear family's boundaries as well as to integrate himself and his new child into the family where he is both father and son. Haley (1973) acknowledged how the birth of the first child changes things for the new parents: "They are now more individuated as adults and less children themselves, but the child brings them further into the total network of relatives as old bonds change their nature and new ones are formed" (p. 53). Shapiro (1978), who studied 20 couples in transition to parenthood, found that all couples seemed engaged in a process of defining a relationship to both families of origin which balanced two crucial dimensions: maintaining the autonomous boundaries of their nuclear family and maintaining the support of extended family connections.

Nursing practice and research has been broadened to include grandparents in the conceptualization of family childbearing experiences. For example, Maloni, McIndoe, and Rubenstein (1987) developed prenatal education interventions that included grandparents—a strategy that encouraged the elder generation's support of the expectant couple in the prenatal period. Horn and Manion (1985) described grandparents' participation in the childbirth experience as an opportunity to enhance bonding among the generations. In addition to these clinical interventions, nurse researchers have studied grandparental involvement in their children's childbearing experiences. Flaherty, Facteau, and Garven (1987) described the grandmother's essential function in low-income extended Black families and in the maternal role process of her adolescent daughter. Grandparental responses and roles related to premature infant care as well as categories of three-generational family nursing assessment were delineated by Blackburn and Lowen (1986a, 1986b). Rempusheski (1990) studied grandparent experiences in families with preterm infants, from which 10 conceptual categories emerged that described grandparental perceptions about the nature, quality, and dynamics of their relationship with a prematurely born grandchild. These studies acknowledged the existence of crucial intergenerational family processes which are interconnected with the birth of a child and attested to the importance of conducting nursing research to develop a knowledge base of these family processes that is relevant for nursing practice.

METHODOLOGY

The grounded theory method of research was used to generate new knowledge of intergenerational family processes related to the birth of the first child. The grounded theory method provides an inductive, phenomenological strategy for the generation of new hypotheses and theoretical concepts and the discovery of basic social processes (Glaser, 1978; Glaser & Strauss, 1967). Grounded theory is guided by the symbolic interactionist perspective which focuses on the social context and interactional matrix of symbolic meaning and behavior from which basic social processes can be inferred (Chenitz, 1986).

The purpose of grounded theory is to generate theory from empirical data rather than to test existing theory (Glaser & Strauss, 1967; Knafl & Howard, 1984). Theory grounded in data is of particular value because it increases the chance that theory and the empirical world will match. Grounded theory is also called the method of constant comparative analysis because it is based on the concurrent processes of data collection, coding, and analysis of data which directs subsequent data collection. Thus data and the emerging theory are in relationship to each other in a recursive and ongoing process of inquiry and analysis.

Sample

Interview and observational data were collected from 3 families, which consisted of 3 infants, their parents, and 6 sets of grandparents. Each family participated in the study for a period of 15 months, beginning with the last trimester of their first pregnancy and ending on the child's first birthday. In each family, the expected baby was the couple's first child and the first grandchild of at least one set of grandparents. The families were chosen from a maternity clinic population and had the following characteristics: Each family consisted of a married couple with an ongoing relationship with maternal and paternal in-laws. They were defined as "healthy" by virtue of the fact that no family member had experienced or was currently suffering from a major physical or mental illness. Ethnically, 2 families were of second- and third-generation Western European and Mediterranean heritage; the third family immigrated from South America. Six of the couples were Roman Catholic and 4 were Protestant. Average annual incomes ranged from $16,000 to $45,500. All study participants, with the exception of 1 grandmother, were employed outside of the home before and after the birth of the baby. The grandparent generation was represented by various pairings: Of the 6 pairs, 4 were married, 1 was widowed, and 1 was divorced, with 1 of the divorced spouses having remarried. Parents ranged in age from 21 to 28 years, and grandparents' ages ranged from 38 to 66 years. Two girls and 1 boy were born to the families in the study. These variations in characteristics enhanced the potential for comparison among families.

Ethical Considerations

The sample was selected from a group of families identified by their nurse midwife as being interested in participating in the study. Subjects were told that the purpose of the study was to discover how families experience the birth of their first child. No deception was used in the methodology. Each family was assured confidentiality and anonymity in all oral and written research reports. It was agreed that the researcher would not share information from one family member with other family members; rather, the families were assured confidentiality among subsystem interviews vis-à-vis the researcher. The families were informed that the researcher respected their right to choose what information to divulge in the study and that they could discontinue participation in the study at any time without penalty. Because the families were informed that the researcher was also a nurse, it was therefore important that a separation of research and clinical roles be made clear. The nature of the research role was delineated, and it was agreed that the researcher would not be available for clinical consultation but would refer the family to their health care providers for medical problems. Consent forms were signed by all parents and grandparents who participated in the study.

Data Collection

Initial interviews prior to the baby's birth included both parent and grandparent generations together, which allowed the researcher to observe interactional patterns among children, parents, and in-laws as well as to learn about family beliefs, traditions, expectations, and past experiences related to the anticipated birth event. After the baby's birth, family members were interviewed individually, in dyads, and in small groups as the developing hypotheses indicated the need. Thus data were collected through theoretical sampling, which allowed for the intentional selection of subjects for the facilitation of the constant comparative analysis, and became the basis for developing and refining the research question and related hypotheses (Strauss, 1987).

Interviews and participant observation occurred in parental and grandparental homes, on the hospital maternity ward, and at a Catholic baptism ceremony and the subsequent family celebration. In addition, semistructured telephone interviews were conducted to clarify data and to check the validity of the researcher's developing hypotheses so that the emerging theory reflected the lived experience of the families.

Data collection began with the initial research question: *How does the family as an intergenerational system respond to the birth of the first child-grandchild?* The first family interviews were conducted with Family A, which consisted of (a) a couple in their late 20s who had been married for 4 years; (b) their parents, who consisted of a couple in their late 50s and a widower in his 60s; and (c) the baby, who was the result of a planned pregnancy. Prenatal interviews included a conjoint meeting with the expectant parents and their parents, an interview with the expectant couple, and three telephone conversations with the expectant mother. The goal of these initial sampling interviews was to provide data for an open coding process, the aim of which is to discover, name, and categorize phenomena so as to uncover as many potentially relevant categories as possible (Strauss & Corbin, 1990).

The grounded theory method begins not with a preconceived theoretical framework but with a research problem set within a partial framework of concepts with which to begin data collection. These concepts are referred to as *local concepts,* which indicate a few principal features of the structures and processes to be studied and give the research its initial direction (Glaser & Strauss, 1967). The local concepts used in this study were based on two major assumptions about families in the process of expanding to include a new baby: First, that *attachment behaviors* will be demonstrated in relation to the new baby and, second, that *family reorganization* will occur among family members' roles and relationships.

The initial interviews indicated that expectant parents and grandparents in Family A had begun to develop attachments to the fetus, which was expressed in a number of ways. For instance, a grandmother showed her concern for the baby's welfare (e.g., "How's my baby today?"), and a father demonstrated a sense of obligation to and for the baby (e.g., "We don't allow anyone to smoke around the baby"). In terms of family reorganization, the expectant parents had begun anticipating the need for role shifts in household duties, child care, and work roles after the baby was born.

In addition to the data collected about the initial local concepts, a multitude of other information was collected, coded, and categorized. Initial categories differentiated data into family structure, family process, and discussion content categories. A highly salient theme which emerged from the initial data was that of the *anticipatory preparation* for the baby, which was occurring among parents and grandparents in a highly organized way. The data collected from Family A indicated the strong family norm of planning for change; indeed, the pregnancy itself was planned carefully by the expectant couple to occur when they had obtained a measure of financial and occupational stability. Whether or not a pregnancy is planned and how this planning affected the family's experience became a potential variable in the developing theoretical formulations.

The focus of the sampling changed to include a family whose first pregnancy was unplanned. Family B included the couple, a 21-year-old wife and 26-year-old husband, who accelerated their wedding plans to marry in the second month of the pregnancy. The maternal grandfather was in his late 40s and was divorced; the maternal grandmother was in her early 40s and had remarried. Paternal grandparents were in their early 50s. Data were collected in conjoint family, couple, and individual interviews, which were then subject to axial coding, the aim of which is to relate categories more specifically that were uncovered during open coding and to find evidence of variation and process with reference to them (Strauss & Corbin, 1990). Data analysis indicated that the unplanned pregnancy was not a deterrent to the family's anticipatory preparation for the birth of the baby. This conclusion was based on the fact that although the pregnancy was unplanned, it was not unwanted. Although this family struggled with in-law conflicts related to the precipitous marriage, both parents and all grandparents were eagerly and happily anticipating the birth of the unexpected child. Family B engaged in preparatory processes similar to those of Family A, despite the variation in the timing of the pregnancy.

The developing hypothesis was further tested by including a family for theoretical sampling in which there was conflict about the desirability of the pregnancy. The third family chosen for continued variational sampling differed from the other families on two dimensions: First, the pregnancy was wanted initially by the wife and not by the husband, and second, the family was of South American origin, providing a cultural contrast to the two American families. Family C consisted of a married couple in their mid 20s, the paternal grandparents, who lived in a duplex conjoining the couple's residence, and the maternal grandmother, aged 38, who lived in a large city 150 miles away. The paternal grandfather lived in South America. This family was interviewed conjointly with the expectant parents and the paternal grandparents; the expectant couple and the wife alone were also interviewed prenatally. The pregnancy became an issue of contention between the couple in the third year of their marriage because the wife wanted to have a baby, whereas the husband wanted to postpone parenthood for another year until the couple was, in his opinion, more financially stable. The wife decided to discontinue contraception without informing her husband and surprised him with the news of the pregnancy. All of the prospective grandparents supported the couple during their marital conflict around this issue, and in spite of this conflict, Family C demonstrated preparatory activities which were very similar to the other 2 families.

Postnatal interviews included meetings with the 3 new parent couples, separate interviews with a grandparent pair, a grandmother, and a grandfather, and frequent telephone interviews with the new mothers for ongoing discussion and verification. A termination interview was conducted with all families, which was attended by parents, grandparents, and baby, with the exception of Family C's maternal grandmother, who could not travel to the final meeting.

Data Analysis

Analysis of data was conducted as a continuous, ongoing process which was integrated with data collection and coding. Interviews were audiotaped, transcribed, and coded line by line. Kinship genograms were drawn for each family to obtain both historical and intergenerational relational data. One three-generation family interaction was videotaped to provide recorded nonverbal as well as verbal data for coding. Field notes from participant observation were included in the coded data. Coded data were clustered into related categories and were compared with one another and with new data to discover the relationships among the data in order to continually refine or discard emerging hypotheses (Stern, 1986). Specific questions helped to focus the process of constant comparative analysis: What interactional patterns occur among the generations in response to the anticipation and presence of the baby? How do family members participate in the evolving interaction among the generations and in-laws vis-à-vis the baby? How does the family handle convergent and divergent needs and expectations for interaction with one another and the baby? What basic social process is reflected within intergenerational family transactions related to the birth of the first child-grandchild? Through the process of constant comparative analysis, the research question was reformulated to reflect the family processes which were emerging from the data: *How do families create the conditions necessary to include the first child-grandchild into their ongoing family life?*

Reliability and Validity

Reliability and validity of the research results were built into the method of grounding theoretical observations in actual data. Reliability was enhanced by data collection within the naturalistic home setting and the cross-coding and categorization of data. Interrater reliability was determined by concurrent data categorization performed by a family therapist, who coded initial interview data and achieved 90% agreement with the researcher's coding. In addition, verification of interrater reliability was achieved by comparison of researcher and rater coding of interview data by calculating the Index of Qualitative Variation (IQV), which measures dispersion in a nominal distribution (Crittendon & Hill, 1971, p. 1073). According to the IQV formula, perfect reliability is represented as 1.0. An IQV score of 95% was reached between researcher and family therapist rater, indicating a healthy reliability in the coding process. Data which received discrepant coding were discussed until consensus was reached.

Validity was enhanced by ongoing contact with participating families over the 15-month duration of the study and by use of the participants' language in coding, categorizing, and theory writing. Concurrent validation, considered by Brink (1991) to be the most crucial validation procedure in qualitative research, was achieved through the use of multiple data collection methods over time. Face validity of the data categorizations (i.e., structure, process, and content categories) was supported by the high level of agreement between the researcher and rater. Construct validity was maintained by continuous review of the developing categories with the participating families to assure that the data represented their lived experience. Finally, 3 parent and 3 grandparent couples corroborated the validity of the emergent theory in their poststudy review of the research report.

Theory Writing

Memo writing was conducted concurrently with data collection, coding, and categorizing to record the researcher's theoretical analysis of the data. Memos served to advance the data from the empirical to the theoretical level of abstraction necessary for the identification of the core category and the description of the basic social process reflected by the data (Glaser, 1978).

FINDINGS: THE PROCESS OF MAKING PLACE

The data revealed the evolution of a family process which began before birth and allowed for the incorporation of the new baby into the family's ongoing life. The families were reorganizing their interpersonal patterns not only with the new baby but with each other as they expanded the boundaries of their relationships to include the presence of the new member. The core category is the set of variables which account for the phenomena observed and was identified as the process of "making place."

Making place is defined as the process occurring in a family through which a newborn individual receives recognition as a member of that family. It is an integrative process in that it facilitates the creation of new relational connections within the family as well as gives new meaning to existing ones. The families made place for the new and expanded relationship, for the infant, and among each other in two major domains of experience: physical place and social place.

Making Physical Place

The families expanded and restructured physical space to make room for the new baby through *nesting* behavior. The phenomena of nesting has been researched as a maternal behavioral phenomena related to hormonal changes in pregnancy and is considered one of the maternal tasks of pregnancy (Rubin, 1975). However, family members other than the expectant mothers became involved in preparing space for the baby: Two grandmothers prepared a play space for the expected child and "baby-proofed" their kitchen and bathroom cabinets to prevent injury when the baby became mobile; another grandmother bought a crib for her house in anticipation of overnight visits; and a retired grandfather remodeled bedroom space for the baby while his daughter and son-in-law worked. Nesting included expanding space, rearranging existing space, and cleaning. It began as early as the second trimester and as late as the last month of pregnancy in 2 families who believed that it was "bad luck" to begin preparation prior to reasonable assurance that the baby was healthy and viable. All of the families had created room for the infant before birth. The meaning of this potential space to the family was evidenced by their frequent visits to the prepared room. The baby's presence had developed a reality prior to the birth, and the creation of the baby's room was a major step in acknowledging the new member.

Making Social Place

Creating social place involved family interaction that either established or acknowledged an ongoing relationship among adults and the baby and included three intergenerational activities: naming, attributing, and welcoming. Naming reflected the interactional process of deciding on and conferring the unique personal referent for the baby and respective referents for new parental and grandparental roles. Attributing reflected the process of describing the baby's and family members' characteristics in a way that reflected similarities, differences, or relationships within the family. Welcoming invited interaction among family members.

Naming the baby was a specific task within the larger family process of reorganizing roles and identifications and was recognized as primarily the task of the expectant parents. The parents became involved in naming the baby as early as the first trimester and involved other family members in ways which reflected the uniqueness of each family system within its ethnic and cultural traditions. For example, Family C gave their baby an American name, different from all other existing family names, which was congruent with the new parents' goals to be thoroughly Americanized. Families A and B conferred a unique first name on their infants but chose a relative's name for the middle names as a gesture of intergenerational connection. The process of naming also included the adults' reorganization of their identities vis-à-vis the new baby and each other as they anticipated the roles of parent and grandparent. The adults practiced their new roles even before the baby was born by referring to each other as "Mom," "Grandpa," and so forth. Maternal and paternal grandparents were differentiated from each other by selection of different affectionate titles (e.g., Granny or Grandma, Poppa or Pepe). When speaking to the baby, the adults made frequent reference to each other according to their new role identification, thus confirming and affirming each other's expanded relationships within the family.

Attributing behaviors were those in which characteristics were ascribed among family members. These behaviors have direct influence on the quality and development of affiliative bonds. Attributions were manifested on two dimensions: a complimentary derogatory dimension and a similarity-difference dimension.

The complimentary-derogatory dimension included attributions of positive or negative quality. Complimentary attributions reflected desired or admired characteristics of another member: for example, "He is a good father." In contrast, derogatory attributions expressed negative or undesirable qualities: for example, "She is meddlesome and self-centered." It is significant that derogatory attributions, which signaled family conflict, were confined to the adults in the family. The baby, either in utero or after birth, was never the object of derogatory attributions, even in the face of an unplanned pregnancy, financial hardship, or family discord.

Additionally, family members ascribed attributions to self and each other in terms of perceived similarities and differences among them, which accounted for another dimension of attribution. Generally, members expressed a relaxed tolerance for the differences which they saw between themselves and others as well as a comfort with characteristics which were perceived to be shared. Attribution about similarities ("The baby looks just like her daddy") both acknowledged and reinforced relational bonds between family members. Family members enjoyed connecting with the baby through attribution of similarities and used this process to establish the baby's identification as a member of the family. The families' cultural and relational issues were clearly reflected in how they engaged in the attributing process. For instance, one family actively competed to determine what "side of the family" the baby most resembled, reflecting this family's conflict between parental loyalties to their families of origin. In the South American family, the parental couple actively espoused enculturation into American norms and rejected ties to "the old country and the old ways"; the parents stressed the uniqueness of the baby's personality ("He's his own person").

Welcoming activities acknowledged the existence of the new baby, whether actual or potential in relationship with others. This relational space making was seen in three ways: gift giving, greeting, and invitations for interaction.

Gift giving was "welcoming in action." Baby gifts were given in all families as early as the fourth month of the pregnancy. Parents and grandparents also received gifts which affirmed their new roles and acknowledged their new status. The baby shower was the epitome of "welcoming in action" and represented familial and social acknowledgment of the baby's presence and the commitment to contribute to his or her care. The shower marked a turning point for the expectant mothers: "I finally feel ready for the baby." This cultural and family ritual provided formal public acknowledgement of the family's transition to a new status and set of relationships and responsibilities.

Greeting acknowledged the existence of another person and indicated a desire for interaction. Family members began greeting the expected baby during the pregnancy, both directly and indirectly. For instance, a family member's patting the expectant mother's abdomen and saying "Hi, baby" was a direct greeting. The baby was also greeted indirectly by being included in the parents' greetings: "How are the three of you today?" After the baby's arrival, he or she was greeted consistently with an enthusiasm not always extended among adults. Conflicts and tensions among adults were reflected in avoidance or distancing maneuvers, such as delayed greetings or averted eyes. However, the infant enjoyed unambivalent affirmation in family greetings. Additionally, members were greeted with verbal acknowledgment of their new family roles: for example, "How's the new father doing?" Finally, relational connections were asserted and affirmed in greetings: for example, "How's Grammy's little girl?" Thus greetings reflected the structural changes that had occurred in family relationships among the generations.

Invitations for interaction expressed a desire for relationships among family members and included (a) outstretched arms which invited embrace, (b) eye contact and smiling, (c) offering to share food or a toy or a book, or (d) a verbal request for another person's presence. These verbal and nonverbal actions built and maintained social space among members and contributed to the evolution of enduring affiliations in the family.

Changes in relational connections among existing family members and to the newborn member reflected the evolution of two functions of this process, namely, intergenerational affiliation and continuity, which represent the space-time dimensions of making place.

Affiliation is defined as a state of relational connectedness resulting from human interactional processes. The anticipation and presence of the new baby created a focus of consensual interest, precipitated the development of new roles and relationships among all members, and intensified existing bonds and new attachments with the newborn. The transition to parenthood and grandparenthood included the reorganization of relationships between the new parents and their parents in relation to the new baby. For instance, parents and grandparents renegotiated their relationships to a more egalitarian status, as sons and daughters assumed parental responsibility, and grandparents developed roles of support and nurturance for both their grown children and their grandchild. The baby became a focal point between the elder generations which created opportunities for the enrichment of their relationships. One new father commented, "Now that the baby has arrived, I have more to talk about with my in-laws. It's more interesting to be together enjoying the baby."

In addition to intensified pleasure, the families' affiliative bonds tolerated stress and conflict. For example, a conflict between members in 2 of the 3 families resulted in temporary withdrawal from interaction, whereas in the third family, confrontation and "clearing the air" was the preferred response to interpersonal difficulties. As one new mother stated, "We've all changed since the baby's birth. It had to be. There is a new person here, and he's important to all of us. We have to be willing to give and take." Although conflict contributed to various distancing or stressful confrontive maneuvers, these families were organized so that relational distance could be negotiated while maintaining affiliative bonds.

Continuity is represented in individual experience as a sense of "self through time." All of the grandparents were happy knowing the family or the family name would "go on" through the life of the grandchild. One grandmother expressed her sense of having been blessed to witness the arrival of her grandson and was sad that her own deceased mother was deprived of the experience. Thus family continuity, as the experience of "self through time" within relational connectedness, is considered a desirable state which promotes individual and family survival and well-being. The families in this study continued to build on what Weiss (1974) described as "reliable alliance," a situation in which there were expectations of future connection based on past and present bonds and shared experiences. It is through the process of making place that the new generation is incorporated into the ongoing life of the family, both as a valued member in the present and as a bearer of the family's future.

DISCUSSION

The research data pointed to a definition of the family as a relational field in constant transformation in which human existence is supported for growth. This relational field is the primary context or environment in which shared social reality is created through affiliations over time. These intergenerational affiliations provide opportunity for attachments, which, according to Weiss (1974), are essential to meaningful, satisfying, and healthy social relationships. Attachment is provided within relationships from which participants gain a sense of security and place. In this study, the infant was not the only family member who benefited from the process of making place: Parents and grandparents found pleasure in their new attachments with the baby and each other. Weiss pointed out that social bonds which afford the opportunity for nurturing others enhance interpersonal bonds because adults obtain satisfaction from having responsibility for the well-being of a child or another person. Attachment theorists have traditionally focused on the maternal-child bond (Ainsworth, Blehar, Waters, & Wall, 1978). Although this primary attachment is of central importance to individual well-being, other intimate relationships provided by the extended family are essential to full human competence. Marris (1982) observed that unless children learn early that there can be several unique nurturing figures in their lives who have a particular, special love for them, they cannot create the conditions for mature adult attachments. Thus it is crucial that nursing's view of individual and family health be expanded to include the extended family relationships in which intimate experiences are embedded.

Current family nursing research on the experience of pregnancy has included an intergenerational focus. Rempusheski (1990) identified grandparents' intense interest and involvement in the care of their preterm infant grandchildren. Mercer, Ferketich, DeJoseph, May, and Sollid (1988) found that strong family ties and relationships with extended kin mitigate the effect of stress on expectant couples during pregnancy. The importance of relational research in describing family pattern and reorganization in childbearing families was suggested by Fawcett (1989). The need for prospective longitudinal studies of healthy families was documented by Murphy (1986), and the need for family research as a base for evolving nursing theory was asserted by Whall and Fawcett (1991). The concept of making place adds to existing literature in its uniqueness as a model of intergenerational relationship development grounded in longitudinal data from healthy families. In addition, the process of making place reflects three key family tasks which were identified by Friedemann (1989) within her control-congruence model for mental health nursing of families. These tasks include creating and sharing space, the provision of bonding, and the acceptance of similarities and differences among the members in supporting both togetherness and individuation. The process of making place reflects a synthesis of these tasks, which occurs when a family has successfully reorganized to contain the new relationships that the birth of the first child engenders in the family system.

Limitations of the Study

This study included data from a small group of families who were maritally intact, relatively financially stable, and whose extended family was geographically available. Theoretical sampling among more families with ethnic, socioeconomic, and membership variability is needed to further saturate and densify the theory of making place. Although the study included 2 families in which there was initial conflict about the timing of the pregnancies, the study sample did not provide an opportunity to examine the potential effects of an unwanted baby on the process of making place. Also, the effects of marital and in-law conflict on this process need to be explored in order to develop an understanding of relational impediments to making place.

There was evidence in the study of another experiential domain that could be labeled "psychological place." This domain includes intrapsychic realities related to the internalization of object relationships, the development of the self system, and the nature and quality of the individual's emotional life. This research was limited to an exploration of interactional phenomena and, as such, did not generate adequate information about the inner life of family members. Family theorists have divergent views on the compatibility of family systems and individual theories. For instance, Kerr (1981) stated that family systems and individual thinking are two distinctly different ways of conceptualizing human behavior, and attempts to mix them reflect a failure to appreciate their difference. Epstein, Baldwin, and Bishop (1982) hypothesized that structural, organizational, and transactional patterns of family functioning are more important in determining behavior than are intrapsychic variables. However, this researcher is in agreement with Fogarty (1976), who asserted that a comprehensive theory about the family must include a map of the relationships between people—the external system—and the processes that go on inside a person—the inner system—because they both exist and form a continuum. Data from this research were inadequate for description of the intrapsychic dimensions of making place.

Recommendations for Practice and Research

The concept of making place offers a useful focus for family nursing, namely, the importance of the relational context of family health. Making place creates the conditions for structural changes in family relationships and roles that allow for human growth and development. It could be inferred that without a family's making place for a new baby, healthy maturation can be compromised. Therefore, perinatal nursing assessment and intervention should include focus on how the family reorganizes its relationships and roles to receive the new baby. Assessment of a family's making place will address the following areas of family experience:

1. *What are the family's patterns of affiliations?* What is the quality of in-law relationships? What are the family's patterns of contact? What forces (socioeconomic, cultural, or emotional) are sources of conflict and tension? How is conflict resolved? Who is included or excluded from planning for or interacting with the new baby? How does the process of naming the baby reflect the family's affiliative patterns?
2. *How are attributions made among members?* How do family members describe themselves and each other? Are similarities and differences acknowledged? Are attributions complimentary or derogatory, and between whom in the family system? Are negative attributions a source of conflict among the generations?
3. *How is physical space being made for the baby?* How are the parent and grandparent generations interacting around creating space for the baby? Is the space adequate for the baby's needs? Are there conflicts about space making?

The nurse's awareness of the importance of the entire family's response to the first child's birth will assist in the identification of problems related to making place. The results of this study indicate the importance of grandparents in the birth experience, yet, as Rempusheski (1990) observed, they are rarely included in the health care system's organization of care for expectant parents and their babies. Even if grandparents are not actively included in perinatal activities (i.e., expectant parent classes, prenatal and postnatal visits, and so forth), their changing relationships with the new parents and their contributions to the quality of family life are important for comprehensive and accurate assessment and intervention in the perinatal period.

Nursing research would be useful in identifying the process of making place in various family configurations. How place is made for second- and later-born children could provide valuable information regarding birth-order variations and the family processes with which they are related. Single-parent, adoptive, divorced, and remarried families may be studied for variations of making place for the new infant. Research on nuclear families who are geographically separated from their families of origin might illuminate the influence of generational proximity in the process. How family conflict affects the process of making place needs further exploration. Studies of various cultural patterns of making place could support more effective transcultural nursing interventions. Families incorporating members other than babies (i.e., spouses, stepchildren, or aging grandparents) might reveal varied patterns of making place that reflect family expansion over the lifespan. Finally, it is important to study the context of relational expansion in families at risk for development of physical or mental health problems. Adolescent parents or parents with a history of psychiatric illness or who are in a state of situational crisis, such as the birth of a sick or developmentally challenged infant, could be studied in terms of how less than ideal circumstances influence the process of making place. Theoretical sampling among these diverse family constellations would assist the effort to discover whether making place reflects the basic social process which is characteristic of all expanding relational family systems.

CONCLUSIONS

This study has broadened the context of birth from the nuclear to the extended family and has provided longitudinal data about intergenerational processes which function to expand relational boundaries to include the firstborn child. How new parents and grandparents expand their relationships to include new role functions and responsibilities is described in the model. The importance of grandparents in preparation for and incorporation of the new infant into the family was a major finding. The family is central to nursing's conceptualizations of human development and health and, as such, is an important focus for continuing nursing research.

REFERENCES

Ainsworth, M.D.S., Blehar, M. C., Waters, E., & Wall, S. (1978). *Patterns of attachment*. Hillsdale, NJ: Lawrence Erlbaum.

Barnhill, L. R., Rubenstein, G., & Rocklin, N. (1979). From generation to generation: Fathers-to-be in transition. *Family Coordinator, 22*, 229–236.

Blackburn, S., & Lowen, L. (1986a). Grandparents in NICU's: Support for parents. *American Journal of Maternal Child Nursing, 11*(3), 190–192.

Blackburn, S., & Lowen, L. (1986b). Impact of an infant's premature birth on grandparents and parents. *Journal of Gynecologic and Neonatal Nursing, 15*(2), 173–178.

Brink, P. (1991). Issues of reliability and validity. In J. M. Morse (Ed.), *Qualitative nursing research: A contemporary dialogue* (pp. 164–185). Newbury Park, CA: Sage.

Carter, E., & McGoldrick, M. (1980). The family life cycle and family therapy: An overview. In E. Carter & M. McGoldrick (Eds.), *The family life cycle: A framework for family therapy* (pp. 3–28). New York: Gardner.

Chenitz, W. C. (1986). Getting started: The research proposal for a grounded theory study. In W. C. Chenitz & J. M. Swanson (Eds.), *From practice to grounded theory: Qualitative research in nursing* (pp. 39–47). Menlo Park, CA: Addison-Wesley.

Cowan, C. P., Cowan, P. A., Cole, L., & Cole, J. D. (1978). Becoming a family: The impact of the first child's birth on a couple's relationship. In W. B. Miller & L. F. Newman (Eds.), *The first child and family formation* (pp. 296–324). Chapel Hill: University of North Carolina Population Center.

Crittendon, K. S., & Hill, R. J. (1971). Coding reliability and validity of interview data. *American Sociological Review, 36*, 1073–1080.

Duvall, E. M. (1974). *Family development* (5th ed.). Philadelphia: Lippincott.

Epstein, N. B., Baldwin, L. M., & Bishop, D. S. (1982). McMaster model of family functioning. In F. Walsh (Ed.), *Normal family processes* (pp. 115–141). New York: Guilford.

Fawcett, J. (1989). Spouses, experiences during pregnancy and the postpartum: A program of research and theory development. *Image, 21*, 149–152.

Flaherty, M. J., Facteau, L., & Garven, P. (1987). Grandmother functions in multi-generational families: An exploratory study of black adolescent mothers and their infants. *Maternal-Child Nursing Journal, 16*(1), 61–73.

Fogarty, T. F. (1976). Systems concepts and the dimensions of self. In P. J. Guerin, Jr. (Ed.), *Family therapy: Theory and practice* (pp. 144–153). New York: Gardner.

Friedemann, M. L. (1989). Closing the gap between grand theory and mental health practice with families, Part 2: The control-congruence model for mental health nursing of families. *Archives of Psychiatric Nursing, 3*(1), 20–29.

Glaser, B. (1978). *Theoretical sensitivity: Advances in the methodology of grounded theory*. Mill Valley, CA: Sociology Press.

Glaser, B., & Strauss, A. (1967). *The discovery of grounded theory*. Chicago: Aldine.

Haley, J. (1973). *Uncommon therapy*. New York: Norton.

Hill, R. (1964). Methodological issues in family development research. *Family Process, 3*(1), 186–206.

Horn, M., & Manion, J. (1985). Creative grandparenting: Bonding the generations. *Journal of Gynecological and Neonatal Nursing, 14*(3), 233–236.

Kerr, M. E. (1981). Family systems theory and therapy. In A. S. Gurman & D. P. Knister (Eds.), *Handbook of family therapy* (pp. 226–266). New York: Brunner/Mazel.

Knafl, K., & Howard, M. (1984). Interpreting and reporting qualitative research. *Research in Nursing and Health, 7*(1), 17–24.

Larsen, V. L. (1966). Stresses of the childbearing year. *American Journal of Public Health, 56*(1), 32–36.

LeMasters, E. E. (1957). Parenthood as crisis. *Marriage and Family Living, 19,* 352–355.

Maloni, J. A., McIndoe, J. E., & Rubenstein, G. (1987). Expectant grandparent class. *Journal of Obstetric and Gynecological Nursing, 16*(1), 26–29.

Marris, P. (1982). Attachment and society. In C. M. Parkes & J. Stevenson-Hinde (Eds.), *The place of attachment in human behavior* (pp. 185–204). New York: Basic Books.

Mercer, R. T., Ferketich, S. L., DeJoseph, J., May, K. A., & Sollid, D. (1988). Effect of stress on family functioning during pregnancy. *Nursing Research, 37,* 268–275.

Murphy, S. (1986). Family study and nursing research. *Image, 18*(4), 170–174.

Rempusheski, V. F. (1990). Role of the extended family in parenting: A focus of grandparents of preterm infants. *Journal of Perinatal and Neonatal Nursing, 4*(2), 43–55.

Rubin, R. (1975). Maternal tasks in pregnancy. *Maternal-Child Nursing, 4*(3), 143–153.

Russell, C. S. (1974). Transition to parenthood: Problems and gratifications. *Journal of Marriage and the Family, 26,* 294–301.

Shapiro, E. R. (1978). *Transition to parenthood in adult and family development*. Unpublished doctoral dissertation, University of Massachusetts, Amherst.

Stern, P. N. (1986). Conflicting family culture: An impediment in stepfather families. In W. C. Chenitz & J. M. Swanson (Eds.), *From practice to grounded theory: Qualitative research in nursing* (pp. 169–180). Menlo Park, CA: Addison-Wesley.

Strauss, A. (1987). *Qualitative analysis for social scientists*. Cambridge: Cambridge University Press.

Strauss, A., & Corbin, J. (1990). *Basics of qualitative research: Grounded theory procedures and techniques*. Newbury Park, CA: Sage.

Weiss, R. S. (1974). The provisions of social relationships. In Z. Rubin (Ed.), *Doing unto others* (pp. 17–26). Englewood Cliffs, NJ: Prentice-Hall.

Whall, A. L., & Fawcett, J. (1991). *Family theory development in nursing: State of the science and the art*. Philadelphia: F. A. Davis.

Mary Anne Bright is an assistant professor in the School of Nursing at the University of Massachusetts.

Chapter 9

Historical Research Approach

Caring for clients includes the acquisition of a nursing history. Without collecting background data, decisions regarding a client's current health care need and future chance of achieving a higher level of wellness would be greatly jeopardized by ignorance. Historical understanding is crucial to providing nursing care because of nursing's essential holistic nature. Looking at the whole person requires recognition of multiple factors that influence the person. Similarly, decisions regarding the nursing profession today risk failure and inadequacy of response if history is ignored.

All knowledge has a historical dimension; conversely, historiography provides individuals with a way of knowing. Tholfsen (1977) explained that "the past is present in every person and in the cultural and institutional world that surrounds [them]" (p. 248). This, Tholfsen continued, means that the historian must know the historical conditions of the period being studied. Knowledge of the past helps to inform most other research designs that include explanatory background information establishing an understanding of the phenomenon to be studied. Selecting a historical research design as the methodology requires that the researcher have an understanding of what history is; a knowledge of various social, political, and economic factors that impact events, ideas, and people; an interest in the subject; and creativity in approach (Christy, 1978; Rines & Kershner, 1979).

Qualitative Research in Nursing: Advancing the Humanistic Imperative by Helen J. Streubert and Dona R. Carpenter. Copyright © 1995 by J. B. Lippincott Company.

DEFINING THE MEANING OF HISTORY

Many definitions and explanations exist as to the meaning and nature of history. Austin (1958) defined history as "an integrated, written record of past events, based on the results of a search for the truth" (p. 4). Kruman (1985) explained history as "facts (ideas, events, social, and cultural processes) filtered through human intelligence" (p. 111). Kruman referred to an *objective relativism* which permits the objective reality of one historian to coexist with different historical interpretations of others and thus to promote change in ideas and advances in historical inquiry. Matejski (1986) conceived of history "as a past event, a record, or account of something that has happened" (p. 175). Furthermore, Matejski explained history as a field of study with its own set of criteria and methods that enables the researcher to collect data and interpret findings. Developing its own method often borrowed from other disciplines, historical inquiry examines the interaction of people, activities, and "multiple variables" (p. 77) affecting human thought and activity. The narrative that results from a historian's findings must creatively weave the many factors together into a readable and interesting story.

Historical research opens windows into the past, creating new ideas and reshaping human thinking and understanding. Ashley (1978) explained the crucial role historical research plays in the foundation of nursing scholarship by defining history as "the study of creative activity in human behavior [that] gives one the courage to create and respond to what is new without fear of losing one's identity with the whole of humanity" (p. 28).

Like nursing, history is an art and science. The discipline of history requires the use of scientific principles to study the interrelationship of social, economic, political, and psychological factors that influence ideas, events, institutions, and people. Yet in order to explain the findings of historical inquiry, balancing the rigors of scientific inquiry and the understanding of human behavior, a historical researcher must revert to the "art of contemplation, speculation, and of interpretation" (Newton, 1965, p. 24).

A researcher who chooses historical method must exhibit more than just a curiosity about the past. The researcher formulates a thesis about the relation between ideas, events, institutions, or people in the past. Chronologically ordering events over time does not explain the links and ties established between them. Probing for explanations between historical antecedents requires questioning, reasoning, and interpreting, Christy (1978) explained that "healthy skepticism becomes a way of life for the serious historiographer" (p. 6). The historiographer seeking to discover meanings in the past must sift through data and examine each piece closely for clues.

When studying the past, the historical researcher uses a variety of sources such as private letters, personal journals, books, magazines, professional journals, and newspapers. The researcher travels in time and explores these materials, seeking a relation between ideas, events, institutions, or people. The purpose of such a study is not to predict. Instead it is to understand the past in order to explain present or future relations. From historical documents, the historiographer derives insight from past lived experiences that can be adapted to generate new ideas (Barzun & Graff, 1985).

Researchers use a historical design if they believe something from the past will explain something in the present or the future. Conflict between what the researcher thinks and what may be written about a particular topic also influences the decision to do historical research. For example, misconception regarding nurses' participation in the late 19th century women's movement led Lewenson (1990, 1993) to study the relationship between the woman's suffrage movement and the four nursing organizations that had formed in America between 1893 and 1920. To dispel the tension between contemporary understanding of the past or a *present-mindedness,* which omitted nursing's political response to the events of the late 19th and early 20th century, required a historical inquiry.

Present-mindedness refers to using a contemporary perspective when analyzing data collected from an earlier period. This analysis of data is stigmatized as *unhistorical* and leads to inaccurate conclusions when ideas and lived experiences of people in the past are compared with events that come later (Tholfsen, 1977, p. 247). Although Tholfsen warns historians to be careful of absolutes and the dangers of present-mindedness, he argues that "the best history is rooted in a lively interest in the present" (p. 247). Nevertheless, history refers to constant change, and this change is what "produces the endless diversity characteristic of the historical world" (p. 248). Each period must be studied within the context of its age to avoid judging or interpreting the past without respect to changes made overtime. Hence, differences found in every age must "be understood in its own terms" (p. 248).

Nurses and history make a good match. Nurses come from rich, diverse backgrounds, with many human contacts which can be used to better understand and explain human behavior. Nurses, adept at studying human behavior, are well suited to historical inquiry where they study human behavior in the context of an event, a place, a person, an institution, or an idea in the past. Like historians, nurses identify and interpret patterns of behavior that occur over time.

ELEMENTS AND INTERPRETATIONS OF THE APPROACH

To understand the wholeness of the past, the nurse historian selects a framework to guide the study. However, as Lynaugh and Reverby (1987) warn, no one formula or specific method exists for doing historical research. Tholfsen (1977) contends that "history lacks a coherent theoretical and conceptual structure" (p. 246). No one theoretical framework exists for which to study history. History is a discipline with many structures that Cramer (1992) describes as "permanent or semipermanent relations of elements that determine the character of the whole" (p. 6). Superimposed structure enables the researcher to organize the data. For example, when using geography to frame a study, the researcher may write a regional history, or when using a particular topic to organize a study, the researcher may focus on women's work (Cramer, 1992).

Society asks historians to analyze an experience and use that experience to explain and prepare society for similar events in the future (Hofstadter, 1959). Hofstadter illustrated this by explaining how historians study the records of war so that society can learn something that will help in future wars. Writing for a specific function creates further tension between the dual nature that exists within the historian's role: the writing of a historical narrative and the writing of a historical monograph. According to Hofstadter, the former tells a story but often is disappointing in analysis, and the latter approximates a scientific inquiry but lacks in literary style and frequently offers insufficient analytical data. However, both of these functions are enriched by interrelating social sciences and historical inquiry. Hofstadter believed that combining social science and historical research produces fresh ideas and new insights into human behavior.

Historians look at other disciplines to help inform and structure their work. To understand the development of nursing education in America and to provide a theoretical framework, the historian might use research from women's history and educational history in the United States. Knowledge of American labor history, important to nursing history because of nurses' apprenticeship role in hospitals, would also be a useful framework for the historiographer to organize the data conceptually To study history using a variety of approaches, such as philosophical, national, psychohistorical, or economical, allows the researcher to explore a point in time with a conceptual guide from a particular discipline (Ashley, 1978; Matejski, 1986).

Nurse historians ponder different theoretical frameworks that structure historical research. At the Fourth Invitational Nursing History Conference held in 1991, the agenda included the study of three different theoretical approaches: biographical, social, and intellectual.

Doing a *biographical history,* that is, the study of an individual, opens a wide vista to an entire period (Brown, D'Antonio, & Davis, 1991). At the Fourth Invitational Nursing History Conference, historian Laurie Glass (1991) explained that biography uses the story of a person's life to understand the "values, expectations, tensions, and the conflicts of the time and the culture within which he or she lived" (Brown, D'Antonio, & Davis, 1991). Interpretation requires historians to familiarize themselves with the period so that meanings can be derived from within the particular time frame rather than superimposed from a later contemporary distance. For example, to understand the life of the early 20th century nurse and birth control activist Margaret Sanger, it is essential to understand society's beliefs about woman's roles and beliefs about procreation.

Social history explores a particular period and attempts to understand the prevailing values and beliefs by exploring the everyday events of that period. Historian Vern Bullough (1991), at the same conference, described a strategy used in doing social history. Bullough explained that the usefulness of using specific quantitative data in understanding the life experiences of "'ordinary' men and women" (Brown, D'Antonio, & Davis, 1991, p. 3). Analysis of census data, court records, and municipal surveys, for example, assists the historian to go beyond the boundaries of class, ethnicity, economics, and race, hence enabling the historian to gain a broader understanding of the subject being studied.

Intellectual history, where "*thinking* is the event under analysis," lends itself to several approaches (Brown, D'Antonio, & Davis, 1991, p. 2). Historian Diane Hamilton (1991), another presenter at the Fourth Invitational Nursing History Conference, provided suggestions for doing an intellectual history. The historian may explore the ideas of an individual considered to be one of the intellectual thinkers of a period, such as studying the ideas of public health nurse Lillian Wald; or the historian may explore the history of ideas over time, such as the ideas exercised by nursing leaders that influenced the development of nursing education in America; and yet another approach may be the exploration of the attitudes and ideas of people who are not considered the intellectual thinkers of that period, such as the ideas of the practicing nurse. Hamilton cautioned historians using this approach of the possible conflict that may arise between the ideas and the contextual backgrounds that gave rise to them (Brown, D'Antonio, & Davis, 1991; Hamilton, 1993).

The historical researcher must be ready to "live in permanent struggle with conceptual ambiguities, missing evidence and conflicting viewpoints" (Lynaugh & Reverby, 1987, p. 4). The historian continually faces a methodological polarity whereby tension exists between the "general and the unique, [and] between the particular and the universal" (Tholfsen, 1977, p. 249). However, this tension and ambiguity are essential to history because they mirror human experience with all of life's contradictions and ambiguities (Tholfsen, 1977). When approaching historical research, the researcher must expect ambiguity of design as well as data. The researcher must decide on a particular theoretical framework and understand the conflicting views and ideas regarding the approach. With this in

mind, historians can begin to construct a creative design that addresses
their research interest.

APPLICATION OF THE APPROACH

Although no single historical method exists, Lynaugh and Reverby (1987)
point out, essential guideposts and rules of evidence ensure the credibility and usefulness of the historian's findings. In search of an approach,
Barzun and Graff (1985) wrote that "without form in every sense, the facts
of the past, like the jumbled visions of a sleeper in a dream, elude us"
(p. 271). The next section offers a guide to direct the beginning researcher
in developing a historical design. As in any process, the researcher must
allow fluidity between the steps of this guide and easily move from one
step to another, in both directions. For example, the data collected may
direct the literature review and the literature review may in turn determine the thesis.

DATA GENERATION

Title

The title tells the reader what to expect from the study and delineates
the topic being studied, the time frame, and the purpose of the study.
Although the title appears first in a completed study and concisely
describes what the research is about, it may be the final step the
researcher takes.

Statement of the Subject

To begin the application of a historical design, the researcher must define
the topic to be studied and prepare a statement of the subject (Kruman,
1985). A clear, concise statement tells the reader what will be studied and
the reasons for selecting this subject. An explanation of a researcher's
interest in the topic and justification of its relationship with other topics
must be presented. In addition, the researcher establishes the purpose
and significance to nursing and nursing research in this section (Rines &
Kershner, 1979).

   When selecting a topic, Austin (1958) suggested that the subject be
"part of a larger whole, and one which can be isolated" (p. 5). By isolating a part of the topic, it becomes a more manageable study. It may be
easier to study the curriculum of three nurse training schools in 1897 than
to tackle all of nursing education in the late 19th century.

   Historical study does not predict outcomes so there is no hypothesis. The thesis guides the study and moves the research toward a particular field or discipline. Researchers base their ideas on background infor-

mation they have obtained. Patterns that emerge in the initial fact-finding and knowledge-building step aid in the creative formation of a thesis statement. For example, instead of predicting the effect of apprenticeship training on the development of nursing education, historians identify themes or theses about nursing education and use these themes to convey their ideas on the subject such as the study done by Hanson (1989) on the emergence of liberal education in nursing education.

To accomplish this important step, researchers must gather information regarding the period to be studied. They must have a working knowledge of the social, cultural, economic, and political climate that prevailed and how their subject is influenced by these factors. This helps establish patterns and identify relevant points regarding the subject and justifies the selection of historical method.

Literature Review

A good starting point for a literature review is to identify major works published on the topic selected. If the historian wants to study the history of critical thinking, then one must assess what has been written on the subject and identify the themes and ambiguities related to critical thinking that exist in the literature. Part of the review includes identifying the problems connected with the topic, for example, the ambiguities that have arisen over time in defining and evaluating critical thinking. The anticipation of problems that may arise with methodology or with the interpretation of data allows the historical researcher time to plan how one would resolve these problems. Searching the literature for references from several periods allows for greater understanding of the subject. Various computer data bases now exist that provide a means by which to obtain some of the data needed in the literature review.

A literature review helps the researcher formulate questions that need to be addressed, delineate a time frame for the study, and decide on a theoretical framework. In addition, the review affords the researcher an opportunity to learn what type of materials are available to them. For example, the researcher learns whether primary sources or firsthand accounts of an event, such as the letters written by an individual living during the period being studied, can be obtained; the researcher also learns of secondary sources or secondhand accounts of an event, such as histories or newspapers that have already been written on the particular subject being studied.

Based on the literature review, the historian formulates questions regarding events that influenced the chosen subject; questions beginning with how, why, who, and what are asked in light of the ideas, events, institutions, individuals that existed, and thus may shed light on the subject. If a topic such as public health nursing in the United States is narrowed to the study of the public health nurses living at the Henry Street Settlement, then questions such as "How did the Henry Street Settlement begin? Who began the Henry Street Settlement? What is a settlement house? Why was Henry Street the location?" may all guide the direction of the literature search. These questions may prompt the researcher to examine biographies of people who participated in the settlement house movement during the late 19th and early 20th centuries. Or to better understand life at that time, the historian might read city records regarding population statistics; or he or she might examine material already published to understand another historian's perception of women's roles, education, work, and life at that time. Newspaper accounts, written histories, proceedings of minutes, photographs, biographies, letters, diaries, and films may be helpful to the historian in search of greater understanding of a particular subject.

During the literature review, the historian must develop an organizing strategy that will help in the analysis of the data. Some facts that are obtained may seem trivial in the beginning of the project but become crucial to explaining or connecting events learned later in the study. Thus, careful documentation, whether using an index card filing system or establishing a directory in a word processing program, will help the researcher retrieve the information at a later time (Austin, 1958; Barzun & Graff, 1985). The bibliographic entry should include the author, title, abstract, place of publication, date, and particular archive or library where the information was found. Any pertinent information should be included in the notes so that during analysis of the data the researcher will be able to easily retrieve important information or go back to the original source if necessary.

During this phase of the project, the historian begins to develop a bibliography. Using historical source materials from libraries, archives, bibliographies, newspapers, reviews, journals, and associations, the researcher begins to comprehend the extent of the subject under investigation (Matejski, 1986).

To accomplish this important step, the historian uses collections found in libraries and archives. Libraries and archives contain different types of reference materials that require different methods of storage and classification. To enable the researcher to use each one appropriately, it is necessary to be familiar with both.

Libraries contain published materials often used as secondary materials. To locate the material, the researcher uses a card catalog or computerized catalog system that identifies the work with a call number. This number designates each volume's unique location in the library, usually arranged by subject. Many of the books have been purchased and are permitted to circulate (Termine, 1993) as opposed to archives where materials remain on site.

Archives differ from libraries in their holdings, cataloging, and circulating policies. Archives contain unpublished materials that are considered primary source materials. These can be the "official records of an organization or persons . . . [and] are preserved because of the value of the information they contain" (Termine, 1993). In an archive, instead of using a card catalog to find a book, the researcher uses a finding aid. A finding aid is a published book or catalogue that tells the researcher what is in the archive or repository. The finding aid identifies a collection using a record group, a series, and a subseries. However, the collections are not stored according to these designations. Instead, the collections are stored haphazardly, within aisles, shelves, and box numbers. Libraries contain a discrete number of volumes while archives contains linear (cubic) feet of records. Archives acquire their material by collections. For example, many organizations cannot store or maintain their records and transfer this task to archives. Unlike libraries where books are circulated, archives require that researchers use the materials in the archives. In most archives, the researcher may only use pencil and paper to collect data, or in some places a laptop computer may be used. Most archives require that researchers make an appointment so they can discuss their project with the archivist. Researchers use archives for research and references. In addition, archives provide materials and memorabilia that can be used in exhibitions such as the history of an organization or a person. Because of the fragile nature of some of the primary source materials, archivists will only permit scholars engaged in historical research to use the collections (Termine, 1993).

Archivists and librarians assist researchers to access materials and render an important informational service. However, because of the differences between libraries and archives, the work of these two professional groups varies. While archivists work with the records, papers, manuscripts, and non-printed materials found in the collections, librarians manage the books and publications (see Table 9.1) (Termine, 1993).

DATA TREATMENT

Sources

Unable to go back in time physically, the historical researcher must find some way to understand what actually occurred during an earlier period. In order to research historical antecedents, the researcher must identify

TABLE 9.1   TERMINE'S DIFFERENCES BETWEEN LIBRARIES AND ARCHIVES

	Library	Archives
HOLDINGS	Published materials	Unpublished materials: records, manuscripts, papers.
LOCATORS	Card catalog Call number	Finding aid Record group, series, subseries
	Unique location by subject	Haphazard, location of "boxes" by aisle, shelf, box number
STORED	Volumes (titles)	Linear (cubic) feet
ACQUIRED	Purchased by volume or issue	Donated or purchased collections
USE OF MATERIALS	Circulating	Non-circulation; use of paper and pencil only or laptop computer

Note. From Presentation, "A Talk About Archives," J. Termine, March 31, 1993, State University of New York, Health Science Center at Brooklyn, College of Nursing. Adapted by permission.

sources from the period. Primary sources give firsthand accounts of a person's experience, an institution, or an event, and may lack critical analysis. However, some primary sources, such as personal letters or diaries, may contain the author's interpretation of an event or hearsay. Thus, it is up to the researcher to analyze and interpret the meaning of the primary source.

Ulrich (1990) wrote about Martha Ballard, an 18th century midwife from Hallowell, Maine. Using Ballard's diary as a primary source, Ulrich wrote a rich biographical account of Martha Ballard as well as a historical rendering of everyday life during that period. Ballard's diary, kept daily for over 27 years, connects "several prominent themes in the social history of the early Republic" (Ulrich, 1990, p. 27). More importantly, Ulrich explained, "it [the diary] transforms the nature of the evidence upon [which] much of the history of the period has been written" (p. 27). Prior to Ulrich's use of the diary as a primary source, other historians did not see the potential it had for uncovering historical data about this period in the United States. They perceived Ballard's daily record of the deliveries she assisted with, the travel she endured to reach laboring women, the stories she wrote about other people, and the accounts of her own family as trivial and too filled with daily life to be of any importance. However, Ulrich, when viewing the same diary, believed that it reached directly to the "marrow of eighteenth century life" (p. 33). The "trivia that so annoyed earlier readers provides a consistent, daily record of the operation of a female-managed economy" (p. 33).

Unlike primary sources that are authored by persons directly involved in the event, secondary sources are materials that cite opinions and present interpretations. Newspaper accounts, journal articles, textbooks from the period being studied can be used as secondary sources to place the researcher within the context of that period. Newspaper accounts of the 1893 Columbian World Exposition held in Chicago adds authenticity to the story about the founding of the American Society of Superintendents of Training Schools for Nurses (known today as the National League for Nursing). However, it is important to note that these same secondary sources can be used as primary sources depending on the questions the researcher asks or the purpose of the study (Austin, 1958). For example, although newspaper articles give secondary accounts of what has happened, they also offer insight into what was considered important during the late 19th century. Thus, if insights of individuals present at a particular point in history are being studied, then newspaper accounts can be used as primary as well as secondary sources. Chaney and Folk (1993), for example, used cartoons found in the American Medical Association's published journal, *American Medical News* as a primary source in their study, "A Profession in Caricature: The Changing Attitudes Towards Nursing" in the *American Medical News,* 1960–1989."

Genuine and Authentic

When selecting primary sources, the genuineness and authenticity become important issues. Barzun and Graff (1985) explained that historians are responsible for the verification of documents, thus assuring that they are genuine and authentic. Genuine means that a document is not forged, and authentic means that the document provides the truthful reporting of a subject (Barzun & Graff, 1985). Authenticating sources requires several operations, none of which are fixed in a specific technique. The researcher relies on "attention to detail, on common-sense reasoning, on a 'developed' field for history and chronology, on familiarity with human behavior, and on ever-enlarging stores of information" (Barzun & Graff, 1985, p. 112). Authenticity of letters or journals becomes even more important when the researcher finds them in an attic or a closet of a school of nursing. More than likely, primary sources found in archival collections have already been found to be genuine and authenticated by the institution in which they are housed. Nevertheless, the researcher is responsible for the final authenticity of the document; careful reading of the document, the type of paper, the condition of the material, and an extensive knowledge of the period can all help the researcher verify the document as authentic.

The validity of historical research relies on measures that address matters concerning external and internal criticism. External criticism questions the genuineness of primary sources and assures that the document is what it claims to be. Internal criticism of the data concerns itself with the authenticity or truthfulness of the content. Kerlinger (1986) stated that internal criticism "seeks the 'true' meaning and value of the content of sources of data" (p. 621). The researcher must ask: Does the content accurately reflect the period it is said to be written in? Do the facts conflict with historical dates, meanings of words, and social mores?

Spieseke (1953) said that when determining the reliability of the contents, it is important for researchers to evaluate when authors of primary sources wrote their account, whether it was close to the event or 20 years later. Other questions that must be raised are: Did a trained historian or an observer write the story? and Were facts suppressed, and if so why? To insure the accuracy of the writer, Spieseke suggested the researcher check for corroborating evidence, look for another independent primary source that supports the data, and identify any disagreements between sources. Ulrich (1990), for example, authenticated Ballard's diary by corroborating some of Ballard's entries regarding feed bills with other sources from the town in which she lived.

Data that can be externally validated as genuine, however, can be found to be inconsistent when their contents are examined. For example, letters may have been written by an individual in the 19th century, but the content may conflict with known facts of that period and pose serious questions regarding the *truth* of the content (Kerlinger, 1986). Nevertheless, external criticism "ultimately . . . leads to content analysis or internal criticism and is indispensable when assessing evidence" (Matejski, 1986, p. 189). Austin (1958) illustrates this point by explaining that learning the date of a source (external criticism) helps to determine if the content reflects the period in which it was written (internal criticism) and vice versa.

Data Analysis

Analysis of the data relies on the statement of the subject including the questions raised, the purpose, and the conceptual framework of the study. The themes developed by the researcher direct the data analysis. The researcher frames the findings according to research questions that are generated by the thesis. According to Spieseke (1953), the purpose of the study often directs the analysis of the data. If the researcher wanted to teach a lesson, answer a question, or support an idea, then selection of relevant data is organized accordingly. How the researcher analyzes the material depends, in part, on the thematic organization of conceptual frameworks used in the study. Using social, political, economic, or feminist theory will structure the data and enable the researcher to concentrate on particular areas.

In data analysis, the researcher must deal with the tension between these conflicting truths so that some interpretation or understanding regarding the subject can be found. In some way the researcher must strike a "balance between conflict" (Tholfsen, 1977, p. 246). Questions such as the following need to be asked: Is the content found in the primary and secondary sources congruent with each other or are there conflicting stories? and If the conflict does exist, is there supporting evidence to justify either side of the argument?

Another important aspect of analysis is the researcher's bias regarding the subject and its influence on the interpretation of data. Awareness of the researcher's bias helps to identify a particular frame of reference that may limit or direct the interpretation of the data. Moreover, self-awareness promotes the researcher's *honesty* in finding the truth and decreases the influence of the bias on the interpretation (Austin, 1958; Barzun & Graff, 1985).

Analysis should develop new material and new ideas based on supporting evidence rather than just *rehash* ideas (Matejski, 1986). The researcher seeks to discover new truths from the facts assembled. However, each individual, when given the same data, will analyze the data differently and will thus contribute to the tentative nature of interpretation (Austin, 1958). In order to interpret the findings and get at a truth, the historian must be conscious of the role ideology plays in analysis. The researcher questions how ideology, or any set of ideas, influences the analysis of a particular event. A paternalistic ideological view of the nurse's role in the health care system may starkly contrast with the interpretation of the same data when using a feminist one. Awareness of ideological influence forces the researcher to study the full impact ideas have on an event and to avoid accepting ideas on face value. Tholfsen (1977) argued that history will suffer if taught from any one ideological stance; instead its aim should be the "commitment to the disinterested pursuit of truth, accompanied by an openness to continuing debate and discussion" (p. 255). With this understanding, the researcher analyzes and sorts out the data, and tries to find new truths that can be supported by the evidence produced by the data.

Analysis occurs throughout the process of data collection. The historian looks for evidence to explain events or ideas. By interpreting primary and secondary documents, the researcher forms a picture of a historical antecedents. However, these documents become part of history, only when "they have been subjected to historiography that bridges the gap between lived occurrences and records" (Matejski, 1986, p. 180).

Researchers, in search of true meanings and bridging the gap, must be aware not only of their own bias, and that of ideology, but also of bias from the sources themselves that may impede interpretation. For example, in biographical research, the use of informants through interviews and the use of materials found in archival collections raises issues regarding the accuracy and validity of the data. Historians doing a biographical study need to be cautious of interviews that often present a bias or one-sided view of the individual being studied. Archival holdings of an individual's papers also may be suspect to bias because of the subject's predetermination of what should be included in the collection (Brown, D'Antonio, & Davis, 1991).

An ethical concern regarding the use of an institution's or individual's private papers relates to the right to privacy versus the right to know. Although it is beyond the scope of this chapter to delve into this issue, it is important for the historical researcher to be aware of this dilemma. The researcher must have a clear idea of the kinds of information that need to be obtained from the data. If the source is found in an archive, then the archivist is responsible for seeing that "policy, regulations, and rules—governing his action do exist and are effective" (Rosenthal, 1982, p. 3). However, the scholar has the ultimate responsibility of using the data appropriately. If the goal of the historiographer is further understanding of social, political, or economic relations between individuals, institutions, events, or ideas, then one must question what purpose is served if exploiting or embarrassing details are exposed. Future access and preservation of primary sources are discouraged by the misuse and sensationalism generated by historians who "present conclusions regarding motives and behavior that transcend the evidence . . . [and] turn an ordinary book into a best seller" (Graebner, 1982, p. 23). If this involves the past, then only a historical reputation is damaged; however, if this involves people who are still living or their immediate ancestors, then the right to access is questioned and future contributions of papers from other families or institutions are at risk. When determining how the data should be used, Graebner (1982) suggested that:

> decisions, events, and activities which affect the public welfare or embrace qualities of major human interest—and thus add legitimately to the richness of the historic record -set the acceptable boundaries of historical search and analysis (p. 23).

Interpreting the Findings

The historical narrative is the final stage in the historical research process. This is the stage where the researcher tells the story that interprets the data and engages the reader in the historical debate. Synthesis occurs and findings are connected, supported, and molded "into a related whole" (Austin, 1958, p. 9). Decisions regarding what to include and what to emphasize become important. In historical exposition the researcher explains not only what happened but how and why it happened. Relations between events, ideas, people, organizations, and institutions must be explored and interpreted within the context of the period being studied. The political, social, and economic factors set a stage or backdrop for which to compare and contrast the historical data collected. Historical judgments, based on historical evidence, must pass through the filter of "human understanding of human experience" (Cramer, 1992, p. 7). However, to accomplish this the researcher must be sensitive to the material, must show genuine engagement in the subject, and must balance the forces of self-interest, societal interest, and historical interest. Along with these attributes, the researcher needs creativity in order to achieve a coherent, convincing, and meaningful account (Ashley, 1978; Spicscke, 1953).

When writing the narrative, the researcher is charged with creatively rendering the events, explaining the findings, and supporting the ideas. It requires discipline, organization, and imagination on the part of the historian to accomplish this Herculean task. The historiographer must set aside time to write daily; find a quiet place to concentrate and contemplate the data; use a detailed outline to direct the writing of the manuscript; plan the story using the thematic framework that was established earlier in the study; and use time and place as landmarks to give balance and direct the flow of the story while critically interpreting the findings (Austin, 1958).

The historian weaves together historical facts, research findings, and interpretations influenced by the conceptual framework into a coherent story. To guide the researcher in the writing process, the narrative can be divided into chronological periods. Or, use of geographical places such as regional areas in the United States, thematic relationships, research questions, or political, social, cultural or economic issues also can be used to organize the narrative. These *ad hoc inventions* are determined by the researcher and thus are subject to the researcher's interest, bias, and understanding of the historical method (Cramer, 1992; Fondiller, 1978).

In the writing of history, the writer may want the readers to *hear* the words spoken during the period being studied and uses direct quotes to do so. Direct quotations also provide corroboration of and credibility to the researcher's interpretation. However, while authentic quotes are a useful narrative tool, overquoting must be avoided. It is better to paraphrase the person's words and use limited direct quotes to give the narrative a flavor of the person.

Historiography displays the researcher's creativity and imagination as the story unfolds. Creativity connects thoughts, quotes, and events into a readable story and gives birth to new ideas (Christy, 1978). The interpretations and response to the themes and questions rely on the historian's ability to go beyond the known facts and develop new ideas and new meanings. No two historians will view the same data and respond in exactly the same way. The human filter, through which all information passes, will alter the researcher's response to the data and provide the catalyst for the creation of new ideas (Barzun & Graff, 1985; Christy, 1978).

SUMMARY

The nursing profession needs the infusion of new ideas, new meanings, and new interpretations of its past to explain its place in history and its direction in the future. Ashley (1978) confirmed that connection when she wrote,

> [W]ith creativity as our base, and with strong historical knowledge and awareness, nurses can become pioneers in developing new types of inquiry and turn inward toward self-knowledge and self-understanding (p. 36).

The historical method gives the qualitative researcher tools to explore the past. Using certain guideposts along the way, historiographers formulate ideas, collect the data, validate the genuiness and authenticity, and narrate the story. However, to make the research meaningful, historians must relate the research questions and the findings to the present.

REFERENCES

Ashley, J. (1978). Foundations for scholarship: Historical research in nursing. *Advances in Nursing Science, 1*(1), 25–36.

Austin, A. (1958). The historical method. *Nursing Research, 7*(1), 4–10.

Barzun, J., & Graff, H. F. (1985). *The modern researcher*, 4th ed. San Diego, CA: Harcourt Brace Jovanovich.

Brown, J., D'Antonio, P., & Davis, S. (1991). Report on the Fourth Invitational Nursing History Conference. Unpublished report, Philadelphia, PA.

Bullough, V. (1991). *Social history.* Paper presented at the meeting of Fourth Invitational Conference on Nursing History: Critical Issues Affecting Research and Researchers, Philadelphia, PA.

Chaney, J. A., & Folk, P. (1993). A profession in caricature: The changing attitudes towards nursing in the *American Medical News,* 1960–1989. *Nursing History Review, 1,* 181–201.

Christy, T. (1978). The hope of history. In M. L. Fitzpatrick (Ed.), *Historical studies in nursing* (pp. 3–11). New York: Teachers College Press.

Cramer, S. (1992). The nature of history: Meditations on Clio's Craft. *Nursing Research, 41*(1), 4–7.

Fondiller, S. (1978). Writing the report. In M. L. Fitzpatrick (Ed.),. *Historical studies in nursing* (pp. 25–27). New York: Teachers College Press.

Glass, L. (1991). *[Biographical history].* Paper presented at the meeting of Fourth Invitational Conference on Nursing History: Critical Issues Affecting Research and Researchers, Philadelphia, PA.

Graebner, N. A. (1982). History, society, and the right to privacy. In *The scholar's right to know versus the individual's right to privacy: Proceedings of the first Rockefeller Archive Center Conference, December 5, 1975* (pp. 20–24). Pocantico Hills, NY: Rockefeller Archive Center Publication.

Hamilton, D. (1991). *Intellectual history.* Paper presented at the meeting of Fourth Invitational Conference on Nursing History: Critical Issues Affecting Research and Researchers, Philadelphia, PA.

Hamilton, D. B. (1993). The idea of history and the history of ideas. *Image Journal of Nursing Scholarship, 25*(1), 45–50.

Hanson, K. S. (1989). The emergence of liberal education in nursing education, 1893 to 1923. *Journal of Professional Nursing, 5*(2), 83–91.

Hofstadter, R. (1959). History and the social sciences. In F. Stern (Ed.), *The varieties of history* (pp. 359–370). New York: Meridan.

Kerlinger, F. N. (1986). *Foundations of behavioral research,* 3rd ed. New York: Holt, Rinehart & Winston.

Kruman, M. (1985) Historical method: Implications for nursing research. In M. M. Leininger (Ed.), *Qualitative research methods in nursing* (pp. 109–118). Orlando, FL: Grune & Stratton.

Lewenson, S. B. (1990). The women's nursing and suffrage movement, 1893–1920. In V. Bullough, B. Bullough, & M. Stanton (Eds.), *Florence Nightingale and her era: A collection of new scholarship* (pp. 117–118). New York: Garland Publishing.

Lewenson, S. B. (1993). *Taking charge: Nursing, suffrage and feminism, 1873–1920.* New York: Garland Press.

Lynaugh, J., & Reverby, S. (1987). Thoughts on the nature of history. *Nursing Research, 36*(1), 4–69.

Matejski, M. (1986). Historical research: The method. In P. L. Munhall & C. J. Oiler (Eds.), *Nursing research: A qualitative perspective* (pp. 175–193). Norwalk, CT: Appleton-Century-Crofts.

Newton, M. (1965). The case for historical research. *Nursing Research, 14,* 20–26.

Rines, A., & Kershner, F. (1979). *Information concerning historical studies.* Unpublished. New York: Teachers College Columbia University, Department of Nursing.

Rosenthal, R. (1982). Who will be responsible for private papers of private people?: Some considerations from the view of the private depository. In *The scholar's right to know versus the individual's right to privacy: Proceedings of the first Rockefeller Archive Center Conference, December 5, 1975* (pp. 3–6). Pocantico Hills, NY: Rockefeller Archive Center Publication.

Spieseke, A. W. (1953). What is the historical method of research? *Nursing Research, 2*(1), 36–37.

Termine, J. (1993). *A talk about archives.* Paper presented at the State University, Health Science Center at Brooklyn College of Nursing, Brooklyn, New York.

Tholfsen, T. R. (1977). The ambiguous virtues of the study of history. *Teachers College Record, 79*(2), 245–257.

Ulrich, L. T. (1990). *A midwife's tale: The life of Martha Ballard based on her diary 1785–1812.* New York: Vintage Books.

Historical Research Approach Applied to Nursing Education, Practice, and Administration

When historiography should be used and who should use it raises questions regarding the appropriate selection of this method. The historical method has been used to study nursing education, administration, and practice when historical understanding of relations in these areas has been needed. Chapter 10 highlights how researchers in nursing education, administration, and practice utilize historical methodology. It offers support to future historians by identifying attributes needed by the researcher and by explicating the criteria for evaluating completed research from the steps in the historical research process discussed in Chapter 9. To illustrate the appropriateness of this method in these varied professional settings and to encourage further research, this chapter explores potential areas for application of historiography and critiques some of the historical studies already completed in nursing education, administration, and practice. A reprint of the Poslusny (1989) study can be found at the end of the chapter to assist the reader in understanding the critiquing process.

ATTRIBUTES REQUIRED OF THE HISTORIOGRAPHER

Although few formal guidelines exist to direct the historical researcher, some attributes are needed by the researcher to assist in the process. The historiographer searches for facts and evidence that will unveil the nature and relations regarding historical events, ideas, institutions, or people. To accurately assess historical meanings, the researcher must assure the reader of external validity that confirms that the source is what it claims to be. At the same time, the internal validity of the source must be established, verifying the consistency between the genuineness of the primary source and the authenticity of the data. Following these steps, the historiographer must organize the ideas and make connections, while acknowledging personal and ideological bias. The researcher must interpret the material making sense of the data as the story unfolds; this requires narrative and explanatory skills.

Accuracy is important to the historiographer and requires skill. Helpful in this process are the systems the researcher develops to maintain accuracy. How the researcher collects data, organizes the bibliography, and numbers the different drafts of the narrative assists in the accurate accounting of the story. The historiographer must organize the data and tell the story in a logical fashion. The researcher must address questions that arise from the data honestly, trying to understand and explain what the data are describing. The researcher must be prepared to answer questions such as: Did an event noted in a source actually happen? or Could it have happened as it was noted in the primary source? Throughout the study the historiographer must be true to the data, allowing them to unfold and bring a better understanding of the subject. This requires a self-awareness of the researcher's own bias and honesty in relation to the findings. Does the researcher's own bias hinder discovery of new meanings that may be revealed? Essential among the attributes needed by the researcher is imagination. Imagination lets the researcher make connections in the data and create a story that assists in learning more of the truth (Barzun & Graff, 1985).

According to Spieseke (1953), the historical researcher must be able to locate and collect data, analyze the reliability of the data, organize and arrange the data into a pattern, and express "it [the data] in meaningful and effective language" (p. 37). The narrative should show the successful attainment of these four important skills, thus providing a method to evaluate the process. The narrative not only tells the story but allows the researcher (and others) to critique the study as well.

Table 10.1 organizes the data presented in Chapter 9 and suggests some criteria to use when evaluating historical research. Later in this chapter, the criteria are used to review some of the published studies in the areas of nursing education, administration, and practice. However, it is important to note that because published historical research should read as an interesting narrative, analysis using a specific instrument such as Table 10.1 is inhibiting. The reviewer needs to know that any guide is just a guide to follow, not an absolute rule. Headings may not clearly delineate primary or secondary sources or personal bias (as perhaps it would in a historical dissertation or in other forms of reported research). Nevertheless, used as a guide, Table 10.1 highlights important features of historical research and helps the consumer critique its worth more effectively.

An answer to the question of what came first, the chicken or the egg? epitomizes the dilemma in deciding whether to use the historical method first, or to let the area of interest guide the decision regarding choice of method. Why select historical method in nursing education, administration, or practice when so many other methods have worked in the past and continue to serve many researchers well? The research questions or conflicts that need historical explicating determine this. Armed with the appropriate historians' attributes, the historical researcher (or historiographer) ventures into these unstudied areas and formulates specific questions. However, following the selection of the subject, the topic must be narrowed to enable the researcher to study the area fully. To create and build a wealth of historical knowledge requires teamwork or the linkage of several historical studies that will eventually fill gaps and offer a fuller understanding of history (Bloch, 1964). The historian probes historical antecedents in broad areas of nursing education, administration, and practice in order to explain relations, ideas, or events that influenced nursing's professional development in these areas. Review of previous studies helps the researcher determine his/her own course of study and stimulates imagination.

HISTORICAL STUDIES IN NURSING PRACTICE

Nursing education has such close historical ties with nursing practice that to study one means studying the other. During the late 19th century and well into the 20th century, hospitals relied heavily on student nurses to provide patient care. Change in the traditional, apprenticeship educational model and the move to university-based educational settings dramatically and economically altered the delivery of care in hospitals and nursing practice. Prior to these changes, graduate nurses, upon completing their training, were rarely hired to staff hospitals and were forced to look elsewhere for jobs. Graduate nurses worked outside of hospitals as private duty and public health nurses.

In 1928, Wolf (1991) addressed the National League of Nursing Education (now known as the National League for Nursing) regarding the transition of graduate nurses employed by hospitals. Wolf explained how graduate nurses who provided patient care as opposed to student nurses would be advantageous to hospital administrators, nursing educators, and to the graduate nurses. Aside from stabilizing nursing service, providing an excellent service, and profiting the employer and employee, Wolf (1991) argued that hiring graduate nurses would improve the value society placed on nursing service. Wolf believed that graduate nurses faced undue criticism from hospital administrators who believed that student nurses were more "buoyant, resilient, and enthusiastic" (Wolf, 1991, p. 140) than graduates.

TABLE 10.1   HISTORICAL RESEARCH QUESTIONS TO BE ADDRESSED

Generation of Data

Title	1. How does it concisely reflect the purpose of the study?
	2. How does it clearly tell the reader what the study is about?
	3. How does it delineate the time frame for the study?
Statement of the Subject	1. Is the subject easily researched?
	2. What themes and theses are studied?
	3. What are the research questions?
	4. Are there primary sources available to study the subject?
	5. Has it been studied before?
	6. What makes this study different or similar than others?
	7. What is the significance to nursing?
	8. What is the rationale for the time frame for the study?
Literature Review	1. What are the main works written on the subject?
	2. What time period does the literature review cover?
	3. What are some of the problems that may arise when studying this subject?
	4. Can primary sources be identified?
	5. Was the subject narrowed during the literature review?
	6. What research questions were raised during the literature review?

Treatment of Data

Primary Sources	1. How were primary sources used?
	2. Were they genuine and authentic?
	4. How was external validity determined?
	5. How was internal validity determined?
	6. Were there inconsistencies between the external validity and internal validity?
	7. Does the content accurately reflect the period of concern?
	8. Do the facts conflict with historical dates, meanings of words, and social mores?
	9. When did the primary author write the account?
	10. Did a trained historian or an observer author the source?
	11. Were facts suppressed, and if so, why?
	12. Is there corroborating evidence?
	13. Identify any disagreements between sources.
Secondary Sources	1. What were the secondary sources used?
	2. How were secondary sources used?
	3. Do they corroborate the primary source?
	4. Can you identify any disagreements between sources?

(cont'd.)

TABLE 10.1 (CONT'D.)

Data Analysis

Organization
1. What conceptual frameworks were used in the study?
2. How would the study be classified: intellectual, feminist, social, political, biographical?
3. Were the research questions answered?
4. Was the purpose of the study accomplished?
5. If conflict exists within the findings, was there supporting evidence to justify either side of the argument?

Bias
1. Was the researcher's bias identified?
2. Was analysis influenced by a present-mindedness?
3. What were the ideological biases?
4. How did bias affect the analysis of the data?

Ethical Issue
1. Was there any infringement on historical reputation?
2. Was there a conflict between the right to privacy versus the right to know?
3. Did the research show that decisions, events, and activities of an individual or organization affected the public welfare or embraced qualities of major human interest?

Interpreting the Findings

Narrative
1. Does the story describe what happened, including how and why it happened?
2. Were relations between events, ideas, people, organizations, and institutions explained, interpreted, and placed within a contextual framework?
3. How were direct quotations used (too limited or too long)?
4. Was the narrative clear, concise, and interesting to read?
5. Was the significance to nursing explicit?

Guidelines for evaluating historical research

Yet, Wolf argued that "the graduate nurse sees more to be done for a patient than a student, she knows better what to do" (p. 140).

Wolf's (1991) speech provides the historian with a perspective of someone personally involved in the changes that occurred in nursing practice history which had profound effects on the shape of things to come. Historical research in the development of nursing practice might examine nursing practice in hospitals, private duty, or in public health. External factors such as wars, economic depressions, advances in medicine and science affected the development of nursing practice and pose an infinite number of ways to approach the study of nursing practice. Primary and secondary sources can be found in speeches presented at various professional meetings, in minutes of professional meetings, and in graduation addresses. Archives of hospitals, schools of nursing, and visiting nurse services contain data that tell the story of nursing practice.

Discussions in the literature defining nurses' roles, specialization, and society's value of care find its origins in history. Bullough (1992) explained that "clinical specialization started in the early twentieth century as nurses with advanced knowledge and training were needed to care for groups of patients with special needs"(p. 254). Specialties emerged in nursing such as nurse anesthetist, nurse-midwifery, public health nursing, and critical care nursing that demanded additional education, practical experience, and in some instances certification. Unanswered questions raised regarding the development of different specialties and the needed qualifications for each lend themselves to historical inquiry.

CRITIQUE OF A STUDY IN NURSING PRACTICE

In a recently published article, "Watchful Vigilance: Nursing Care, Technology, and the Development of Intensive Care Units," Fairman (1992) analyzed the active role nurses played in the development of intensive care units (ICUs). The first part of the title articulates the type of care, watchful vigilance, while the second half includes the areas to be compared, contrasted, and studied—nursing care, technology, and the development of intensive care units. Fairman found after a review of historical studies on the development of ICUs that nursing care had not been studied, "rendering nurses' work invisible and unacknowledged" (Fairman, 1992, p. 56). Fairman clearly identified for the reader two areas nursing had contributed to the development of the ICUs. The first was the "traditional practice of intensive observation and triage" (p. 56), that provided the model of care used in ICUs in the 1950s; the second was the ICU nurse's increased status in the work environment and newly gained expertise as he or she sought more experiences and education in this specialty.

Traditional nursing roles, observation, and triage provided the prototype for the model of care in the newly developed ICUs. The "watchful vigilance" of the private duty nurse and the triage of patients according to physiological stability served as the model and thus, according to Fairman (1992), represented "a continuity rather than a novel approach in the care of the critically ill" (p. 56).

Fairman (1992) narrated the history of the origins of the ICUs clearly and comprehensively. One of the earliest sources used to describe observation and triage by nurses begins with the passage from a Civil War nurse and author, Louisa May Alcott, who described how she had divided the ward into three rooms, "my duty room, my pleasure room, and my pathetic room. . . ." (Alcott quoted in Fairman, 1992, p. 56). Later developments in the United States such as the rise in the use of hospitals, and an "increasingly complex patient population" (Fairman, 1992, p. 56) contributed to the development of these special care units. Multiple factors affecting the use of hospitals and the type of patient receiving care altered the delivery of nursing care and created a need for an open space to provide the critically ill patient with the traditional nurse's role of observation and triage.

Throughout the narrative, Fairman (1992) provided a critical analysis of the evolution of ICUs. Changes in hospital architecture removed patients from the easily observable open ward and placed them in private and semi-private rooms, forever altering the way nurses delivered care. When the importance of close observation by private duty nurses and triage by nurses for critically ill patients became apparent to hospital administrators and physicians, they opted to develop units that used this model. However, Fairman (1992) notes that hospital administrators and physicians selected the ICU as a way to improve hospital conditions rather than support other possible strategies such as increasing nurses' pay and reducing the high turnover rate.

Fairman (1992) used descriptions from ICU nurses to provide and support the historical account depicting the care nurses gave in ICUs and the introduction of new technology. Primary and secondary sources such as taped interviews, books, dissertations, and photographs are evidenced within the text of the article. Those nurses selected to work in the early ICUs gained status in the hospital social hierarchy. Moreover, families of patients in ICU had higher expectations of these nurses than they did of the staff nurses on general wards. In addition, ICU nurses, because of additional experience and training, felt somewhat apart from the other nurses (Fairman, 1992).

Fairman (1992) explained that once ICUs became established in hospitals, physicians claimed ownership of the space, forcing nurses and doctors to renegotiate their relationships in this area. Shared expertise developed and collaborative agreements formed between the two groups as they worked closely in these areas. With an increase in the number of ICUs in the 1960s and 1970s, and with increasing reliance on technology, the close observation and triage role of the nurse underwent further changes. Fairman argued that the "watchful vigilance of patients was obscured by enthusiasm for machines as the ICU became a technological repository" (p. 58). However, Fairman noted that as society is becoming uncomfortable with the technological takeover, the ICU is rediscovering its roots and developing an appreciation of nurses' significant influence in the ICU through their traditional practices. These practices, Fairman explained, have led to the success in the care of the critically ill patient, and thus have "empowered nurses in the political process of health care decision, validating nurses' work" (Fairman, 1992, p. 58).

Fairman's (1992) clear and interesting account of the contribution nurses made in the care of the critically ill patient and in the success and development of the ICU is one example of historical research in nursing practice. In each area of nursing practice, a history exists that can be studied and used to explain an important aspect of that practice today.

HISTORICAL STUDIES IN NURSING EDUCATION

Researchers interested in nursing education concern themselves with varied aspects of this subject such as an analysis of nursing texts (Davis, 1988a), a history of educational funding (Hardy, 1988), the development of university education in nursing (Baer, 1992), or the biography of an important figure in nursing education (Downer, 1989). Topics in nursing education ranging from curriculum design to control of education can be addressed using historical frameworks. This approach not only provides background descriptive information but also answers relevant questions regarding issues that concern nursing today.

Currently, several areas such as adult learners, critical thinking, and cultural diversity concern nursing educators. However, the historian may question the idea of adult learners being new in nursing education and attempt to understand this topic by studying the nursing student of the past. One way to do this is to return to past records of nurse training schools or professional studies of nursing. For example, the 1923 Goldmark study entitled "Nursing and Nursing Education in the United States" noted that in 1911 about 70% of the training schools required students to be 20 or 21 years old for admission; however, within seven years, the age requirement had dropped to 18 or 19 years. Why did the admission age drop at that time and why did training schools initially believe older women would be better training school candidates? What teaching strategies worked better with older women than with younger ones? Both question the past and yet relate to pertinent issues surrounding the adult learner of today.

Another contemporary issue, encouraging critical thinking among nursing students, has its roots in nursing's history. For example, in 1897, Superintendent of Bellevue Training School [Agnes] Brennan addressed the Superintendent's Society and said:

> An uneducated woman may become a good nurse, but never an intelligent one; she can obey orders conscientiously and understand thoroughly a sick person's need, but should an emergency arise, where is she? She works through her feelings, and therefore lacks judgement (Brennan, 1991, p. 23).

Was Brennan referring to critical thinking when she reasoned that nurses needed to have the knowledge and theory regarding pathology to understand the appropriate care of the sick? Brennan believed it was equally important for nurses to spend time in clinical practice, learning the "character of the pulse in different patients or finding out just why some nurses can always see at a glance that this patient requires her pillow turned" (Brennan, 1991, p. 24). She firmly believed that a trained nurse required both the theoretical and the practical and that without both something would be missing in the nursing care given. To Brennan, "theory fortifies the practical, practice strengthens and retains the theoretical" (Brennan, 1991, p. 25). Brennan discussed clearly her views on the theory/practice dichotomy that still baffles nursing educators today. However, Brennan firmly believed that nurses must be educated to think in order to practice.

Historiography addresses the contemporary issue of cultural diversity by studying racial tensions in nursing and in society and allowing the researcher a better understanding of the conflicts involved. Historians may question, Was there cultural diversity in nursing? or Where did the nursing student at the beginning of the nineteenth century come from? or What socio-economic-political background did the student bring to nursing?

Hine (1989), in the book *Black Women in White: Racial Conflict and Cooperation in the Nursing Profession, 1890–1950,* described the opening of training schools for African-Americans who were excluded from most of the existing nurses training schools in the United States. While all schools did not racially discriminate, many schools that admitted African-Americans did so using quotas. The very origins of the National Association of Colored Graduate Nurses in 1908 speaks to the early exclusion of African-Americans from the first two national nursing organizations, the American Society of Superintendents of Training Schools for Nurses (renamed the NLNE in 1912), and the Associated Alumnae of the United States and Canada (renamed the American Nurses' Association in 1911). The historian needs to look at what was, as well as what was not, to better understand historical events. For example, how did nursing handle cultural diversity? When did the profession welcome people of different race, color, and creed into the profession? and Who were the advocates of an integrated society?

The historian who searches for answers may learn that two years before the founding of the National Association of Colored Graduates Nurses (NACGN) in 1908, nursing political activist Lavinia Dock spoke out against prejudicial treatment of any professional nurse; Dock (1910) cited the need for practical ethics to be demonstrated in nursing and ardently hoped that the nursing association [the ANA] would not ever "get to the point where it draws the color line against our negro sister nurses" (p. 902). She always believed that the Nurses' Association was one place in America where color boundaries were not drawn. However, as the

ANA expanded, Dock witnessed "evidences" that made her think "that this cruel and unchristian and unethical prejudice might creep in here in our association" (p. 902). Dock said that under no circumstances should nurses emulate the cruel prejudices displayed by men and urged nurses to treat each nurse of color "as we would like to be treated ourselves" (p. 902). She supported black nursing leader Adah Thoms who became president of the NACGN and a politically active nursing leader who in 1929 wrote the history of African-American nurses in a book entitled *The Pathfinders* (Davis, 1988b).

Questions raised by conflicting ideas in the data and omission of information in the narrative suggest new areas for historical inquiry. One such example of this is a recent historical doctoral dissertation by Mosley (1992) entitled "A History of Black Leaders in Nursing: The Influence of Four Black Community Nurses on the Establishment, Growth, and Practice of Public Health Nursing in New York City, 1900-1930." Mosley included a section specifically addressing institutional racism as it existed in nursing during the first 30 years of this century. To understand the prejudice experienced by African-American nurses, Mosley focused on the lives and contributions of four leaders in public health nursing: Jessie Sleet Scales, Mabel Staupers, Elizabeth W. Tyler, and Edith M. Carter.

CRITIQUE OF A STUDY IN NURSING EDUCATION

Historical research explores and analyzes past events as society's values and beliefs influenced nursing education. In the recently published study entitled "Aspirations Unattained: The Story of the Illinois Training School's Search for University Status," Baer (1992) described how "against a backdrop of one century's turning into another, with attendant changes in the garb of charity and the power of medicine . . . nursing got caught between shifting social priorities" (p. 43). Baer used the history of the Illinois Training School (ITS) and its unattained goal for university status to illustrate nursing's predicament at being caught between society's shifting values in charity and the increasing power of medicine. Baer's title tells the reader what the subject of the discourse is, unattained aspirations of ITS, as well as introduces the notion of nursing's historical efforts to move toward university education for nurses. Although the dates of the study are not included in the title, the period is established during the time when the Illinois Training School sought university status.

Baer (1992) set the time frame of the study between the Civil War and the Great Depression and located it at the ITS in Chicago, Illinois. Several archival repositories provided Baer with primary source materials to study the ITS' attempt to become a school within the University of Chicago. Diaries, "Memorandum of Agreement," Annual Reports of the

ITS, papers, and letters were some of the primary sources that Baer used in the study. Supporting secondary sources included published historiographies such as *Ordered to Care: The Dilemma of American Nursing, 1850–1945* by Reverby (1987) and *"The Physician's Hand" Work Culture and Conflict in American Nursing* Melosh (1982). In addition, newspaper accounts from the period as well as the 1923 Goldmark report provided Baer with further evidence for the study. Today, when several different entry levels into practice confound the definition of the professional registered nurse, it is significant to see the difficulty that one nurses training school had in offering a university-based education.

Baer (1992) juxtaposed nursing in the late 19th and early 20th century against a backdrop of the declining role philanthropists played in supporting social welfare programs. The shift in the United States away from individual philanthropic support toward other areas of financial support led the ITS to seek new sponsors. The ITS, chartered in 1880, became one of the important training schools in America. Among the superintendents who ran the ITS were such notable nursing leaders as Isabel Hampton, Isabel McIsaac, and Laura Logan. Successful at several fund-raising efforts, over time the ITS underwent expansion and acquired real estate properties. According to Baer, by 1926 the ITS's "real estate and other assets reached a value of $500,000" (p. 45). The Goldmark Report (Goldmark, 1984), funded by the Rockefeller Foundation and several notable nursing leaders, supported the movement toward university-based nursing education. The Chicago University had planned to open a school of medicine and a school of nursing. In 1927, the University of Chicago Medical School and Billings Hospital opened; however, the planned school of nursing never materialized. While the medical school was being planned, negotiations between the university and the ITS were under way. An agreement reached in 1926, called the 1926 Memoranda Agreement, provided for the transfer of the ITS assets to the University of Chicago, allowing for the development of a university-based program. It was planned that bachelor's degrees would be awarded to nurses who completed the program and that the official merger would take place three years later in December 1929.

Baer (1992) narrated the story of the ITS merger with the University of Chicago explaining the many problems that plagued the ill-fated agreement. While the University of Chicago had already claimed the assets of the ITS, the Great Depression, beginning only one month before the agreement was to begin, decreased the size of the ITS assets. As a result, the promised university-based school of nursing never opened as agreed upon in 1926. Baer identifies several factors that allowed opponents of the plan to prevent the formation of the school, such as the over production of nurses during the 1920s, changes in "key university personnel,

diminishing loyalties among ITS constituents, the absence of a unified
national nursing education position, and a radically altered economic
environment" (p. 47). In one day the ITS became the Cook County School
of Nursing and the agreement with the University of Chicago never mate-
rialized. It was not until 1949 that the newly formed Cook County training school embraced collegiate education when it merged with the University of Illinois.

Baer (1992) fluidly described the plan for the University of Chicago
School of Nursing as well as offering a rich critique of the events.
Although the merger between the school of nursing and the university
failed to occur, the proposed plan gave nurses an "educational presence"
(p. 47) that they probably would not have had otherwise. Nevertheless,
Baer continued,

> lost in the valley between two women's movement, two world wars,
> altered national beliefs about benevolence, and rolling economic circum-
> stances, the ITS Board, faculty, and graduates neither provided the nec-
> essary leadership nor protested the university's failure to comply (p. 47).

Baer explained the relationship between the factors that inhibited the con-
summation of the merger agreement and presented the contextual background to do so. For example, nursing leadership was divided on the
issue of whether to move professional education from hospital-based
schools into colleges and universities. This division resulted in little support for the proposed ITS plan or a united protest when the plan failed.
Baer's narrative is clear, concise, and interesting to read. It used direct
quotes sparingly throughout the text to expand or support an idea. Baer's
work offers insight into the effect historical events influenced by society's value has on the development of nursing education in America.

HISTORICAL STUDIES IN NURSING ADMINISTRATION

By now it should be clear to the reader that doing historical research
requires creativity. One can select a topic of interest and study it using different approaches. Studying the history of nursing organizations founded
by nursing leaders provides the researcher with a fertile field of study.
An example of a nursing administration research study would be the study
of the beginnings of the National League for Nursing which epitomizes
the efforts of nurse administrators to organize and control nursing education and practice (Birnbach & Lewenson, 1991). The National League
for Nursing began in 1893 when a group of nursing superintendents in
charge of nurses training schools met in Chicago at the Columbian Exposition. Superintendents throughout the United States met and founded

the American Society of Superintendents of Training Schools for Nurses of the United States and Canada. In 1912 this organization became the National League of Nursing Education, and in 1952 it became the National League for Nursing. Superintendents started this organization so they could collectively address the issues confronting the developing profession. They advocated reforms such as improving educational standards, developing uniform training school curriculums, decreasing working hours, and increasing the number of years of training. Through their efforts, the organization developed needed educational reforms in nursing and fostered the control of practice.

To study nursing administration, the researcher might use biographies of nursing leaders. Biography offers insight into the characteristics as well as the role of the person.

Biography need not be limited to one person but may compare and contrast the relationships of a group of leaders, such as in the study by Poslusny (1989).

CRITIQUE OF A HISTORICAL STUDY IN NURSING ADMINISTRATION

Poslusny (1989), in the published article, "Feminist Friendship: Isabel Hampton Robb, Lavinia Lloyd Dock, and Mary Adelaide Nutting," examined the friendships among three nursing leaders during the late 19th and early 20th century. The title clearly indicates the type of relationship— feminist friendship—that these three women shared. Introducing the subject, Poslusny, established the social and political texture of the period and provided an overview of nursing's contributions. Amidst the backdrop of movements that advocated woman suffrage, social reform, and motherhood, nursing was identified as the first professional group of women to organize, to publish a journal, and to belong to the international community of women. Poslusny argued that some women entered nursing as a "way of entering the battle against male-dominated social structure" (p. 64). However, she observed that nurses in the early 20th century woman movement (woman movement is reflective of early 20th century terminology) were rarely credited for their feminist positions, and seldom do feminists and nurses in the late 20th century feminist movement support the goals of each group.

Poslusny (1989) defined *feminist friendship* as interpersonal support among women that becomes "a dialectic between struggle and victory, between nurture and empowerment" (p. 64). Although this relationship did not reflect the ideology of the woman's movement, Poslusny believed it reflected women's support for each other while striving for recognition and influence in the world. Poslusny clearly explained that feminist friendship served as the "framework for unity and progress in nursing at the turn of the century" (p. 64).

Poslusny (1989) studied Robb, Dock, and Nutting because of their significant role in nursing practice, education, and administration. Their professional relationship began at the Johns Hopkins Hospital Training School for Nurses (JH). Robb was superintendent of nurses there in 1889 and invited Dock, whom she had known while a student at Bellevue School of Nursing, to be her assistant. While at JH, Robb and Dock met Nutting, one of the nursing students at the school. As a framework for the study Poslusny used the social context of the Progressive Era, drawing attention to women's lives and social relations within a Victorian society and the economic status of women in a newly industrialized society. Poslusny drew parallels between the nursing profession and women's roles, and used this to describe the relationship among Robb, Dock, and Nutting.

Poslusny (1989) used several secondary sources that offer a contemporary feminist analysis of the period such as Cook (1979), Cott (1984), Ehrenreich and English (1973), and Smith-Rosenberg (1975). This builds upon earlier feminist critiques of social and economic institutions such as Mill (1970) and Gilman (1966). Other secondary sources that contribute to the work include biographical material such as Noel's (1980) doctoral dissertation on Robb and Marshall's (1972) biography of Nutting. Primary source documentation is extensive and reveals letters, personal notations, books, professional journals, and speeches of the three women studied.

Dock's close ties with women such as Lillian Wald (a trained nurse) and Jane Addams, activists in the social settlement movement, corroborated Poslusny's (1989) thesis that women sought support from other women for empowerment. Poslusny furthered this thesis in the relationship established among Robb, Dock, and Nutting. Different than the settlement house workers who lived and worked together, Robb, Dock, and Nutting developed close bonds because of similar ideology regarding the growth of the nursing profession. Like other professional women of this era, Robb, Dock, and Nutting shared a commonality of ideas that established their relationship. Poslusny explained that the idea of friendship was somewhere between the Victorian tradition and the platonic ideal. The relationship shared by Robb, Dock, and Nutting, stretched further than intimacy or empowerment. They found purpose and unity for their friendship in the profession they shared.

Poslusny (1989) presented biographical descriptions of each of the women studied and used several quotes from each to highlight the relationship they established. Poslusny described Robb as a visionary, Dock as a revolutionary, and Nutting as an administrator. Poslusny analyzed the nature of their relationship, connecting it to ideas regarding feminist friendship. Poslusny presented divergent views on feminist friendship and the contributions to nursing practice, education, and administration made by the three women. Both personal and political dimensions were included in the discussion of the professional relationship, and Poslusny furthered the discussion by relating it to contemporary issues such as networking, mentoring, and collaboration. Change in society requires a "unified commitment to intervene personally in the socioeconomic conditions and the political structure . . .[and] has been made in the context of personal support" (p. 67). Poslusny argued that feminist friendship is the "framework for unity and progress" (p. 67) and suggested that the relationship among Robb, Dock, and Nutting provides an excellent example of this type of friendship.

SUMMARY

In each area, nursing practice, education, and administration, historians have an opportunity to study different facets of nursing. Creativity, an open mind, and fortitude assist the historical researcher in finding new sources to study, to make connections between events, ideas, and people, and to analyze the findings critically. No less important to this process is the ability to write an interesting narrative that holds the reader's attention and permits the flow of ideas. Equipped with this knowledge and the correct attributes, the researcher interested in writing history may begin.

REFERENCES

Baer, E. (1992). Aspirations unattained: The story of the Illinois Training School's search for university status. *Nursing Research, 41*(1), 43–48.

Barzun, J., & Graff, H. F. (1985). *The modern researcher,* 4th ed. San Diego, CA: Harcourt Brace Jovanovich.

Birnbach, N., & Lewenson, S. (Eds.) (1991). *First words: Selected addresses from the National League for Nursing 1894–1933.* New York: National League for Nursing Press.

Bloch, M. (1964). *The historian's craft.* New York: Vantage Books.

Brennan, A. (1991). Comparative value of theory and practice in nursing. In N. Birnbach & S. Lewenson (Eds.), *First words: Selected addresses from the National League for Nursing 1894–1933* (pp. 23–25). New York: National League for Nursing Press. Original speech presented in 1897.

Bullough, B. (1992). Alternative models for specialty nursing practice. *Nursing and Health Care, 13*(5), 254–259.

Cook, B. W. (1979). Female support networks and political activists: Lillian Wald, Crystal Eastman, Emma Goldman. In N. F. Cott & E. H. Pleck (Eds.), *A heritage of her own: Toward a new social history of American women.* New York: Simon and Schuster.

Cott, N. F. (1984) Passionless: An interpretation of Victorian sexual ideology, 1790–1850. In J. W. Leavitt (Ed.), *Women and health in America: Historical readings* (pp. 57–69). Madison, WI: University of Wisconsin Press.

Davis, S. (1988a). *Evolution of the American nursing history text: 1907–1983.* Columbia University Teachers College, Ed.D. UMI order #PUZ8906485.

Davis, S. (1988b). Adah Belle Samuels Thoms. In V. Bullough, O. M. Church, & A. P. Stein (Eds.), *American nursing: A biographical dictionary* (pp. 313–316). New York: Garland Publishing.

Dock, L. (1910). Report of the thirteenth annual convention. *American Journal of Nursing, 10* (11), 902.

Downer, J. L. (1989). *Education for democracy: Isabel Stewart and her education, 1878–1963.* Columbia University, Teachers College, Ed.D. UMI order # PUZ9013541.

Ehrenreich, B., & English, D. (1973). *Complaints and disorders: The sexual politics of sickness.* New York: Feminist Press.

Fairman, J. (1992). Watchful vigilance: Nursing care, technology, and the development of intensive care units. *Nursing Research, 41*(1), 56–60.

Gilman, C. P. (1966). *Women and economics: A study of the economic relation between men and women as a factor in social evolution.* New York: Harper Torchbooks. Original work published in 1898.

Goldmark, J. (1984). *Nursing and nursing education in the United States.* New York: Garland Publishing. Original work published in 1923.

Hardy, M. A. (1988). Political savvy or lost opportunity? Evolution of American Nurses' Association policy for nursing education funding 1952–1972. *Journal of Professional Nursing, 4*(3), 205–217.

Hine, D. C. (1989). *Black women in white: Racial conflict and cooperation in the nursing profession, 1890–1950.* Bloomington, IN: Indiana University Press.

Marshall, H. E. (1972). *Mary Adelaide Nutting: Pioneer of modern nursing.* Baltimore: Johns Hopkins University Press.

Melosh, B. (1982). *The physician's hand: Work, culture and conflict in American nursing.* Philadelphia: Temple University Press.

Mill, J. S. (1970). *The subjection of women.* Cambridge, MA: MIT Press. Original work published in 1869.

Mosley, M .O. P. (1992) A history of black leaders in nursing: The influence of four black community health nurses on the establishment, growth, and practice of public health nursing in New York City, 1900–1930. (Doctoral dissertation, Teachers College, Columbia University, 1992.) *Dissertation Abstracts International,* Vol. 53/02-B, 774.

Noel, N. L. (1980) Isabel Hampton Robb: Architect of American nursing. (Doctoral dissertation, Teachers College, Columbia University, 1979) *Dissertation Abstracts International, 41*(1), 132B.

Poslusny, S. (1989). Feminist friendship: Isabel Hampton Robb, Lavinia Lloyd Dock, and Mary Adelaide Nutting. *Image: Journal of Nursing Scholarship, 21*(2), 64–68.

Reverby, S. M. (1987). *Ordered to care: The dilemma of American nursing 1850–1945.* London: Cambridge University Press.

Smith-Rosenberg, C. (1975). The female world of love and ritual: Relations between women in nineteenth-century American. *Signs, 1*, 1–29.

Spieseke, A. W. (1953). What is the historical method of research? *Nursing Research, 2*(1), 36–37.

Wolf, A. (1991). How can general duty be made more attractive to graduate nurses? In N. Birnbach & S. Lewenson (Eds.), *First words: Selected addresses from the National League for Nursing 1894–1933* (pp. 138–147). New York: National League for Nursing Press. Original speech presented in 1928.

Research Article

Feminist Friendship:
Isabel Hampton Robb,
Lavinia Lloyd Dock
and Mary Adelaide Nutting

Susan M. Poslusny

Three nurses who met at the Johns Hopkins School of Nursing were the architects of professional nursing education and the founders of the major professional organizations in nursing: Isabel Hampton Robb, Lavinia Lloyd Dock and Mary Adelaide Nutting. Their relationship was an important part of the context in which feminism, social reform and nursing came together at the turn of the century. This paper explores the social context that structured their professional interests as well as their personal relationships.

> Why should there be this lack of harmony in our nursing ranks ... we are beginning to feel an increasing necessity for some definite moral force or laws that shall bind us more closely together in this work of nursing, and that will bring us into more uniform and harmonious relations. (Robb, 1900, pp. 10–11)

Nurses were the first group of professional women to organize and form professional associations, to publish a professional journal and to establish a federation of health care professionals at the international level. Nurses such as Lillian Wald, Lavinia Dock, and Margaret Sanger were

---

SUSAN M. POSLUSNY, R.N., M.S.N., Delta Gamma, is Nurse Educator at St. Mary's Hill Hospital, Milwaukee, Wisconsin, and a doctoral student at the University of Illinois at Chicago College of Nursing. The work for this article was partially supported by a professional nurse trainee-ship. The author gives special thanks to Laurie Glass for her help in guiding the work on which this manuscript is based. Correspondence to University of Illinois at Chicago, College of Nursing, 845 South Damen, (M/C 802), Chicago, IL 60612.

Reprinted from Poslusny, S. M., Feminist friendship: Isabel Hampton Robb, Lavinia Lloyd Dock, and Mary Adelaide Nutting, *IMAGE: Journal of Nursing Scholarship,* 21:2, pp. 64–68, with permission of Sigma Theta Tan © 1989.

leaders in the twentieth century movements of social reform, women's suffrage and voluntary motherhood. Florence Nightingale and Clara Barton became heroines in a society that did not often recognize the unique contributions of women (Bullough & Bullough, 1984). Development of the nursing profession proceeded simultaneously with the profession's involvement in issues of social change. Women who entered nursing often saw it as a way of entering the battle against male-dominated social structures. Yet nurses are rarely recognized as being feminists and leaders in the fight to obtain equal rights and position for women. Liberal feminist advocates strove for parity with men in the man's world, while nurses worked to gain separate recognition as women through the development of a women's profession. Feminists and nurses have not eagerly supported each other in recent years on the issues that confront their respective organizations. Each group as a social movement has had difficulty in finding a cause or issue that could unite their organizations and memberships.

Unity and progress for women have been intimately linked with that of nurses. The early progress of women in securing legal rights is closely related in time to the progress of nurses in establishing themselves as a profession. Interpersonal support among individual women is an essential feature of the leadership in the movements toward unification both of women and of nurses. Such support has been characterized as "feminist friendship." Feminist friendship takes the form of a dialectic between struggle and victory, between nurture and empowerment (Pogrebin, 1987). This relationship does not necessarily reflect a particular doctrine of the "women's movement," but it does reflect the efforts of women to achieve recognition and influence in the world while maintaining a spirit of support for each other. In retrospect, it was feminist friendship that created the framework for unity and progress in nursing at the turn of the century.

Johns Hopkins Hospital Training School of Nurses was the birthplace of a professional relationship among three women that would grow to a personal friendship and would eventually influence the direction that the nursing profession would follow in the twentieth century. Isabel Hampton (Robb) became Superintendent of Nurses at Johns Hopkins in 1889. She took as her assistant Lavinia Lloyd Dock, whom she had known at Bellevue Training School. That same year Mary Adelaide Nutting entered Johns Hopkins for training. During the eleven years that followed, these three women maintained close personal contact, as evidenced by joint projects and professional collaboration as well as warm and friendly personal correspondence. They would become the architects of nursing education at Teachers College, the founders of the major professional organizations in nursing including the Society of Superintendents, the Associated Alumnae of Trained Nurses, the International Council of Nurses, and the creators of the *American Journal of Nursing* (Christy, 1969, 1975). Their relationship with each other was an important part of the context in which feminism, social reform and nursing came together at the turn of the century. Each woman brought a unique perspective to the work of unification in nursing and each shared that perspective with her peers, gaining the support needed to see those ideas to completion. Understanding the context for the creation of that framework may illuminate some of the issues that face nursing today.

Women at the Turn of the Century

One of the features of the post-Civil War era was the increasing disparity between social classes. The major developments in that society were experienced very differently by the advantaged classes than by the disadvantaged classes. Major shifts in the social, economic and political structure created change in social roles and personal morality. Because of their traditional dependence on others, women were more affected by these social changes. Change enabled advantaged women to alter their traditional roles and to improve their status in society, while change led to a greater oppression of disadvantaged women.

Social Relations in Victorian Society

Victorian society had created a world of social relations that institutionalized social convention and emotional distance, segregated men and women and restricted the activities of women to the home (Smith-Rosenberg, 1975). Victorian society also dictated that it was "unladylike" to perform any work, to think, or to display any part of the anatomy or movement that could be construed as "sexual" (Ehrenreich & English, 1973). Women were expected to be "passionless" and asexual (Cott, 1984).

The conditions of Victorian existence encouraged the further exploitation as well as the interdependence of women. The "cult of female invalidism" created the impression that advantaged women were chronically sick (Ehrenreich & English, 1973). Physicians, who would benefit from the medicalization of women's health, treated women for real and constructed sicknesses (Lovell, 1981). Women, with other women in attendance, took lengthy convalescence in bed for "nervous ailments." Sickness fit the image of the ideal Victorian woman—frail, long-suffering and pious. Sickness became identified as a feminine attribute, and nursing became identified as a woman's responsibility. Nightingale's (1860/1969) *Notes on Nursing* was written with the assumption that every woman was a nurse because all women had charge of someone's health at some point.

The repressiveness and segregation of the society contributed to the interdependence of women in another way. Women created a culturally distinct homosocial world. As described by Smith-Rosenberg (1975) in her classic exploration of female friendship in the Victorian era, this homosocial world was accompanied by elaborate rituals for many of the events that marked passage or family responsibility for a woman: naming of children, schooling, courtship, betrothal, marriage, birth, sickness and death. The mutual interdependence of women for these events and their physical isolation from men created the context for a subculture of women. The subculture provided for the introduction and socialization of new members and the transmission of its own institutions to new generations of women. Unabashed expressions of love and endearments between women were a reflection of the Platonic ideal. Romantic dialogue remained separate from desire.

Other events signaled that society was facing a major transition that would affect the status of women and in turn the character of their relationships with each other. Florence Nightingale (1852/1979) had published her essay on the plight of women: "Why have women passion, intellect, moral activity—these three—and a place in society where no one of the three can be exercised?" (p. 25). She followed this with her text of nursing knowledge. The text outlined the framework for the first legitimate profession for women outside of a religious vocation or self-selection as a healer or midwife. (Nightingale, 1860/1969). Shortly thereafter, John Stuart Mill (1869/1970) and Charlotte Perkins Gilman (1898/1973) published their thoughts on the status of women, creating the framework for feminist critique of social and economic institutions. The turn of the century promised significant change and opportunity for women.

Economic Relations in an Industrial Society

The Industrial Revolution occurred in the context of abundant human and natural resources and the humanistic belief in man's ability to control those resources. The turn of the century saw a rapid growth in the nation's population from the influx of European immigrants. Immigrants and farm laborers settled in the cities, where work was readily available. All members of the family including women and children became part of the working class. Mechanization of labor created a manufacturing economy that relied on the availability of workers. Long hours yielded low wages. Extreme poverty and discontent became concentrated in urban areas. The advantaged woman who was no longer able to perform her own labor, sew, or engage in sexual activity was attended and replaced by the growing class of domestic servants, garment workers and prostitutes (Ehrenreich & English, 1973). The wealth of the nation grew, but little of that wealth was realized by the working class. Poverty and disease were the major effects of industrialization for the working-class woman.

The public health movement was a response to the very visible and immediate problems of the urban ghetto—poverty and disease. Public health consisted of disease control and population control. "District nursing" was an important part of the public health movement and was centralized in the settlement houses that were established in major urban areas. The settlement houses represented the first viable option for secular women to live communally for the purpose of mutual support and aid.

The settlement houses were homes for women social reformers who lived and worked together. The women used a sense of moral obligation and a desire to become active participants to challenge the patriarchal political structures. Women such as Jane Addams, Lillian Wald and Lavinia Dock also found the settlement house to be a means of recreating the intimate support of the homosocial world and to empower women. The affection that each women felt for her female friends was characteristic of the social settlement movement. "Service to humanity and leadership in public life were constantly refueled by their female support communities and by personal relationships with women who gave them passionate loyalty and love" (Cook, 1979, p. 441).

The Personal is Political

The affiliation of Isabel Hampton Robb, Lavinia Lloyd Dock and Mary Adelaide Nutting reflected the changing character of women's relationships into this century. Women, educated and liberated from traditional roles, required a different kind of support from their peers. Ideology was as important as was affection for the new professional woman. Propriety and altruism tempered familiarity. Friendship in this era represented a new ethic for the professional woman.

The factors that influenced the friendship between Robb, Dock and Nutting include commonality of beliefs and complementarity in professional ability and focus. Each shared a sense of history, a common frustration with the exploitation of nurses, a mutual concern for the rights of women, a common goal of unity for the profession. Each worked to develop the major professional nursing institutions; each also maintained a unique professional focus. This blend of interests, abilities and focus within the context of a strongly supportive, professional relationship created the force and power in the early years of the profession.

Isabel Hampton Robb was the visionary leader. Isabel Stewart commented on the years at John Hopkins:

> I have always wondered how far we would have gone in nursing if that group of able dynamic leaders—Mrs. Robb, Miss Nutting, Miss Dock, and others of the same little circle—had not come into nursing at the right moment to get the group started off on progressive educational and organizational lines. Mrs. Robb seems to have been the chief dynamo in the early days and she probably did much to charge the others.[1]

A former student at Johns Hopkins interpreted things somewhat differently as students sometimes do, "Isabel Hampton dominated Adelaide Nutting ... Hampton blossomed and bloomed when Miss Dock was with her."[2] Lavinia Dock (1910a) remembered:

> ... the truly original and creative character of Miss Hampton's mind, for during the three years that we were together there [at Johns Hopkins] I saw her conceive and develop all the various ideas which are now embodied in living groups of persons and in broad lines of organization ... It was this reality to her of visions of the future that made her so delightful to live with and gave her her great fascination. (p. 17)

Mary Adelaide Nutting (1910) observed that "she was in every sense of the word a leader." (p. 19).

Indeed it is possible that Robb mentored each of the others into positions where it was possible for them to show their leadership ability. After meeting Dock at Bellevue, Robb later invited Dock to become her assistant at Johns Hopkins and to participate in the organization of the training school for nurses (Dock, 1910a). She also arranged that Dock should participate as a regular guest lecturer for the course at Teachers College.[3] Robb met Mary Adelaide Nutting as one of the first students in the new training course for nurses at Johns Hopkins. Nutting later became Superintendent when Robb married. Robb's continued support of Nutting is reflected in the fact that she recommended Nutting to replace Miss Allerton as administrator of the Hospital Economics Course at Teachers College.[4] In their various positions at Johns Hopkins primarily, and later at Teachers College, Robb enabled, encouraged and supported the efforts of these great women.

Despite her marriage, Robb did not forsake her commitment to nursing. The marriage infuriated many of her colleagues since married women of a privileged position were not supposed to work. Dock, in a private reflection on Isabel Robb's life, commented, "Miss Hampton's early life was uneventful—her nursing period short; her marriage a mistake and an anticlimax; her subsequent activities no different from those of many married nurses."[5] Contrary to Dock's bitter comment, Robb remained active in nursing. She delivered many papers on different subjects: professional education for nurses (Hampton, 1893/1949), the role of women on hospital boards (Robb, 1902), and the need for unity and organization among nurses (Robb, 1900). She provided the challenge and stimulus to form major professional associations: The Society of Superintendents of Training Schools for Nurses and The Associate Alumnae of Trained Nurses. She participated in funding, organizing and inaugurating the *American Journal of Nursing.* She wrote one of the first nursing textbooks in 1893, *Nursing: Its Principles and Practice,* and the first ethics text, *Nursing Ethics* in 1900. Noel (1980) evaluated Robb's contribution to nursing: "She needed to compromise in order to fulfill both home and professional responsibilities, yet she continued to be the most productive, versatile, and visionary nurse of her time" (p. 134).

Dock was the revolutionary spirit: a feminist, suffragette and socialist. One of the first public health nurses of the settlement house movement, Dock felt that nursing and women's issues were intimately related if not inseparable. At one point she was to speak to the nursing students at Teachers College about the history of nursing in Europe:

> I was quite young and I'd never seen Miss Dock … I was sure I'd know her when I met her, because she'd be tall and angular and intellectual looking. Who should turn up at the door but this small, short sort of roly-poly little person with curly hair. She'd just been at a suffrage meeting, and she had "Votes for Women" across her hat and "Votes for Women"

across her chest. She said, "Now what am I going to talk about?" I said
... "you were to talk about nursing on the Continent." "Oh," she said,
"very bad. It'll not be any better till they get the suffrage. I'll talk about suffrage." (Isabel Stewart cited in Christy, 1969, p. 50).

Through 23 years of participation as Honorary Secretary in the International Council of Nurses, Dock brought women's issues into nursing
and helped to unify nurses at an international level (Dock, 1900a; 1904;
1910b; Nutting, 1903). Along with Robb, she was one of the founding
members of the International Council of Nurses, which grew out of their
participation in the International Congress on Women. She wrote extensively on the need for political action in nursing (Dock, 1900b; 1906a).
In 1903 she boldly challenged the fledgling Society of Superintendents
of Nursing to recognize its political power:

> The society, in all these rather abstract but most important ways, has not
> done what it might do; has not made itself a moral force; is not a public
> conscience; takes no position on large public questions; is not feared by
> those of low standards; allows all manner of new conditions and devel-
> opments in nursing affairs to arise, flourish, succeed, or fail without tak-
> ing any notice whatever of them, apparently not even knowing about
> them ... Yet this society, as one body, would often be astonished at the
> actual extent and weight of its influence if its whole latent and at present
> unsuspected power were actually to be systematically exerted in an intel-
> ligent and energetic manner. (p. 99).

Dock was a prolific writer, bringing her perspectives on women,
nursing and politics to the profession. She authored a number of articles
on various types of public health nursing: visiting nursing (1906b), rural
nursing (1907), almshouse nursing (1908a; 1908b), mountain medicine
(1909), and the patient with "small means" (1906c). She authored the first
pharmacology text for nurses, *Materia Medica* (1890); and coauthored
the *History of Nursing* (1907–1912) with Nutting, and *The Short History of
Nursing* (1920) with Stewart. She also wrote the then controversial book,
Hygiene and Morality (1910/1985), which examined the issues of prosti-
tution and venereal disease.

Nutting was the administrative leader. She entered nursing somewhat
later than did Dock and Robb but worked to effect many of the ideas
generated by her friends. Having succeeded Robb as Superintendent at
Johns Hopkins School, she was able to effect significant change and
improvement in the education of nurses. She succeeded in incorporating a third year of training in the theory of nursing at Johns Hopkins, an
idea proposed by Robb (Hampton, 1893/1949, p. 8). She went on to advocate the development of preparatory academic education for nurses (Nutting, 1900).

At Teachers College, she and Dock were volunteer lecturers in Economics. Later, as Professor of Domestic Administration in the Department
of Domestic Economy, the first nurse to become a university professor,

Nutting began her work toward the implementation of full university education for nurses. She succeeded in getting the Hospital Economics Course endowed, an effort begun by Robb (Noel, 1980, p. 169). She later saw the status of nursing change at Teachers College. The Department of Domestic Economy became the Department of Nursing and Health in 1910 and the Department of Nursing Education in 1923.

Her dedication to educational aims often prevented her involvement in other activities. For example, she was unable to contribute to the premier issue of the *American Journal of Nursing,* or become involved in the suffrage movement with her friends, Wald and Dock (Marshall, 1972). She did collaborate extensively with Dock, however, in writing the first two volumes of *The History of Nursing*. She also compiled the papers and correspondence of the nursing leadership from Teachers College for the archives at Columbia University (Nutting Papers, 1985).

Robb, Dock and Nutting maintained a close, interdependent, professional relationship, as evidenced by the collaboration, mentorship and joint projects. Evidence of affection among these three great women is not as extensive as evidence of their professional collaboration and support. Their letters to each other are expressive in style and tone of their distinctive personalities: Robb was very familiar in her correspondence, whereas Nutting was more formal, and Nutting sent thoughtful gifts.

> Many thanks dear Adelaide for the charming little Walts possession! I went to see his collection in the Tail Gallery last summer but missed one of my favorites—"The Slumber of the Apes"—one of the most wonderful pictures painted by the hand of men. It has the whole history of womankind in it and still this old world is blind and will not see—I wish you could have been with us ... Heres to the new year may it team with blessings for you in the ways you want them most—As ever yours affectionately.[6]

Dock's correspondence with Nutting was filled with detail about her travel, her political activities and business relating to the writing of *The History of Nursing*. Her correspondence with Nutting, which could be quite pithy at times, reflected a more personal tone than used with Robb, perhaps reflecting greater parity in stature and relationship.

> My dear Adelaide—you will be arriving at New York about noon and I am sure you will be homesick, lonely, and scared enough at first. You must go down to the Settlement early and get a little friendly cheer and comfort into you.[7]

The friendship that characterized the personal relationship between these women reflected the ethic proposed by Nightingale (1893/1949). The ethic, promoted by Robb focused on the importance of unity and an "esprit de corps" among nurses but discouraged the formation of smaller "cliques." As Robb wrote in 1900:

> Any tendency towards the formation of cliques in a school is to be dis-
> couraged; they are harmful to the best development of a true class spirit;
> are narrowing and apt to render unduly and unfairly critical those who are
> [a] member of them. Sentimental, intense personal friendships are a mis-
> take, and are rarely productive of good. In some instances they must be
> regarded as forms of perverted affection; they are always unhealthy, since
> they make too great demands upon the emotions and nerve force, and are
> likely to assume undue proportions, so as to interfere with the proper dis-
> charge of one's duties ... A good steady, common sense friendship will be
> more helpful to both parties and will assuredly last longer. (pp. 139–140)

Friendship had become for nurses a question of ethical behavior that
existed somewhere between the Victorian tradition of romantic friendships and the Platonic ideal. Ethical behavior for friendship between
nurses retained the same character as proposed by Robb for a number
of years (Aikens, 1935). Beyond thinking that women's friendships would
create a sense of purpose in one's life and would be the only source of
emotional sustenance, these professional women found that unity in the
profession was the new purpose for the friendship between the women.

Feminist Friendship

Among the nursing leadership at the turn of the century, interpersonal
support was a means to achieve unity and "esprit de corps" in the profession. The interpersonal support among Robb, Dock and Nutting played
an important role in the progress of the profession toward its educational,
organizational and practice goals. In fact Bullough and Bullough (1984)
suggested that the professional activities of that period may reflect the
special interests of that small group rather than the needs of the profession at large. This is not to suggest that the profession did not benefit
from the visionary, revolutionary and administrative talents of these nursing leaders. It does suggest that in determining professional goals and in
mustering commitment to those goals, personal needs were as important
as social context, political climate and altruism. Friendship and support
can contribute to the personal satisfaction that is experienced by individual nurses and nursing leaders (Chinn, Wheeler, Roy, & Wheeler, 1987).
Personal satisfaction helps sustain the investment in professional activities
that are sometimes tedious and unrewarding and in professional issues
that seem not to change.

Feminist friendship engages personal and political dimensions of the
professional relationship. It is more than simply an "alliance of the weak,"
although this is not an uncommon; nor is it an entirely inappropriate characterization of any relationship between women. More than a moral "esprit
de corps," feminist friendship creates a political context for social change.
The political dimension is the one that is difficult for many nurses because
they are not used to participating in the political struggle for change. The
tradition of nursing is one of service and dedication to morality and public welfare, not politics and the dialectic of power relations. We must learn

from history: socioeconomic conditions and politics contrive consistently to affect the health of the nation, but remedy has not been found in the exercise of additional power. Rather change has occurred as a result of a unified commitment to intervene personally in the socioeconomic conditions and the political structure that maintain the poverty and oppression of disadvantaged groups. That commitment has been made in the context of personal support; however, it was not made in isolation.

Interpersonal support in nursing has recently received considerable attention in the literature. Mentoring (Darling, 1985), collaboration (Charleston Faculty Practice Conference Group, 1986), and networking (Persons & Wieck, 1985) are advocated as ways of achieving position or advancement for nurses and attaining group goals. Power strategies have had even less influence on the poverty, homelessness and pandemic that afflict the nation's health.

Feminist friendship is more than a political statement about relations between women. It is a framework for unity and progress that finds historical example in the leadership that emerged from Johns Hopkins at the turn of the century. It has contributed to the development of nursing as a profession. It has contributed to the empowerment of women. And it has contributed to the health of a nation engulfed in poverty, disease and destitution. No better example today could exist for nurses in our struggle for unity and progress.

Notes

[1] Personal notation of Isabel Stewart, dated March 23, 1938. Nutting Papers, Teachers College, Columbia University.

[2] Letter to Isabel Stewart from Mrs. A.R. Colvin, Johns Hopkins Class of 1892, dated November 15, 1940. Nutting Papers. Note from Stewart on letter: "not in keeping with MAN and LLD."

[3] Schedule of lectures noted in correspondence by Isabel Hampton Robb, 1901–1902. Nutting Papers.

[4] Letter to Miss Banfield from Isabel Hampton Robb, dated February 17, 1902. Nutting Papers.

[5] Letter to Miss Bean from Lavinia Lloyd Dock, dated July 17, 1940. Nutting Papers.

[6] Letter to Adelaide Nutting from Isabel Hampton Robb, dated December 29 [year not recorded]. Nutting Papers.

[7] Letter to Adelaide Nutting from Lavinia Dock, dated October 6, 1903. London. Nutting Papers.

References

Aikens, C. A. (1935). *Studies in ethics for nurses*. Philadelphia: W. B. Saunders.

Bullough, V. L., & Bullough, B. (1984). *History, trends, and politics of nursing*. Norwalk, CT: Appleton-Century-Crofts.

Charleston Faculty Practice Conference Group (1986). Nursing faculty collaboration viewed through feminist process. *Advances in Nursing Science, 8*(2), 29–38.

Chinn, P., Wheeler, C. E., Roy, A., & Wheeler, E. M. (1987). Just between friends. *American Journal of Nursing, 87,* 1456–1458.

Christy, T. E. (1969). *Cornerstone for nursing education: A history of the Division of Nursing Education of Teachers College, Columbia University, 1899–1947.* New York: Teachers College Press.

Christy, T. E. (1975). The fateful decade, 1890–1900. *American Journal of Nursing, 75*(7), 1163–1165.

Cook, B. W. (1979). Female support networks and political activism: Lillian Wald, Crystal Eastman, Emma Goldman. In N. F. Cott & E. H. Pleck (Eds.), *A heritage of her own: Toward a new social history of American women.* New York: Simon and Schuster.

Cott, N. F. (1984). Passionlessness: An interpretation of Victorian sexual ideology, 1790–1850. In J. W. Leavitt (Ed.), *Women and health in America: Historical readings* (pp. 57–69). Madison: University of Wisconsin Press.

Darling, L. A. (1985). Mentors and mentoring. *Nurse Educator, 10*(6), 18–19.

Dock, L. L. (1900a). The International Council of Nurses. *American Journal of Nursing, 1,* 114–115.

Dock, L. L. (1900b). What we may expect from the law. *American Journal of Nursing, 1,* 8–11.

Dock, L. L. (1903). The duty of this society in public work. *American Journal of Nursing, 4,* 99–101.

Dock, L. L. (1904). The Congress of Women in Berlin. *American Journal of Nursing, 4,* 817–820.

Dock, L. L. (1906a). The progress of registration. *American Journal of Nursing, 6,* 297–305.

Dock, L. L. (1906b). Training for visiting nursing. *American Journal of Nursing, 7,* 109–111.

Dock, L. L. (1906c). Central directories and sliding scales. *American Journal of Nursing, 7,* 10–13.

Dock, L. L. (1907). Rural Nursing. *American Journal of Nursing, 3,* 181–182.

Dock, L. L. (1908a). Almshouse nursing. *American Journal of Nursing, 8,* 361–363.

Dock, L. L. (1908b). The crusade for almshouse nursing. *American Journal of Nursing, 8,* 520–523.

Dock, L. L. (1909). Mountain medicine. *American Journal of Nursing, 9,* 181–183.

Dock, L. L. (1910a). Recollections of Miss Hampton at the Johns Hopkins. *American Journal of Nursing, 10,* 15–19.

Dock, L. L. (1910b). The London meeting of the International Council and Congress of Nurses. *American Journal of Nursing, 10,* 15–21.

Dock, L. L. & Stewart, I.M. (1920). *A short history of nursing.* New York: Putnam.

Dock, L. L. (1985). *Hygiene and morality.* In J. W. James (ed.), *A Lavinia Dock Reader.* New York: Garland. Original published in 1910.

Dock, L. L. (1890). *Textbook of materia medica for nurses.* New York: Putnam.

Ehrenreich, B., & English, D. (1973). *Complaints and disorders: The sexual politics of sickness.* New York: Feminist Press.

Gilman, C. P. (1973). Women and economics: A study of the economic relation between men and women as a factor in social evolution.

Hampton, I. A. (1949z1893). Educaitonal standards for nurses. In L. Petry (Ed.), *Nursing of the sick, 1893* (pp. 1–12). Papers and discussions from the International Congress of Charities, Correction and Philanthropy, Chicago, 1893. New York: McGraw-Hill.

In A. L. Cooper & S. M. Cooper (Eds.), *The roots of American feminist thought* (pp 193–217). Boston: Allyn and Bacon. Original published in 1898.

Lovell, M. C. (1981). Silent but perfect "partners": Medicine's use and abuse of women. *Advances in Nursing Science, 3*(2), 25–40.

Marshall, H. E. (1972). *Mary Adelaide Nutting. Poineer of modern nursing.* Baltimore: Johns Hopkins University Press.

Mill, J. S. (1970). *The subjection of women.* Cambridge, MA: MIT Press. Original published in 1869.

Nightingale, F. (1949). Sick nursing and health nursing. In L. Petry (Ed.), *Nursing of the sick, 1893* (ll. 24–43). Papers and discussions from the International Congress of Charities, Correction and Philanthropy, Chicago, 1893. New York: McGraw-Hill.

Nightingale, F. (1979). *Cassandra: An essay.* New York: Feminist Press. Original published in 1852.

Noel, N. L. (1980). Isabel Hampton Robb: Architect of American nursing. (Doctoral dissertation, Teachers College, Columbia University, 1979). *Dissertation Abstracts International, 41*(1), 132B.

Nutting, M. A. (1900). The preliminary education of nurses. *American Journal of Nursing, 1,* 416–424.

Nutting, M. A. (1903). Our relations to the National Council of Women. *American Journal of Nursing, 11* 900–903.

Nutting, M. A. (1910). Isabel Hampton Robb: Her work in organization and education. *American Journal of Nursing, 11,* 19–25.

Nutting, M. A. & Dock, L. L. (1907–1912). *A history of nursing, Volumes I–IV.* New York: Putnam.

Nutting papers (1985). *History of nursing* Volume two. The Archives of the Department of Nursing Education, Teachers College, Columbia University (series 3). Ann Arbor, MI: University Microfilms International.

Persons, C. B., & Wieck, L. (1985). Networking: A power strategy. *Nurse Economist, 3*(1), 53–57.

Pogrebin, L. C. (1987). *Among friends: Who we like, why we like them, and what we do with them.* New York: McGraw-Hill.

Robb, I. H. (1900). Address of the president. *American Journal of Nursing, 1,* 97–104.

Robb, I. H. (1920). Nursing ethics: For hospital and private use. Cleveland: Koeckert. Original published in 1900.

Robb, I. H. (1893). Nursing: Its principles and practice for hospital and private use. Philadelphia: W. B. Saunders.

Robb, I. H. (1902). Women on hospital boards. *American Journal of Nursing, 2,* 252–257.

Smith-Rosenberg, C. (1975). The female world of love and ritual: Relations between women in nineteenth-century America. *Signs, 1,* 1–29.

Chapter 11

New Generation Research Approaches

New generation research approaches are an unorganized group of research methodologies that share common beliefs about the goals and purposes of scientific investigation. Naturalistic inquiry, action research, and life history are described in this chapter as research methodologies available to the new generation nursing scientist. Unlike their predecessors, new generation nursing scientists place less emphasis on research methodology and instead hold prime certain non-methodological beliefs. Those beliefs are that nursing is a human and technological science, that nursing is a practice discipline, and that scientific investigation has ethical and moral implications (DeGroot, 1988; Gortner, 1990; Gortner & Schultz, 1988; Moccia, 1988). Not only do new generation nursing scientists acknowledge these three assumptions about nursing and nursing research but they then carry out nursing research using methodologies that facilitate allegiance to those assumptions. Thus, research methodology to the new generation researcher provides a vehicle for gaining new knowledge and understanding and for actualizing other more humanistic beliefs. A discussion of the philosophical basis of new generation research can help to clarify the intent of the three diverse methodologies included in this chapter.

PHILOSOPHICAL CONSIDERATIONS

Assumptions underlying new generation research derive from and extend the philosophical beliefs of post-empiricism described in Chapter 1. To be specific, many philosophers of science now find the goal of empiricist

Qualitative Research in Nursing: Advancing the Humanistic Imperative by Helen J. Streubert and Dona R. Carpenter. Copyright © 1995 by J. B. Lippincott Company.

research injudicious because of its emphasis on explanation and prediction through methodology. In addition, these philosophers find the goal of post-empiricist research lacking because of its singular attention to understanding as the primary product of science. Instead, new generation nursing scientists believe research should emphasize three goals. The first goal is to rise above competition between qualitative and quantitative research methodologies and recognize that nursing is both a technological and humanistic profession where multiple research approaches have equal applicability. The second goal is to place a greater value on research that directly improves nursing practice than on theory-generating research. Theory-generating research is useful to the new generation nursing scientist as a means to a practical end, but is not an end in itself. The final goal that characterizes a new generation nursing scientist is to have certain ethical and moral principles guide all phases of the research process.

The ideas of multiple research approaches, research for practical purposes, and ethical and moral principles are not unique to new generation scientists. Other philosophers of science have also subscribed to them to some extent. The difference lies in the importance of these goals to new generation scientists over the value of allegiance to method. As a result, the research approaches chosen for discussion in this chapter were included not because they are new or unique to new generation ideology. Instead they were chosen because they are methods some researchers have used to achieve the goals of the new generation. Each of the goals of new generation research is discussed in turn.

Nursing Research Should Emphasize Both the Humanness and the Technology of Nursing

New generation nurse researchers accept the changing beliefs of philosophers of science that phenomena have multiple realities, that multiple truths exist, and that there is no one correct methodology for scientific inquiry (Feyerabend, 1970; Habermas, 1975; Laudan, 1981; Toulmin, 1985). These philosophers believe the methodology of scientific inquiry should be guided by the type of problem that arises and that each of the competing philosophical paradigms offer different kinds of insight, all of which may be appropriate.

The phenomena of concern to nurse scientists are complex and multifaceted (DeGroot, 1988) and include both human and non-human factors. Human factors include patients, nurses, and other health care personnel. Non-human factors include the vast technology available to nurses and the physical environment in which patients and nurses exist. Thus, in recognizing both the human and technological nature of nursing, the new generation nurse researcher utilizes both quantitative and qualitative methods of data gathering to answer nursing research questions. Some research questions may relate to mainly human factors and thus require predominantly qualitative methods of data generation, concentrating more on a deep understanding and de-emphasizing explanation. Other research questions may relate to predominantly technologic factors and necessitate quantitative methods of data generation with an emphasis on explanation, prediction, and control. Most often nursing research questions are multi-faceted and require a combination of data generation methods to reveal the comprehensive nature of phenomena under study. This combination of data generation methods within a single study is often referred to as methodological triangulation (Duffy, 1987). Triangulation is gaining acceptance among new generation researchers as a vehicle for providing understanding of complex phenomena of concern to nurses. Hence, new generation nurse scientists seek research methodologies that permit use of a variety of methods and facilitate comprehensive, multifaceted understanding and explanation.

In addition to believing that phenomena of concern to nursing are comprehensive and multifaceted, new generation nurse researchers subscribe to dialectic belief (Rowan, 1981). The dialectic places its emphasis on change and recognizes that phenomena are in a constant state of change. In *dialectical* thinking change is greatly influenced by opposites. New generation researchers view the relationship between phenomena as dialectical. They see this relationship as a process that is always changing as it seeks to reconcile the contradictions within it. For example, a dialectical thinker researching a phenomenon such as pain would search a data set for contradictions. This search might reveal that pain involves both positive and negative forces: that is, pain is both a protective mechanism and a powerful force that causes great discomfort. As the dialectical thinker studies pain, the apparent contradiction between the protective and harmful aspects becomes reconciled, resulting in a greater understanding of this dynamic concept. Reconciliation occurs as the thinker realizes that in specific instances pain warns individuals of impending danger or harm, while at other times pain ceases to serve a protective function. By studying these apparently opposing facets of pain, the dialectic thinker comes to a fuller, more meaningful understanding of its nature. Thus, a researcher believing in the dialectic embarks on a scientific investigation guided by certain theoretical formulations having only a preliminary idea of the research design. As the study unfolds, the new generation researcher investigates the contradictions in the data, allowing the theory to change and reshape as the study progresses. Similarly, the research protocol is shaped and guided by the data emerging from the continuing investigation.

Nursing Research Should Aim To Improve Nursing Practice

New generation nursing researchers and researchers in other disciplines believe that social change is a desired outcome of research. In the social sciences the desire for social change translates to a desire for changes in practice (Argyris, Putnam, & Smith, 1985). In nursing, social change is interpreted as changes in nursing practice, administration, and educational arenas. The extent to which changes in nursing practice are an actual part of an investigation varies with the strategy chosen. Researchers using action research, a methodology discussed in this chapter, believe that a scientific investigation must include strategies for changing practice. Other methodologies recognize that change in practice may be the ultimate goal, and thus strive to create results that are valid for practitioners, but they do not implement findings in practice as a part of the actual study. Most simply stated, the goal of new generation research is to narrow the theory-practice gap through considerations of application to practice as a crucial entity in the scientific investigation.

Nursing Research Should Be Guided by Certain Ethical and Moral Principles

Ethical and moral principles that guide new generation research include a belief in social responsibility and belief in the democratic ideal. New generation nurse researchers believe that research methodology should provide for allegiance to these two moral and ethical ideals (DeGroot, 1988; Gortner & Schultz, 1988; Gortner, 1990). Thus, new generation nurse researchers choose methodologies because they remain true to certain moral and ethical principles.

Traditionally, scientists have not always been answerable for the social implications of their investigations, in either research process or research product. A goal of a socially responsible science represents a radical change to many empiricist and post-empiricist philosophers of science who believe science should be value free. Yet, this reaction is not difficult to understand when one considers that traditional research has been successful in producing a tremendous knowledge and technology explosion with little consideration of social, political, or economic implications (Toulmin, 1985). The technology explosion has not remedied some of our most nagging problems such as quality of life in the presence of high technologic care, or the cost of high technology health care and accessibility of that health care to the poor and underprivileged. In fact, some may consider that the knowledge and technology explosion has contributed to these social problems. New generation researchers believe that investigators have the responsibility to consider the social, political, moral, cultural, and economic implications and significance of the theoretical and action outcomes of their research (Reason, 1988; Toulmin, 1985).

Thus, socially responsible new generation researchers should consider the impact of the outcomes of a proposed investigation at the outset, during the planning phase. If the expected outcomes of a study are projected to be detrimental to society, the morally responsible new generation researcher will redesign the study or possibly abandon the idea. Socially responsible researchers will also consider the moral implications of study outcomes at the completion of the study. The research report will include a discussion of the social, political, moral, cultural, and economic effects of the study's outcomes. When making recommendations for application of a study's outcomes to nursing practice, the researcher will carefully consider these social implications. If the researcher determines a potential negative or harmful effect, the recommendation might be to not implement the findings or to investigate the problem further before implementation is considered. Recommendations for further study might then include additional studies of the social effects of the study outcome.

For example, a new generation researcher might choose to study a new method of nursing care delivery. Being a socially responsible scientist, the researcher carefully considers the social implications of the new method. If it is determined that the new method is financially costly or that it might potentially harm a cultural minority group of patients, the idea might be abandoned or redesigned. At the least the researcher will discuss those potentially costly or harmful implications in the research report and make a morally responsible recommendation.

Morally responsible new generation researchers also support the democratic ideal in their research. Research participants are considered partners in the research relationship who should be actively involved in the planning and implementation of the study. In addition, as equal partners, research participants are not taken advantage of or used by the researcher to achieve research ends. Instead participants should benefit from participating in the study and be empowered by the study.

The roots of new generation belief in supporting democratic ideals in scientific investigations lie in *critical theory*. Critical theory is a philosophical belief system expressed by Marxist philosophers, such as Jurgen Habermas (1971, 1975). Following his critique of philosophy of science, Habermas recognized that previous paradigms offered valuable insight into the nature of reality, yet they failed to recognize the influence and constraint of unrecognized forces controlling human action. These controlling forces could be in the form of cultural expectation, tradition, political forces, or ideology. The value of recognizing the influence of external control, according to Habermas, is that individuals potentially can be liberated from the control once insight is gained. Hence, researchers following the assumptions of critical theory seek to empower study participants in a scientific investigation by creating a mutually beneficial, collaborative relationship between researchers and those researched. New generation researchers believe the collaborative research relationship can be the vehicle for empowering study participants (Heron, 1981; Reason, 1988). New generation researchers use the term *research participants* to signify the collaborative relationship.

A second belief system, *holism,* underlies the need for a collaborative relationship between researchers and participants in a new generation study (Reason, 1988). Followers of holism believe that systems, including human systems, have a characteristic wholeness about them and that their wholeness is more than the sum of their parts. Followers of holism believe further that it is impossible to understand any of the parts of an individual system without an understanding of the wholeness of that system. In addition, each individual system differs from all other systems. As such, systems have common characteristics, but taken as a whole, each individual system is unique. Followers of holism believe further that to know or understand the wholeness of a system requires participation in or with that system (Gadamar,1989; Heidegger, 1962; Kuhn, 1970; Lakatos, 1981; Toulmin, 1985). Through collaborative participation the researchers and the participants come to a deep understanding of phenomena under study.

The extent of collaboration between researchers and participants in the methodologies described includes every stage of the research process. Each of these methodologies also has the potential of being used in a non-collaborative way; however, the collaborative approach will be emphasized for the new generation nurse researcher.

New generation nursing research methodologies, then, represent a change from traditional approaches to inquiry. The emphasis shifts from a search for ultimate truth to a search for practical truths that empower participants and cause no other social, cultural, or economic harm. The choice of method for a scientific investigation in the new generation realm then shifts from a desire for control to one of practical and social responsibility. Gortner (1990) suggests that because nursing is a practice discipline, the ability to prescribe nursing practice should remain a goal of nursing research. New generation researchers would agree that prescribing nursing practice is a worthy research goal; however, it is not the ultimate goal. Morally responsible new generation researchers strive to discover prescriptive patterns and regularities while empowering research participants and protecting social, cultural, and environmental welfare.

SELECTING AN APPROACH

Nurse scientists will choose to do new generation research because they accept its underlying philosophical beliefs. Any nursing problem or research question has the potential of being answered through application of new generation research methodology. Since new generation research is an emerging research approach, it is represented in several contemporary research methodologies. In this chapter naturalistic inquiry, action research, and life history are presented as methodologies by which new generation goals can be achieved. The methodologies to be described differ in that they stress differing parts of the belief system as prime in their methodological approach. Understanding the uniqueness of each methodology can assist the aspiring new generation nursing researcher in choosing an appropriate methodology.

APPLICATION OF NATURALISTIC INQUIRY

Natural Inquiry is a research methodology wherein the researcher implements beliefs of the naturalistic domain. Two tenets describe the naturalistic domain: investigating phenomena as they occur naturally and deriving research outcomes inductively. Researchers investigate a phenomenon as it occurs naturally by observing it in its natural setting or by listening to individuals describe their experience of the phenomenon as it occurs for them. Naturalistic inquirers need to investigate a phenomenon in its natural setting because in that setting the phenomenon remains part of the context that surrounds it. Phenomena are inextricably intertwined with their context and can only be understood within that context. When a phenomenon is controlled or taken out of its natural setting, it becomes a part of a new context, the controlled study situation, which is not natural to the phenomenon.

Also, when phenomena are investigated as they occur naturally, the investigator refrains from manipulating them in any way. Furthermore, studying phenomena as they occur naturally allows new generation researchers to observe and describe phenomena as they occur over a period of time. Observations over time facilitate description of the sequence of a phenomenon's events and delineation of the pattern of change or growth in its relationships (Denzin, 1989). The naturalistic inquirer strives to study a phenomenon as it exists in its natural context in the most non-intrusive way possible so that the study changes the phenomenon as little as possible.

The research outcomes from a naturalistic inquiry range from an interpretative description to a form of theoretical formulation. Elden (1981) describes the theoretical formulation as *local theory*. The term local implies that theoretical formulations emerging from a specific naturalistic inquiry are unique to the data set in that particular investigation and are not generalizable to the same phenomenon in another situation or circumstance.

Further, in the naturalistic domain the local theory is derived inductively (Lincoln & Guba, 1985). Inductive theory emerges from a research study rather than being preconceived prior to the investigation. Inductive theory builders acquaint themselves with knowledge about a particular phenomenon prior to beginning a naturalistic inquiry. Then when the study begins, they put their knowledge aside and through observation piece together bits of information about the phenomenon inductively, creating a local theory about the phenomenon. The local theory describes that phenomenon as it occurs within the context in which it was investigated.

If the context of a particular phenomenon changes, the specifics of the local theory change. Thus, the theory that emerges from a naturalistic inquiry is the local theory that explains the particular inquiry, making generalization to other contexts or settings unlikely or impossible. The goal of naturalistic inquiry is to describe the context in sufficient detail that other nurse scholars reading the research report might generalize specifics to their settings as they deem appropriate.

In a similar way, the design of a naturalistic inquiry emerges from the study rather than being preconceived by the researcher (Lincoln & Guba, 1985). The naturalist domain dictates an emergent design because of a belief in phenomena as consisting of multiple, context dependent realities. Only after the realities become apparent to the naturalistic inquirer can the most appropriate design for the study be determined. The new generation nurse researcher retains control of a naturalistic inquiry by planning the study in phases. Prior to beginning the investigation, the researcher identifies the focus for the study. The focus may be stated in the form of a research question, a program or activity to be evaluated, or a policy to be analyzed (Lincoln & Guba, 1985; Guba & Lincoln, 1989). The natural setting for the study should be readily apparent after identification of the focus. Likewise, the unit or units of study for the investigation should then flow naturally from the identified focus. Examples of units of study might include patients or a patient population, nurses, time, social interactions between two or more groups of people, and attitudes, meanings, and language of the people in the study.

For example, imagine that a nurse researcher wants to study ethical decision making in home care nurses. The purpose of the study is to understand how home care nurses approach ethical decision making and to understand the meaning of ethical decision making to these nurses. To study ethical decision making within the context of its natural domain, the nurse researcher chooses to observe home care nurses as they make decisions in their daily practice and talks to them about the decisions they make routinely. The focus of the study in this situation is ethical decision making. The unit of study is the home care nurse. As the researcher conducts the study, the unit of study may broaden to include other individuals involved in the ethical decision-making situation, such as patients, physicians, and nurse administrators.

Conducting the Naturalistic Inquiry

Phase I. After identifying the focus of the study, its natural setting, and the units of study, the naturalistic inquirer enters phase I of the investigation. Lincoln and Guba (1985) term phase I the "orientation and overview" (p. 325) phase. During this phase, the researcher enters the field of study and interacts with the people in that setting to determine what is important to study and follow up in more detail. To accomplish this orientation, the researcher interviews selected individuals related to the focus of study asking them open-ended questions about what they see as important for the researcher to know. In our example of ethical decision making in home care nurses, the researcher would first identify one or two currently practicing home care nurses to interview in phase I. The purpose of this interview would be to acquaint the researcher with the home care nurse's perceptions and experience of ethical decision making in his or her practice. Specific salient elements that surface from these interviews might be time, the nurse's experience with decision making, or specifics of the patient situation. Data are analyzed following phase I so that the researcher can identify the elements salient to the focus and plan for phase II. Thus, information gained in phase I provides the groundwork for the emerging research design.

Phase II. The purpose of phase II is "focused exploration" (Lincoln & Guba, 1985, p. 235). During phase II, the researcher uses various methods of data generation to obtain in-depth information about the elements identified in phase I. At this time the researcher identifies methods of data generation, the composition of the sample from which to gather the data, and the instruments to be used for data generation. Lincoln and Guba (1985) pointed out that the major instrument for data generation will be the human instrument because only a human being has the capacity to process the multiple realities present in a phenomenon. Other instruments may be utilized, but the human instrument will be primary.

In phase II of our example of ethical decision making in home care nurses, the researcher might decide to gather data from practicing home care nurses by interviewing them about their ethical decision-making experiences. The researcher might also observe home care nurses giving patient care to see firsthand how ethical decisions are made.

Phase III. Data generated in phase II are analyzed and a report is written in preparation for phase III. In phase III, the report is given to the participants in the study for them to verify. During phase III, "the task is to obtain confirmation [from participants in the study] that the report has captured the data as constructed by informants, or to correct, amend, or extend it."(Lincoln & Guba, 1985, p. 236).

The phases of a naturalistic inquiry are not as discreet and finite as their description makes them seem. In reality, the researcher often cycles back and forth between phases, returning to a previous phase at times to follow up on a piece of information uncovered. For example, the participants may disagree with a portion of the report during phase III, causing the researcher to re-enter phase II to generate additional data about the element in question. Likewise, researcher collaboration with participants may occur at any or all phases in the study. Collaboration may include confirmation of findings and participation in choosing the specific methods to be used in the study.

Data Generation

Data are generated in a naturalistic inquiry using a variety of methods. Methods of data generation may include interviewing or observing human sources, surveys, documents, and records. No limits are placed on the methods of data generation that may be utilized, including both qualitative and quantitative data. Yet, interviews and observation of human beings activities are the primary method of data generation in nurse researchers' use of naturalistic inquiries. Interviews and observations during phase I of a study will be unfocused and unstructured, while in phase II they will be more focused and structured based on the findings in phase I.

The naturalistic inquirer chooses the sample for a study to achieve maximum variation. The purpose is to generate as much information as possible to "detail the many specifics that give the context its unique flavor" (Lincoln & Guba, 1985, p. 201). Lincoln and Guba also suggested serial selection of sample units.

Successive units of research participants are chosen for a specific purpose. For example, in our ethical decision-making study the researcher chose two or three home care nurses for the purpose of learning about their experience of ethical decision making in phase I. As it became apparent in phase II that physicians played a role in some ethical decisions nurses make, physicians might be added to the study sample. The researcher might interview several physicians about their experiences making ethical decisions with home care nurses. This additional information from physicians will help the researcher clarify what the nurses have said. A likely source for successive participants is nomination by the previous participants. Sampling ends when information obtained becomes redundant.

Data Treatment and Analysis

Lincoln and Guba (1985) recommended the *constant comparative method of data analysis* developed by Glaser and Strauss (1967) for analyzing data generated in a naturalistic inquiry. The majority of data generated will be textual data, either transcripts of interviews or recordings of field notes. Lincoln and Guba stressed, however, that when using the constant comparative method for naturalistic inquiry, the purpose is not to generate a theory that will "enable prediction and explanation of behavior" (Glaser & Strauss, 1967, p. 3) as Glaser and Strauss originally intended. Rather, the constant comparative method is used in naturalistic inquiry simply to process data. The eventual outcome of the analysis will be a case report of the study describing what the researcher has learned about the phenomenon. The outcome from this use is a local theory, theoretical formulations that apply only to the study situation and are not necessarily generalizable to instances of the phenomenon in other circumstances.

To do constant comparative data analysis, naturalistic inquirers begin by reading through a text and identifying units of data. Units should have two characteristics. They should be "heuristic, that is, aimed at some understanding or some action that the inquirer needs to have or to take . . . [and] they should be the smallest piece of information about something that can stand by itself" (Lincoln & Guba, 1985, p. 345). Units may be as small as a few words or a sentence to as large as a paragraph or two. Units of data can be managed using either a computerized data management system or an index card system. Useful computer data management programs are listed in Table 11.1.

After identifying units in the data set, researchers begin reading each unit and assigning it to a category on a "feels right" or "looks right" basis (Lincoln & Guba, 1985, p. 340). As researchers assign units to categories it is vitally important that they compare each successive unit with previously identified units. As researchers proceed through the identified units and assign them to emerging categories, rules of inclusion for the category will begin to appear. When this occurs, researchers should stop and write a note describing the category as it is conceptualized at this point.

The task of identifying units of data and forming them into categories can be frustrating and ambiguous, especially for the neophyte qualitative researcher. Many researchers may be tempted to utilize an existing theory to aid in identifying categories. This temptation should be avoided, or once recognized by the researcher, abandoned. The goal is to identify categories that emerge from the data and assign them labels and rules of inclusion based solely on the data.

Researchers proceed through the data until all units are assigned to a category. Then categories are reviewed and refined. Refinement may include breaking some categories into smaller categories or combining like categories into one larger category. As researchers proceed through

TABLE 11.1 **COMPUTERIZED QUALITATIVE DATA MANAGEMENT PROGRAMS**

Computer Program	Source
MS-Dos Programs	
Atlas-Ti	Qualitative Research Management 73425 Hilltop Road Desert Hot Springs, CA 92241 (619) 320-7026
Ethnograph (Version 3.0)	Qualis Research Associates P.O.Box 2070 Amherst, MA 01004 (415) 256-8835 $150.00
Hyper Research for Windows	Qualitative Research Management 73425 Hilltop Road Desert Hot Springs, CA 92241 (619) 320-7026 $275.00
Martin (Version 2.0)	Martin School of Nursing University of Wisconsin-Madison 600 Highland Avenue Madison, WI 53792 (608) 263-5336 $250.00
Textbase Alpha	Qualitative Research Management 73425 Hilltop Road Desert Hot Springs, CA 92241 (619) 320-7026 $150.00
Macintosh Programs	
HyperQual 2	Qualitative Research Management 73425 Hilltop Road Desert Hot Springs, CA 92241 (619) 320-7026 $180.00
Hyper Soft	Qualitative Research Management 73425 Hilltop Road Desert Hot Springs, CA 92241 (619) 320-7026 $175.00
Nudist (Version 3.0)	Learning Profiles, Inc. 2329 W. Main Street, #330 Littleton, CO 80120-1951 (800) 279-2070 $275.00

category refinement, relations between categories will become apparent. Some categories will be identified as missing or incomplete and will be earmarked for follow-up with more data generation. Denzin (1989) cautioned against discarding or disregarding deviant or negative cases from the categorization. It may be equally important to the phenomenon under study to describe normal as well as deviant or irregular behavior. For a full description of the constant comparative method of data analysis the reader is directed to Lincoln and Guba (1985) or to Glaser and Strauss (1967).

Researchers can analyze quantitative data generated in the naturalistic inquiry using traditional techniques. Having an expert in quantitative data analysis on the research team greatly facilitates this process.

At this point the reader should realize that the researcher cycles between data analysis and data generation (Guba & Lincoln, 1989). Analysis reveals the need for further data generation. The researcher collaborates with the participants throughout data generation and data analysis for verification of perceptions and interpretations. Participants aid in clarifying categories and in determining subsequent data generation methods.

A pertinent question for many researchers is "When do I stop generating data?" Lincoln and Guba (1985) identified three criteria for ending data generation and analysis: (1) when data sources are exhausted, i.e., when no new information emerges about a category; (2) when the researcher and participants feel a "sense of integration" (p. 350) about the data; or (3) when new data are far removed from current data and not contributing to the understanding of the phenomenon under study.

The Case Study Report

The last step in the naturalistic inquiry cycle is to write a case study report that should include the following: a description of the research problem; a description of the context and setting for the study; a description of key participants in the setting, their interactions, and how they influence the phenomenon under study; a discussion of the emerging categories, their importance, and interrelationship; and a discussion of the implications of the findings in the study. The case study should be written so that the reader gains a thorough understanding of the phenomenon as it occurs in this particular setting to facilitate readers judging the advisability of transferring findings in the study to other settings. Last, Lincoln and Guba (1985) suggested that a description of research methods and steps for assuring trustworthiness be appended to the case study for interested readers. Methods for assuring *trustworthiness* in new generation nursing research are discussed at the end of this chapter.

The value of this inductive, emergent approach for nursing is that it allows for the illumination of new ideas or novel ways to conceptualize and solve old problems. Naturalistic inquiry allows the researcher to be truly creative in the approach to problem solving. To this end, naturalistic inquiry is an especially useful tool to the new generation nurse researcher looking for creative approaches to nursing problems. It has the value of freeing the researcher from the past and from old ways of thinking.

This approach is not free of anxiety. Entering a research study unrestrained by theoretical formulation can be anxiety producing to the uninitiated. Waiting to see what naturally evolves from the interaction can feel uncertain, but the reward is the freedom to see phenomena in a new light and to discover creative approaches to old problems.

APPLICATION OF ACTION RESEARCH

Action research most simply defined is a systematic method of learning from experience. Contemporary action researchers learn from experience in two ways, with or without an outside facilitator (MacDonald, 1992). The use of an outside facilitator is emphasized in the foregoing discussion.

Kurt Lewin (1946) first conceived of action research as a method of interacting with or participating in a system for the dual purposes of learning about the system and effecting a change in the system. Through interaction with the system, the researcher also contributes to the body of scientific knowledge about the system. Thus, the action researcher serves two masters, if you will, theory and practice. Lewin's change theory is familiar to many. Action research differs from change theory in that it utilizes principles of change theory to effect a change in a system, but at the same time systematically investigates the process and results of the change as a form of research.

Action researchers aim to serve the practice master by studying a particular practice or system in collaboration with the key practitioners in that system. The inquiry includes learning about the practice from those involved in it, planning for changes in the practice, implementing those changes, and evaluating the success of the changes. The direct result of action research is the generation of practical knowledge that has the potential of helping a particular system improve. The knowledge generated is practical because it relates directly to the problems and concerns idiosyncratic to an individual system. An indirect result of action research is that practitioners learn about their system and learn to implement change to improve their own practice (Susman & Evered, 1978). As action research progresses, the practitioners learn strategies for helping themselves.

Action researchers serve the theory master by gaining access to knowledge in specific situations that may otherwise be difficult to obtain. Gaining this privileged information provides the researcher with the opportunity to refine existing theories or to generate new theories using knowledge derived from practice (Clark, 1972).

Action researchers do not provide a highly prescriptive methodology as a guide for prospective new generation researchers. The aim of learning through action for action remains paramount, while the choice of method depends on the peculiarities of the situation. Action researchers describe their craft as a cyclical process involving collaboration between researchers and participants throughout. Winter (1989), in reviewing the action research process, pointed out that action researchers do not agree completely on the form the cyclical process takes. The elements common to all forms of the cyclical processes of action research are an analysis of current practices and implementation of change. Researchers differ in their approach as to which comes first, analysis or implementation. If analysis comes first, the action research process begins with review of the problem situation, progresses to diagnosis and planning for change, followed by implementation of the change and evaluation of the effects of the change. This conception of the action research process closely parallels the steps of the nursing process and is thus most easily understood by nurses.

The extent of collaboration between researchers and study participants also varies among action researchers (Susman & Evered, 1978). Collaboration ranges from the review of the problem and diagnosis only, to full collaboration at all stages of the research. Action researchers who facilitate collaboration at all stages of the action cycle submit that they are able to obtain the most practical solutions to the problems identified (Whyte, 1991).

Data Generation

Data are generated during all stages of the action research cycle using a variety of methods, but most researchers are not specific about how data should be generated. Argyris, Putnam, and Smith (1985) suggested that the overriding purpose of data gathering in action research should be to gain information about the actions taken by practitioners and to ascertain the reasons or intentions for those actions without threatening or constraining the practitioners. To achieve the goal of understanding the reason for action, the researcher combines interview with observation and qualitative with quantitative methods. Winter (1989) provided a broad overview of data generation techniques that might be used in an action research study. He stressed that data generation needs to be meticulous with detailed record keeping to facilitate a deep understanding of practice. Techniques include keeping detailed diaries of subjective impressions of interactions with practitioners and field notes of meetings and observations of practitioners carrying out their work. In addition, researchers utilize documents relating to a situation, such as nurses' notes, time sheets, or nursing care plans, and surveys of practitioners' attitudes, preferences, or experiences. Interviews with nursing practitioners and other individuals related to their work are also valuable methods of data generation.

Other informants may include other health care practitioners with whom nurses must collaborate and support personnel working with nurses.

Data generation begins in a broad, comprehensive way at first, but, as the research progresses, emerging insights guide and focus successive data generation. Data generated are in the form of facts and interpretations or explanations of those facts. Interpretations and explanations make "implicit claims to be authoritative, to be firmly embedded in a competence to understand the situation, and thus to make judgments as to normality, relevance, and causation" (Winter, 1989, p. 43). Authoritative interpretations are based on "professional authority and practical authority" (Winter, 1989, p. 43). Professional authority derives from expertise of some sort, while practical authority is based on everyday common-sense experience.

In the initial planning stage, researchers and participants decide which methods of data generation are valuable for a particular situation. As data are gathered, researchers and participants begin to form tentative interpretations. These interpretations then are used to focus successive data generation sessions. The researchers and participants together also decide on techniques for recording data, such as tape recordings, video recordings, note taking, or photographs and slides. The choice depends on the intrusiveness of the technique and the level of accuracy and detail it produces. Tape recording and videotaping are generally more intrusive, but provide greater accuracy of detail; although note taking and photographs are less intrusive, they also provide less accurate detail.

Winter (1989) stressed that researchers and research participants should plan for at least three different methods of data generation so that each method "can partly transcend its own limitations by functioning as a point of comparison with another" (p. 22). Two methods of data generation might result in polarized opinions or insights, while the addition of a third method might allow for a third interpretation that reconciles the polarization. Hence, through *triangulation of data generation* techniques, researchers and participants can insure more meaningful problem solving.

Throughout the action research cycle, the researcher serves as the expert in data generation techniques. As such, the researcher should be armed with a detailed understanding of a variety of techniques and their application. The decisions about generation will remain collaborative, with the researcher serving the role of expert facilitator. Most agree that a team of researchers is the most effective way to provide the needed expertise.

Data Treatment and Analysis

Action researchers are equally unclear about data treatment and analysis as they are about data generation, if not more so. Most authors do not identify methods of data treatment and data analysis. Winter (1989) suggested reflexive and dialectical critique as methods of analyzing qualitative data. A discussion of each of these concepts is in order.

Remember that the goal of data generation in action research is to make observations of action and to determine the purpose or intention of the action. All statements made during data generation are subject to reflexivity. That includes written and verbal language of both participants and researcher/observers of practitioners. Reflexivity is used here to describe the belief that the language individuals use to describe an experience reflects the experience being described and also all other experiences in the individual's life. Knowing that observations and interpretations are reflexive creates two assumptions for the action researcher. The first is a rejection of the idea of a single or ultimate explanation for an observation or interpretation. Instead, the belief is that many explanations exist for any one observation. The second assumption is the belief that making the various explanations for an experience explicit increases the researchers' and participants' understanding of those observations and interpretations.

When engaging in *reflexive critique* the researchers and participants probe for the reflexive basis of data generated. Alternative explanations or interpretations are made explicit. The goal in making the reflexive explanations explicit is to establish that a number of alternative explanations could be relevant and equally important. Reflexive critique facilitates discussion between the researchers and participants, a path to greater insight.

For example, action researchers might implement a new method of nursing care delivery in an intensive care unit. The researchers evaluate the implementation of the new method by interviewing nurses on the unit to determine their degree of satisfaction with the new method. Several nurses state that they do not find the new method helpful because it takes them too much time to implement. When using reflexive critique to analyze this information, the researchers and several participants would think about all information they have about implementing the new method and brainstorm possible explanations for the findings. Explanations might be that the nurses are unfamiliar with the system or that nurses are lacking in a basic skill to carry out the new method. It is imperative that both researchers and participants engage in this reflexive critique together. Together they can decide upon the most likely explanation, or they might decide on several good possibilities, engage in further data collection about the possibilities, and re-examine their findings.

Action researchers engage in *dialectical critique* by probing data generated to make explicit their internal contradictions. By probing the discrete elements of a phenomenon and exposing their contradictory nature, the researchers and participants can come to a clearer understanding of the nature of change inherent in a particular phenomenon.

If the researchers evaluating the implementation of a new method of patients care delivery in the above example were to use dialectic critique, they would also meet with several research participants to discuss data related to time needed to implement the new method. The researchers would probe the data for conflicting information related to time. In doing so they might discover that inexperienced nurses say the new technique takes more time to implement, while experienced nurses say the new technique takes less time to implement. Or they may discover that the new techinique takes more time to implement on the day shift than on the night shift. Discussing and probing these opposites will give the researchers further insight into the complex factors influencing implementation of the new method.

The Case Report

In the next step of the action research cycle, the researchers prepare a report of the data generated and the results of data analysis for the practitioners who collaborated with the researchers for the study. Remember that the result of data analysis is a plurality of explanations for phenomena observed. The report includes many explanations and also questions for further consideration. The report is not intended to be a prescription for action. Instead, its purpose is to provide its consumers, the practitioners, with a spring board for dialogue. Discussions among practitioners and between the researchers and participants about the report and subsequent course of action will ensue. The course of action in this case comes from the practitioners with guidance from the researcher. The action is implemented with continued evaluation of its effectiveness, with or without the continued guidance of the researcher (Argyris, Putnam, & Smith, 1985; Whyte, 1991; Winter, 1989).

Action research as described above remains true to the beliefs of new generation nurse researchers. New generation researchers should choose to use an action research methodology when a change in nursing practice is desired. A change to participative management in a nursing unit, implementation of a new teaching method for orienting new staff, or a change in methods of surveying patient populations for high-risk behaviors are examples of changes in nursing practice amenable to action research. Choosing the methodology of action research as described will facilitate the new generation nurse researcher in creating changes in practice that are specific to the practice situation in question, that empower the practitioners in process, and that are socially responsible.

APPLICATION OF LIFE HISTORY

Life history is a collection of research methods designed to elicit the "experiences and definitions held by one person, one group, or one organization as this person, group, or organization interprets those experiences (Denzin, 1989). It is the telling of a life story or stories for the purpose of gaining insight into the realities of those individuals' lives. Insight is gained by having participants tell the story of their life, including subjective feelings, intentions, motivations, and thoughts associated with a particular behavior or set of events (Armstrong, 1987). New generation researchers, such as nurses, use the life history method to gain an insider's view of a particular phenomenon of concern to the practice. The result is nursing practice grounded in the life experiences of its participants, patients, nurses, or students.

Life history as a research method was derived from *symbolic interactionism* in the 1930s and 1940s (Armstrong, 1987; Denzin, 1989; Faraday & Plummer, 1979). Followers of symbolic interactionism believe that humans learn about and define their world through interaction with others. Symbols, such as words, meanings, and language, are learned through interaction and are used by the interacting individual to represent the individual's evolving definition of any given situation. Researchers, then, learn about humans through observations of their interactions with others and through interpretation of their symbols (Denzin, 1989).

Life history, like action research and naturalistic inquiry, has the potential of being equally beneficial to both researchers and participants alike. Armstrong (1987) observed that participants in his life history studies have benefitted from the telling of their stories by gaining critical insight into their situations and through consciousness raising.

Life history is not, however, considered a form of therapy. It is conducted for the purpose of research, not for therapeutic purposes such as reminiscence therapy. Thus, benefit through insight may occur with the life history method, but that is not its intention. At the same time, the telling of the life history may be painful to the teller. The life history researcher keeps this fact in mind when recruiting potential participants to a life history study. Participants are told that the telling of their stories may create pain or may result in insight and understanding. Because the telling may create pain, participants also are informed that they should not feel obliged to discuss anything they wish not to. Using volunteers in the study helps the researcher assure that participants feel in control of their telling. If certain individuals are reluctant to explore the past, they should not be recruited into the study.

Thus, the telling of a life history may be therapeutic to the teller. At the same time, the researcher benefits from hearing the life history by being able to construct accounts of phenomena grounded in the life experience of individuals living with the phenomena under study. The knowledge gained by the researcher is therefore grounded in life experience and practical. For this reason, life history can be an extremely useful methodology for gaining knowledge embedded in patient experiences of phenomena of interest to nursing. The result should be derivation of practically applicable clinical nursing theoretical formulations. The theory produced might be a local theory with some postulations that generalize to other individuals experiencing the same phenomenon.

The value of the life history method is, first, its ability to describe in detail the lived experience of a particular phenomenon from the subjective perspective of the individuals involved. Second, the life history method makes it possible for the new generation researcher to gain an appreciation of the process or the sequence of events surrounding a phenomenon. As individuals relate their life stories, the researcher is privy to the time sequence of the events leading to and subsequent to a particular phenomenon (Armstrong, 1987).

Denzin (1989) provided the clearest outline of how to go about completing a life history. According to Denzin, the life history researcher begins by identifying the focus of the inquiry or the research question to be answered by the life history. The researcher then selects the participant or participants from whom the life history will be generated and the form the life history is to take. It is important to make clear at this juncture that a life history can take the form of a single or multiple case studies. In selecting participants, the researcher needs to decide whether a single case or multiple cases are appropriate to construct the life history and answer the research question. Deciding between single or multiple cases is a question of balancing detail of description with the ability to abstract general themes. The single case provides the greatest detail but does not support abstraction of themes; while multiple cases will be edited and thus less detailed, they do provide for abstraction of common themes between cases (Armstrong, 1987).

Denzin (1989) identified two forms the life history can take. The complete life history relates the story of the participant's entire life. The topical life history, in contrast, is concerned with a phase in the participant's life relating to the focus of the study. For example, a nurse researcher may wish to study the development of non-compliance by studying participants' entire life, including how early childhood factors led to the development of non-compliance and how the non-compliance progressed once it became apparent. Or, the nurse researcher may choose to focus only on the phase in the participant's life when the non-compliance became apparent. The nature of the research question will guide the researcher in choosing between a complete or topical life history.

Next, Denzin (1989) said the life history researcher records the events in the participants' lives including, subjective responses to those events. The researcher also will record the participants' interpretations of the events and experiences in their lives, including their perceptions as to causation and sequence. As data are generated, the life history researcher also assures that sources are valid. Firsthand sources are usually the most valid, accurate representations of what actually occurred. Denzin (1989) pointed out, however, for a variety of reasons firsthand sources may distort their telling or perceptions about their life. He suggested using a variety of sources and checking one source against the other to increase the validity of the findings. For example, a nurse researcher might want to research living with AIDS. To do so, the researcher would certainly interview individuals diagnosed with AIDS using the life history approach. If the individual with AIDS said that having AIDS was emotionally draining, resulting in frequent crying episodes, the researcher would then interview someone who lives with the individual with AIDS to verify that indeed the AIDS individual did experience frequent crying episodes.

The researcher analyzes the life stories case by case as they are generated. Cycling back and forth between data generation and data analysis facilitates focusing the emerging life history. If the researcher collaborates with participants as each case is analyzed, this also will help to focus the emerging life history and assure that it represents the reality of the participants.

The final report of the life history is prepared by the researcher and returned to participants for verification. If needed, the researcher may return for additional data generation to clarify discrepancies identified by participants. The researcher then relates the findings of the life history to existing or emerging theory.

Data Generation

The life history researcher may generate data from a variety of sources. The most common sources will be persons who have experienced the focus of the study. Data may be generated from verbal or written accounts of participants who have experienced the phenomenon firsthand by written account in the form of written life stories or "life lines" (Woodhouse, 1992) or through oral interviews. Oral interviews may take the form of individual interviews or focus group interviews. To do the life line exercise described by Woodhouse (1992), the participant draws a straight line on a sheet of paper and records along the line the significant events in his or her life that influenced or related to the focus of the study. The life line exercise is a method of helping participants to remember and organize the significant events in their lives and may be a good starting point for the life history. Armstrong (1987) stated that he prefers the written account for at least beginning the life history because it provides more time for thought for the participant.

A combination of written and oral accounts is often required for a comprehensive accounting of the participant's life history. Repeated interviews are frequently necessary to get an accurate accounting. Oral accounts will usually be tape recorded for later transcription. A researcher may decide not to tape record if the recording provides too great a distraction or intrusion to the participant.

Other sources of data include: public records, such as actuarial records, political and judicial reports, governmental documents, media accounts; and private archival records, such as autobiographies, diaries, and letters (Denzin, 1989). Denzin described a reasonable approach to generating data for life histories. He described the natural history, interpretive approach as follows:

> The natural history, interpretive approach . . . isolates critical experiences and locates them in the subject's social world. It isolates the critical others in the subject's life. It secures personal experience narratives from the subject and his or her significant others, using these stories to fill in the subject's life and bring the subject alive. This approach recreates the subject's life history and then illuminates that history with life stories and self stories. These narratives are fitted to the oral history of the subject. The subject then becomes a case study, whose personal history is compared with the histories of other subjects. This approach realizes that lived time is not linear; it is circular and interactional. The objective temporal division between past, present, and future blurs in the telling of a life story, or personal experience narrative (p. 199).

The natural history, interpretive approach to data generation is especially useful at the beginning of a life history study since it allows the researcher to identify key features of the life history that can then be followed up later for greater detail.

Data Analysis

Data are usually analyzed as qualitative descriptions, although Armstrong (1987) cited instances of the subjective data in a life history being converted to quantitative data and analyzed statistically. The constant comparative technique method of data analysis is the most frequently recommended for life histories. The method is carried out just as described in the naturalistic inquiry section of this chapter. The result of the constant comparative analysis will be a local theory or model as described in naturalistic inquiry.

Armstrong (1987) recommended using the *analytic induction method of data analysis* when the researcher desires generalization beyond the life history, that is, if the researcher is interested in applying themes to individuals other than those participating in the life history investigation. To complete analytic induction the researcher proceeds as in constant comparative analysis and develops a theory or model that explains and describes the relations between themes and categories of information found in the data. Elden (1981) uses the word *local* to describe a theory specific to the data set in an investigation. Then, the researcher looks for negative cases to falsify the local theory or model. In the example of using life history to understand the experience of living with AIDS, the researcher might interview a number of individuals with AIDS and formulate a local theory describing examples of coping mechanisms used by participants in the study. If the next individual interviewed uses a coping mechanism not already described in the investigation, that individual would represent a negative case. Each time a negative case is found, the local theory is revised to account for the negative case. The search for negative cases continues until no more negative cases are found.

Woodhouse (1992) described a method of life history data analysis of multiple life stories using a combination of approaches. She began the analysis by organizing data into three categories as suggested by Mandelbaum (1973): "aspects of the person's life, the principal events in the person's life and conditions in his or her life when these events took place, and how the person adapted" (Woodhouse, 1992, p. 267). Data within each category then are coded according to Miles and Huberman's (1984) first level codings. First level codes are descriptive names the researcher assigns to meaningful word segments in a data set. The word segments may be a phrase, a sentence, or a paragraph in the transcript of field notes that the researcher believes have a particular meaning. The name the researcher uses to label the word segment helps in categorizing the data set into meaningful pieces. Next the researcher contextualizes "the roles, events, relationships, and meanings that the [participants] reported" (p. 268) into schema(ta) following the guidelines of Lofland and Lofland (1984). The schemata include the following elements: acts, activities, meanings, participation, relationships, and settings. The schemata aid the researcher in clustering first level codes or categories together into meaningful patterns. As the researcher pulls categories into meaningful patterns, themes emerge from the data (Goetz & LeCompte, 1984). Woodhouse (1992) provided an excellent example of how the life history research approach can use a variety of qualitative data analysis methods to achieve stated goals.

Reporting the Life History

The life history is reported in a narrative style containing long verbatim descriptions. The goal is to capture as clearly as possible participants' interpretations of the events and experiences in their lives surrounding the focus of the study. The life history, in short, will read very much like a novel. It tells a story, a story that informs.

New generation nurse researchers may choose the life history methodology as an end or as a means to an end. As an end, the life history methodology provides the new generation researcher with a method of gaining knowledge that informs practice and remain true to underlying moral and ethical beliefs. As a means to an end, the life history can be an example of a method of data gathering in either a naturalistic inquiry or an action research study. When used in combination with other methods of data generation, the life history as method can aid the new generation researcher in gaining a unique understanding of the human factors related to the phenomenon under study.

TRUSTWORTHINESS

Lincoln and Guba (1985) provided excellent guidelines for assuring that naturalistic inquiry is trustworthy. They said that an inquiry is trustworthy if the researcher can convince the consumer that the results are "worth paying attention to, worth taking account of" (Lincoln & Guba, 1985, p. 290). Guidelines for assuring *trustworthiness* are equally applicable to all research methodologies described in this chapter and are presented here as guidelines for assuring trustworthiness for new generation nursing research.

The purpose of a new generation nursing research is to uncover the truth of a phenomenon as the practitioners in the identified setting see it. The new generation researcher assures that the representation is true by being immersed in the setting for a prolonged period and repeatedly observing and interacting with practitioners. Second, the truth of a phenomenon is assured through collaborative research methods that involve the participants in data analysis as well as data generation. Triangulation of data generation methods and continual search for negative cases are additional methods of assuring a true representation of the phenomenon under study (Lincoln & Guba, 1985; Denzin, 1989).

The new generation researcher assures that findings can be replicated by laying what Lincoln and Guba (1985) call an "audit trail" (p. 319). To lay an audit trail, the researcher keeps accurate records of all raw data generated, methods of generation, and sources of data. In addition, records are kept of data analysis and the emerging research process. The audit trail should make it possible for another research team to repeat the same inquiry in the same setting, should one choose to do so.

SUMMARY

New generation research represents a shift in philosophy of science. Traditionally assumptions underlying scientific investigations have been concerned with allegiance to a particular research methodology. Traditional researchers believe following a particular research method, whether quantitative or qualitative, results in truth. New generation research, in contrast, abandons reliance on method to provide scientific truth. New generation researchers view scientific problems as multifaceted and complex, thus often requiring multiple research methodologies. New generation research is based on the assumptions that: scientific problems are multifaceted and require multiple research approaches; all research should contribute to practice; and that researchers are ethically responsible to their research participants and for the product of their research.

Naturalistic inquiry, action research, and life history research methodologies have the potential of meeting the assumptions of the new generation research approach. Both naturalistic inquiry and action research facilitate the use of quantitative and qualitative methods of data generation to answer the complex questions posed by nurse researchers. Action research is specifically designed to change practice, while naturalistic inquiry and life history have the potential to change practice but do not explicitly provide for changes within their research strategies.

All three methodologies facilitate collaboration between researchers and participants and can be equally beneficial to both parties. Participants can be actively involved in planning the emerging research design of a naturalistic inquiry. Active involvement of research participants in an action research study results in a positive response to change and in teaching research participants to be change agents. The life history methodology benefits research participants by providing an avenue for them to gain insight and new understandings about their lives.

Researchers, in following new generation assumptions, may use multiple research methodologies to answer their research questions. In addition, new generation researchers freely revise and redesign research methodologies to answer their research questions adequately. In the new generation of research, provision of practice-related research and ethical responsibility to research participants are prime considerations.

Chapter 12 discusses nursing research studies using new generation approaches. New generation approaches to research are in their infancy in nursing research. A review of current research practice with these approaches aids the reader in applying these exciting methodologies to nursing research.

REFERENCES

Argyris, C., Putnam, R., & Smith, D. M. (1985). *Action science*. San Francisco: Jossey-Bass Publishers.

Armstrong, P. F. (1987). *Qualitative strategies in social and educational research: The life history method in theory and practice*. The University of Hull School of Adult and Continuing Education, Newland Papers, Number 14, Hull, U.K.

Clark, P. (1972). *Action research and organizational change*. New York: Harper & Row, Publishers.

DeGroot, H. A. (1988). Scientific inquiry in nursing: A model for a new generation. *Advances in Nursing Science, 10*(3),1–21.

Denzin, N. K. (1989). *The research act: A theoretical introduction to sociological methods.* Englewood Cliffs, NJ: Prentice Hall.

Duffy, M. E. (1987). Triangulation: A vehicle for merging quantitative and qualitative research methods. *Image: The Journal of Nursing Research, 19,* 130–133.

Elden, M. (1981). Sharing the research work: Participative research and its role demands. In P. Reason & J. Rowan (Eds.), *Human inquiry: A sourcebook of new paradigm research* (pp. 253–266). New York: Wiley & Sons.

Faraday, A., & Plummer, K. (1979). Doing life histories. *Sociological Review, 27,* 773–798.

Feyerabend, P. (1970). Consolations for the specialist. In I. Lakatos & A. Musgrave (Eds.), *Criticism and the growth of knowledge* (pp. 197–230). Cambridge: Cambridge University Press.

Gadamar, G. (1989). *Truth and method,*2nd ed., J. Weinheimer & D. Marshall (Trans). London: Sheer & Ward.

Glaser, B., & Strauss, A. (1967). *The discovery of grounded theory.* Chicago: Aldine Publishing Co.

Goetz, J., & LeCompte, M. (1984). *Ethnography and qualitative design in educational research.* New York: Academic Press.

Gortner, S. R. (1990). Nursing values and science: Toward a science philosophy. *Image: Journal of Nursing Scholarship, 22,* 101–105

Gortner, S. R., & Schultz, P. R. (1988). Approaches to nursing science methods. *Image: Journal of Nursing Scholarship, 20,* 22–24.

Guba, E. G., & Lincoln, Y. S. (1989). *Fourth generation evaluation.* Newbury Park, CA: Sage Publications.

Habermas, J. (1971). *Knowledge and human interest,* J. Strapiro (Trans.). Boston: Beacon Press.

Habermas, J. (1975). A postscript to knowledge and human interest. *Philosophy of the Social Sciences, 2,* 157–189.

Heidegger, M. (1962). *Being and time.* J. Macquarrie & E. Robinson (Trans.). New York: Harper & Row.

Heron, J. (1981). Philosophical basis for a new paradigm. In P. Reason & J. Rowan (Eds.), *Human inquiry: A sourcebook of new paradigm research* (pp. 19–36). New York: Wiley & Sons.

Kuhn, T. (1970). Logic of discovery or psychology of research? In I. Lakatos & A. Musgrave (Eds.), *Criticism and the growth of knowledge* (pp. 1–24). Cambridge: Cambridge University Press.

Lakatos, I. (1981). History of science and its rational reconstructions. In I. Hacking (Ed.), *Scientific revolutions* (pp. 107–127). Hong Kong: Oxford University Press.

Laudan, L. (1981). A problem-solving approach to scientific progress. In I. Hacking (Ed.), *Scientific revolutions* (pp. 144–155). Hong Kong: Oxford University Press.

Lewin, K. (1946). Action research and minority problems. *Journal of Social Issues, 2,* 34–46.

Lincoln, Y. S., & Guba, E. G. (1985). *Naturalistic inquiry.* Newbury Park, CA: Sage Publications.

Lofland, J., & Lofland, L. (1984). *Analyzing social settings: A guide to qualitative observation and analysis*, 2nd ed. Belmont, CA: Mayfield.

MacDonald, J. (1992). Project 2000 curriculum evaluation: The case for teacher evaluation. *Nurse Education Today, 12*, 101–107.

Mandelbaum, D. (1973). The study of life history: Gandhi. *Current Anthropology, 14*, 177–206.

Miles, M., & Huberman, A. (1984). *Qualitative data analysis*. Beverly Hills, CA: Sage Publications.

Moccia, P. (1988). A critique of compromise: Beyond the methods debate. *Advances in Nursing Science, 10*(4), 1–9.

Reason, P. (1988). Introduction. In P. Reason (Ed.), *Human inquiry in action* (pp. 1–17). Newbury Park, CA: Sage Publications.

Rowan, J. (1981). A dialectical paradigm for research. In P. Reason & J. Rowan (Eds.), *Human inquiry*, (pp. 93–112). New York: John Wiley & Sons.

Susman, G. I., & Evered, R. D. (1978). An assessment of the scientific merits of action research, *Administrative Science Quarterly, 73*, 582–603.

Toulmin, S. (1985). Pluralism and responsibility in post modern science. *Science, Technology, and Human Values, 10*, 28–37.

Whyte, W. F. (1991). Participatory action research: Through practice to science in social research. In W. F. Whyte (Ed.), *Participatory action research*. Newbury Park, CA: Sage Publications.

Winter, R. (1989). *Learning from experience: Principles and practices in action-research*. Philadelphia: Falmer Press.

Woodhouse, L. D. (1992). Women with jagged edges: Voices from a culture of substance abuse. *Qualitative Health Research, 2*, 262–281.

Chapter 12

New Generation Research Approaches Applied to Nursing Education, Practice, and Administration

Nurse philosophers of science have begun to suggest the use of new generation research approaches for nursing research (DeGroot, 1988; Gortner, 1990; Gortner & Schultz, 1988; Moccia, 1988). Assumptions underlying new generation research approaches are: a belief that nursing research should emphasize both the humanness and the technology of nursing; a belief that the primary purpose of nursing research should aim to improve nursing practice; and a belief that nursing research should be equally beneficial to researchers and research participants. In this chapter a critical review of published nursing research studies using new generation approaches reveals the extent to which nurse researchers have adopted the beliefs of new generation research.

Appendix 12.1, found at the end of the chapter, provides an overview of all research studies published in the nursing literature since 1984 using new generation methodologies. Although the studies are few in number, they do represent each of the new generation research methodologies. In addition, the studies also represent the three areas of nursing practice: clinical, administrative, and educational nursing practice.

Because few examples of new generation research methodology were found in the published literature, a review of nursing dissertations is included to represent the use of new generation approaches by beginning nurse researchers. Appendix 12.2, found at the end of the chapter, summarizes examples of nursing dissertations using new generation research approaches.

The majority of dissertations presented use the naturalistic inquiry approach. The studies are predominantly in the area of clinical nursing practice. The dissertations related to nursing practice were written to gain insight and understanding of clients and of phenomenon of concern to clients, such as sexuality (Lion, 1992), homelessness (Heusel, 1990), and independence (Morrissey, 1984). Rarely do the authors of the dissertation abstracts explicitly describe the relation of the study findings to clinical practice. One exception is the study by Thorne (1990) in which the author explicitly states the purpose of the study is to effect a change in health policy. Only one dissertation (O'Quinn-Larson, 1989) was related to nursing education. Its focus was the understanding of nursing students, specifically those nursing students with a chemical dependence. The single dissertation (Thorpe, 1989) related to nursing administration focused on nursing educational leadership.

Beginning nurse researchers are using new generation research methodologies during their doctoral studies. It is impossible to determine whether or not these beginning researchers have chosen their methodologies because they support new generation belief since they to not discuss their reasons for choosing these research methodologies in their published abstracts.

NEW GENERATION RESEARCH APPROACHES AND CLINICAL NURSING PRACTICE

Clinical nursing practice problems are complex and multifaceted. They often include both technological aspects and human system factors. Nurse researchers following the assumptions of new generation research recognize that nursing clinical practice problems are complex and for this reason they may choose new generation research approaches to answer their research questions. The studies were critiqued in this section using criteria identified in Table 12.1 A report of the Kelly (1991 study can be found at the end of this chapter to assist the reader in understanding the critiquing process.

Life History Methodology

An excellent example of new generation nursing research related to nursing clinical practice is the study "Emily: A Study of Grief and Bereavement" by Kelly (1991). The research report is reviewed here as an example of a new generation approach, life history, to clinical nursing practice scientific investigation.

Kelly (1991) embarked on this research study seeking to understand and explain what appeared to be an intense grief reaction in an 83-year-old

TABLE 12.1 CRITERIA FOR CRITICAL REVIEW OF NEW GENERATION RESEARCH APPROACHES

1. Does the study provide for a collaborative effort between researchers and research participants in planning and implementing the research?
2. Does the researcher use data generation techniques appropriate to the research questions asked?
   a. Are qualitative techniques used when human qualities are studied?
   b. Are quantitative techniques used with technological factors?
   c. Are multiple techniques of data generation used?
3. Is at least one of the aims or purposes of the study to improve clinical,administrative, or educational nursing practice?
4. Does the researcher describe the benefit of the study to research participants?
5. Has the researcher discussed ethical and moral implications of the study results?
6. What theoretical framework guides the study?
7. Is sufficient contextual detail provided to facilitate the reader's judgment about transfer of findings to similar settings and situations?
8. Are methods for assuring trustworthiness of the findings described?

widow recently admitted to a nursing home. Kelly chose the life history approach to answer the research question because she believed this woman's life events would provide insight into her current intense grief reaction.

Kelly (1991) gained insight into Emily's intensive grief reaction through the life history approach. Through a series of interviews with Emily, Kelly discovered that Emily had experienced several dependent relationships, followed by loss in her life. Her first dependent relationship was with her mother. When Emily lost her mother through death, she became intensely insecure and grief stricken. Rather than learning to be independent without her mother, Emily quickly married a man upon whom she also became very dependent. When Emily's husband died, her grief reaction was extremely intense because she had never learned the skills of independent living. She was unable to develop a dependent relationship after her husband's death and thus experienced intense, prolonged grief.

The life history study of Emily is an excellent example of a single-case, topical life history. The single case is represented by one grieving woman, Emily. The topic of the life history study is grief and bereavement as exemplified through Emily's telling the story of her grief. Emily's story also provides an excellent example of how the life history method facilitates explication of timing and sequencing of events in an individual's life to gain understanding of a phenomenon, such as grief. Through

Emily's story, Kelly (1991) is able to trace the beginning of Emily's grief reaction to her childhood relationship with her mother. The life history clearly describes the sequence of events in Emily's life and how those events help to explain Emily's current grief reaction. The events begin with Emily's relationship with her mother, move to her mother's death, her marriage, her relationship with her husband, and the death of her husband. Each of these events in turn helps the reader to understand Emily's current state of grief.

Kelly (1991) told us the purpose of her study is to "better understand . . . the events and behavior complicating the adjustment to the loss of a spouse" (p. 138) as experienced by Emily. Although the stated purpose is to develop a local theory describing Emily's bereavement, Kelly also identified nursing implications of the study results. She described important factors for the nurse to assess in order to facilitate the grieving process in any patient. Although she did not discuss it in the research report, Kelly may have directly influenced nursing practice if she had communicated her findings to the staff caring for Emily in the nursing home and discussed with the staff methods for using this information in Emily's nursing care. The findings had the potential to assist the nurses in caring for Emily and also could have taught the staff to use similar assessments when providing supportive bereavement care to other grieving patients.

Kelly (1991) used grief and bereavement theory to guide her thinking but did not use the theory as a framework for interpretation of data generated in the study. She allowed the local theory to emerge inductively from the study.

In very subtle ways, Kelly (1991) provided for active participation of Emily in the emerging research method. After meeting Emily, Kelly revised her original intention to be consistent with Emily's current state. She abandoned her original idea of assessing Emily's adaptation to the nursing home to instead "listen to whatever was uppermost in her [Emily's] mind" (p. 140). This very sensitive nurse researcher recognized that following Emily's needs would allow her to achieve her research aim of understanding Emily. Had she persisted with her original plan, her research purpose never would have been achieved and Emily would have suffered in the process. This subtle collaboration with the research participant is an excellent example of how new generation research methods emerge as the researcher collaborates with the research participant.

Kelly (1991) used a series of interviews to answer her research question, understanding a human being. Only qualitative methods could have provided this unique understanding of Emily. By listening to Emily's words, the researcher was able to gain an understanding of Emily's current feelings and perceptions, and of the interrelation between past related events and feelings and Emily's current state. Only Emily's words could have provided this insight.

Kelly (1991) provided sufficient contextual detail to allow the reader to judge whether findings about Emily's grief can be transferred to other patients with similar grief reactions. In reporting her findings, Kelly provided the reader with great detail about the story, frequently quoting Emily's words.

Although she does not list methods of providing trustworthiness, Kelly (1991) described her method in sufficient detail to give at least some insight into the trustworthiness of her findings. Kelly provided for trustworthiness by meeting with Emily repeatedly over an extended period, by recording field notes after each interaction with Emily, and by seeking peer review of her findings and interpretations. Additional methods of providing trustworthiness might have been to corroborate the accuracy of events as Emily described them through interviewing an outside source such as Emily's son or friends. Kelly also could have demonstrated the accuracy of Emily's story by verifying the accuracy of dates and sequencing of events with public record of those events if available, i.e., the date of her husband's illness, elapsed time between illness and death of her husband, and elapsed time between death of her husband and loss of her home. Kelly also could have provided for trustworthiness of her data by verifying her perceptions and interpretations with Emily to assure their accuracy. Kelly never told us that she completed this verification; however, it likely could have occurred as a natural consequence of Kelly's communication with Emily.

Kelly (1991) very clearly described the benefits of this life history research to Emily. In Emily's words, "Oh, my dear, am I any help at all to you? It seems as if you are here to help me instead of the other way around" (p. 140). Kelly did not discuss the ethical and moral implications of her study in the research report.

The life history of Emily's grief is an excellent example of a new generation research approach in nursing clinical practice. The life history methodology has provided understanding and meaning of Emily's grief. The study is related to clinical nursing practice and has been implemented in such a way that it is equally beneficial to the researcher and the research participant.

Action Research

A second study of clinical nursing practice is presented as an example of the use of action research in nursing. The study, "Primary Nursing and the Role of the Nurse Preceptor in Changing Long-Term Mental Health Care: An Evaluation," is reported in the *Journal of Advanced Nursing* by

Armitage, Champney-Smith, and Andrews (1991). The purpose of this action research study was to implement and evaluate the change to primary nursing on two psychiatric patient units.

The principal investigator in this study, a nurse educator, served as the outside facilitator for this action research study. The study began with an exploratory survey (Armitage, 1986) of the current nursing care practices on a psychiatric unit. The researcher used patient record review, interviews of nurses working on the unit, a survey assessment of the nurses' perception of patients' survival skills, a five-minute interval timed-analysis of patient and nurse activity on the unit, and participant/observation of four patients for one entire day. This intense observation revealed that methods of nursing care delivery on the unit were "custodial and outmoded" (Armitage, Champney-Smith, & Andrews, 1991, p. 414), resulting in very little rehabilitation of the patients housed on the unit. Following the exploratory study, the researcher concluded that institution of a primary nursing method of nursing care on the unit might help to rectify the situation. The authors of the research report did not state whether or not the nurses collaborated in the decision to institute the system of primary care.

This initial exploratory study also provided excellent detail about the contextual factors in one of the patient units. No information was provided about contextual factors in the second unit. Sufficient detail was provided to facilitate reader judgment about transferability of the study methodology to a similar psychiatric patient care unit.

The research team identified a number of patient and nurse related indicators of success of the planned change. These indicators were measured prior to the introduction of the change to primary care to establish a base line. The methods of evaluation included observation of nurses giving patient care and holding clinical meetings and surveys of nursing staff satisfaction, attitudes, and opinions of the atmosphere on the unit. Patients were interviewed to determine their satisfaction with care on the unit. Additionally, nursing care was audited through a retrospective analysis of nursing records. These methods of generating data for evaluating the change were very appropriate to the outcome measures.

The researchers reported giving considerable attention to collaboration with nursing staff to facilitate implementation of the planned change. They recognized at the outset that the change would not be effective unless the staff giving nursing care were involved in making those decisions. A nurse change agent position was created on each unit to facilitate decision making with the staff. The nurse change agent implemented quality circles on the units to involve the staff nurses directly in planning for the change in care delivery.

Trustworthiness was not discussed by the researchers. However, the study methodology is an excellent example of the use of triangulation of data generation methods to provide for credibility of findings. In addition, sufficient information was provided to audit the research process in this study.

The post-change evaluation measures used in the study clearly point out the benefit of the nurses participating in the research study. Staff completed a very detailed questionnaire that assessed their level of work satisfaction following the implementation of the change. The researchers did not discuss ethical and moral implications of the change to primary nursing.

Naturalistic Inquiry

Naturalistic inquiry methods of research can be used to gain understanding of phenomena of concern to nurses in clinical practice, as has been demonstrated by several abstracts of doctoral dissertations. Yet, no published reports of naturalistic inquiry were found in the published nursing literature related to clinical nursing practice.

NEW GENERATION RESEARCH APPROACHES AND NURSING ADMINISTRATION

Problems of concern to nurses researching nursing administration are complex and multifaceted. New generation research approaches can be used to answer nursing administration research questions and to improve the practice of nursing administration. An example of the use of a new generation approach to nursing administration research is the study "Life and Career Pathways of Deans in Nursing Programs" by Redmond (1991). This study is the single published report of a naturalistic inquiry found in the nursing literature.

In this study Redmond (1991) used naturalistic inquiry to describe the "life and career paths of women who became deans of nursing programs" (p. 228). Redmond used three methods to gather data from the deans: life history interview, document search of the deans' curriculum vitae, and survey. The researcher did not offer an explanation as to why she chose the three data collection methods. The use of life history in this study is one method of data collection using the naturalistic inquiry approach, in contrast to Kelly's study (1991) where the life history was the sole methodology of the study. In this case, the life history is a multiple-case life history. The topic for the life history in this study is preparation for the nursing deanship.

Redmond's (1991) purpose in completing a naturalistic inquiry of the deans was to "identify how present deans obtained the special knowledge and skill to deal with the demands of their current administrative positions" (p. 228). Her purpose in choosing the approach was that it allowed her to describe "the deans' perspectives on the people, relationships, events, and experiences that were important factors in their lives and careers, and that influenced them in their assumption of the dean's position" (p. 228). This approach allowed Redmond to identify a local theory of the deanship grounded in the perspective of currently practicing deans. Redmond did not extend her study to influence the practice of the nursing deanship, but she did identify practice implications for her findings. She identified a need for existing deans to groom and mentor select faculty members for the deanships. She also suggested that specific programs and networks be developed for the purpose of grooming and mentoring future deans.

Redmond (1991) clearly identified a developmental model based on the work of Erickson (1950, 1968), Morgan and Farber (1982), and Levinson (1978) as the theoretical framework for her study. In addition, she explained at the outset how she used the theoretical framework to link childhood factors with adult qualities in the deans. Although Redmond identified and used a theoretical framework, she allowed the data to diverge from the theory, refining and revising her theoretical formulations as the data dictated. In this way, Redmond was successful in creating a local theory of the deanship grounded in perspectives of the deans in the study.

Redmond (1991) indirectly involved nursing school deans in the planning of her study and directly collaborated with the dean participants in implementing her study. Redmond began the study by surveying 53 deans of nursing for demographic characteristics and data related to life and career relationships and experiences. This initial step represents phase I of the naturalistic inquiry, providing Redmond with insight into the deans' perspectives of these key areas. Although she did not choose to do so, Redmond also could have asked the deans if there were additional crucial areas that should be considered and how she might go about obtaining those data.

Following the initial survey, Redmond (1991) interviewed 6 deans of nursing and reviewed their curriculum vitae. Following her interpretation of data gained from the interviews and document search, Redmond gave the interpretative description to each dean participant to review for accuracy. The researcher also met again with each dean after they read the interpretative description to assure that her interpretations accurately reflected the deans' experiences and perceptions.

Redmond (1991) stated her research question: "What life and career experiences and relationships do deans of nursing programs identify as significant factors in their pathway to the deanship?" (p. 229). This research question related to human factors in the deans' experiences and relationships, and is appropriately researched through the qualitative methods of life history interview and survey. The researcher did not report on the specifics of the survey in the article, but it appears that she used the survey to provide both qualitative and quantitative demographic data for the study.

Further, Redmond (1991) identified four major domains important in the pathway to the deanship: significant others, educational experiences, occupational experiences, and personal events. She described examples from the deans' life stories for each of these domains. The examples are in the words of the deans and include sufficient contextual data for reader understanding and judgment about the transferability of findings.

Describing it as validity and reliability, Redmond (1991) provided a comprehensive description of assurance of trustworthiness. She provided a well-documented theoretical framework upon which she based her study. She also carefully described how she developed her survey and interview protocol through pilot testing and revision. A very detailed description of how the researcher analyzed her data provided for auditing of the procedures. It is clear to the reader how the researcher arrived at a domain from the deans' life stories. In addition, the researcher clearly listed the various subdomains as they were derived from the deans' stories. Redmond assured the credibility of her findings by using interview and document search methods of data gathering, by repeatedly interviewing each dean, and by having the dean participants validate the accuracy of the researcher's interpretations.

Redmond (1991) mentioned in the report that she considered the dean participants as "co-researchers" (p. 231), but she did not describe how the study directly benefitted the participants. It would be interesting to know if the deans felt that they were benefitted by participating in the study. Ethical and moral implications of the study were not discussed by the researcher.

Redmond's (1991) study of nursing deans provided a fine example of a naturalistic inquiry used to answer a nursing administration practice question. She expressed some assumptions related to new generation belief. She provided implications of the study results for administrative practice, designed her methods to answer the question asked, and considered the participants as partners in her study. It was not clear whether the participants view themselves as partners or as subjects in this study.

Both Redmond (1991) in her published study and Thorpe (1989) in her dissertation demonstrated that naturalistic inquiry can provide valuable insights for nurse administrators. Both have used new generation research approaches to provide insights into leaders of nursing education. Redmond concentrated on development of leaders, while Thorpe emphasized leader performance. Both represent a beginning and at least an indication that new generation research has potential benefit to nursing administration.

NEW GENERATION RESEARCH APPROACHES AND NURSING EDUCATION

Nurses researching nursing education have barely begun to take advantage of new generation approaches to nursing research. The one published study found in the nursing literature is reviewed to provide an example of how new generation approaches can provide valuable insight and understanding for nurse educators. The study is an action research study completed by McCaugherty (1991). He titled his report of the research, "The Use of a Teaching Model to Promote Reflection and Experiential Integration of Theory and Practice in First-Year Students: An Action Research Study."

McCaugherty (1991) embarked on this study because he wanted to improve the practice of nursing education. Specifically, he wanted to develop a teaching model that would facilitate the integration of theory and practice in the first year student. McCaugherty is a nurse educator who completed his action research study in several phases to achieve his aim. He began by searching the literature related to integration of theory and practice and based on his findings developed a tentative teaching model that would achieve his aim. The teaching model was guided by a theoretical framework based on the Kolb Learning Cycle (Kolb, 1984).

In the second phase of the study, McCaugherty (1991) became a teacher and participant/observer researcher to create the most effective teaching model possible. Following Lewin's action research, McCaugherty put his teaching model, a "ward tutorial" (p. 537), into action with small groups of students and evaluated its effectiveness in the process. Developing the teaching model through teaching allowed McCaugherty to involve his students in the implementation of the research study. Evaluation was accomplished through a teacher-recorded diary of each teaching session and teacher-conducted semi-structured interviews with students.

In the final phase of the study McCaugherty (1991) used a "static group comparison" (p. 538) research design to evaluate the effectiveness of the ward tutorial teaching model in achieving integration of theory and practice for nursing students. Through this design he compared students on one patient ward who were not exposed to tutorial teaching to students on another ward who were exposed to tutorial teaching. He used "spot checks" (p. 538) of students' knowledge and rationale for the care they provided their patients to evaluate the effectiveness of the teaching model in achieving integration of theory and practice. The spot checks occurred on both wards without warning to students. McCaugherty reported that he used a "qualitative approach" (p. 535) in analyzing the spot checks, diaries, and student interviews, but he offered no details as to how this was accomplished.

McCaugherty (1991) reported only the results of the spot checks analysis. Although he stated that he analyzed the spot checks qualitatively, he reported the results quantitatively in the form of a histogram, listing categories of student response as "good, satisfactory, or poor" (p. 538). Reporting examples of the students' actual responses to the spot checks and an identification of themes as they occurred in the students' responses would have provided valuable insight to the reader specifically related to how the students actually performed. As McCaugherty reported his data, the reader is left with no insight into the student response to the teaching model, except to know that the researcher categorized them as good, satisfactory, or poor.

McCaugherty (1991) was successful in reporting qualitative response of the teacher to the teaching method, although he did not tell us how these data were gathered. The report is random rather than systematic, but does provide the reader with insight into the strengths and weaknesses of the teaching method from a teacher and curriculum perspective.

A second weakness of this study is the researcher's failure to provide the reader with contextual detail of the teaching environment in which the study occurred. Without this detail the reader cannot judge whether the results might transfer to another setting.

The researcher did discuss the "validity" (p. 539) of the spot checks as accurate measures of student ability to integrate theory and practice. He concluded that the spot checks were not "indicator[s] of nursing care . . . however, [they] provide some indication of the students' understanding" (p. 539). He did not discuss ethical and moral indications of the study.

This study provides an excellent example of the use of action research to evaluate an innovative model of teaching. The researcher was successful in designing a study that was equally beneficial to researcher and participants and that directly benefitted the practice of nursing education. This study is not a good example of the use of qualitative methods of data analysis to provide meaning and understanding. The researcher's method of converting qualitative data to quantitative data for presentation deprived the reader of valuable insight into the students' ability to integrate theory and practice.

McCaugherty's (1991) study demonstrates that new generation research approaches have potential benefit to nurse educators through development of student and clinical practice appropriate teaching methodologies. In addition, O'Quinn-Larson (1989) in her dissertation demonstrates that naturalistic inquiry can be a new generation approach to providing understanding of nursing students. These studies represent at least a beginning use of new generation research approaches to benefit nursing education.

SUMMARY

Naturalistic inquiry, life history, and action research approaches to new generation research are being used by nurse researchers. Their use is evident in clinical nursing practice, nursing education, and nursing administration. Evidence exists that at least some of the researchers have followed the assumptions of new generation research in their use of these approaches. Many researchers state their desire to create equal benefit to research participants in their research reports. Also, many studies have the aim of improving nursing practice. Most of the studies use only qualitative methods of data collection and analysis; however, a few examples do recognize the complexity of nursing problems and include both quantitative and qualitative methods of data generation.

Most researchers reported that they chose a new generation method of research because of its consistency with the humanness of nursing. Yet, very few researchers reported using new generation methodologies for the direct purposes of improving nursing practice, supporting a belief in social responsibility, or empowering research participants. The failure of many nurse researchers to justify their choice of new generation methodologies because of beliefs in social responsibility and the democratic ideal may reflect the newness of new generation research ideas and the slow acceptance of those beliefs among nursing scholars. As with any novel thought, acceptance of new ideas about research comes gradually.

REFERENCES

Armitage, P. (1986). The rehabilitation and nursing care of severely disabled psychiatric patients. *International Journal of Nursing Studies, 23,* 113–123.

Armitage, P., Champney-Smith, J., & Andrews, K. (1991). Primary nursing and the role of the nurse preceptor in changing long-term mental health care: An evaluation. *Journal of Advanced Nursing, 16,* 413–422.

Bramwell, L. (1984). Use of the life history in pattern identification and health promotion. *Advances in Nursing Science, 7*(1), 37–44.

DeGroot, H. A. (1988). Scientific inquiry in nursing: A model for a new generation. *Advances in Nursing Science, 10*(3), 1–21

DesRosier, M., & Cantanzaro, M. (1992). Living with chronic illness: Social support and the well spouse perspective. *Rehabilitation Nursing, 17,* 87–91.

Erickson, E. (1950). *Childhood and society.* New York: Norton.

Erickson, E. (1968). *Identity and youth, in crisis.* New York: Norton.

Ford, S. (1989). Home care clients' meanings of home. *Dissertations Abstracts International, B 50/10*, 4452.

Gortner, S. R. (1990). Nursing values and science: Toward a science philosophy. *Image: Journal of Nursing Scholarship, 22*, 101–105.

Gortner, S. R., & Schultz, P. R. (1988). Approaches to nursing science methods. *Image: Journal of Nursing Scholarship, 20*, 22–24.

Gustafson, D. C. (1988). Signaling behavior in stage I labor to elicit care: A clinical referent for Wiedenbach's need for help. *Dissertation Abstracts International, B49/10*, 4230.

Heusel, K. J. (1990). The experience of homelessness viewed through the eyes of homeless school-age children. *Dissertation Abstracts International, B 51/10* , 1991.

Jenks, J. M. (1993). The pattern of personal knowing in nurse clinical decision-making. *Journal of Nursing Education, 32*, 399–405.

Jacavone, J., & Dostal, M. (1992). A descriptive study of nursing judgment in the assessment and management of cardiac pain. *Advances in Nursing Science, 15*(1), 54–63.

Kelly, B. (1991). Emily: A study of grief and bereavement. *Health Care for Women International, 12*, 137–147.

Kenner, C. A. (1988). Parent transition from the newborn intensive care unit (NICU) to home. *Dissertation Abstracts International, B 49/08*, 3105.

Kolb, D. A. (1984). *Experiential learning.* Englewood Cliffs, NJ: Prentice Hall.

Levinson, D. J. (1978). *The seasons of a man's life.* New York: Alfred A. Knopf.

Lion, E. M. (1992). Sexuality of the dying: What dying participants, their spouses and their caregivers teach us about the sexuality of the dying. *Dissertation Abstracts International, B51/10*, 4779.

Mayo, K. (1992). Physical activity practices among American black working women. *Qualitative Health Research, 2*, 318–333.

McCaugherty, D. (1991). The use of a teaching model to promote reflection and the experiential integration of theory and practice in first-year student nurses: An action research study. *Journal of Advanced Nursing, 16*, 534–543.

Moccia, P. (1988). A critique of compromise: Beyond the methods debate. *Advances in Nursing Science, 10*(4), 1–9.

Morgan, E., & Farber, B. (1982). Toward a reformulation of the Ericksonian model of female identify development. *Adolescence, 17*, 199–211.

Morrissey, S. M. (1984) Resources and characteristics of elderly women living alone in a community. *Dissertation Abstracts International,* 280.

O'Quinn-Larson, J. B. (1989). Registered nurses' perceptions of factors related to chemical dependency in nursing students. *Dissertation Abstracts International, B 50/06*, 2341.

Poslusny, S. M. (1990). Women's friendship in depression: The lived experience of depressed and non-depressed friends. *Dissertation Abstracts International, B 52/03* 1356.

Redmond, G. M. (1991). Life and career pathways of deans in nursing programs. *Journal of Professional Nursing, 7*, 228–238.

Roe, M. L. (1989). Relationships between professional interactions and patient care behaviors. *Dissertation Abstracts International, B 52/03*, 906.

Rosenbaum, J. N. (1991), The health meanings and practices of older Greek-Canadian widows. *Journal of Advanced Nursing, 16*, 1320–1327.

Sachs, B. A., Poland, M. L., & Giblin, P. T. (1990). Enhancing the adolescent reproductive process: Efforts to implement a program for black adolescent fathers. *Health Care for Women International, 11*, 447–460.

Thompson, J. (1991). Exploring gender and culture with Khmer refugee women: Reflections on participatory feminist research. *Advances in Nursing Science, 13*(3), 30–48.

Thorne, S. E. (1990). Navigating troubled waters: Chronic illness experience in a health care crisis. *Dissertation Abstracts International, B 51/12*, 5811.

Thorpe, K. M. (1989). *Interpreting the activities of nursing educational administrators: A leadership perspective.* Unpublished doctoral dissertation, University of Alberta, Canada.

Webb, C. (1990). Partners in research. *Nursing Times, 86*(32), 40–44.

West-Sands, L. D. (1990). Embracing the ugly child within: Life history of an incest survivor. *Dissertation Abstracts International, B 51/12*, 5812.

Whyte, D. (1992). A family nursing approach to the care of a child with a chronic illness. *Journal of Advanced Nursing, 17*, 317–327.

Author/Pub.Date	Method	Why Method Chosen	Purpose	Data Analysis
Clinical Nursing Practice				
Bramell, L. (1984)	Full, multi-subject life history	Retains nursing's holistic perspective	Gain holistic perspective of human patterning; theory development	Qualitative
Rosenbaum, J. N. (1991)	Life history: ethnography	Little knowledge known about the subject	To discover meaning of health care to this culture of women	Qualitative
Thompson, J. (1991)	Life history: feminist participatory	Gain understanding of women's experience and women's struggles	Explore psycho-social adjustment within a cultural context in refugee women	Qualitative
Whyte, D. (1992)	Life history: ethnography	Little known about the phenomenon, providing support	Gain new knowledge about providing nursing in practice	Qualitative
Sachs, B. A., Poland, M. L. Giblin, P. T. (1990)	Action research	Integrate research into ongoing programs while continuously monitoring those programs	Evaluate a program designed to involve adolescent fathers in child-bearing and child rearing	Not described
Webb, C. (1990)	Action research	To motivate nursing staff to change	Implement a change in nursing practice	Qualitative and quantative
DesRosier, M., Cantanzaro, M., & Piller, J.	Naturalistic inquiry	Not addressed by the authors	Describe experience of women caring for their husbands with debilitating muscular sclerosis	Qualitative

283

(cont'd.)

APPENDIX 12.1 (CONT'D.)

Author/ Pub.Date	Method	Why Method Chosen	Purpose	Data Analysis
Clinical Nursing Practice				
Jacavone, J., & Dostal, M. (1992)	Naturalistic inquiry	Gain new knowledge about nurse decision making	Gain practice based knowledge of nurse clinical decision making about cardiac pain	Qualitative
Jenks, J. (1993)	Naturalistic inquiry	Gain new understanding of nurse clinical decision making	Gain practice based understanding of nurse clinical decision making	Qualitative
Mayo, K. (1992)	Naturalistic inquiry	To understand physical activity from an emic perspective	Understand how black women man- age a program of physical activity within the context of their daily lives	Qualitative

Author/ Abstr. Date	Research Methods	Purpose	Methods of Data Collection	Data Analysis
Clinical Nursing Practice				
Morrissey, S. M. (1984)	Naturalistic inquiry	Describe the role of health and other variables in maintaining the independence of the elderly	Interview	Qualitative
Kenner, C. A. (1988)	Naturalistic inquiry	Describe parental response to caring for newborns at home following discharge from a critical care unit	Interview	Qualitative
Ford, S. (1989)	Naturalistic inquiry	Explore and describe the concept of home from the perspective of clients	Life history interview	Qualitative
Roe, M. L. (1989)	Naturalistic inquiry	Describe the relationships between nurse-physician interactions and patient care behaviors in emergency rooms and neonatal units	Interview, video, observation	Qualitative
Gustafson, D. C. (1988)	Naturalistic inquiry	Describe verbal and nonverbal cues indicating a call for help in laboring women	Interview, video, observation	Qualitative
Heusel, K. J. (1990)	Naturalistic inquiry	Describe the experience of homelessness from the child's perspective	Interview	Qualitative
Poslusny, S. M. (1990)	Naturalistic inquiry	Describe the meaning of friendship to clinically depressed women	Interview questionnaire	Qualitative
Thorne, S. E. (1990)	Naturalistic inquiry	Describe and analyze chronic illness to effect a change in health care policy	Unstated	Qualitative

(cont'd.)

APPENDIX 12.2 (CONT'D.)

Author/ Abstr. Date	Research Methods	Purpose	Methods of Data Collection	Data Analysis
Clinical Nursing Practice				
Lion, E. M. (1991)	Naturalistic inquiry	Gain understanding and insight into the sexuality of the dying	Interview, observation, document review	Not described
West-Sands, L. D. (1990)	Life history	Describe the lived experience of incestuous abuse	Interview	Qualitative
Nursing Education				
O'Quinn-Larson, J. B. (1989)	Naturalistic inquiry	Describe the phenomenon of chemical dependency in nursing students	Interview	Qualitative
Nursing Administration				
Thorpe, K. M. (1989)	Naturalistic inquiry	Derive insight into nursing educational leadership through an interpretative description of activities and meanings of administrators in nursing educational institutions	Interview	Qualitative

Emily: A Study of Grief and Bereavement

Brighid Kelly, RN, C, PhD

The author's purpose in presenting this article is to describe and interpret the phenomena that contributed to a state of extended bereavement in an 83-year-old widow. The problem concerned a newly admitted nursing home resident who appeared to be experiencing profound grief at the loss of a husband who had died 12 years earlier. The method was qualitative, specifically, ethnographic. This case study focuses on the life history of one individual as she perceived it. The question posed for the study was what are the factors contributing to a grief reaction in an elderly widow 12 years after her husband's death? To answer this question a series of interviews were conducted with the informant. The data were then analyzed for meaning in light of current theory in grief and bereavement. The findings, presented in the informant's words, highlight the importance of suddenness, multiplicity of losses, relationship with the deceased spouse, and personal characteristics of the bereaved.

Loss and its accompanying grief are no strangers to the old. By the time they have reached their 70th birthday, most adults have experienced significant losses. One of the most devastating is the death of a spouse. Few persons are prepared for it, least of all dependent women like Emily. Emily said she had a wonderful life. Her husband took care of everything. She never had to concern herself with anything beyond cooking the meals. She did not drive, so the shopping was done with her husband. She said, "He carried me around on a pillow and the only bill I ever paid was the paper boy." It was reasonable to expect that Emily's bereave-

BRIGHID KELLY: College of Nursing and Health, University of Cincinnati, Cincinnati, Ohio.

Reprinted from Kelly, B., Emily: A study of grief and bereavement, *Health Care for Women International, 12*, pp. 137–147, with permission of Taylor and Francis, Inc. © 1991.

ment would be painful and lengthy, but Emily's husband has been dead for 12 years and Emily still grieves.

She had resided in a nursing home for 5 days when I first met her. She was a small woman of 83 who, when told that I was interested in talking with her about her adaptation to the home, quickly said that she was hoping to return to her apartment when she improved. She had been admitted because her arthritic condition made the use of her walker hazardous. Emily's acute grief was apparent. She was intensely preoccupied with the memory of her dead husband, whom she said had been deceased for 6 years. She cried continuously, sobbing and wailing intermittently. She was restless and exhibited lack of concentration, memory loss, and loss of appetite. She had severe tremors of her hands, and her mouth shook so badly that she often slurred her words. The staff of the nursing home believed she was experiencing withdrawal from pain medication abuse. There was no doubt that she was experiencing a crisis. However, as Dimond (1981) has pointed out, although episodes that might be termed crises occur at various stages in the bereavement process, conceptualizing grief under the narrow framework of crisis theory substantially limits the possibility of explaining the phenomenon. The events and behavior complicating the adjustment to the loss of a spouse have been described by others as a period of psychosocial transition (Caplan, 1975; Parkes, 1970). Psychosocial transitions are "major changes in life space that are lasting in their effects" and that result in permanently altered attitudes about the world (Parkes, 1971, p. 445). To better understand these major changes, the central question posed for this study was what were the contributing factors to a state of extended bereavement that was unresolved after 12 years? To answer this question, I conducted a series of conversations with Emily and analyzed her responses, using grief and bereavement theory.

Bereavement is "a total response pattern, psychological and physiological, following the loss of a significant object, usually a loved one" (Averill, 1968). It has two components, grief, which is a set of physiological, psychological, and social reactions, and mourning, which is behavior determined by cultural mores and customs. Grief, the normal reaction to the death of a loved one, has been described by Glick, Weiss, and Parkes (1974) as having three phases. The initial phase lasts about 2 weeks and is characterized by feelings of numbness, emptiness, disbelief, and profound sorrow. The intermediate phase lasts approximately 1 year and is characterized by obsessional review of the death, searching for meaning and in some cases searching for the deceased. The recovery phase is the final phase and begins when the bereaved becomes more socially active and demonstrates new coping behavior.

Barry (1973) has said that the work of mourning or grief after a loss is designed to free the sufferer from emotional attachment to the loved object. This work is modified by many variables: the previous structure and personality of the bereaved, the nature of the relationship to the loved one, and the social climate in which the loss occurs. Barry said that a combination of factors that interfere with the work of mourning may result in prolonged grief. Atypical grief reactions have been discussed by several researchers (Barry, 1973; Hauser, 1983; Hodgekinsons, 1982; Marris, 1958; Parkes, 1985). Delayed or inhibited grief, for whatever reason, may surface unexpectedly years later. Persons exposed to an unexpected loss are subject to increased psychiatric morbidity and constitute a high-risk group (Lundin, 1984).

Dimond (1981) described three intervening variables thought to be critical to successful adaptation following bereavement in the elderly. These are supportive social networks, concurrent losses, and coping skills. *Supportive network* is defined as "that set of personal contacts through which the individual maintains his/her social identity and receives emotional support, material aid and services, information, and new social contacts" (Walker, McBride, & Vachon, 1977). The second major set of intervening variables, *concurrent losses,* is in essence the cumulative effect of several losses. People are often relocated after the death of a spouse, which may result in a number of other losses (i.e., home, friends, neighborhood, life-style, etc). In essence, one is unable to adjust to one loss before one is confronted by the effects of others. The way in which individuals manage such crises is a function of their past experience and the skill and competencies they have acquired in managing previous life crises. These adaptive behaviors are called *coping skills.* It is reasonable to believe that successful coping in previous crises is the foundation of subsequent adaptation to future crises. Lopata's studies (1973, 1975) have revealed that a sense of personal control is critical to successful adaptation to widowhood. She identified two principal tasks to be accomplished by the aged widow. These are (a) learning to live independently and (b) successful interaction in society as a single person.

METHOD

An ethnographic approach was used. Ethnographic research uses several methods of data collection, such as interviews, life histories, event analysis, and participant observation (Bogdan & Taylor, 1975). In this case, I concentrated on the life history of one individual, based on the belief that the attitudes and perceptions of people concerning past events are of greater importance than verification of their data. My aim in using this research strategy was to seek themes in the data that provide meaning and understanding of the phenomena experienced by the informant.

When I first met Emily, my intention was to interview her over a period of weeks to assess her adaptation to the nursing home environment. However, her preoccupation with her losses and her anxiety were so great I decided to listen to whatever was uppermost in her mind. I visited Emily 6 days of each week for the next 7 weeks. I did not take notes in her presence. Field notes were taken immediately after each interaction. These field notes were then analyzed for meaning and categorized according to themes arising from the data, such as suddenness, loss, or Emily's character. Initially these categories were simply high-lighted in the text with a notation, but gradually, as more data were collected, data fitting under these categories was transferred to index cards. Subsequently, the raw data and these categories were read by two qualitative research experts who were asked to comment on the validity of the categories. Suggestions made by these readers helped corroborate the validity of findings and also assisted in finding new meaning in the data.

Emily had agreed to be an informant and was aware of the purpose of my visits. Thus, as our relationship progressed and I became her therapist, she would frequently grab my hand and ask, "Oh, my dear, am I any help at all to you? It seems as if you are here to help me instead of the other way around." This statement, I believe, reveals a facet of Emily's character. She is so eager to please and sensitive to the needs of others that even in her extreme pain and agitation she was aware of my needs. The outcome of these talks, I believe, is a mixture of Emily's present and her past.

FINDINGS

Emily's initial substantive loss was the death of her husband. In our talks, she returned time and time again to speak of him and their life together. On most of these occasions, she would begin by talking about some happy event and then her eyes would fill with tears. She would say, "It was all so sudden, he was sick only a week," and at that point she would break down and cry. At first, I sat and held her hand until she had regained control. Then later she began telling the story of how her husband died. The story never changed; the facts were always the same except that with each subsequent telling, more detail was added. Her confusion about exactly how long her husband had been dead lasted about 2 weeks. It seems that Allen, her husband, found blood in his stool and they called the doctor. He was admitted to the hospital and after a week of tests, he had surgery. On the day of the surgery she and their son, Allen, Jr., their only child, were sitting in a long hallway. The surgeon who had just completed the surgery came to speak to them. He said everything was fine and recommended that Emily go home as her husband would be in recovery for some time. She remembers that she stood up to go and Allen, Jr., was helping her on with her coat when all of a sudden the hallway seemed full of loud ringing and nurses and doctors rushing toward the recovery room. The surgeon ran also. "It was Allen," Emily said. "He had just died." She looked past me sighing and sobbing bitterly. "It was all too sudden." She wept, "I never could get used to the idea that he was gone."

Emily's subsequent losses included mobility, her physical ability to use her hands, and eventually her home. When Emily was admitted to the nursing home, she said it was "too sudden" also.

One day they called to say there was a bed and the next day, here I was. I didn't have time to get used to the idea. My son told me that this was the best nursing home in the whole area and if I passed up this opportunity I might not get in here.

I found it noteworthy that Emily described her two greatest losses as "sudden." I wondered if the suddenness and trauma of finding herself in a nursing home was the catalyst for the grief reaction she was now experiencing. I had no way of knowing what Emily had been like in the intervening years since her husband's death, but I suspected that her grief had not been as acute as it now appeared. I asked her about this. She said,

> I have always mourned. My friends would say to me, "Emily, you should be happy that you had such a wonderful marriage and such a happy life," and I would respond "That's why I'm sad. Why, if he were not so wonderful, I would not miss him so much."

Emily's losses were concurrent. After her husband's death, she immediately moved in with her son, his wife, and their three young children. I asked her one day why she gave up her home so quickly. She replied, "I couldn't manage on my own. There were two acres of land. I didn't know how to handle the furnace if anything went wrong. You see, I never had to do anything. I was frightened to be alone."

When Emily moved in with her son she lost the opportunity to attend church each day. She often referred to this and spoke of the kindness of two of her son's neighbors who, on learning that she liked to attend mass daily, began taking her each day. Several years later, when Emily moved to her own apartment, she chose one solely on the basis of its being across the street from her church. Emily was deeply religious. It was her most manifest coping mechanism. Yet, although she accepted the loss of her husband as the will of God and saw it all as a cross she had to bear, she apparently never sought meaning beyond this except that she had been "too happy" or her husband had been "too good." I never perceived anger in Emily and wondered if this was in any way connected to her apparent acceptance of God's will.

Emily had also experienced compound losses of a symbolic nature. She lost her wedding rings and all the material possessions that reminded her of her marriage. One day when we were talking, she showed me a habit she has of exploring the ring finger of her left hand. I asked her where her rings were. She replied, "They are in the bank; Allen, Jr., thought they would be safer there. The eternity ring has diamonds all around and the engagement ring is a carat and a half. He thought they might be stolen."

At other times she would want to show me a piece of furniture or china to illustrate an anecdote and her eyes would fill with tears when it registered that she was not at home. It began to dawn on me that Emily had lost everything. She had nothing but the clothes she was wearing, her prayer book, and a family picture on the wall. Her financial affairs had been taken over by her son. It occurred to me that she would probably never see her rings or her apartment again.

Emily's losses, both concurrent and subsequent, were cumulative. At this point in time, she longed for someone to understand her, someone who would be as kind and patient with her as her husband had been. She often referred to his kindness, patience, and understanding. She spoke of having had migraine headaches throughout her life and that her husband had always been solicitous. I wondered about her support network.

Emily's relationship with her son remains obscure. In all our conversations, she rarely spoke of him except in conjunction with her care or his visits. Although she never said anything that might lead one to think her son was not kind to her, it was obvious she did not want to upset him. Shortly after I began visiting her, I found she had been moved to another room. Her son had thought that it would be more comfortable and less noisy. Emily was miserable. She grabbed my hand and whispered that she really had not minded the screaming of the woman next door because she could look out the window. Now she did not have a window and her roommate was deaf. Her roommate kept shouting questions at her but could not hear her replies. Emily was in anguish. Clinging to my hand, her mouth shaking uncontrollably, she said, "Oh! My son will be so angry with me. He'll say he tried to do what's best for me and I don't appreciate it. Oh, what will I do? I hate this room."

I could not help contrasting Emily's references to her son with those to her husband. I wanted to pursue this difference, but I sensed that she would protect her son and might be threatened by further questioning in this area. My suspicion that her son was often impatient with her was supported by the charge nurse, who said,

> Her son yells at her. You can hear him down the hall. He tells her she doesn't appreciate anything he does for her. He tells her she needs to make a greater effort to like the place. I told him quite frankly that if she doesn't want to go to the dining room to eat, she doesn't have to.

Although I was reluctant to ask Emily questions that might result in the termination of our relationship, I began thinking of ways to have her put into words some of her thoughts about her son. One day, I asked her how she would compare her husband to her son. She replied,

> I really don't know how to answer that. As you know, my son is under a great deal of pressure from his job. I would have to say that my son sees things as either black or white. There are no grays. Everything is either right or wrong. My husband saw a whole range of possibilities and he was so-ooo patient and compassionate.

The subject of support from friends arose without questioning. Emily often referred to the kindness and loyalty of her friends. She would often say, "I have such wonderful friends," and support this with an anecdote of one of her friend's kindnesses. She told me of how they had always included her from the time of Allen's death. Intertwined in these accounts was a note of sadness at their eventual inability to continue listening to her talk about her husband. She provided ample examples of how they would try to have her think of the present and not dwell on the past. Yet she evidenced no animosity about this, apparently accepting that she alone had suffered the loss, and she did not expect her friends to experience her pain. She also laid great store in the fact that she had so many old friends. She told of two friends with whom she had attended grade school who still called weekly. Emily's sensitivity to the needs of others, kindness, and graciousness were demonstrated often in the times I visited. Her concern for those around her was genuine. Every once in a while, I visited Emily at the dinner hour. She introduced me to those around her and, if she did not remember someone's name, she would apologize for it. On these occasions she regretted that she could not offer me some refreshment. I came to know her well and found that she had very good insight into her behavior and her dependency. Emily would be the first to acknowledge her dependency. Once she referred to herself as "Mommy's girl" and when I asked if she was an only child she replied,

> No! I had a brother and sister who were older than I, but I always did what I was told. This may sound hard to believe—my friends could never believe it—but I had a job as a stenographer and I turned my paycheck directly over to my mother and then she would give me my pocket money. I did that until I was married. I believe that contributed to my dependency.

Referring to herself as "a ninny," she followed up with some story about how she could never be assertive. In attempting to clarify this, I asked her what exactly she meant by the term *ninny*. She answered, "Well, it means that I'm not aggressive. I have no courage to stand up to people. I sometimes think that things might have been different had I been stronger."

This was not the only time that Emily talked about how things could have been different. She recalled when Allen, Jr., had been a little boy and the time she began to drive until one day she went off the road. She never really drove again, although she had attempted it years later. In telling this, she laughed heartily as the humor of it all returned. One could imagine that this had always been a humorous subject in their family.

Emily's good sense of humor is another strong coping skill. This became more and more evident as I came to know her. She often told stories of silly things she had done, and it was evident that she could laugh at herself. Once she abruptly said to me with a twinkle in her eye, "What is hell?" I responded, "It's hot," and she went on,

> You often hear it's hot as hell;
> 'Tis sometimes said it's cold as hell;
> When rain pours down, "it's hell," they say
> It's also hell when it is dry.
> We hate like hell to see it snow
> It's a helluva wind when it starts to blow.
> Now how in the hell can a person tell

What is meant by this word hell.
That married life is hell they say
When you come home late, there's hell to pay.
Hell yes; hell no; and Oh hell; too.
The hell you don't, the hell you do
And what the hell, and oh hell where
And what in hell do you think I care.
And the hell of it is and it sure is hell
We still don't know what in the hell is
this place called HELL.

We both laughed heartily, and I asked who the author was. She laughed again and said, "I just don't know. It was posted on the inside of the back page of my fifth grade math book." Emily loved poetry and quoted it often. One day she recited "Thanatopsies" from beginning to end. I was not familiar with this poem but was struck by the death imagery in it. The final stanza goes like this:

So live, that when thy summons comes to join
The innumerable caravan, which moves
To that mysterious realm, where each shall take
His chamber in the silent halls of death,
Thou go not, like the quarry-slave at night,
Scourged to his dungeon, but, sustained and soothed
By an unfaltering trust, approach thy grave
Like one who wraps the drapery of his couch
About him, and lies down to pleasant dreams

William Cullen Bryant
(1794–1878)

It occurred to me then that perhaps Emily wished for death. I raised the issue of her death, and she said simply, "I'm not afraid to die. In fact, I often wish it would come and take me from here." Emily wanted to be courageous and often said, "Each morning I offer up my sufferings and pain and then I cry about them all day." She would then laugh in a tearful way, once more making fun of her own weakness. Her deep spirituality appeared to be her only consolation. I attempted to explore past crises in order to understand how Emily had coped with these in her earlier life. When asked, however, she said she did not believe she had had any. She believed her life had been very smooth. She sometimes said she believed that was one reason why she now had so much pain. She had been "too happy."

DISCUSSION

Although Emily is, of course, unique, I found her to be representative of many nursing home residents whom I have met and come to know. Many of these women personify what happens to individuals who never develop as independent persons.

Emily's references to her mother and their relationship suggest a symbiotic relationship. Mahler (1972) discussed this concept as separation-individuation, in which, she says, growing up is a life-long mourning process. "Inherent in every step of independent functioning is a minimal threat of object loss" (Mahler, 1972, p. 333). Emily transferred her dependence from her mother to her husband without assuming responsibility for her own life. When Emily lost her mother, the trauma was manageable because by then the transfer was complete and her husband was there to support her in her grief. Her problems appear to have begun with the death of her husband. He died so suddenly that she had little time to develop a dependence on her son. Perhaps her relationship with her son made such a transfer impossible.

Emily's bereavement was complicated by an accumulation of losses that Kastenbaum (1969) has called *bereavement overload*. Emily lost her husband, with whom she had a "wonderful" relationship, and also lost her identity as his wife. Thus, all her relationships were affected. In Emily's world, in which a woman's identity is centered around the marital role, where does one go for a new identity? Emily reconstructed her identity as that of grieving widow possibly because, as Lopata (1975, p. 51) has pointed out, she had "no place to go." Yet, although this role provided much solicitude for years, even her most loyal friends tired of her constant references to and sanctification of her husband. Concurrent losses were her home and all that it symbolized of her married life, her freedom, and her social milieu. Subsequently she lost her mobility and the possessions symbolic of her married life.

Emily's admission to the nursing home was sudden. She was not given time to prepare for it, just as she had not had time to prepare for the loss of her husband. In these strange surroundings she found no comfort. Seeking comfort appears to be an important coping mechanism in grieving (Carter, 1989). Perhaps Emily reached out to her dead husband for comfort, recalling his solicitude yet at the same time aware that he could not be with her. Emily also sought comfort from those material things that reminded her of her "happy" life. Instead she was surrounded by strangers and strange rituals. Consequently, she experienced an acute grief reaction that lasted about 3 weeks.

Emily's greatest strength is her spirituality. She "offers up" her sufferings, thus finding meaning in her pain. She believes that her husband is in Heaven and that she will be reunited with him. She finds great consolation in her memories. She is proud of her friendships, especially that which has lasted 70 years. She also has the ability to laugh—even tearfully. She is a caring person for whom it was easy to care and thus she is relatively well cared for by the nursing home staff.

Nursing implications of this study are that one cannot assume that grief is associated only with death or even that grief has predictable stages that occur for a period following a particular loss. It would appear that grief takes many forms, and recurrences of acute grief reactions should be viewed as part of a bereavement process that has not been resolved.

Listening to the bereaved describe their loved one and obtaining a personal history of the bereaved and the quality of the relationship with the loved one, as well as the events surrounding the death, are all important assessment factors in attempting to understand bereavement and facilitate the grieving process. These factors were supported in a recent study of grief themes (Carter, 1989).

REFERENCES

Averill, J. (1968). Grief: Its nature and significance. *Psychological Bulletin, 70,* 721–748.
Barry, M. (1973). The prolonged grief reaction. *Mayo Clinic Proceedings, 48,* 329–335.
Bogdan, R., & Taylor, S. (1975). *Introduction to qualitative research.* New York: Wiley.
Caplan, G. (1975). *Support systems and community mental health.* New York: Behavioral Publications.
Carter, S. (1989). Themes of grief. *Nursing Research, 38*(6), 354–358.
Dimond, M. (1981). Bereavement and the elderly: A critical review with implications for nursing practice and research. *Journal of Advanced Nursing, 6,* 461–470.
Glick, I., Weiss, R. S., & Parkes, C. M. (1974). *The first year of bereavement.* New York: Wiley.
Hauser, J. (1983). Bereavement outcome for widows. *Journal of Psychiatric Nursing and Mental Health, 21,* 23–31.
Hodgkinson, P. (1982). Abnormal grief. The problem of therapy. *British Journal of Medical Psychology, 55,* 29–34.
Kastenbaum, R. (1969). Death and bereavement in later life. In A. Kutcher (Ed.), *Death and bereavement* (pp. 25–54). Chicago: Thomas Spring.
Lopata, H. (1973). *Widowhood in an American city.* Cambridge, MA: Schappa Press.
Lopata, H. (1975). On widowhood grief work and identity reconstruction. *Journal of Geriatric Psychiatry, 144,* 41–55.
Lundin, T. (1984). Morbidity following sudden and unexpected bereavement. *British Journal of Psychiatry, 144,* 84–88.
Mahler, M. (1972). On the first three subphases of the separation-individuation process. *International Journal of Psychoanalysis, 53,* 333.
Marris, P. (1958). *Widows and their families.* London: Routledge & Kegan Paul.
Parkes, C. (1970). The first year of bereavement. *Psychiatry, 33,* 444–467.
Parkes, C. (1972). *Bereavement: Studies of grief in adult life.* New York: International Universities Press.
Parkes, C. (1985). Bereavement. *British Journal of Psychiatry, 146,* 11–17.
Walker, K., McBride, A., & Vachon, M. (1977). Social support networks and the crisis of bereavement. *Social Science and Medicine, 11,* 35–41.

Chapter 13

Challenges Facing Qualitative Researchers

Developing a qualitative research study is a significant activity. Identifying a problem suitable for qualitative investigation, following through with data collection and analysis, and disseminating the findings can be a lengthy process. Researchers using qualitative designs will need a degree of tenacity to complete a qualitative project. However, the enthusiasm generated from completion of the first study will certainly support continuing work within the qualitative paradigm.

Sharing the results of a qualitative investigation with other nurse researchers becomes a reality at the completion of the study. This is an exciting opportunity to provide new insights, receive thoughtful critiques, and learn from others with similar interests.

Once the qualitative researcher develops a degree of comfort with research activities involved in the conduct of a qualitative project, interest in developing a grant proposal using qualitative approaches may emerge. Grant writing requires the qualitative researcher to develop additional skills. The development of these skills is worth the time when researchers have their ideas validated through the receipt of grant funds.

This chapter is designed to inform the qualitative researcher about important differences in submission of a qualitative manuscript for publication, to offer suggestions regarding the submission of a qualitative proposal for grant funding, and to share creative strategies for presenting qualitative research findings.

PUBLISHING

Dissemination of research findings is the responsibility of all researchers. Sharing results with one's colleagues is an exciting event. Whether sharing ideas in a journal article or in a public forum such as a conference, qualitative researchers need to be aware of what their audiences will expect as well as the way to offer their insights best.

Identifying an Audience

When a study is finished and it is time to document results, it is important to identify for whom one is writing. If the audience is composed primarily of qualitative researchers, the manuscript will look very different than if the audience is nurse educators interested in the research. Be clear from the start who the audience is. One way to do this is to review current journals and see which journals provide a format supportive of qualitative approaches. Some nursing journals publish more qualitative research than others. Regular review of major research journals is necessary in order to become familiar with journals that publish qualitative research on a regular basis. Examples of journals that publish qualitative studies include: *Advances in Nursing Science, Image: The Journal of Nursing Scholarship, Nursing Science Quarterly, Qualitative Health Research, Research in Nursing and Health* and *Western Journal of Nursing Research*. This list is in no way meant to be exhaustive. Nor is it offered to suggest that other journals do not publish qualitative studies. The purpose is to share the journals that have demonstrated a sustained and ongoing commitment to the publication of qualitative research.

In addition to identifying a journal that will be receptive to qualitative research approaches, it is essential to identify a journal with a focus on the content area of the study. For instance, *Qualitative Health Research* has as its purpose to disseminate qualitative research; however, the journal is focused on practice issues in health care and does not usually publish nursing education research articles. Therefore, an education study that utilizes qualitative methods would best be reported in an education journal such as *The Journal of Nursing Education* or *Nurse Educator*.

When the potential journal has been identified, obtaining a copy of the journal's *guidelines for authors* is essential. This document will assist the researcher in developing a manuscript that meets the editorial expectations of the journal chosen. Most guidelines for authors do not offer specific recommendations for presentation of qualitative findings. Reading qualitative studies published in these journals is the best way to develop an understanding of how to meet editorial guidelines when submitting results of a qualitative study for publication. There are some important guidelines qualitative researchers should follow regardless of the journal in which findings are published.

As offered earlier, be sure to define the audience. Each group of readers have a specific purpose in reading a particular journal. Speak to what the important facets of the research are. These should reflect the journal's purpose. For example, if writing in a scientific journal such as *Nursing Research,* detailing method(s) and data analysis will be as important as sharing the findings. In contrast, if publishing in *Home Health Care Nurse,* the findings and implications for practice will be more important to the readership than the actual method(s) for conducting the study.

Most novice scholars are educated to submit query letters. Many journal editors now are saying that query letters are not necessary and may actually prolong the time of publication because of the response time from submission of the query letter to response by journal staff. Often a phone call will suffice to confirm whether the topic is of interest to the readership of a particular journal. Most importantly, remember, when developing a manuscript, to be certain that the research is well presented. Poorly prepared manuscripts can set the stage for a rejection letter even if the study has significant merit.

Once submitted, editorial staff members will review a new submission and decide whether the content reflects the journal's purpose and is well written. If not, the manuscript will be returned. It then will be the researcher's responsibility to identify a more suitable periodical. If a manuscript has not been returned or accepted within a reasonable period, the author should follow up with a phone call or letter.

Developing the Manuscript

The hardest thing about writing is starting. Researchers usually learn through conduct of their projects that it is not hard to write notes for one's self, but it is very difficult to set personal ideas to paper that will be read by others. This is particularly true with qualitative research. The very nature of the data collection and analysis requires the researcher to write. This type of writing is personal; it usually will not be scrutinized by others. Documenting one's feelings, perceptions, observations, theoretical directions, or insights is part of the implementation of the qualitative research experience. Developing diaries, memos, or transcripts into a scientific manuscript requires a fair amount of rigor and determination. It also requires keen synthesis abilities.

Qualitative research generates a large amount of hard data. The data in their raw form are interesting but unusable for the purpose of research reporting. The qualitative researcher must condense and synthesize for the reader the importance of the research while not losing the richness of the findings. This can be a very real challenge because of the prolonged and intimate involvement of the researcher with the participants.

One way to focus on research for publication in a journal is to break the study up into parts. More than one manuscript can be developed from a qualitative research study. If, for example, the culture of an open heart surgery unit is studied over a one-year period, the researcher could develop a manuscript to look at access and ethical considerations in this type of setting. Another manuscript could be developed that would focus on the nurses and their activities and artifacts. Still another article could look at the interactions between patients, their families, and institutional structures. Additionally, description of the process of conducting such an inquiry could be developed into another manuscript. Ideally, a book or a chapter for a book would provide the researcher with the best opportunity for presenting the entire study. However, time and opportunity may limit publication in this format. If the researcher is not interested in publishing the study in parts, then certainly he or she could develop the study in such a way that it will be of greatest interest to individuals who will read it. For instance, using the above example, findings could be presented in the context of practice implications in critical care journals. Publishing in a practice journal would not require a great deal of emphasis on method or analysis but would require significant attention to findings and implications. Knafl and Howard (1984) offer additional guidelines for interpreting and reporting qualitative research.

The most difficult obstacle to overcome in developing a qualitative manuscript for publication is the need to report the study in a 12- to 15-page article. Remember, it is more important to be focused and logical than to try to report the whole study.

Once the journal has been identified and the focus has been determined, the next step is to develop the ideas logically that the researcher wishes to convey. "An outline provides guidance in writing" (Field & Morse, 1985, p. 130). The purpose of the outline is to keep the writer focused. It is very easy to drift away from the core of the manuscript without an outline. Depending on the preference of the author, the outline can be more or less detailed.

When writing begins, remember to organize ideas in a logical manner but also in a way that provides the reader with an appreciation of the richness of the data. For example, in a grounded theory article by Jordan (1990), she describes a man's experience of his wife's pregnancy and what Jordan describes as feelings of being a "stagehand" (p. 14). The raw data included in the article to exemplify this idea were as follows:

> It's always in reference to how [my wife] is doing, and I feel like I have resigned myself more to just responding to what they are asking and

that is to say how [she] is doing as opposed to me and how I am doing.
. . . I really tried to initially go out . . . and open myself up and really
share . . . but, so much of the response is, "You've just got to stick it
out. There is no recognition. I don't feel like I should deny my feelings
and deny what's going on for me. The message is clear . . . 'You need
to focus on her." I just haven't found anybody that [sic] is real understanding, like "What is the experience like for you."

This excerpt provides the reader with an insider's (emic) view of
what it is like to be the husband of a pregnant woman. It gives the reader
a "feel" for or depth of the experience. The excerpt articulates one way
that qualitative reporting is different from quantitative reporting. Qualitative reporting demands documentation of ideas or conclusions in words
rather than numbers. Using words to justify one's position takes a significant amount of skill because, unlike presentation of statistics, significance
of the findings is found in the writer's syntax, not in statistical manipulation of numerical values.

When the manuscript is completed, colleagues should be asked to
critique the ideas presented. Too often, a neophyte qualitative researcher
makes the mistake of believing that because much time has been spent
immersed in the data that writing it up is merely a technicality. Qualitative research manuscripts are subjected to rigorous review. It is essential
that the ideas be clear and demonstrate important findings to the nursing community. Review by knowledgeable colleagues will assist in assuring the logic, consistency, and importance of the findings.

Once submitted, the researcher should be ready to revise as
requested by the reviewers. Few manuscripts, qualitative or quantitative,
sustain juried review without requests for revision. If the unfortunate circumstance occurs and a rejection letter is received, do not throw away the
manuscript. Look carefully at the critique, use the comments to improve
the manuscript, and try another journal. It is acceptable also to use the comments, revise the manuscript, and resubmit it to the same journal. Quality
research should be published. At times, it takes a fair amount of tenacity to
see ideas through to publication. But once published, the researcher enjoys
a feeling of accomplishment and the satisfaction of having the work available in print for those interested in the topic and research approach.

CONFERENCE PRESENTATION

Publication of the manuscript is just one part of the responsibility of the
researcher in dissemination of the findings. In addition to getting one's
ideas in print which takes between 10 to 18 months, the researcher should
be engaged in presenting the findings to the scholarly community using

other forums. One of the best ways to share results in an efficient and effective way is through formal presentation. This can occur through a paper or poster presentation.

Whether presenting findings in a paper or poster, some important considerations need to be addressed specifically for the qualitative researcher. Most formal presentations result from a *call for abstracts*. The call for abstracts requires the researcher to submit a synopsis of the research in a few paragraphs limited to between 150 and 500 words. Research abstracts serve several purposes. Specifically, they:

1. Provide peer review panels with information about an investigator's work so that the quality and relevance may be determined;
2. Quickly communicate the key points of the research to assist planners of scientific meetings to organize cohesive relevant scientific sessions; and
3. Provide an effective way for information to be packaged and printed uniformly for proceedings of scientific meetings (Lindquist, 1993, p. 47).

Guidelines for abstract submissions generally are available from the group sponsoring the research conference or workshop. It is essential that responses to the call reflect the theme of the conference and meet the criteria for presentation. The guidelines for abstract submission usually include the purpose of the study, the method used to conduct the inquiry, the sample, the findings, and the significance of the findings to nursing. Inclusion of the information requested will greatly improve the chances for having the abstract accepted. However, the results of a qualitative study are *rich and dense,* so the question becomes: "How do I demonstrate the richness of my work and the significance in 150 to 500 words when I have trouble writing it in 15 pages?"

The most important point in submission of any abstract is to convince the reviewer that the work was done well, it will be interesting, and it is significant to the profession. It is impossible to share the richness of the work in an abstract. What the researcher should be striving for is to "whet the appetite" of the reviewers so they say, "We want to know more about this inquiry." Finally, attention to appearance of the abstract will help to make a favorable impression on the reviewer. If the abstract presentation is sloppy, the reviewers may anticipate a poor quality presentation, and rejection will result (Lindquist, 1993).

Call for abstracts generally ask researchers in which format they prefer to present, poster or paper presentation. Neophyte researchers would be wise to indicate either. Podium presenters often are individuals who have demonstrated their ability to engage a group successfully in their work. For individuals who have never presented orally before large groups, poster presentations offer the opportunity to discuss the findings in a comfortable, relaxed atmosphere. The poster presentation provides the neophyte researcher with the chance to develop skill and confidence in presenting research findings.

Oral Presentation

If accepted for an oral presentation, there are important aspects of sharing the results that should be kept in mind. Qualitative research should be presented in such a way as to engage the conference participants in the work. Presentation of a portion of the work will allow the researcher to share the dense findings. Because the average length of podium presentation is between 20 and 30 minutes, be careful not to spend too much time discussing the approach used to conduct the inquiry. Although this is essential information, the audience will be most interested in the findings. Provide the audience with just enough information about the method so that they have the context and direction of the study but do not share so much that the presentation of the findings needs to be rushed. It is essential not to hurry presentation of quotations from informants. These are the findings of the study. They should be shared thoughtfully, giving the audience time to absorb the words. Slides or overheads provide a visual representation of the quotes, giving the audience additional time to assimilate the meaning of the words. Photographs and illustrations of findings add to the presentation as well. Finally, be sure to leave an adequate amount of time for questions. If the research has been presented well, the audience will want to know more because their interest has been aroused. During the question and answer period, a unique opportunity is available to share additional findings and some of the anecdotal information.

Poster Presentation

Presenting qualitative research in poster format is a unique challenge, but certainly one that can be met successfully. Poster presentations should be displayed so that in a glance, interested individuals can determine whether they want to know more or whether they prefer to move to the next poster. Anyone who has ever attended a poster session knows that the sheer volume of posters available limits interested parties from spending time with each poster presenter. Therefore, the poster must capture the attention of its audience immediately.

For this reason, the most important part of the poster will be its title. The presentation of the title, its color, size of print, and content should catch the passerby's interest first. It is essential to present a title that immediately lets the reader know what the topic and approach to the research is. For instance, "The Near Death Experience" as a title would attract individuals interested in the topic. This title is brief. In a moment, individuals passing by can determine whether they want to know more. Similarly, a title such as "Male Nursing Students' Perceptions of Clinical Experience: A Phenomenological Inquiry" quickly tells what the subject matter and the research approach is.

In addition to title, the content should be presented in an appealing way. Pictures and illustrations capture the passerby's attention and gives the presenter the opportunity to share results verbally. There are many good articles on the mechanics of preparing and presenting a poster to which the interested reader can refer (Beal, Lynch, & Moore, 1989; Bushy, 1991; Gustafson, 1981; Sexton, 1984; Sweeney, 1984). Specifically, for the qualitative researcher, there is benefit in providing the interested individual with an abstract or a hand-out that highlights the important findings in the research and/or the exhaustive description if appropriate. Included on the printed material that the audience will take away should be the name and address of the researcher so that nurses interested in the findings or the method can contact the researcher for additional information.

In addition to using a matted poster format, some qualitative researchers have used audiovisual materials such as a slide projector with tape player to give an added dimension to their presentation. The inclusion of sound and changing visuals connects the consumer to the work. Presenting a poster using audiovisual equipment, however, requires access to electricity and additional space. The researcher interested in presenting a poster in this format needs to contact the conference planners to see whether there is accessible electricity and adequate space to present in this way.

Creativity is the key to successful presentation of any idea. Presenting qualitative research lends itself to creativity because of the nature of the data, the data collection strategies, and the dense data that result. The researcher presenting a poster demonstrating a qualitative research approach should take advantage of the possibilities open to sharing his or her findings and use them to share the interesting and exciting data revealed in the conduct of the inquiry.

GRANT WRITING

With the completion of one or more qualitative research studies, the development of a grant proposal should be seriously considered. This is the next logical step in the development of a research career regardless of the type of research conducted.

The development of a competitive research proposal requires the researcher to develop the project in such a way as to convince a panel of reviewers that the applicant has the necessary knowledge, experience, and commitment to complete the proposed project. Reviewers will be looking at the researcher's credentials, the scientific merit of the project, and its potential contribution to the profession (Cohen, Knafl, & Dzurec, 1993; Sandelowski, Davis, & Harris, 1989).

Funding Sources

One of the first steps in considering the development of a competitive proposal is to identify potential funding sources. There are a number of funding sources available to the nurse interested in conducting qualitative inquiry. Each organization has available materials detailing the types of projects funded and submission guidelines. For researchers seeking their first funding dollars, small grants are the most useful and are generally easier to access. Examples of small grant programs include college or university funds. These monies are accessible through small grant proposals available on a competitive basis within institutions. The monies generally come from allocations to faculty development budgets or result from foundation or alumni gifts for this purpose. In addition to college or university funding, several nursing organizations offer small grants. These include but are not limited to the following: Sigma Theta Tau International, National League for Nursing Council for Research in Nursing Education, American Nurses Foundation, American Association of Critical Care Nurses, and the Association of Rehabilitation Nurses. Many businesses also offer small grants. These include product organizations such as infant formula or durable medical equipment companies. Health care organizations frequently fund research as well. Hospitals and community health organizations are two examples.

The nurse interested in receiving funding needs to identify the variety of resources available. This will require a moderate amount of time first to determine the funding sources available and then to select the one most interested in funding the project. If available and accessible, use resource libraries found in universities that have established nursing research centers to identify potential funding sources. These institutions generally have a plethora of diverse materials and experienced staff to assist in locating the appropriate resources and assisting in proposal development. Organizations such as the American Association of Colleges of Nursing, the National League for Nursing, Sigma Theta Tau International, and the American Nurses Association have resource materials available to help focus the search if a university-based nursing research center is not available.

Individuals interested in developing larger projects should have completed and published results of small funded projects before seeking funding from organizations offering larger funding support. Organizations that fund large projects include but are not limited to the National Institute of Nursing Research, National Institute of Health, American Education Association, Kellogg Foundation, Robert Wood Johnson Foundation, and National Science Foundation. In addition, many non-profit organizations such as the American Heart Association, the National Arthritis Foundation, and the American Cancer Society provide moderate to large funding for projects. The critical ingredient to receiving larger sums of money in addition to submission of a well-developed project is experience. Organizations that make large awards do not do so unless single researchers or research teams have significant documented experience.

Developing the Proposal

There are several good books that have specifically been written to focus on proposal development and grant writing so that this section will not address the specific mechanics of developing a research proposal for funding. Instead, what is intended is to give the qualitative researcher some ideas about the challenges and potential pitfalls in developing a qualitative grant proposal. As Morse (1991) states:

> In comparison to the WYSIWYG (what you see is what you get) presentation of the quantitative application, the qualitative proposal is vague, obscure, and may even be viewed as a blatant request for a blank check (p. 148).

The idea of developing a proposal for funding knowing beforehand that all the ambiguities cannot be written out of the grant presents a unique but not insurmountable challenge. Researchers interested in receiving funding for a qualitative study must convince the reviewers not only of the merits of the project, which may seem obscure and undirected, but also of the experience of the researcher.

In a qualitative proposal, pilot work serves very little purpose (Brink, 1990). In a quantitative study, it demonstrates the potential strengths and weaknesses of the design. In qualitative proposals, the number of participants is determined by saturation of data which can include as few as two or more than 50 people. In a quantitative study, the number of subjects is determined by the design, projected outcome, and the number of variables under study. Based on these parameters a precise number of subjects for inclusion can be established. In qualitative studies, data collection and analysis require flexibility. In quantitative studies, the data collection and analysis are largely objective. The purpose of these comparisons is to focus on the precise and often predictable nature of a quantitative research proposal versus the very imprecise and unpredictable nature of a qualitative proposal.

Morse (1994) recommends "the first principle of grantsmanship is to recognize that a good proposal is an argument—a fair and balanced one"

(p. 226). Therefore, the qualitative researcher must clearly and persuasively present evidence which will convince the grant reviewers that the proposal is worth funding. To facilitate a clear understanding of the research ideas, the proposal's author "should assume nothing and explain everything" (Morse, 1994, p. 227).

The second principle of grant writing offered by Morse (1994) "is that one should think and plan before starting to write" (p. 227). Planning before writing will give the proposal author the opportunity to delineate clearly the research plan, beginning with development of the research question and ending with distribution of the research results. In addition to assisting with writing the actual proposal document, planning conclusively before beginning to write allows the author time to draft a complete budget. Because the budget is the part of the proposal that will allow the researcher to operationalize the project fully, it is essential that it be well developed and that all expenses be detailed. The type of items which will be included in the budget are: personnel, such as research assistants, transcription service, secretary, consultant; equipment, such as tape recorder, computer, data analysis program; supplies, such as paper, tapes, photocopying; and travel, including mileage for travel between research sites, conference travel and presentation fees, and consultant travel. Carefully laying out the project will assist greatly in developing a proposal that is clear, succinct, and fundable.

Investigator Qualifications

The challenge in obtaining funding for qualitative research is for prospective grant recipients to demonstrate their abilities by illustrating to the reviewers that a track record in scholarly publication, presentation, consultation, and success in acquiring small awards makes them a risk worth taking. "Granting bodies must [be made to] recognize the process nature of the research and that they are funding the *investigator* rather than the *proposal* per se" (Morse, 1991, p. 149). As Morse (1991) stated, "[F]or major grant applications, evaluation of the *investigator* is critical and should be most heavily weighted" (p. 149). This is not to say that the research project does not need to have scientific merit and must be described as fully as possible, but rather to illuminate the nature of the process, which is decidedly imprecise when compared to a quantitative proposal.

Human Subjects

In addition to qualitative researchers clearly identifying their expertise and qualifications, it is important that qualitative research proposals conclusively identify the mechanisms for assuring human subjects protection. One of the strengths of qualitative approaches is the unique opportunity to get to know individuals, groups, or communities. This strength creates its own potential hazards where protection of human subjects is concerned. The nature of the data, personal descriptions, precludes qualitative researchers from maintaining confidentiality, particularly when quotes are published or used as references in publications (Munhall, 1989). However, qualitative researchers can assure anonymity. It is essential to demonstrate how the identities of the informants will be protected. There are situations such as in the use of ethnography where identification of the participants may actually contribute significantly to the position of the group or their ability to access resources. In these cases, qualitative researchers must document that participants have agreed to have their identities made public.

Developing mechanisms for assuring confidentiality and anonymity contribute significantly to the proposal; however, it is also important to clarify for institutional review boards and funding agencies that mechanisms are in place to deal with potentially sensitive outcomes. For example, if a researcher is living with a community and discovers that one of the rituals of the group is physically to isolate and abuse children who do not excel in academics, the researcher must be able to clearly define steps that will be taken to protect the vulnerable group. It is essential to try to identify all the potentially sensitive situations and develop mechanisms to intervene or to have intervention available.

Audiotaping and taking photographs is another example of a potential violation of human subjects' rights. As addressed earlier, permission must be documented for such activities.

ETHICAL CONCERNS

The discussion of human subjects is an important part of any research proposal. However, the issue of ethics in conducting qualitative research is important whether the project is funded or not. Researchers are required by ethical principles in all professions to safeguard the rights of the public. The principles related to the conduct of research are a direct result of the 1974 National Research Act which established the National Commission for the Protection of Human Subjects in Biomedical and Behavioral Research (Schoen, 1988). Part of the act was the establishment of institutional review boards. These review boards have primary responsibility for safeguarding the rights of individuals who participate in research studies. The qualitative researcher has the responsibility of acquiring institutional review for the conduct of research studies.

Protection of human subjects is essential in the conduct of research. Individuals have the right to self-determination. This means that they have the right to be informed about research in which they participate.

Informed consent, an ethical principle that requires researchers to obtain voluntary consent including description of the potential risks and benefits of participating, is required of qualitative research studies. Munhall (1988) recommends "process consent" (p. 156) rather than the traditional consent which is signed in the beginning of most studies and not revisited unless participants question their obligations related to the study. Process consent or "consensual decision-making" (Ramos, 1989, p. 61) means that the researcher renegotiates the consent as unforeseen events or consequences arise (Munhall, 1988; Ramos, 1989). By providing the opportunity to renegotiate the consent and be part of the decision making as the study develops, the qualitative researcher is affording participants the chance to withdraw or modify what they initially agreed to.

For instance, a phenomenologist decides that he or she is interested in studying the birth experience. Consent is obtained to observe and record the labor and delivery experience of first-time parents. The laboring couple initially agrees to and states that they are comfortable with observation and recording of the laboring experience. As the birth experience continues, the couple demonstrates noticeable uneasiness during the videotaping of the delivery. Using the idea of process consent and mutual decision making, the researcher would find a way of validating the couple's continuing interest in having their experience observed and recorded. When the couple is given the opportunity to renegotiate their initial agreement, the researcher is functioning in the best interest of the participants. Research participants should be provided with opportunities to renegotiate their agreement should an experience be different than they initially perceived it to be.

Qualitative studies, like quantitative studies, should be conducted with the highest ethical standards. Qualitative researchers must consider their informants. What impact will participation in the study have on the informants? For instance, in studying a phenomenon such as grieving in parents who have lost children, the nurse researcher may see the findings of such a study greatly informing the caring practices of nurses who work with these individuals. However, what will the impact be on the parents who share their experiences? Will they be placed in vulnerable emotional situations and how will the researcher protect them? Grieving parents may, in fact, agree to participate and sign informed consents. However, the full understanding of what describing this phenomenon to a qualitative researcher could be must be completely understood before the study begins. This is not to say that the research should not be conducted but rather that the researcher needs to have a fully developed plan related to how these parents can be cared should the description of their experiences result in psychological trauma. One way to handle this particular situation is to employ a psychologist with grief experience as a consultant. In this way, a plan is in place should grieving parents be placed in a vulnerable situation as a result of the research.

Fully communicating the objectives of the research study and exploring the potential risk with the informants will help to assure a complete understanding of the research. Further, once the study begins, the researcher has the responsibility of insuring that the "therapeutic imperative of nursing (advocacy) takes precedence over the research imperative (advancing knowledge) if conflict develops" (Munhall, 1988, p. 151). Because of the intimate nature of qualitative data collection and the researcher as instrument, those engaged in qualitative studies must always be aware of the intertwining role of caring professional and the scholarly researcher. Neither role can, nor should be, suspended in the conduct of nursing inquiry.

SUMMARY

Qualitative research is an exciting opportunity to create meaningful nursing knowledge from individuals' lives and experiences. To make the knowledge accessible, findings must be shared in a significant way. Presenting a qualitative project in an article, poster, speech, or grant proposal requires imagination and refined presentation skills. Qualitative researchers have a responsibility to their consumers and developing qualitative scholars to present their ideas in a clear and acceptable manner. Their research should be shared in a way that illustrates the richness and value of conducting research using the approaches described in this text.

The development of qualitative research projects and the refinement of social science approaches to human inquiry appropriate to nursing science establish a major research focus for the profession. Nurses interested in these projects have the unique opportunity to be on the cutting edge of the developments. It is an exciting time for nurses and for research. There is a vast and expansive qualitative research landscape waiting for interested nurse researchers. It is a landscape of imagination, one colored by the lives and experiences of those individuals with whom nurses interact: clients, students, and other nurses. It is essential to document these unique experiences and share them with each other in order to explore and describe the human experience fully. The challenge awaits those who are willing to participate.

REFERENCES

Beal, J. A., Lynch, M. M., & Moore, P. S. (1989). Communicating nursing research: Another look at the use of poster sessions in undergraduate programs. *Nurse Educator, 14*(1), 8–10.

Brink, P. J. (1990). Dialogue: The granting game. In J. M. Morse (Ed.), *Qualitative nursing research: A contemporary dialogue,* rev. ed. Newbury Park, CA: Sage.

Bushy, A. (1991). A rating scale to evaluate research posters. *Nurse Educator, 16*(1), 11–15.

Cohen, M. Z., Knafl, K., & Dzurec, C. L. (1993). Grant writing for qualitative research. *Image: Journal of Nursing Scholarship, 25*(2), 151–156.

Field, P. A., & Morse, J. M. (1985). *Nursing research: The application of qualitative approaches.* Rockville, MD.: Aspen.

Gustafson, M. (1981). Poster presentation—more than a poster on a board. *Journal of Continuing Education in Nursing, 12*(2), 28–30.

Jordan, P. L. (1990). Laboring for relevance: Expectant and new fatherhood. *Nursing Research, 39*(1), 11–16.

Knafl, K. A., & Howard, M. J. (1984). Interpreting and reporting qualitative research. *Research in Nursing and Health, 7,* 17–24.

Lindquist, R. A. (1993). Strategies for writing a competitive research abstract. *Dimensions of Critical Care Nursing, 12*(1), 46–53.

Morse, J. (1991). Editorial. On the evaluation of qualitative proposals. *Qualitative Health Research, 1*(2), 147–151.

Morse, J. M. (1994). Designing funded qualitative research. In N. K. Denzin & Y. S. Lincoln (Eds.), *Handbook of qualitative research* (pp. 220–235). Thousand Oaks, CA: Sage.

Munhall, P. L. (1988). Ethical considerations in qualitative research *Western Journal of Nursing Research, 10*(2), 150–162.

Munhall, P. L. (1989). Institutional review of qualitative research proposals: A task of no small consequence. In J. M. Morse (Ed.), *Qualitative nursing research: A contemporary dialogue.* Rockville, MD: Aspen.

Ramos, M. C. (1989). Some ethical implications of qualitative research. *Research in Nursing and Health, 12,* 57–63.

Sandelowski, M., Davis, D. H., & Harris, B. G. (1989). Artful design: Writing the proposal for research in the naturalist paradigm. *Research in Nursing & Health, 12,* 77–84.

Schoen, D. C. (1988). Ethical issues in nursing research. *Orthopaedic Nursing, 7*(4), 47.

Sexton, D. (1984). Presentation of research findings: The poster session. *Nursing Research, 33,* 374–375.

Sweeney, S. (1984). Poster sessions for undergraduate students: A useful tool for learning and communicating nursing research. *Western Journal of Nursing Research, 6*(1), 135–138.

Glossary

ARCHIVES Contain unpublished materials that often are used as primary source materials.

A PRIORI Form of deductive thinking in which theoretical formulations and propositions precede and guide systematic observation.

ACTION RESEARCH A research method characterized by the systematic study of the implementation of a planned change to a system.

ACTORS Individuals within a particular cultural group who are studied by ethnographic researchers.

ANALYTIC INDUCTION A method of qualitative data analysis wherein the researcher seeks to refine a theory through the identification of negative cases.

AUDITABILITY The ability of another researcher to follow the methods and conclusion of the original researcher.

AUTHENTICITY Term used to describe the mechanism by which the qualitative researcher ensures that the findings of the study are real, true, or authentic. In historical research refers to assuring that a primary source document provides the truthful reporting of a subject.

BIOGRAPHICAL HISTORY Studies the life of a person within the context of the period in which that person lives.

BRACKETING A methodological device of phenomenological inquiry that requires deliberate identification and suspension of all judgments or ideas about the phenomenon under investigation or what one already knows about the subject prior to and throughout the phenomenological investigation.

CATEGORY Classification of concepts into broader categories following comparison of one category to another. Broader categories serve as an umbrella under which related concepts are grouped.

CODING The process of data analysis in grounded theory whereby statements are grouped and given a code for ease of identification later in the study.

313

CONCEPTUAL DENSITY   Data generation that is exhaustive and comprehensive and provides the researcher with evidence that all possible data to support a conceptual framework has been generated.

CONFIRMABILITY   This is considered a neutral criterion for measuring the trustworthiness of qualitative research. If a study demonstrates credibility, auditability, and fittingness, the study is also said to possess confirmability.

CONSTANT COMPARATIVE METHOD OF DATA ANALYSIS   A form of qualitative data analysis wherein the researcher makes sense of textual data by categorizing units of meaning through a process of comparing new units with previously identified units.

CORE VARIABLE   The central phenomenon in grounded theory around which all the other categories are integrated.

CREDIBILITY   A term that relates to the trustworthiness of findings in a qualitative research study. Credibility is demonstrated when participants recognize the reported research findings as their own experiences.

CRITICAL THEORY   A philosophy of science based on a belief that revealing the unrecognized forces that control human behavior will liberate and empower individuals.

CULTURAL SCENE   An anthropological term for culture. It includes the actors, the artifacts, and the actions of the actors in social situations.

DEDUCTIVE   The process of moving from generalizations to specific conclusions.

DEPENDABILITY   This is a criterion used to measure trustworthiness in qualitative research. Dependability is met through securing credibility of the findings.

DIALECTIC   A form of logic based on the belief that reality is represented by contradiction and the reconciliation of contradiction.

DIALECTICAL CRITIQUE   A form of qualitative data analysis wherein the researcher engages in dialogue with research participants to reveal the internal contradictions within a particular phenomenon.

DISCIPLINE OF HISTORY   Both a science and an art that studies the interrelationship of social, economic, political, and psychological factors that influence ideas, events, institutions, and people.

DWELLING   A term used to demonstrate the degree of dedication a researcher commits to reading, intuiting, analyzing, synthesizing, and coming to a description or conclusion(s) about the data collected during a qualitative study. Also called immersion.

EIDETIC INTUITING Accurate interpretations of what is meant in the description.

EMBODIMENT (OR BEING IN THE WORLD) The belief that all arts are constructed on foundation of perception, or original awareness of some phenomenon (Merleau-Ponty, 1956)

EPISTEMOLOGY The branch of philosophy concerned with how individuals determine what is true.

ESSENCES Elements related to the ideal or true meaning of something that gives common understanding to the phenomenon under investigation.

EXTERNAL CRITICISM Questions the genuineness of primary sources and assures that the document is what it claims to be.

FIELD NOTES Notes recorded about the people, places, and things that are part of the ethnographer's study of a culture.

FITTINGNESS A term used in qualitative research to demonstrate the probability that the research findings have meaning to others in similar situations. Fittingness is also called transferability.

FREE IMAGINATIVE VARIATION A technique used to apprehend essential relations between essences and involves careful study of concrete examples supplied by the participant's experience and systematic variation of these examples in the imagination.

GENUINE When a primary source is what it purports to be and is not a forgery.

GRAND TOUR QUESTION(S) General opening question(s) that offer(s) overview insights of a particular person, place, object, or situation.

HISTORY Webster's New International Dictionary defines history as "a narrative of events connected with a real or imaginary object, person, or career... devoted to the exposition of the natural unfolding and interdependence of the events treated." History is a branch of knowledge that "records and explains past events as steps in human progress.. [it is] "the study of the character and significance of events." Barzen and Graff (1985) describe history as an "invention" and as an "art."

HISTORIOGRAPHY Historiography requires that historiographers study and critique sources and develop history by systematically presenting their findings in a narrative. Historiography provides a way of knowing the past.

HISTORIAN/HISTORIOGRAPHER   Balances the rigors of scientific inquiry and the understanding of human behavior; develops the skill of speculation and interpretation to narrate the story.

HISTORICAL METHOD   Application of method or steps to study history systematically.

HOLISM   A belief that wholes are more than the mere sum of their parts.

IMMERSION   A term used to demonstrate the degree of dedication a researcher commits to reading, intuiting, analyzing, synthesizing, and coming to a description or conclusion(s) about the data collected during a qualitative study. Also called dwelling.

INDUCTIVE THEORY BUILDING   Theory derived from observation of phenomena.

INDUCTION   The process of moving from specific observations to generalizations.

INTENTIONALITY   Consciousness is always consciousness of something. One doesn't hear without hearing something or believe without believing something.

INTUITING   A process of thinking through the data so that a true comprehension or accurate interpretation of what is meant in a particular description is achieved.

INTERNAL CRITICISM   Concerns itself with the authenticity or truthfulness of the content.

INTELLECTUAL HISTORY   Studies ideas and thoughts over time of a person believed to be an intellectual thinker, or the ideas of a period, or the attitudes of people.

LIFE HISTORY   A research method wherein the researcher listens to the telling of life story for the purpose of understanding a particular aspect of the individual's life.

LOCAL THEORY   A theory that describes a particular group or sample that can't be generalized to a larger population.

NATURALISTIC INQUIRY   A research methodology based on a belief in investigating phenomena in their natural setting free of manipulation.

PHENOMENOLOGICAL REDUCTION   A term meaning recovery of original awareness.

PRESENT-MINDEDNESS Use of a contemporary perspective when analyzing data collected from an earlier period of time.

PRIMARY SOURCES Firsthand account of a person's experience, an institution, or of an event, and may lack critical analysis; examples include private journals, letters, records.

REFLEXIVE This term refers to being both researcher and participant and capitalizing on the duality as a source of insight.

REFLEXIVE CRITIQUE A form of qualitative data analysis wherein the researcher engages in dialogue with research participants to reveal each individual's interpretation for the meanings influencing behavior.

RELIABILITY The consistency of an instrument to measure an attribute or concept that is was designed to measure.

SATURATION Repetition of data obtained during the course of a qualitative study. Signifies completion of data collection on a particular culture or phenomenon.

SECONDARY SOURCES Materials that cite opinions and present interpretations from the period being studied such as newspaper accounts, journal articles, and textbooks.

SOCIAL HISTORY Explores a particular period of time and attempts to understand the prevailing values and beliefs through the everyday events of that period.

SELECTIVE SAMPLING In a grounded theory investigation, selecting from the generated data those critical pieces of information relevant to the current investigation, and avoiding incorporation of material that is not connected to the current investigation.

SITUATED A term that reflects the position of the researcher within the context of the group under study.

SOCIAL SITUATION The activities carried out by actors (members of a cultural group) in a specific place.

SYMBOLIC INTERACTIONISM A philosophical belief system based on the assumption that humans learn about and define their world through interaction with others.

TACIT KNOWLEDGE Information known by members of a culture but not verbalized or openly discussed.

THEME Used to describe a structural meaning unit of data that is essential in presenting qualitative findings.

THEORETICAL SAMPLING   Sampling on the basis of concepts that have proven theoretical relevance to the evolving theory (Strauss &Corbin, 1990).

THEORETICAL SENSITIVITY   Personal quality of the researcher that is reflected in an awareness of the subtleties of meaning of data (Strauss & Corbin, 1990).

TRANSFERABILITY   A term used in qualitative research to demonstrate the probability that the research findings have meaning to others in similar situations. Transferability is also called fittingness.

TRIANGULATION   Method of using multiple research approaches in the same study to answer research questions.

TRIANGULATION OF DATA GENERATION TECHNIQUES   The use of three different methods of data generation in a single research study for the purpose of generating meaningful data.

TRUSTWORTHINESS   Establishing validity and reliability of qualitative research. Qualitative research is trustworthy when it accurately represents the experience of the study participants.

VALIDITY   The degree to which an instrument measures what it was designed to measure.

Index

Page numbers followed by *f* indicate figures; *t* following a page number indicates tabular material.

A

Abstracts
  call for, 302–303
  guidelines for submissions, 302
  purposes of, 302
Act, in social situations, 103
Action research
  application of, 255–259
    to nursing education, 278–280
    to nursing practice, 273–275
  case report in, 259
  data generation in, 256–257
  data treatment and analysis in, 257–259
  definition of, 255, 313
  published studies, 281*t*–282*t*
Activities, in social situations, 103
Actor(s), 99
  definition of, 313
  in social situations, 103
Acute care settings, caring in, phenomenological study of, 51
Ad hoc inventions, in historical research, 209
Adult learning theory, 130
Aesthetic knowing, 3–4
Amalgamated language, 100
Analytic induction, definition of, 313
Analytic induction method, of data analysis, 263–264
Anonymity, assuring, 307–308
Anthropology, 89
A priori, definition of, 313
Archives, 203, 204*t*
  definition of, 313
Audiotaping, 101
Auditability, 63, 65
  critiquing guidelines for, 53*t*
  definition of, 313
  in ethnographic research, 117
Audit trail, 26, 265
Authenticity, definition of, 313

B

Basic social psychological process(es), 149, 157
Battered women, healing in, phenomenological study of, 51
Being-in-the-world, 33–34
  definition of, 315
Bereavement, definition of, 288
Bereavement overload, 295
Bias, in historical research, questions on, 216*t*–217*t*
Biographical history, 198–199
  definition of, 313
Bio-physical knowledge, 18
Bracketing, 22, 33, 40, 47
  definition of, 313

C

Call for abstracts, 302–303
Card sorting contrast question, 107
Cared-for-ness, phenomenological study of, 58*t*–59*t*
Caregivers, experience of, phenomenological study of, 60*t*
Caring
  among nursing students, phenomenological study of, 64
  meaning of, phenomenological study of, 54*t*–55*t*
  phenomenological study of, 56*t*–57*t*
Caring behaviors, phenomenological study of, 54*t*–55*t*
Caring nursing student-patient experience, themes of, phenomenological study of, 54*t*–55*t*
Case report, 259
Case study report, 254–255
Category, definition of, 313
Childlessness, evaluation of meaning of, 74
Coding
  definition of, 313
  in grounded theory research, 156–157
  theoretical, 159
Commitment to nursing, lived experience of, phenomenological study of, 58*t*–59*t*

319